Sacred Places, Civic Purposes

Sacred Places, Civic Purposes

Should Government Help Faith-Based Charity?

E. J. DIONNE JR.
MING HSU CHEN
editors

BROOKINGS INSTITUTION PRESS
Washington, D.C.

Library of Congress Cataloging-in-Publication data

Sacred places, civic purposes : should government help faith-based
charity? / E.J. Dionne, Jr. and Ming Hsu Chen, editors.
    p. cm.
Includes bibliographical references and index.
    ISBN 0-8157-0259-0 (pbk. : alk. paper)
    1. Church charities—United States. 2. Church charities—Government
policy—United States. 3. Government aid—United States. 4. Church and
state—United States. I. Dionne, E. J. II. Chen, Ming Hsu.
    HV530 .S25 2001
    361.7'5'0973—dc21

                                                              2001006142

9 8 7 6 5 4 3 2 1

The paper used in this publication meets minimum requirements of the
American National Standard for Information Sciences—Permanence of Paper for
Printed Library Materials: ANSI Z39.48-1992.

Typeset in Adobe Caslon

Composition by Cynthia Stock
Silver Spring, Maryland

Printed by R. R. Donnelley and Sons
Harrisonburg, Virginia

For all who dedicate themselves to others, particularly those who gave so much to bring comfort and hope to those afflicted by the terrible events of September 11, 2001, and in memory of those who perished

Foreword

Long before there was a welfare state, religious congregations worked to alleviate poverty. They continued their efforts following the establishment of government programs to assist the poor, and now congregations commonly collaborate with government agencies to help feed, clothe, and care for the needy; run afterschool programs; provide teen pregnancy counseling; and develop programs to prevent crime.

On some issues, such as that of school choice, adversaries have engaged in polarized battles involving both high principles and special interests. But much church-state cooperation has continued with limited challenge in the courts. Although to many among the poor the church and the government are both essential institutions, they rely on the church not only for assistance but also for a sense of community, power, and meaning.

In recent years a new dialogue has begun regarding the proper role of congregations in lifting up the poor and the proper nature of their relationship to government. The new debate has at times been deeply divisive, but it also has created an opening for new points of departure from the old debate and, at least occasionally, new opportunities to heal old breaches. The issue was addressed in the 2000 presidential campaign, when both Texas Governor George W. Bush and Vice President Al Gore proposed expanding cooperation between government and "faith-based organizations." After having been in office only a few weeks, President Bush created the White House Office of Faith-Based and Community Initiatives and proposed new legislation on government support for faith-based efforts.

The seeds of the new dialogue were sown in an earlier Brookings compilation, *What's God Got to Do with the American Experiment?* edited by E. J. Dionne Jr. and John J. DiIulio Jr., who served as the first director of the White House Office of Faith-Based and Community Initiatives through the fall of 2001. The possibility of a new debate became clear in a December 1997 conference, "Sacred

Places, Civic Purposes," funded by the Pew Charitable Trusts and sponsored by Brookings in cooperation with Partners for Sacred Places. The result was the beginning of a lively conversation that crisscrossed every party line and ideological divide.

Sacred Places, Civic Purposes: Should Government Help Faith-Based Charity? has evolved from that conversation. The volume focuses on five specific challenges: teen pregnancy, crime and substance abuse, community development, education, and child care. The objective is to explore what faith-based groups are doing, how government can help them without getting in the way, and when government involvement might be mistaken or counterproductive, from the standpoint of both the religious groups themselves and the constitutionality of the involvement.

The concerns of this book would have been well appreciated by Robert Brookings, the St. Louis businessman who founded the Brookings Institution. Although the Institution has become known mainly for its application of social sciences to public policy issues, the broader social concerns of its founder have been honored over the years. And, of course, there is a long and honorable tradition of the engagement of social science in the study of religious institutions. This book—which explores how sacred places have been empowered to serve civic needs and purposes—is very much at home in the broader tradition of Brookings scholarship. It presents the views of a politically and religiously diverse group of individuals—social scientists as well as clergy, government officials as well as neighborhood activists. Its goal is to describe, with an evenhanded treatment of the issues and an emphasis on problem solving, the tangible achievements of faith-based organizations.

The views expressed here are solely those of the authors and should not be attributed to the trustees, officers, or other staff members of the Brookings Institution.

MICHAEL H. ARMACOST
President, Brookings Institution

Washington, D.C.
September 2001

Acknowledgments

This book is a tribute to the authors whose work it comprises. In every case, those authors took time out of extremely demanding schedules to consult on the project, to participate in conferences, and to write their essays and continually revise them to reflect the ever-changing context of faith in public life. We thank them for their contributions to this project—for the wide variety of opinions, broad range of expertise, and depth of insight that they have enabled us to present—and for their years of hard work on behalf of charity and justice. Our hope is that by presenting all of their voices—harmonious and discordant alike—we will foster a more open, rigorous, and rich national dialogue on the valuable contributions that faith-based organizations make and on what government's relationship to them should be.

In particular, we thank Avis Vidal and Joan Lombardi for serving as wise and able advisers and for helping to coordinate the voices in the areas of community development and child care, respectively—this on top of their duties as conference participants and authors. This book is far better because they shared their expertise and advice. We also thank Belle Sawhill, John DiIulio, Melissa Rogers, Bill Galston, Bruce Katz, Bill Dickens, Michael Cromartie, and Peter Steinfels for serving as informal consultants.

This book would not exist and this project would never have gotten off the ground without the extraordinary work of Staci Simmons. With intelligence and great ingenuity, she helped to conceive this project and then gracefully managed all aspects of the conferences on teen pregnancy, crime, and community development before leaving to take on another creative task in helping to establish the Pew Forum on Religion and Public Life. Ming Hsu Chen took responsibility for the last two conferences and for editing all of the papers.

Most of the voices here were enlisted through the conferences, which were held thanks to the support of the Pew Charitable Trusts. Special thanks go to

Luis Lugo of the Trusts, who also helped to conceive this project. He saw the importance of these issues long before they made the front pages of newspapers and the talk shows. Luis understands as well as anyone in the country the civic possibilities of America's diverse religious communities. We also are deeply grateful to the president of the Pew Trusts, Rebecca Rimel, and to Kimon Sargeant, Barbara Beck, Diane Winston, and Julie Bundt. The opinions expressed here are, of course, those of the authors and do not necessarily reflect the views of the Pew Charitable Trusts.

The conferences engaged some 500 people of diverse professional, political, and theological backgrounds in sometimes groundbreaking, often challenging, and always illuminating discussions. But anyone who has worked in event planning knows that it takes a team to do it right. The conferences ran more smoothly because of the very competent people at the Brookings Institution and the Pew Forum on Religion and Public Life. Susan Stewart and her staff provided valuable administrative and financial oversight. Andrea McDaniel, Melissa Rogers, Amy Sullivan, and Andrew Witmer volunteered boundless enthusiasm, support, and labor. Andrea in particular helped us through all troubles—and, more important, helped us avoid trouble in the first place. Stacey Rosenstein and Esperanza Valencia, along with their staffs in Conference and Catering Services, were true professionals, ensuring the smooth operation of all of the events.

At the conclusion of the conferences, we had more than 30 hours of discussion and several memorable presentations that nonetheless had to be transformed into a publishable form. Nothing would have come out right without Kayla Meltzer Drogosz. Kayla, whose knowledge of the subject is broad and deep—and whose commitment to social justice is lifelong and enduring—came on as the book was reaching its final stages. She acted as if it were her own, corralling final manuscripts from a far-flung group of authors, making sure that last-minute improvements saw the light of day (and print), and offering superb advice to all, including especially the editors.

Then the staff of the Brookings Press, along with Christina Counselman, Tommy Ross, and Ari Selman, performed magic. Tommy and Ari were critical in checking the final manuscripts. Eileen Hughes made large substantive and editorial improvements for which we are deeply grateful, and she did so with great sensitivity to the diverse views of our authors. Tanjam Jacobson provided invaluable assistance in revising the many chapter notes. Larry Converse creatively spun the pieces together into an attractive layout. Susan Woollen directed the design of a cover that we loved at first sight. Becky Clark made sure that the book would reach the hands of those who care about these issues. Robert Faherty lent leadership and vision to the project in innumerable ways.

And speaking of leadership, publication of this book could not have occurred without the leadership, vision, and encouragement of Michael Armacost, Paul Light, and Thomas Mann of the Brookings Institution. We feel blessed to have carried out this work in the exciting, collegial, and genuinely friendly environment they have created.

Most of these essays were completed before the events of September 11. But we are sure that all of the authors share the sentiments we express in our dedication.

Our thanks, above all, to Mary Boyle; to James, Julia, and Margot Dionne; to Stephen Chen; and to our parents, families, and many friends who lived through this with us. They help make faith, hope, and love believable propositions.

E. J. Dionne Jr.
Ming Hsu Chen

Contents

PART FOUR
The Role of Faith-Based Organizations in Education

FURTHER COMMENTS

PART FIVE
The Role of Faith-Based Organizations in Child Care

PART SIX

Should Government Help Faith-Based Charity?

Sacred Places, Civic Purposes

CHAPTER ONE

When the Sacred Meets the Civic: An Introduction

E. J. DIONNE JR. and MING HSU CHEN

How can anyone oppose government help for religious congregations working so hard to shelter the homeless and battle crime in inner cities, to provide child care for poor children, and to bring investment to the neighborhoods they serve? Why shouldn't government do all it can to nurture these islands of hope?

How can anyone who believes in the First Amendment's promise of religious freedom support giving *any* government money to religious institutions that might use the funds to advance a particular faith? Why should government channel aid to the poor through congregations that might use a disadvantaged person's vulnerability as an opportunity for recruitment and conversion?

These are tendentious, but not necessarily unfair, questions. The fact that many Americans might see *both* sets of questions as reasonable helps explain why our great national debate over government help to faith-based organizations arouses such passion and engenders such division. It is not as simple as the country being split into hostile camps; Americans, as individuals, are often divided within *themselves*.

Large majorities like the idea of supporting the community work of religious congregations because they respect what they do and believe that religion can transform people's lives. They believe that greater choice in social programs will lead to better services and that faith-based providers are especially caring and compassionate.[1]

Yet majorities *also* worry that such programs might force recipients to take part in religious practices against their will. They are concerned that government might become too involved in religious organizations. And most Americans oppose allowing government-funded religious groups to make hiring decisions on the basis of an applicant's faith.[2]

In principle, Americans want the government to help faith-based organizations. In practice, they worry about what that help might mean.

As Peter Steinfels argues in his powerful closing chapter of this book, the current interest in the work of religious congregations reflects the confluence of many currents in American political thought going back some forty years. On this issue, the left's long-standing interest in granting power to grassroots organizations controlled by the poor meets the right's desire to find alternatives to government provision of social assistance. A general disaffection with government's performance meets a widespread belief that programs to uplift the needy must convey values and virtues as well as money. Our rendezvous with this issue, as Steinfels argues, now seems inevitable.

Those who sympathize with the work of religious congregations thus include people motivated by very different impulses and points of view. Some see social problems as the result of individual failures and disabilities. They see the poor as being poor primarily because they have made bad personal decisions. This view emerges at times in President Bush's rhetoric, which emphasizes the importance of individual conversion as a means of overcoming personal failures. He speaks quite honestly of the importance of conversion in his own life. Seen in this optic, supporting faith-based institutions means strengthening efforts to encourage the poor to make appropriate moral choices.

Others who sympathize with faith-based groups agree that the disadvantaged should be seen as morally responsible for themselves. But they insist that often the poor are poor because of unjust social structures, discrimination, government policies, and economic changes over which they have little control. Those who hold this view see religious congregations not only as a source of personal strength for individuals but also as "prophetic interrogators"—a phrase from Jim Wallis, another contributor to this book—who challenge social injustice. Those who believe this also want to strengthen the religious community, but they do not want government funding to still dissident voices in the congregations. Faith-based groups, after all, are often the most powerful advocates for those who are left out and among the only institutions over which the poor have control.

Related to this distinction is another, between those who see congregations primarily in individualistic terms and those who see them as builders of community. In one view, religion is fundamentally about saving people one soul at a time. Those who believe this and advocate government funding for faith-based services do so because they believe religion will strengthen *individuals*. In the other view, religious congregations are builders of *community* and civil society. As Mark R. Warren has put it, religion is seen as providing "an initial basis of cooperation by grounding such action in a set of common values, goals, and commitments to the public good. . . . At its best, religion has provided a moral basis to conceive of our place in a larger human society and inspired people to work for racial equality, social justice, and democracy."[3]

Some who support the work of religious congregations do so because they hope to win converts to their faith. Others believe that their faith requires them to serve those in need, whether the needy convert or not. Many believe both these propositions at the same time.

Finally, there are those who hope that religious congregations might take over important parts of the welfare state. Others see congregations' work as indispensable, but supplementary to the tasks of government. Those in the first camp are deeply skeptical of government and would like to reduce its role in American life. Those in the second camp believe profoundly in government's essential role in providing health care, education, supplementary income, and training to those who fall on hard times. But they believe that congregations can do things government cannot and reach people in a way no government employee, however well intentioned, ever could.

It must be added, of course, that many—including members of *all* of these groups—insist that congregations are not primarily about social work *or* community organization, but places of worship, instruction, and service to God.

And almost all of these distinctions may oversimplify the motivations of the competing camps. But to make them is to underscore one of the central purposes of this book: to suggest that seeing the work of religious congregations through a narrow ideological prism—conservative or liberal, "accommodationist" or "separationist," Republican or Democratic, religious or secular—is to miss the richness of their contribution to American life. It is also to miss the richness of the debate over what government should and should not do to encourage their work.

OPENING UP THE DEBATE

Our purpose here is not to impress upon readers a particular, dogmatic viewpoint or to give one and only one answer to the question posed in our subtitle. On the contrary, in an area where the lines are drawn sharply and harden quickly, this is very consciously *not* a party-line book. It is intended to open up the debate, not to narrow it.

We hope that even the staunchest critics of government funding for congregations might come away with a better understanding of why this idea appeals to many and with a better appreciation of the large contributions that congregations make. And we hope that even the strongest supporters of government assistance for these groups might better appreciate that serious questions about this idea are not simply the product of extreme secularist minds closed to religion altogether, but reflect genuine concerns about civil rights and religious freedom.

This book began taking shape well before President Bush took office and made the work of faith-based organizations a centerpiece of his administration. It grew out of a series of conferences held between 1999 and 2001 at the Brookings Institution with the support of the Pew Charitable Trusts. This volume is designed neither to praise nor to condemn the president's efforts; you will find both praise and criticism here. Most of the essays are concerned with problems that transcend the particulars of one administration's efforts, on the theory that we will be debating the role of religious institutions in our public life long after this administration ends.

The project reflects a certain frustration with the way the issue of government aid to faith-based organizations is usually confronted. In 1997, one of the editors and John DiIulio—who served as the first director of the White House Office of Faith-Based and Community Initiatives before his departure in August of 2001—put together a series of meetings to discuss what churches, synagogues, and mosques do to alleviate poverty and assist the marginalized. The meetings were highly productive and led to publication of the volume *What's God Got to Do with the American Experiment?*[4]

What became clear during those discussions is that, too often, advocates of competing viewpoints retreat too quickly to first principles. The word *retreat* is chosen intentionally. Of course, it is good to argue about first principles. But participants in this debate are so comfortable with disputes over what the First Amendment does or does not mean that they sometimes give short shrift to examining the actual contributions of religious congregations to social well-being.

Many insights are lost when this happens, among them the role of congregations as providers of service, as the creation and creators of community, and as organizers of efforts to push government and society to do more on behalf of social justice. The fact that much government money has long flowed in, through, and around religious institutions is ignored. And, as we have seen, important differences among those who admire the work of the congregations get lost, too.

The *Sacred Places, Civic Purposes* project was organized to put problem solving at the forefront and to deal with the broader constitutional and cultural issues in the context of the *specific* and important work that congregations do. You could say that we enter the discussion through a side door, beginning with the social problems and what can be done about them. Only then do we ask about the capacity of religious groups to alleviate them, and only after that do we look at government's role. This book is, first, about social problems, especially problems faced by the poor; second, about the contributions that religious groups make to meeting these social needs; and, third, about the ways in which government can help (and may hinder) the efforts of religious groups.

This focus is reflected in the organization of the book and the substance of the essays. The last section deals with the broad argument about government aid to faith-based organizations only *after* a series of essays that examine particular problems in which congregations are closely engaged. We focused on five: teen pregnancy, crime, community development, education, and child care. We know, of course, that the work of congregations extends beyond these areas, but they are particularly instructive and important.

Our goal was to gather together not only specialists on church-state issues but also social scientists, clergy, educators, government officials, social service providers, activists, and business leaders deeply engaged in these issues. We wanted to discuss what faith-based organizations do in the context of the efforts of others to deal with the problems at hand. The sessions, in which some 500 people participated, were notable not just for the work of the formal presenters but also for the quality of our audiences, which were made up of sober analysts, passionate practitioners, and impassioned critics. Some of the essays here grow out of comments from the audience and are not simply the work of those commissioned to write or respond to papers.

The first five sections of the book are organized in roughly the same way, containing two or three major papers from each session, followed by a series of shorter commentaries. This book is not a conference report. Transcripts of the meetings themselves can be found at the Brookings Institution website (www.brookings.edu). Instead, we asked authors to transform their comments into essays. We greatly appreciate their work. Many of the shorter essays are self-contained arguments and occasionally reply as much to each other as to the major papers. The essays by Keith Pavlischek and Julie Segal, for example, grew out of our session on crime, but they offer rich encapsulations of the views on opposing sides in the broader charitable choice controversy.

If we may be permitted a brief point of pride, we believe that the authors gathered in this book are among the best people in their particular fields. They offer a very wide range of viewpoints—religious and denominational as well as political and philosophical. Neither of the editors agrees with all of the essays gathered here, and we suspect that this will be true of virtually anyone who comes to this book. We hope this is one of its strengths. And many of the essays, designed to describe social problems and what is being done to alleviate them, may draw assent *across* ideological and philosophical barriers.

As the book makes clear, supporters of government aid for faith-based social service provision are not always themselves religiously active or even religious at all. Critics of these proposals include some who are now hard at work within the very congregations and faith-based organizations targeted for assistance. On many of these questions, those most involved in faith-based organizations are more interested in achieving a broader and more generous commitment by government to the poor than in receiving any particular help for their own institution.

FAITH-BASED PROBLEM SOLVING

Religious congregations play very different roles on different issues. On the matter of teen pregnancy, there is widespread concern about whether religious congregations are doing *enough*, and different denominations and religious traditions clearly have quite different views on what the content of sex education should be.

This often unnoticed fact should not be surprising. As Isabel Sawhill writes, those engaged in battling teen pregnancy tend to be divided into two broad camps. One camp, which she describes as *moralists*, is concerned primarily with the immorality of premarital sex and its dangers. Those she calls *consequentialists* are concerned primarily with the health consequences and the number of births to teens. She argues that strategies offered by *both* groups are essential to continuing the downward trend of teen pregnancy.

Debra Haffner, a consequentialist in Sawhill's terms, advocates an approach that emphasizes education (including education in contraception). Congregations, she says, should play an important part in supplementing the education that takes place in the home and in schools. Patrick Fagan, a moralist in Sawhill's schema, cautions that liberal approaches to sexuality have failed to produce results and that only a religiously based, abstinence approach can sustain the downward trend. Fagan argues that church attendance itself is powerfully associated with the avoidance of early sexual experience by teens and thus of pregnancy. We do not agree with all of Fagan's views—for what it is worth, our ideas run closer to those of Sawhill. But Fagan's essay underscores that the most important effects of religion often come from practice itself and not from any particular "faith-based program." One can believe this, of course, and still oppose government grants and contracts that directly support the practice of religion.

The control and prevention of crime entail some of the *least* and *most* controversial forms of faith-based engagement. It is impossible not to admire the work congregations have done to patrol neighborhoods, keep at-risk teens from falling into criminality, and help former prisoners rebuild their lives. John DiIulio, George Kelling, the Reverend Eugene Rivers, and Chris Winship, among others, discuss the success of Boston's Ten Point Coalition in grappling with these tasks.

Kelling, a noted criminologist, reflects broadly on the nature of "interorganizational collaborations" in fighting crime, drawing on his two decades of experience working on anticrime and community policing initiatives. As moral authorities that prod communities to take control of the "small things," Kelling argues, congregations play a crucial role in halting the deterioration of neighborhoods and reducing violence.

His criticisms of religious groups for their response to his own initiatives in reducing crime in the New York subway system also point to an aspect of religious engagement in social problems so often ignored in the current debate. As he shows, the interventions of churches, synagogues, and mosques are often on the *liberal* side of the public debate, to the frustration of the very conservatives who are usually so lavish in their praise of faith-based organizations. Whether or not one agrees with Kelling's overall view, he is surely correct in insisting that religious participants in the public debate have an obligation to "get the problem right." They must match their moral witness with an understanding of the practical trade-offs facing those trying to solve public problems. That is good advice to the left, the right, and the center.

One area in which faith-based organizations play a large role in the reduction of crime—the treatment of those addicted to drugs—is likely to be at the heart of the controversy over whether government funding for faith-based efforts is constitutional or not. Many of the most successful drug treatment programs may turn out to be those that place the greatest religious demands on participants. There are, as yet, not enough data to know that for sure, but assume for the moment that this claim is true. If religious conversion is a powerful tool for freeing individuals from drug dependency, and if cost-benefit analysis is to guide the spending of public money on drug programs, what is to be done? The *more* religiously demanding a program is, the *greater* is its potential to violate the First Amendment, a point alluded to by DiIulio.

Supporters of faith-based drug treatment would argue that government should put its money wherever it finds success, a point made forcefully by Pavlischek. But putting government money directly into such programs would almost certainly involve government support for religious conversion. Vouchers are a partial answer to the dilemma, but they do not make it go away.

In the work of community development, local religious institutions are often crucial as organizers who can stand up for the credibility of local organizations. They are the best link many of our poorest neighborhoods have to other institutions, especially those with the capacity to invest capital. "Congregations," writes Jeremy Nowak, "often serve as the most important place within low-income communities for building secular public relationships." Similarly, Avis

Vidal and Nowak both see religious congregations as aiding the typical community development corporation by serving as "incubators and organizers." Congregations provide a base of volunteers, create a direct link to financial resources, and promote public trust. Without necessarily receiving a dime in government funds themselves, congregations play a critical role in persuading investors, public and private, that a particular project is worthy and has authentic community support.

Father Joseph Hacala forcefully argues that community development is a special and especially enlightening case because faith-based institutions serve as far more than "service providers" or Samaritans trying to bind up individual wounds temporarily. In this work, the faith communities deal with the essential issues of social justice. They address the failures of economic structures even as they seek to develop the capacities of individuals. They seek not merely short-term spending to alleviate social problems but also long-term investments to reconstruct communities. Hacala, who headed the office on faith-based work at the Department of Housing and Urban Development during the Clinton administration and before that directed the Catholic Church's Campaign for Human Development, knows whereof he speaks. He underscores the existence of faith-based initiatives long before the current round of attention they've won.

In discussing the role of congregations in education, we consciously *avoid* focusing on the voucher issue. We do so in part because there has already been so much research and debate on this question. We also believe that the argument over vouchers shifts attention away from the many things that *even those religious congregations without schools of their own* already do to enhance the educational opportunities of children. As Ernie Cortes reports, the Industrial Areas Foundation (IAF) has used the churches as a base for organizing parents to demand improved public school curriculums, better teaching, and enhanced provision of child care. Dennis Shirley describes in detail the work of the IAF. "Congregations," he says, "can be powerful allies with schools in the struggle to create a safe environment for urban youth and to provide them with a high-quality education." Mavis Sanders offers a helpful catalogue of partnerships between public schools and faith-based institutions going on *right now*. They undertake their good work without raising constitutional problems or ideological controversy. David Hornbeck, the former school superintendent in Philadelphia, offers eloquent practical testimony about his work with faith-based institutions and his view that the churches, synagogues, and mosques are indispensable allies of *public* education.

All of these examples are important because they suggest one danger in the current debate: *so much attention is being paid to charitable choice programs, including the Bush proposals, that little notice is given to the vast array of activities un-*

dertaken *by the religious institutions that are not constitutionally controversial.* To some degree, both Bush *and* his critics might be faulted for suggesting that faith-based initiatives are much newer and bolder than they are. Bush himself seems to go back and forth on this matter, at times emphasizing the novelty of his program, at others suggesting—in the interest of reassuring critics but also accurately—that he is only building on past achievements.

In truth, Catholic Charities, Lutheran Services of America, and the Jewish Federations—representing religiously affiliated, but independently incorporated, nonprofit organizations—have long received public funds for the provision of secular services. It is worth noting, however, that charitable choice does not require houses of worship to form separate 501(c)(3) organizations to receive direct government grants or contracts. This is one of a number of charitable choice provisions that represents significant change in the relationship between the government and religious institutions, which is why it is controversial. But charitable choice does not represent some sudden entry by religiously affiliated groups into the social service field; such groups have always played a large role.

The case of education, like that of community development, underscores the danger of seeing religious congregations only as potential "service providers." This undervalues their role as community organizers and advocates. As the experience of the IAF and its Alliance schools shows, congregations often make their largest civic contributions as critics of the status quo who seek *not* government funding for themselves, but better and more responsive government for their members and their neighborhoods.

Government partnerships with faith-based organizations in the provision of child care is the subject of the fifth part of this book. This extremely important story is told well by Joan Lombardi, Mary Bogle, and the co-authors Fred Davie, Susan Le Menestrel, and Richard Murphy. The child care case should be playing a much bigger role in our current debate because it represents one of the oldest and most established forms of government partnership with faith-based groups. As Bogle notes, "Congregation-based early childhood programs have been supported by taxpayer dollars for at least thirty years." The Child Care and Development Block Grant, included in the Omnibus Budget Reconciliation Act signed by the first President Bush in November of 1990, provided for vouchers that parents could use in congregation-based facilities.

This is a government-subsidized faith-based program that seems to have worked and for that reason alone deserves study. But the entire area of child care is fraught with difficulty—in part because needs still outstrip available government resources. As Davie, Le Menestrel, and Murphy point out, these programs face enormous staff turnover. Teacher salaries are low. There is "a documented extreme need for after-school programming in schools, especially for low-income families."

One question that deserves further debate is whether the provision of child care piecemeal through vouchers, including vouchers that go to religious programs, may hinder the creation of broader networks of both preschool and after-school care within or attached to public school systems. Another is whether we are focusing so much of the debate on *whether* religious institutions should get public funds that we are evading the broader debate over whether *more* public funds, however spent, are needed for child care. Lombardi makes the trenchant point that faith-based institutions are popular among child-care providers because "religious institutions often have the only spaces available, especially for low-income families." The issue, she says, is often as much about a shortage of *space* as it is about *faith*. The religious congregations are, too frequently, the only nongovernmental institutions to which the very poor can turn, in part because they are often the only institutions over which they exercise a degree of control.

Still, Lisbeth Schorr notes that there may well be something special about faith-based child care because it is built on "the desire to instill the traits, norms, and beliefs of a particular culture or faith." Having faith as a "core value," she says, can allow programs and those who work in them "to persevere in the face of stress, uncertainty, and disappointment." Faith keeps hope alive.

WHAT'S TO BE DONE?

It is only after examining these particular problems that the book turns more squarely toward the contemporary debate over charitable choice and the Bush initiatives. Even here we have tried to introduce arguments that fall outside the usual confrontations over the First Amendment.

Mark Chaves of the University of Arizona has conducted what is perhaps the most extensive national survey of what congregations actually do in the sphere of social services and what they are likely to do with the dawn of charitable choice. His findings should inject a note of realism into the conversation:

> Although virtually all congregations engage in what might be considered social service activities and although a majority—57 percent—support provision of some type of more or less formal social service, community development, or neighborhood organizing projects, the intensity of congregational involvement varies widely.

Although supporters of charitable choice might hope that congregations engage in what he calls "holistic" services, Chaves finds that they stick with the basic and the immediate. On the whole, they do not have vast staffs dealing with social services. Only 6 percent of all congregations—and only 12 percent of congregations reporting some degree of social service involvement—have even one staff person "who devotes at least 25 percent of his or her time to social service projects."

"Congregations," he finds, "are much more likely to engage in activities that address the immediate needs of individuals for food, clothing, and shelter than to engage in projects or programs that require sustained involvement to meet longer-term goals." This is neither surprising nor in the least dishonorable. It does suggest the danger of placing excessive hopes in the transforming power of individual congregations, especially smaller ones, working all by themselves. As Chaves notes, many of the most effective congregational programs are carried out in partnerships with both religious and secular allies. Small may be beautiful, but Chaves finds that "the minority of large congregations provide the bulk of social services carried out by congregations."

African American churches "are more likely to be engaged in certain key types of social services, such as education, mentoring, substance abuse, and job training or employment assistance programs." Not only are African American congregations more engaged in social services now, but they also are more likely to apply for government funds under charitable choice programs in the future. Chaves finds that 36 percent of all congregations would be interested in applying for government money to support their human services programs. This, of course, also means that a substantial majority of congregations do *not* want to apply. But there is a huge difference by race: 64 percent of African American congregations express a willingness to apply for government funds, compared with only 28 percent of white congregations. (And, as John DiIulio has pointed out, inner-city Hispanic congregations are similar to African American congregations in their inclination toward social work and social activism.)

Chaves's findings mean that any realistic discussion of charitable choice and the Bush initiative must be candid about the centrality of African American congregations to this debate.

The Chaves study also finds that Catholic and liberal-to-moderate Protestant congregations are significantly more likely to apply for government social service funds than are conservative or evangelical congregations. This may help to explain why the Bush initiative does not excite the conservative evangelical base of the Republican Party to the degree many expected and has even drawn criticism from its ranks. The paradox of this initiative is that it most interests those congregations *least* likely to be conservative and Republican in their political orientation.

Chaves's conclusions are important. "The assumption that charitable choice initiatives are likely to involve *new* sorts of religious congregations in providing publicly funded social services—those that have not been involved before—is questionable." As we have seen, his findings suggest that religious social service providers are actually *more* likely to engage in holistic, long-term service if they collaborate with secular organizations, including the government.

For anyone who wants a preview of where this debate might go, *In Good Faith* is an excellent place to begin. This is a consensus statement worked out among critics and supporters of expanded government aid to faith-based organizations representing a variety of political perspectives and faith traditions—Protestant, Jewish, Muslim, Catholic, Buddhist, and Sikh. We include the document here. Over several years, some of the most distinguished and engaged parties in this debate hashed out their differences in a spirit of civility and questing. The consensus statement is important not only for where agreement was found, but also for where the points of disagreement were clarified and placed in relief. This group sought to narrow the differences, and its findings suggest that whatever the fate of the Bush initiative, there is broad room for cooperation between government and faith-based groups, even in the eyes of those most committed to church-state separation. Precisely because the participants searched so hard for consensus where they could find it, the points of disagreement they identify are likely to be the core sticking points as Congress and the country work through this issue. Melissa Rogers, one of the signers of *In Good Faith* and now the executive director of the Pew Forum on Religion and Public Life, offers a fascinating tour of areas where there is wide agreement, and places where there is deep dispute. She notes that divisions do not always fall neatly along the lines of left and right. On certain questions, even those who often find themselves allies discover that they have important and principled differences.

Other essays by John DiIulio, Rabbi David Saperstein, and Peter Steinfels provide powerful alternative—but also overlapping—perspectives on the current controversy. They disagree about the proper relationship of government to faith-based charity, but they share a desire to find constitutional and consensual ways of supporting the good works of religious people, their houses of worship, and their organizations.

It is striking, for example, that DiIulio, the Bush administration's point man on the faith-based initiative during its first months, is more concerned with enhancing the capacity of congregations to help the poor than he is with forwarding any particular conception of government's role in this effort. He would happily give way on legislation if he could count on vastly increased private sector support for the indispensable efforts of faith-based groups in improving the lives of the outcast among us. DiIulio has also included an important postscript, written after his departure from the Bush administration. He suggests that there are grounds for conciliation and compromise that might move legislation forward.

After the assaults of September 11, the administration and both parties in Congress were considering a stripped-down version of the president's proposal through which its least controversial provisions might be enacted into law. "What this means is that the time for any kind of complicated or contentious debate is not now," DiIulio told the *New York Times* in mid-October. "The pieces on which there is the broadest agreement should be moved now. There will be time aplenty to accomplish more later on. That is the spirit of the moment."

It is also striking that David Saperstein, a critic of the Bush initiative and a strong advocate of church-state separation, favors efforts to make it easier for congregations to create separate 501(c)(3) status, which could help these organizations to receive government funding. For all their disagreements, DiIulio and Saperstein want to strengthen the religious sector. Both would prefer this to happen in a way that brought the nation together behind efforts to lift up the disadvantaged.

Although we have not tilted this book toward our own conclusions, it is fair to ask what its editors believe about the fundamental questions raised here. We might both be described as cautiously optimistic about expanded government help to faith-based institutions. We are optimistic because, for all the reasons described in this book, it is clear that the faith-based institutions can work wonders—even, occasionally, miracles—and because they are so often the institutions most closely connected to those on society's margins. Without their houses of worship and the sense of personal and community obligation that they instill, many of our nation's neighborhoods would be lost. Faith-based institutions are, quite simply, essential to the achievement of social justice.

But we are cautious because we do not dismiss the constitutional difficulties these efforts raise. Lines have to be drawn somewhere, especially on the questions of whether the most needy might be proselytized against their will and how rules on employment practices can be written to protect both the integrity of religious institutions and the rights of individuals.

It must also be said that charitable choice programs raise different questions in large and religiously diverse metropolitan areas than they do in more religiously homogeneous communities. Charitable choice guarantees, in principle, that no one seeking social services should have to go to a program that he or she objects to on religious grounds. In metropolitan areas, seekers of services may have a wide range of choices among public, private secular, and religious providers. But those choices may not exist everywhere and certainly not in the same profusion. And, as Diana Jones Wilson argues in the case of child care, rural areas often face even larger shortages of resources and facilities than cities or suburbs. Much of the faith-based discussion has focused, for understandable reasons, on inner cities. As Wilson argues forcefully, attention must be paid to rural America as well.

We also are cautious because neither of us believes that enhancing the capacity of religious institutions is any substitute for increased government support to health care, child care, income supplements for the working poor, and education. It would be an injustice to faith-based groups if the controversy over government help for their good works became a distraction from a necessary debate over how our nation's social needs should be met. It is good that President Bush has said, "Government will never be replaced by charities and community groups." But there is more to be said and debated. Some who sympathize with the president's objectives—among them Senator Joe Lieberman—have questioned how much an initiative of this sort could do for the poor absent significant new spending.

This debate entails not just church-state questions. It is also about how government can strengthen civic and community institutions, whether they be secular or religious. After the House passed a version of the president's plan on a largely partisan vote in July of 2001, Lieberman, among others, suggested that the president's ideas would win more support if they were part of a broader effort to reinvigorate civil society and the nation's voluntary associations. And ultimately this is an argument about whether government should do more for—and how it could do better by—the very Americans, the poorest among us, for whom this initiative was created. Compassion is good, but justice is better.

The danger that greater dependence on government aid could still the prophetic voices of the churches in challenging government should therefore be taken seriously. A great debate is going on in the African American church over whether this initiative is designed in part for political reasons—to change the allegiances of the Democratic Party's most faithful allies. A different but parallel fear from some churches is that entanglement with government and government red tape could obstruct the preaching of the whole of their faith.

From the point of view of religious people, there is an additional danger. Will these programs so emphasize the *instrumental* character of religion—its capacity to create social service programs that "work"—that we will stop caring about the truth and validity of what a tradition teaches and preaches, the most important issue to any religious tradition that takes itself seriously? If government aid truly does dilute what makes religious programs special, this program could well turn out to be, as Melissa Rogers has said, "the wrong way to do right."

But these questions and doubts should not obscure the ways in which the new debate over the civic role of sacred institutions has been powerfully good for our nation. It has renewed our appreciation of what religious congregations contribute to the commonweal. It has reminded us of the dual roles of religious leaders as prophetic and critical voices, and as practical and loving service providers. It has led us to consider both religion's social impact and its effect on individuals—and how the two interact.

In his book *The Needs of Strangers*, Michael Ignatieff writes: "We need justice, we need liberty, and we need as much solidarity as can be reconciled with justice and liberty."[5] The current interest in the role of faith-based groups in public policy and the willingness of politicians—George W. Bush, Al Gore, and Joe Lieberman among them—to talk about their faith in public reflect a search for a new public moral language that tries to find a plausible route to Ignatieff's objectives. In that discussion, it is inevitable that the religious will encounter the secular, that the sacred will encounter the civic.

Sacred places serve civic purposes. That is the central theme of this book. But the sacred and the civic both need protection—sometimes from each other. Religion loses its integrity if its value is measured solely in civic terms. The civic life of a free and pluralistic nation can never be dominated by a particular faith, nor can it be stripped of faith. America's religious life has been strengthened, not weakened, by the Constitution's guarantees that the government cannot get in the way of the free exercise of religion, and cannot establish a public faith. Our government, in turn, has benefited from the challenges regularly put to it by people of faith who need not fear retribution for their demands that the state and the society reach for higher standards.

In its first phase, during the first half of 2001, the debate over the Bush initiative proved deeply divisive, and not only in partisan terms. It will be a great loss if the debate over faith-based charity and social action is locked into this frame in the coming years. If this book proves anything, it is that the work of our religious congregations engages the energy and commitment of Americans across all partisan and ideological divides. The challenge is to find ways in which government can foster this good work without so dividing Americans across religious and political lines that the work itself is jeopardized. This won't be easy. Good things often aren't.

Few events more powerfully underscore the relationship between the sacred and the civic than the public response to the terrorist assaults of September 11, 2001. Throughout the nation, citizens spontaneously flocked to their houses of worship in search of consolation, understanding, and solidarity. Prayer and meditation, along with the acts of generosity and mercy that so often followed, partook of both the sacred and civic realms. Americans discussed the urgency of religious toleration and the paradox that religious commitment, depending on how it is understood, can unite communities or divide them from each other. It can lead, we have learned, to love *or* hatred. The terrible events pushed the country toward a new spirit of seriousness and reflection—creating a moment that might allow us to begin anew our national conversation about faith-based initiatives and the meaning of faith in our public life.

NOTES

1. Pew Forum on Religion and Public Life and Pew Research Center for the People and the Press, *Faith-Based Funding Backed, but Church-State Doubts Abound: A Survey for the Pew Forum on Religion and Public Life* (Washington, D.C.: April 10, 2001). See section 1: "Funding for Faith-Based Organizations: Broader Support, Deeper Differences."

2. Ibid.

3. Mark R. Warren, *Dry Bones Rattling: Community Building to Revitalize American Democracy* (Princeton University Press, 2001), p. 27.

4. E. J. Dionne Jr. and John J. DiIulio Jr., *What's God Got to Do with the American Experiment?* (Brookings Institution Press, 2000).

5. Michael Ignatieff, *The Needs of Strangers: An Essay on the Philosophy of Human Needs* (New York: Viking, 1985), p. 141.

PART ONE

THE ROLE OF FAITH-BASED
ORGANIZATIONS IN PREVENTING
Teen Pregnancy

CHAPTER TWO

Framing the Debate: Faith-Based Approaches to Preventing Teen Pregnancy

ISABEL SAWHILL

The role of sacred places in addressing social problems has received heightened attention in recent years. The inclusion of a charitable choice provision in the welfare reform bill of 1996, together with President Bush's advocacy of faith-based approaches to social problems, has catalyzed new conversations about the wisdom and efficacy of these approaches. In my paper, I address five questions that I think we should be asking about faith-based approaches to preventing teenage pregnancy.[1] First, to what extent does our interest in preventing teen pregnancy turn on moral and ethical issues? Second, what is the role of faith-based institutions in resolving whatever moral dilemmas exist? Third, how should we think about the role of faith-based institutions in a specifically American context? Fourth, how should we deal with the conflict engendered by the fact that different faith communities have different views about the best way to reduce teen pregnancy? And, finally, what are the pros and cons of expanding government support for faith-based approaches?

TO WHAT EXTENT DO OUR VIEWS ABOUT TEEN PREGNANCY TURN ON MORAL QUESTIONS?

The basic fact is that four out of ten girls in the United States become pregnant before their twentieth birthday. Nearly everyone thinks that is a problem, but they do not necessarily agree about *why* it is a problem. If I had to simplify, I would say that there are two major camps: the moralists and the consequential-ists. The moralists are people who, even if there were no adverse consequences, would still be concerned about the fact that sex is going on outside of marriage, particularly among those who are very young. The consequentialists are people who are worried about sexual activity among teens mostly because it leads to pregnancy or to disease.

I sometimes ask people to go through a thought experiment in which it is assumed that there is a perfect contraceptive, one that is in no way dependent on human motivation or human self-discipline. And, because there is a perfect contraceptive, there are no adverse consequences—there is no HIV or other sexually transmitted diseases, there is no AIDS, there is no pregnancy; there is just sex. Ask yourself how this set of assumptions might change your view of this issue. Would you be comfortable with your thirteen- or fourteen-year-old son or daughter being sexually active under those circumstances, or would you counsel them to abstain? How would you feel about sex outside of marriage? About sex between a twenty-three-year-old and a fifteen-year-old? About sex on a first date? Would you think sex could be an extracurricular activity like basketball in the schools? How would you view rape? Would you knock it down from a felony to a misdemeanor?

In the process of trying to answer such questions, one can begin to sort out the extent to which concerns about this problem stem from its consequences and the extent to which they relate to people's values and to the contexts in which they believe a sexual relationship between two people is more or less appropriate.

We do not yet have a perfect contraceptive. In fact, contraceptive failure rates are higher than most people realize. Teens who use contraceptives do not use them consistently. And even among consistent users of effective methods, 12 to 15 percent get pregnant in a year's time.[2] If you become sexually active on your fifteenth birthday and remain so for five years, your chances of becoming pregnant before age twenty are quite high (roughly 50 percent). Thus, even if you are a consequentialist, you can believe that abstinence for young people is a good thing. You do not have to moralize about it; you can simply say that it is the only sure way of preventing pregnancy and disease.

In fact, an earlier expectation that the widespread availability of modern methods of contraception would drastically reduce teenage pregnancy turned out to be wrong. The much greater use of contraceptives between 1970 and 1990 was not sufficient to reduce the teenage pregnancy rate. The reason the rate did not fall is because, although teens were increasingly likely to use contraceptives, many more of them were sexually active as well and thus at risk of getting pregnant. This increase in teenage sex was fueled by more permissive attitudes. According to the General Social Survey, in 1970, almost 47 percent of the American public agreed with the statement, "Sex before marriage is always or almost always wrong." By 1990, the share had fallen to 36 percent.[3] That is a huge change in attitude over a relatively short period. Over the same period, the proportion of girls ages fifteen to nineteen who reported ever having had sex increased from 29 percent to 55 percent. The net result was that the teen pregnancy rate rose 23 percent between 1972 and 1990.[4]

More recently, teen pregnancy and teen birth rates have been declining. This good news is the result of both more contraceptive use and less sex among teens. But why are teens, both boys and girls, having less sex? Numerous factors undoubtedly contribute to this trend, especially fear of AIDS and other sexually transmitted diseases, but one reason is a marked shift in attitudes or social norms. In contrast to the long-term trend of relaxing attitudes toward premarital sex, recent polls show that young people are becoming more conservative in their beliefs. For example, the percentage of college freshmen agreeing with the statement "It is all right to have sex if two people have known each other for a short time" decreased to 40 percent in 1999, down from 52 percent in 1987.[5]

My conclusion is that *values matter*. They matter both at the micro level—an individual's religious or moral values can influence that person's behavior, regardless of what others around them think or do—and they matter at the macro level—the social norms or practices of a particular era may reinforce or be in opposition to that individual's own values and behaviors. The two interact in subtle, but potentially powerful, ways. We know, for example, that the likelihood that a teenager will engage in sex is influenced by what that teenager believes his or her friends are doing.[6] These peer influences can cause small initial changes in attitudes and behavior to snowball into much bigger effects as the larger group adopts the attitudes and practices of a trend-setting or influential subgroup. Something like this seems to have happened between the 1950s and early 1990s. Premarital, including teen premarital, sex became increasingly acceptable, which is why, in the battle between sex and safe sex, sex won.

WHAT IS THE ROLE OF FAITH-BASED INSTITUTIONS?

If solutions to the problem of children having children are at least partly based on ethical and moral principles, which institutions should we look to for some answers? Basically there are three teaching institutions in our society: families, churches, and schools.

Public schools, because they are open to all, must teach "lowest common denominator curriculum." In fact, sex education in the schools, as desirable as it is, is often mostly about reproductive biology; it is much less about values and relationships.

Churches, because they consist of people who share certain moral values, can be more specific about such matters, especially about the appropriate context for sexual relationships. And families, because they dispense values on the most basic level of all, can be even more prescriptive. Most families, of course, do not exist in isolation; they tend to band together in congregations that are often defined by a shared set of religious or other beliefs.

So, faith-based approaches are appealing because they address some of the moral and ethical dimensions of teen pregnancy. They deal with the whole person; they do not deal just with the medical or reproductive aspects of the problem. And they do this in an environment—to use Bill Galston's words—of care, connection, and community.

Each faith community is going to do this in its own distinctive way. When the National Campaign produced its Nine Tips for Faith Leaders, we did not say, "Here is a particular curriculum or program that you should adopt in your church or synagogue or mosque." Instead we emphasized the need for different faiths to arm teenagers with a sense of belonging and a framework of values drawn from that faith's particular understanding of sex, love, and marriage and the relationships among them. The idea was to ask each faith community to tend its own garden, not to worry about what was planted in someone else's garden. The task for each faith community is to define when and under what circumstances sexual expression is appropriate and when and under what circumstances it is not.

Some churches have become much more proactive on this front in recent years. For example, consider a program called True Love Waits, sponsored by a loosely affiliated group of Christian ministries. The program encourages teens to take a pledge to remain abstinent until marriage. Several million teens have taken the pledge, and research by Peter Bearman and Hannah Brückner at Columbia University has shown that those who take the pledge are much more likely to remain abstinent than those who do not.[7] The program appears to work by creating a subculture within which virginity is considered "cool." However, the effectiveness of the program disappears once pledging becomes so prevalent that the teens involved no longer feel as if they belong to a special group. This suggests that faith is not just about values; it is also about a sense of belonging to a community that shares those values and about trying to live up to the expectations set by that community.

HOW DO WE THINK ABOUT THIS IN A SPECIFICALLY AMERICAN CONTEXT?

Faith-based solutions are particularly appealing in the United States because of the very high level of religious engagement in this country. In 2001, almost two-thirds of Americans said religion was very important in their personal lives. The proportion is much higher among blacks (85 percent) than it is among whites (61 percent) and somewhat higher among women (71 percent) than among men (55 percent).[8] This high level of religiosity coexists with a tradition of religious tolerance. These are both distinctively American characteristics. A recent issue of *The Brookings Review*, edited by E. J. Dionne Jr. and John J. DiIulio Jr., called "What's God Got to Do with the American Experiment?" contains polling data that make this point well.[9]

On the one hand, the polls suggest that, relative to thirty years ago, the public is much more concerned about the moral failings of the population, particularly what they perceive to be the moral failings of the young. This finding holds even after adjusting for the fact that the older generation *always* tends to disapprove of the younger generation's behavior. What the data show is that the gap is wider now than in the past. In a survey conducted by the National Campaign to Prevent Teen Pregnancy, poor moral values were the most frequent reason given by adults for high rates of teen pregnancy.[10] On the other hand, the data suggest that tolerance is alive and well in the United States; that whatever moral failings people perceive around them, they are very tolerant of other individuals' right to live by their own lights. The challenge, then, is how to bring judgments to bear without doing so in a self-righteous, moralizing, or intolerant manner. How, for example, does one say that teen pregnancy is wrong without stigmatizing or denigrating those who are, or have been, teen mothers?

WHAT DO WE DO ABOUT CONFLICT?

Advocates of reducing teen pregnancy may agree about the importance of the goal but disagree about the best way of achieving it. Some want to focus on abstinence until marriage; others argue that the horse is already out of the barn and that it is far more urgent and realistic to provide teens with the information and contraceptive services that they need to protect themselves against pregnancy and disease.

Researchers have entered the fray with studies that support one view or the other. Some of these studies have been influential, but where the research conflicts with deeply held values it is likely to be rejected. For example, no matter how many times researchers tell those who advocate abstinence that providing contraceptives to teenagers has *not* been found to increase rates of sexual activity, these advocates believe that programs that teach about contraceptives—and especially those that advocate their use—send a very mixed message.

So, conflict is a problem, and it is not going to be resolved simply by looking at the facts. But we are beginning to understand that it is not necessary to convert others to our own view in order to reduce teen pregnancy in the aggregate.

Yes, it would be simpler if we could all agree on what to teach our children, and probably a little less confusing to them as well, but it is simply not true that only one approach will work. Abstinence until marriage clearly works to prevent teen pregnancy if you can convince people to adopt it. Contraceptives also clearly work to prevent teen pregnancy if they are used carefully and consistently. And many different combinations of these two approaches can work as well, including delaying sexual activity until one is through high school and practicing safe sex thereafter, just to take one of many examples. It does not have to be either/or; we should reject such a false dichotomy. Both abstinence and contraception are effective and appropriate in different circumstances.

In addition, a lot of confusion and unnecessary conflict emerges because of the tendency to label programs as either "abstinence-only" or as "comprehensive sexuality education." The reality is that most programs fall on a continuum, and this tendency to categorize and label them as falling into one camp or the other is not very useful. What happens in an actual classroom is much more complicated and nuanced than these labels suggest.

These conflicts are often barriers to collaboration. The National Campaign to Prevent Teen Pregnancy has worked with a number of local communities where disagreements about the best approach have paralyzed their efforts to do much of anything. In fact, the problem is so severe in some places that we have a favorite saying at the campaign: "While the adults are arguing, the teens are getting pregnant." The campaign has discovered that when we work through these disagreements at the local level by bringing everybody to the table and having a frank and open, but respectful, discussion—preferably one including teens themselves—the community can then move forward much more effectively.

The campaign's Task Force on Religion and Public Values, chaired by Bill Galston, has similarly had to work through its own disagreements. It is an enormously diverse group, and it spent two years trying to find common ground. By approaching its task in a positive and open-minded way, but without in any way trying to paper over the differences, it established a model for what needs to happen in the rest of the country.

The good news here is that much more common ground exists among the public at large than among the national political leaders and advocacy groups focusing on this issue. Although the organized groups have the loudest, and often the most strident, voices, polls show that the overwhelming majority of both adults and teenagers have a more middle-of-the-road, commonsense view. They are in favor of abstinence for school-age youth, but they also want contraceptives to be available for kids who need them. Specifically, in a survey released by the National Campaign to Prevent Teen Pregnancy in April 2001, 73 percent of adults and 56 percent of teens believed that teens should not be sexually active, but that those who are should have access to birth control.[11] More than 90 percent of both adults and teens want teens to receive a strong message that they should abstain from sex until they are at least out of high school.[12] The public is saying that we should embrace abstinence as the standard but recognize that not everyone will abide by the standard and that it is important to have a safety net. At the same time, by overwhelming majorities, they reject the view that it is okay for teens to be sexually active as long as they have access to birth control.[13]

WHAT ARE THE PROS AND CONS OF MORE GOVERNMENT SUPPORT FOR FAITH-BASED APPROACHES?

The values component of this issue and the fact that most religions have a point of view on it, together with the importance so many Americans attribute to religion, suggests that faith-based organizations have an important role to play in preventing teen pregnancy. President Bush has made faith-based approaches a centerpiece of his domestic agenda and has suggested that they might be especially effective in combating teen pregnancy. The public seems to agree. According to a Pew Research Center survey in cooperation with the Pew Forum on Religion and Public Life, 70 percent are in favor of government funding for faith-based programs. However, when asked what type of organization—religious, nonreligious, or government—is best equipped to address teen pregnancy, 39 percent thought religious organizations would do the best job, a slightly higher number (42 percent) favored other nonprofit organizations, and only 12 percent wanted the government directly involved.

Since more faith-based initiatives will arise because of the new White House office, a host of issues will need to be resolved. What is the capacity of this sector to deliver the services? Should the funding be provided directly to religious organizations or indirectly through vouchers that can be used to buy services from both sectarian and nonsectarian organizations, or through charitable tax credits for those who give to faith-based programs? Who will monitor the expenditure of funds and hold the recipients accountable for results? How does one maintain the kind of separation of church and state called for in the constitution? The charitable choice provision in the 1996 welfare bill provides one model. Under charitable choice, faith-based organizations can compete for funding on an equal basis with other organizations. Any faith-based program must be open to all, regardless of religious affiliation or belief; applicants for services must be provided with a choice of providers (including nonsectarian providers); and the funds cannot be used for purely sectarian purposes.

Assuming that such issues can be resolved, the question will still be: How much difference would more funding of faith-based programs make? Compared with secular programs, are faith-based programs a more effective means of reducing teen pregnancy? Is the "faith" component of faith-based programs a critical ingredient, or is allowing religious organizations to participate in running programs just one way of expanding program capacity? There is little hard evidence on these questions. A review of fifty research studies indicates that teens who are more religious (variously defined) are more likely to delay having sex, although they also may be less likely to use contraception once they do become sexually active.[14] However, the available research is not of high quality and cannot distinguish between two very different explanations. One is that teens with a commitment to delaying sex are, for a variety of reasons, also more likely to be religious. The other is that church attendance or religious beliefs actually produce this commitment. Because it would be difficult, if not impossible, to assign people randomly to programs with and without a faith component, we may never know with any certainty how important the faith ingredient in faith-based programs really is. In the meantime, many fear that expanding faith-based programs will infringe on people's civil liberties and pierce the wall between church and state or that they will teach about abstinence but leave young people with few defenses should they become sexually involved. Such concerns are not entirely unfounded. But my own view is that, on balance, we should expand the sector in ways that would enable more teenagers to find a faith-based "home" within their community. This contributes to the development of lifestyle values that lead to more responsible behavior by providing teens with the kind of social support and spiritual guidance that too often is missing in their lives.

NOTES

1. In answering these questions, I want to acknowledge my indebtedness to William Galston, Sister Mary Rose McGeady, Douglas Kirby, Pat Funderbunk Ware, Pat Fagan, E. J. Dionne Jr., and John J. DiIulio Jr.

2. Robert A. Hatcher and others, *Contraceptive Technology*, 17th rev. ed. (New York, Ardent Media, 1998).

3. Inter-University Consortium for Political and Social Research (ICPSR), *General Social Survey* (University of Michigan, 1998).

4. National Campaign to Prevent Teen Pregnancy, *Halfway There: A Prescription for Continued Progress in Preventing Teen Pregnancy* (Washington, D.C.: National Campaign to Prevent Teen Pregnancy, 2001), pp. 1, 9.

5. University of California, Los Angeles, "College Freshmen: Acceptance of Abortion, Casual Sex at All-Time Low," *Kaiser Daily Reproductive Health Report*, January 27, 1999, available on-line at report.KFF.org/archive/repro/1999/01/kr990127.6/html.

6. Bradford Brown and Wendy Theobald, "How Peers Matter: A Research Synthesis of Peer Influences in Adolescent Pregnancy," in *Peer Potential: Making the Most of How Teens Influence Each Other*, pp. 27–80 (Washington, D.C.: National Campaign to Prevent Teen Pregnancy, 1999). See also Peter S. Bearman and Hannah Brückner, "Peer Effects on Adolescent

Sexual Debut and Pregnancy: An Analysis of a National Survey of Adolescent Girls," in *Peer Potential*.

7. Peter S. Bearman and Hannah Brückner, "Promising the Future: Virginity Pledges and the Transition to First Intercourse," *American Journal of Sociology*, vol. 106, no. 4 (2001), pp. 859–912.

8. Pew Forum on Religion and Public Life and Pew Research Center for the People and the Press, *Faith-Based Funding Backed, but Church-State Doubts Abound: A Survey for the Pew Forum on Religion and Public Life* (Washington, D.C.: April 10, 2001), p. 31.

9. E. J. Dionne Jr. and John J. DiIulio Jr., eds., "What's God Got to Do with the American Experiment?" *Brookings Review*, vol. 17, no. 2 (1999).

10. National Campaign to Prevent Teen Pregnancy, *With One Voice: America's Adults and Teens Sound Off about Teen Pregnancy* (Washington, D.C.: National Campaign to Prevent Teen Pregnancy, 2001), p. 10.

11. Ibid., p. 5.

12. Ibid., p. 6.

13. Ibid., p. 5.

14. Brain Wilcox and others, *Adolescent Religiosity and Sexual Behavior: A Research Review* (Washington, D.C.: National Campaign to Prevent Teen Pregnancy, 2001).

CHAPTER THREE

Joseph's Promise: Extending God's Grace to Pregnant Teens

DEBRA W. HAFFNER

A young teenage woman is found to be pregnant. She has been denying it to herself for months. It is only now, as her belly swells, that someone else notices. Her boyfriend, to whom she is engaged, decides to leave her quietly. "Not mine," he thinks. She is afraid and alone. She is desperate. Thus opens the Gospel of Matthew, but it is a scene that occurs every day in inner-city America, in rural, small-town America, and in suburban, middle-class America. Her name could be Melissa Dressler, Amy Grossberg, Towanda Cunningham, or Linda Hall. In the Gospel of Matthew, her name is Mary.

Teen pregnancy is so pervasive—and its consequences so far-reaching—that it seems to me that the relevant question is not "Why should faith communities be involved?" but instead "How can they not be?" Faith communities must be involved with helping young people prevent pregnancies. When that fails, they must be involved in helping teen parents raise their children in a loving and supportive environment. More fundamentally, faith communities can give young people the skills and attitudes they need to lay a foundation for healthy adult intimate lives for themselves and their future families. We have known for more than two decades that teenagers need two things to avoid teen childbearing: capacity and motivation. Faith communities can help to provide both. They can promote capacity by helping teens remain abstinent and by helping sexually active young people use contraception. They can promote motivation by pro-

This paper is adapted from the author's publication, *A Time to Speak: Faith Communities and Sexuality Education* (New York: SIECUS, 1998).

viding important adult connections to young people who need guidance and support.

We need to deal with young people holistically. Teen pregnancy, HIV/AIDS, and adolescent sexually transmitted diseases are not separate problems for separate, young individuals; they are all related to adolescent sexuality. Faith communities need to address sexuality and their youth from preventative, pastoral, restorative, scientific, and spiritual views.

I learned in the seminary that the word "gospel" literally means the good news. I am going to focus on the good news about faith communities and teen pregnancy, but I want to offer two caveats. First, the fact that I am going to talk about the good news does not mean that I think that the faith communities are doing enough or that, in every faith community I discuss, all congregations are involved in teen pregnancy issues. The second caveat is that faith communities alone are not the answer to this problem—no more than schools alone, or parents alone, or government alone, or the media alone can be the answer. During the last quarter century, we have searched for the magic bullet. In 1976, we thought that just giving teens information would be enough. Then we thought that just opening school-based clinics would be enough. Youth development and education approaches, whether secular or faith-based, also will not be enough. Every church, every synagogue, and every mosque in this country could be involved in this issue, but we still would have a teenage pregnancy problem in this country.

RELIGIOUS INSTITUTIONS REACH YOUTH

Thirty years ago, the National Council of Churches, the Synagogue Council of America, and the United States Catholic Conference called on churches and synagogues to become actively involved in sexuality education within their own congregations and within their communities. On June 8, 1968, they released a statement that remains remarkable today for the tenor of its call for religious involvement in sexuality issues for young people. They wrote:

> We recognize that some parents desire supplementary assistance from church or synagogues and other agencies. Each community of faith should provide resources, leadership, and opportunities, as appropriate, for young people to learn about their development into manhood and womanhood and for adults to grow an understanding of their roles as men and women in family, society, and in the light of their religious heritage. In addition to parents and the religious community, the school and other community agencies can have a vital role in sex education in two particular ways: first,

they can integrate sound sexual information and attitudes with the total education which the child receives in social studies, literature, history, home economics, and the biological and behavioral sciences. Second, they can reach the large numbers of young people whose families have no religious identification but who need to understand their own sexuality and their role in society. . . .

The increased concern and interest in this vital area of human experience now manifested by parents, educators, and religious leaders are cause for gratitude. We urge all to take a more active role, each in its own area of responsibility and competence, in promoting sound leadership and programs in sex education. We believe it is possible to help our sons and daughters achieve a richer, fuller understanding of their sexuality so that their children will enter a world where men and women live and work together in understanding and cooperation and love.[1]

It would be exciting and much anticipated for those three bodies to reaffirm their commitment to this call, issued more than thirty years ago. Religious institutions have the ability to reach young people, and therefore they have a unique role to play in preventing teenage pregnancy. Indeed, after the schools, religious institutions commit themselves to serving teenagers in this country more than any other community agency. Moreover, they are specifically empowered to do so from a moral perspective. Almost 90 percent of teens report that they have a religion.[2] More than 60 percent of young people spend at least an hour a week in a church or synagogue-based activity.[3] And 75 percent of teenagers say that religion and church are "somewhat important" to them, including almost half who say they are "very important."[4]

Yet young people report that faith communities are ignoring their sexuality issues. Only four in ten young people say they receive support and care from adults in their religious community.[5] That is a remarkable statement: six in ten teens *do not* think that the adults in the faith community are there for them. Four in ten teenagers report that they have spent less than six hours in their lifetime addressing a sexuality issue in their church or synagogue.[6] Only half of young people say that their congregation is doing a "good" or "excellent" job at helping prepare them for life.[7] Only 4 percent of youth workers report that they address sexuality at least once a month with teens.[8]

Involvement in a religious community actually protects young people from risk-taking behaviors, including involvement with sexual intercourse at an early age. Teenagers who say that religion and prayer are important to them are more likely to delay sexual intercourse, less likely to use alcohol, less likely to use tobacco, and less likely to use drugs.[9] Almost half of teens say they have "made a conscious decision to wait to have sex." The more importance a teen boy or girl places on religion, the more likely he or she is to name this as the reason for de-laying intercourse.[10] More than 21 percent of girls who consider religion important make a conscious decision to wait.[11] Boys who consider religion very important in their lives are half as likely to have had sexual intercourse, as compared to boys who do not consider religion important.[12]

Religious commitment is also correlated with whether a teen has engaged in sexual or intimate activities other than intercourse. The more importance a teen places on religion, the less likely he or she is to have engaged in activities such as French kissing and petting.[13]

RELIGIOUS INSTITUTIONS SUPPORT INVOLVEMENT

Although teens see the congregations as caring too little about their struggles with sexuality, religious institutions increasingly *want* to be involved in these issues. Indeed, a majority of Christian and Jewish clergy support religious involvement in sexuality issues. According to a survey by the Religious Coalition for Reproductive Choice, 89 percent of clergy agree that sexuality needs to be part of a congregation's program, 95 percent agree that it is appropriate to speak about sexuality issues in religious programs, and 75 percent consider it a problem that religious programs do not address sexuality issues.[14] More than 2,000 clergy and theologians have endorsed the Religious Declaration on Sexual Morality, Justice, and Healing, which calls for comprehensive sexuality education in congregations, schools, and seminaries.[15]

Many denominations and faith institutions have issued statements strongly supporting sexuality and HIV education, both within their congregations and in their communities. For example, the American Baptist Church, the Central Conference of American Rabbis, the Disciples of Christ, the Episcopal Church, the Mennonite Church, the National Council of Churches of Christ, the Presbyterian Church USA, the Unitarian Universalist Association, the United Church of Christ, the United Methodist Church, and the United Synagogues of Conservative Judaism have passed resolutions supporting sexuality education within their faith community. For example, the Christian Church of Christ adopted this resolution in 1987:

> Whereas the number of teen pregnancies is increasing, and it is evident that there is a need for sexuality education for teenagers and their parents; and, whereas human sexuality is recognized as a gift from God and sexuality is therefore a concern of the Church; and, whereas the Church affirms the basic values of love, respect, and responsibility in all human relationships; therefore, be it resolved that Disciples' congregations will play

a central role in the education of their young people and parents by offering clear and responsible information on human sexuality.[16]

Some faith communities have called for sexuality education in the public schools. The American Jewish Congress, the Conference of American Rabbis, the Church of the Brethren, the Episcopal Church, the National Council of Churches of Christ, the Presbyterian Church, the United Church of Christ, the Unitarian Universalist Association, and the United Methodist Church all call on communities to take a role in this issue. For example, the policy of the Church of the Brethren says:

> Education for family life is appropriate within the public schools. It is needed to supplement instruction in the home and church. Public school instruction should include information about the body, sex organs, the reproductive system, but the emphasis should be on values and relationships. Teachers who are responsible for this task should be well trained themselves, and they themselves should be worthy models of mature and responsible sexuality. The Church supports responsible family life education in the public schools, as long as the religious commitment of all students and residents of the community is respected. Parents should keep themselves informed about the content of family-life education courses in which their children are influenced and use that educational experience to foster open discussion of the topic of sexuality with their children. Parents should also be acquainted with the content of such courses for the purposes of continuing dialog with school officials. In such dialog, parents should clarify their Christian principles to insure that their own ethical values are not undermined. Family-life education will not solve all sex, marriage, and family problems. The task requires the coordinated efforts of home, school, and church.[17]

Several denominations have called on congregations to actively support sexuality and HIV education programs in the community. For example, in 1996, the United Methodist Church passed the social principle:

> All children have the right to quality education, including full sexual education appropriate to their stage of development that utilizes the best educational techniques and insights. . . . We recognize the continuing need for full, positive, and factual sex education opportunities for children, youth, and adults. The church offers a unique opportunity to give quality guidance and education in this area.[18]

Another example is the 1994 Presbyterian Church of the USA resolution:

Whereas, the Presbyterian Church (USA) recognized at the 204th General Assembly (1992) that sexuality education is a positive factor in preventing unintended pregnancies and the need for abortion; and whereas, Christian sexuality education should first be done within the family; and whereas, the Church can support and train parents and other custodial adults, youth directors, and clergy in this important task; and whereas, the church recognizes that the public schools are also an appropriate setting for educating students about sexuality as an important part of human growth and development, especially when that education is not available in the home or church; and whereas, the Presbyterian Church (USA) feels strongly that the public education system should include quality sexuality education as a component of any human growth and development curriculum beginning in the elementary grades; therefore, the 206th General Assembly (1994) of the Presbyterian Church (USA): (1) Supports the United States Department of Health and Human Services and the U.S. Surgeon General in planning and implementing comprehensive school health education that includes age and developmentally appropriate sexuality education in all grades as a part of human growth and development curriculum for youth. (2) Calls upon state legislatures to require that all schools provide comprehensive kindergarten through twelfth grade human growth and development education that is complete, factual, accurate, free of bias, and does not discriminate on the basis of sex, race, national origin, ancestry, creed, pregnancy, marital or parental status, sexual orientation, or physical, mental, emotional, or learning disability. (3) Calls upon the congregations of the Presbyterian Church (USA) to provide additional sexuality education that reflects the values of the Reformed theological tradition.[19]

In summary, many denominations have developed their own curricula and guides for sexuality education in faith communities. A few denominations, including the Presbyterian Church USA, the United Church of Christ, and the Unitarian Universalist Association, have developed life span curriculums. Other denominations have programs for teenagers, including the Church of the Brethren, the Evangelical Lutheran Church in America, the Mennonite Church, the Salvation Army, the Southern Baptist Convention, and the United Methodist Church. The Catholic Church has adopted the Benziger Family Life Program for young people, kindergarten through eighth grades. The United Methodist Church has a curriculum for older elementary school children.

There is a need for life span sexuality programs in faith communities, beginning with parents of pre-schoolers and continuing through programs for the

elderly. One of the frequent mistakes is to treat sexuality information as an immunization given to the early teens once, with an expectation that it will last
them for life. The development of sound sexual values and attitudes begins in
early childhood and continues through adolescence and adulthood. The type of
information and support needed at each stage differs; for adults, the need for information on sexuality at age forty-five is very different than the need at age
eighteen, and it will be very different again at age seventy-eight. And while programs such as those of the Presbyterian Church, the United Church of Christ,
and the Unitarian Universalist Association take seriously the need for faith communities to address sexuality for people throughout their lives, most church-
based and secular programs concentrate their sexuality education programs at
the level of teenagers. Those programs should be broadened for greater effect.

CONGREGATIONAL ACTIVITIES

Faith communities can offer young people many types of support and programs
that could contribute to the prevention of teenage pregnancy. For example, congregations offer young people opportunities for service, a positive peer group,
and a faith-based foundation for decisionmaking. Congregations could support
not only prevention programs but also pregnant teenagers as well. While researching this paper, I found that there have been many reports, going back to
1975, from states, communities, and the National Academy of Sciences on what
congregations should do to *prevent* pregnancy. I could not find a single one that
discussed the role that congregations should play with *already pregnant* teenagers.

Congregations can help to prevent teen pregnancy by encouraging youth
groups to participate in community activities related to sexuality. For example,
a young person might volunteer at an AIDS hospice, work at a hospital nursery, educate or minister to peers, or staff a community hotline. These activities
would offer teens an opportunity for service, while directly adding to the resources that teens can draw on as they continue to learn about themselves, their
sexuality, and the consequences of various sexual behaviors. Congregations also
can hold after-school programs in the church or temple facility for pre-teens
and teenagers. These programs may include sexuality topics as discussed above,
or they may have a primarily recreational purpose. After all, even without sex-
uality-related programming, young people who are involved in after-school activities, particularly in religious institutions, are less likely to become involved in
sexual behavior.

Congregations also can influence peer cultures by implementing a peer education program around sexuality issues. When trained high school youth groups
provide education and information about sexuality to middle school students

and pre-adolescents, both groups benefit. It is no secret that many congregations "lose" their adolescents after their coming-of-age ceremonies. Offering a sexuality education program for high school youth might help to keep them involved. It is important for youth ministers to address sexuality issues, to offer guidelines for youth retreats, sleepovers, and camping trips, and to be explicit about expectations for youth and leaders. In this way, congregations can help youth to learn skills, such as assertiveness, communication, negotiation, and decisionmaking, that will help them to avoid unplanned and premature sexual behavior. They also can provide them with opportunities to explore controversial issues.

Congregations can help young people to find adult mentors and positive role models. Young people need significant adults in their lives in addition to their parents. And congregations can provide important support for parents, who are the primary sexuality educators of their children. Most parents welcome the assistance of their faith community in helping to provide their children with morals and values. In addition to imparting knowledge, congregations can help adults to develop the skills they need to be good parents, and that includes helping them talk to their children about sexuality. Pastors can encourage parent/child communication on sexuality issues. It is important that religious education programs keep parents informed and up-to-date on efforts to educate their youth about sexuality. Parents need an opportunity to review the curricula and materials, meet with the adult leaders, and complete parent/child homework sessions to increase communication about sexuality issues. Life span religious education can hold retreats for middle school students and their parents.

Faith communities have a unique role to play in sexuality education and teen pregnancy prevention within the context of the religious values supported by that denomination. The Southern Baptists' True Love Waits program, which revolves around young people taking virginity pledges, and the United Church of Christ and the Unitarian Universalist Association's Our Whole Lives program differ dramatically. The programs differ vastly in their approach, and yet both are grounded in the faith principles of the denominations, and both reflect the wishes of the parents who attend them. Neither would be appropriate in the public school setting without major adaptation. But within their own faith context, they are appropriate and responsive to the needs of young people.

Congregations also can play a supportive role in helping pregnant teens and their families to cope with pregnancy. Pastors and congregations should reach out with love to families coping with a pregnant teen girl and her partner. Such support might include counseling on pregnancy options; adoption assistance; adoption, prenatal, and abortion referrals; premarital counseling; and support for the newborn and mother, consistent with the values of the religious community.

When we think about safe communities and teen pregnancy prevention, we need not think just about sexuality education and HIV education programs. The faith community is a place where young people can be connected, where they can become involved in volunteer activities, where they can interact with other significant adults in addition to their parents, where they can make friendships, where they can develop relationships, and where they can find mentors. Teenage pregnancy can be prevented when young people are offered hope for their future. Our faith communities do that, even when they do not explicitly address sexuality issues.

GOVERNMENT FUNDING TO FAITH COMMUNITIES FOR TEEN PREGNANCY PREVENTION

Congregations across the United States have been involved in a variety of programs to promote abstinence among teenagers under federal grant programs. Many congregations received funding under the Adolescent Family Life Act demonstration grants (a program known as AFLA) to prevent teenage pregnancy through teaching abstinence and promoting adoption as the appropriate choice for teenagers who become pregnant. In 1983, a group of clergy and other individuals filed suit against AFLA claiming it was administered in a way that violated the Establishment Clause of the First Amendment in the U.S. constitution. The plaintiffs in *Kendrick* v. *Sullivan* claimed that the program constituted a federal endorsement of a particular religious point of view.

Although the Supreme Court ruled that the statute was constitutional on its face, litigation continued over the manner in which the program was administered. In January 1993, an out-of-court settlement stipulated that AFLA-funded sexuality education not include religious references, be medically accurate, respect the principle of self-determination of teenagers regarding contraceptive referrals, and not allow grantees to use church sanctuaries for their programs or give presentations in parochial schools during school hours.[20] The settlement expired in 1998, at the same time that the new Abstinence Only Until Marriage program under Title V, Section 510(b), began. During the first year of implementation of the program, eighteen states made Section 510(b) grants directly to faith-based institutions, and twenty-four states reported that abstinence programs took place in faith-based institutions.[21]

CONCLUSIONS

Let us end where we started: at the opening section of the Gospel of Matthew. The text says that Joseph is going to dismiss Mary quietly. Then he goes to sleep, and he has a dream. In the dream, he is told that the child to be born will fulfill the prophecy of Emmanuel, which means "God is with us." Joseph decides that he will support Mary, marry her, and help her to raise the child.

Our faith communities have a role to play in helping our children understand that our sexuality is a sacred gift of creation and that its power needs to be exercised responsibly. We must extend God's grace to all of our children: to the virgins, but also to the young people who are engaged in sexual activity, to those who struggle with their sexual orientation, and to those who face unplanned pregnancies or sexually transmitted diseases. Our faith communities should provide our welcome, our love, and our support to all teens. "God is with us." Isn't that the promise of every child? Of every teenager, regardless of the circumstances of his or her birth? Are we called to do any less than Joseph?

NOTES

1. National Council of Churches Commission on Marriage and Family, the Synagogue Council of America Committee on Family, and the United States Catholic Conference Family Life Bureau, "Interfaith Statement on Sex Education" (National Council of Churches Commission on Marriage and Family, the Synagogue Council of America Committee on Family, and the United States Catholic Conference Family Life Bureau, 1968).

2. Michael D. Resnick and others, "Protecting Adolescents from Harm: Findings from the National Longitudinal Study on Adolescent Health," *Journal of the American Medical Association (JAMA)*, vol. 278, no. 10 (September 10, 1997), pp. 823–32.

3. P. L. Benson, P. C. Scales, and E. C. Roehlkepartain, *A Fragile Foundation: The State of Developmental Assets among American Youth* (Minneapolis, Minn.: Search Institute, forthcoming).

4. Kaiser Family Foundation and YM Magazine, "National Survey of Teens: Teens Talk about Dating, Intimacy, and Their Sexual Experiences" (Menlo Park, Calif.: Henry J. Kaiser Family Foundation, Spring 1998), pp. 6–7.

5. E. C. Roehlkepartain and P. L. Benson, *Youth in Protestant Churches* (Minneapolis, Minn.: Search Institute, 1993), p. 61.

6. Ibid., p. 108.

7. Ibid., p. 110.

8. E. C. Roehlkepartain and P. C. Scales, *Youth Development in Congregations: An Exploration of the Potential Barriers* (Minneapolis, Minn.: Search Institute, 1995).

9. Resnick and others, "Protecting Adolescents from Harm."

10. Kaiser Family Foundation and YM Magazine, "National Survey of Teens."

11. Ibid.

12. Ibid.

13. Ibid.

14. Rabbi Bonnie Margulis, "Clergy Attitudes towards Sexuality and Reproductive Choice" (Washington, D.C.: Religious Coalition for Reproductive Choice, March 1998).

15. See the website, www.religionproject.org: June 4, 2001.

16. Christian Church of Christ, "Resolution no. 8718: Resolution Concerning Sexuality Education" (Christian Church of Christ, 1987), p. 270.

17. Church of the Brethren, "Annual Conference Statement: Human Sexuality from a Christian Perspective" (Church of the Brethren, 1983).

18. United Methodist Church, "Social Principles" (United Methodist Church, 1996), p. 15.

19. Presbyterian Church USA, "Sexuality Education for Youth" (Presbyterian Church USA, July/August 1994).

20. Daniel Daley, "Exclusive Purpose: Abstinence-Only Proponents Create Federal Entitlement in Welfare Reform," *SIECUS Report,* vol. 25, no. 4 (April/May 1997), p. 4.

21. Daniel Daley, *Between the Lines: States' Implementation of the Federal Government's Section 510(b) Abstinence Education Program in Fiscal Year 1998* (New York: SIECUS, 1999).

CHAPTER FOUR

Conservative Triumph: Successes of Worship and Family in Preventing Teen Pregnancy

PATRICK F. FAGAN

The dust is clearing from the falling rubble of the sexual revolution, and social scientists are measuring the fallout. This paper argues that some of the major conservative tenets on sexual issues are increasingly solid or, at minimum, defensible in social science terms. Conservative, religious approaches to sexual morality have a firmer grasp on what is good for teenagers (as well as adults and society as a whole) than do liberal, secular ideas—and they have a clearer, though not necessarily easier, path to that good. The time is ripe for conservative beliefs on sexual morality to claim their place in the public discussion on sex education because conservatives now have the data to illustrate, even in mere utilitarian terms, the reasonableness of their principles.

I also intend to introduce to participants in the debate on sex education a variable in teenage sexual behaviors that is both powerful and neglected: regular worship of God (with the sociological proxy of "frequency of attendance at religious worship" as the measure of this practice). The weekly practice of worship is not just a major part of comprehensive sex education. It is likely the *most* powerful of all influences in attaining the goals of *liberal* sex education, especially when combined with the influence of parental involvement. This conclusion is different from the new development among liberals (with which I agree) that religious institutions have a significant role to play in the delivery of sex education. But independent of sex education, the practice of religious belief—and especially religious worship itself—is perhaps the most powerful variable for good in the formation of sexual attitudes and habits among young people.

In contrast to the effects of liberal sex education programs, the practice of religious beliefs has strong effects in bringing about desired conduct. When adolescents, their peers, or their parents worship God regularly in congregations, adolescent sexual activity is reduced. When parents and their adolescent children *all* worship together, the effect is even greater.

THE POSITIVE EFFECTS ON SEXUAL BEHAVIOR OF THE WORSHIP OF GOD BY ADOLESCENTS

Personal worship of God by adolescents sharply reduces the incidence of premarital intercourse.[1] The more regularly adolescents worship God, the less they engage in sexual activity outside of marriage. Those who do not worship at all engage in high levels of sexual activity. For example, the association between the frequency of worship by all adolescents ages twelve to seventeen and their rate of virginity is striking, based on data from the National Longitudinal Survey of Adolescent Health (often called Add Health); see figure 4-1. Those who worship weekly are more than twice as likely to be virgins as those who do not.

Figure 4-1. *Sexual Experience and Frequency of Worship, Teenagers 12–17*

Percent virgin/nonvirgin

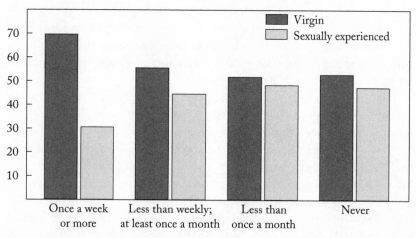

Source: Heritage Foundation domestic policy chart based on data collected 1994–1996 from J. Richard Udry, *The National Longitudinal Study of Adolescent Health* (University of North Carolina at Chapel Hill, Carolina Population Center).

Personal religious practice has a significant and positive impact on the choices that adolescents make regarding their initiation of sexual intercourse. Researchers have found, for example, that the more importance adolescents give to religion and prayer, the longer they retain their virginity.[2] Significantly, this connection between personal religious worship and virginity is noticeable for all adolescent males regardless of their testosterone levels, despite the fact that levels of testosterone normally affect the onset of sexual intercourse among males.[3]

The link between adolescent virginity and personal religious practice is further supported by the findings of Emogene Fox and Michael Young, health educators in Arkansas. In a 1989 survey of 200 freshmen, they find that virgins are significantly more likely than nonvirgins to participate in worship, prayer, and Bible reading and to view the maintenance of virginity as part of God's will for them.[4]

Not only is personal religious practice strongly associated with adolescent sexual abstinence, but the absence of religious practice also is associated with increased premarital sexual involvement. These relationships hold into early adulthood for women (figure 4-2) and for men.

Figure 4-2. *Sexual Experience of Young Adult Females in 1983 and Church Attendance in 1982*

Percent virgin/nonvirgin

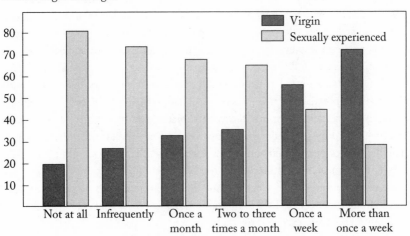

Frequency of church attendance

Source: Heritage Foundation domestic policy chart based on data from *National Longitudinal Study of Youth* (U.S. Department of Labor, Bureau of Labor Statistics). Original analysis by Center for Data Analysis, Heritage Foundation.

Data on the association between the absence of personal religious worship and early adolescent sexual behavior have been available for some time, including a 1991 analysis of the National Survey of Family Growth and a 1989 study by Arland Thornton of the University of Michigan.[5]

Research on adults further confirms the connection between lack of religious practice and high-risk sexual behavior. For example, never-married and divorced adults who have no religious *affiliation* (a much weaker link than regular religious *practice*) are two and three times, respectively, more likely to have multiple sex partners than those who *have* a religious affiliation.[6] These differences play out in higher rates of sexually transmitted diseases.[7]

Similarly, young women who do not worship regularly and who lose their virginity early are more likely to have multiple sex partners.[8] Researchers also have found that the earlier a young woman loses her virginity, the more likely she is to become pregnant. Moreover, among adolescent girls who do lose their virginity, one in five becomes pregnant as an adolescent.[9]

THE POSITIVE EFFECTS OF PEERS WHO PRACTICE THEIR RELIGIOUS BELIEFS

Personal practice is only one religious variable affecting adolescent sexual activity. The religious practice of peers also significantly affects rates of adolescent sexual activity. In the same way that personal religious practice provides a moral compass for adolescents, religious peers act as a community that reinforces religious norms regarding sexual activity. This positive community reinforcement by religious peers has a tremendous impact on the sexual behavior of adolescents.

Both for better and for worse, peer attitudes affect the rates of sexual activity among adolescents. For example, a Utah State University team has found that the combined influence of peer sexual activity and frequency of religious worship is dramatically correlated with subjects' rate of virginity, as shown in figure 4-3.[10] (Figure 4-3 does not, however, separate the effects of frequency of worship and of peer sexual activity.) For example, Best Friends is a peer-based program that teaches abstinence. In the period studied, only 1 percent of program participants became pregnant, and 90 percent remained sexually abstinent throughout adolescence. This is a testament to the power that peer attitudes can have on rates of adolescent sexual activity.

A research team in Philadelphia confirms these findings: the attitudes of peers strongly influence the choices that adolescents make regarding sexual activity. Early sexual intercourse does not happen spontaneously; rather, peers' patterns of dating, premarital sex, and church attendance accurately predict the loss of virginity among young women.[11] Similar results emerge from a 1985 study

Figure 4-3. *Sexual Experience, Peers' Sexual Experience, and Frequency of Worship*

Percent nonvirgin

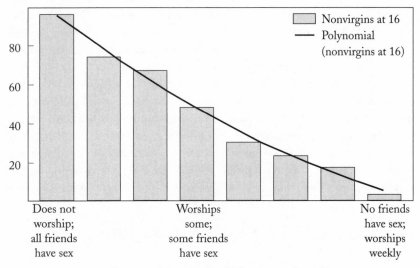

Peer sexual experience and frequency of worship

Source: E. Jeffrey Hill and others, "Religiosity and Adolescent Sexual Intercourse: Reciprocal Effects," unpublished manuscript (Utah State University, 1999).

of black teenagers. The study finds a strong connection between adolescents' frequency of church attendance and their attitudes toward sexual permissiveness. The study also finds a connection between adolescents' judgment of their friends' sexual behavior and their own.[12]

True Love Waits, a faith-based program run by the Southern Baptist Convention, also illustrates the positive influence of religious peers: between 1994 and 2000, more than 2.4 million adolescents between fifteen and nineteen pledged to remain sexually abstinent until marriage.[13] The effects of such programs are appearing in national surveys. According to the National Longitudinal Survey of Adolescent Health, nearly 16 percent of adolescent girls and 10 percent of adolescent boys have made such pledges.[14] When adolescents pledge abstinence until marriage, they are much more likely to delay intercourse.[15] Elayne Bennett, president of Best Friends, reports that of all the girls in the Best Friends program who pledge to delay first sexual initiation, 90 percent intend to abstain until marriage.[16]

THE POSITIVE EFFECTS OF FAMILY RELIGIOUS PRACTICE ON ADOLESCENT SEXUAL BEHAVIOR

Family religious practice is another potent factor in discouraging adolescent sexual activity. Parents have great influence on their children's sexual decisionmaking.[17] They influence their adolescents' sexual behavior in many ways: through their level of religious worship, through the family life they construct for their children, and by their commitment to their marriage.

Family religious practice deters sexual activity among adolescents. As figure 4-4 illustrates, the religious worship of parents is powerfully linked to the sexual behavior of their children. There is a very high connection between a father's religious practice and his children's virginity—even greater than the strong connection between a mother's religious practice and her children's virginity. When both parents worship, the relationship is magnified: there is a powerful, positive relationship with their children's sexual activity.[18] Thus it is not surprising that

Figure 4-4. *Teenagers' Sexual Experience and Frequency of Worship of Mother and Father*

Percent virgin/nonvirgin

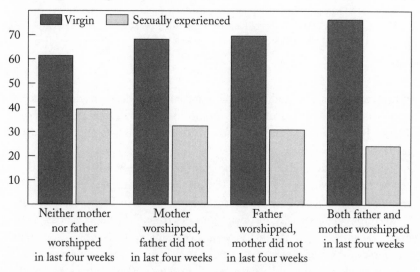

Frequency of worship

Source: Heritage Foundation domestic policy chart based on data collected 1994–96 from J. Richard Udry, *The National Longitudinal Study of Adolescent Health* (Carolina Population Center, University of North Carolina at Chapel Hill).

a faith-based sex education program involving mostly black teenage girls and their mothers in poor Southern communities almost totally eliminated out-of-wedlock births among the high-risk, single-parent population.[19]

Religious families are more likely to encourage sexual abstinence, and this has an effect on the sexual behavior of adolescents. When parents hold strong opinions on sexual abstinence and make sure their children know their views and wishes, adolescents are more likely to maintain their virginity and refrain from becoming pregnant.[20] Conversely, in their 1981 study "Adamant Virgins, Potential Non-Virgins, and Non-Virgins," E. S. Herold and M. S. Goodwin find that "parental acceptance of pre-marital intercourse was more common among the non-virgins [21 percent] than the potential non-virgins [9 percent] or adamant virgins [3 percent] [$p < 1.001$]."[21] After reviewing the recent National Longitudinal Study of Adolescent Health data, Michael Resnick and his colleagues conclude that, for American adolescents in the 1990s, "significant family factors associated with delaying sexual debut include . . . parental disapproval of their adolescent's using contraception."[22]

MARITAL STABILITY AND TEEN SEXUAL ACTIVITY

The literature shows a strong relationship between marital stability and teenage virginity, neatly summed up in Utah State University Brent Miller's rule of a 33 percent increase in sexual initiation for every change in parents' marital status.[23] However, this stability is, in turn, related to the parents' own practice of the worship of God.

The literature repeatedly shows that parents' levels of religious belief and practice clearly influence their own marital stability, happiness, and satisfaction.[24] Researchers back in the 1950s found that couples with long-lasting marriages frequently explained that the practice of religion was the reason for their marital happiness.[25] In the early 1980s Nick Stinnet of the University of Alabama and John DeFrain of the University of Nebraska come to the same conclusion: 84 percent of strong families identify religion as an important contributor to the strength of their family life.[26] More recent systematic reviews of the research literature also confirm that church attendance is the best predictor of marital stability.[27]

Regular worship attendance, rather than the doctrinal teaching on marriage, seems to be the critical factor in marital stability across denominations. For instance, in the 1960s, black Protestants in the South and white Catholics in Massachusetts had similarly low rates of divorce and similarly high rates of church attendance, although they held to very different doctrines on the indissolubility of marriage.[28] When marital separation occurs, the level of worship by each spouse influences reconciliation rates. Rates are higher among regular church attendees, and they are highest when both separated spouses have similarly high levels of church attendance.[29] Furthermore, couples who have some religious belief are less likely to file for divorce. In a study at California State University, sociologists Jerry S. Moneker and Robert P. Ranken analyze records for couples who filed for divorce in California between 1966 and 1971. They find that "couples who report no religious affiliation appear to be at greatest risk of early filing for divorce."[30]

The link between stable home life and family practice of religion has been demonstrated repeatedly. "Middletown," one of the classic sociological research projects of the twentieth century, studied the lives of inhabitants of a typical American town, first in the 1920s and later in the 1980s. Howard Bahr and Bruce Chadwick, professors of sociology at Brigham Young University, conclude on the basis of these studies that "there is a relationship between family solidarity—family health, if you will—and church affiliation and activity. Middletown [church] members were more likely to be married, remain married, and to be highly satisfied with their marriages and to have more children. . . . The great divide between marriage status, marriage satisfaction, and family size is . . . between those who identify with a church or denomination and those who do not."[31]

Arland Thornton, a family sociologist at the University of Michigan, finds the same strong intergenerational transmission of religious belief and practice among Detroit families. He concludes, "These data indicate a strong intergenerational transmission of religious involvement. Attendance at religious services is also very stable within generations across time."[32] Scott Myers published similar findings in the *American Sociological Review* in 1996.[33] There is a connection between religious practice and stable marriage and adolescent virginity.

In 1993, the University of Wisconsin reported on a nationally representative sample survey of 2,441 white women and 1,275 black women. The research team found strong evidence linking the birth of out-of-wedlock children to a "change in family structure" while growing up, controlling for the usual variables of income and education.[34] Adolescents in "high-crime areas" who lost their virginity early had experienced an average of two transitions in their parents' family life (that is, separation/divorce and a "re-partnering" by their parents).[35] By contrast, most virgins had no such family transitions in their lives. Only 18 percent of all adolescents who lost their virginity early were from intact families.[36]

Complementing this finding, Brent Miller and his colleagues find that the rate of adolescent pregnancy increases 33 percent for each change in parents' marital status while the child is growing up.[37]

CONCLUSIONS

Church attendance is correlated with other factors that reduce teen pregnancy: many teens who attend religious services regularly are raised in intact and attentive families. Nonetheless, there is no doubt that high levels of religious worship are very much in the public good. George Washington's advice in his "Farewell Speech to the Nation" is now bolstered by the findings of the social sciences:

> Of all the dispositions and habits which lead to political prosperity, religion and morality are indispensable supports . . . A volume could not trace all their connections with private and public felicity . . . And let us with caution indulge the supposition that morality can be maintained without religion. Whatever may be conceded to the influence of refined education on minds of peculiar structure, reason and experience both forbid us to expect that National morality can prevail in exclusion of religious principle.

The founding traditions of our nation, the common experience of people, and now the findings of the social sciences all point in a clear direction: the regular worship of God in community gives parents and their offspring many strengths, advantages, and benefits, especially in the challenge of directing teenage sexuality. Any honest national strategy of reducing teenage out-of-wedlock births, sexually transmitted diseases, and abortions will place the worship of God squarely within its parameters because of the power of its effects. Such would be a more truly "comprehensive" sex education strategy.

NOTES

1. Bernard Spilka, Ralph W. Hood, and Richard L. Gorsuch, *The Psychology of Religion: An Empirical Approach* (Englewood Cliffs, N.J.: Prentice Hall, 1985). See also Cheryl D. Hayes, ed., *Risking the Future: Adolescent Sexuality, Pregnancy, and Childbearing*, vol. 1 (Washington, D.C.: National Academy Press, 1987); Michael J. Donahue, "Aggregate Religiousness and Teenage Fertility Revisited: Reanalyses of Data from the Guttmacher Institute," paper presented at the Society for the Scientific Study of Religion (Chicago, October 1988); Catherine S. Chilman, "Adolescent Sexuality in a Changing American Society: Social and Psychological Perspectives," NIH Publication 80-1426 (Washington, D.C.: U.S. Government Publications, 1980); L. E. Hendricks, D. P. Robinson, and L. E. Gary, "Religiosity and Unmarried Black Adolescent Fatherhood," *Adolescence*, vol. 19, no. 74 (1984), pp. 417–24; David Larson and others, "The Faith Factor: An Annotated Bibliography of Clinical Research on Spiritual Subjects," Occasional Series Publication, vol. 3, no. 3840 (Rockville, Md.: National Institute For Healthcare Research, 1995), pp. 65–66.

2. Michael D. Resnick and others, "Protecting Adolescents from Harm: Findings from the National Longitudinal Study on Adolescent Health," *Journal of the American Medical Association (JAMA)*, vol. 278, no. 10 (September 10, 1997), pp. 823–32.

3. Carolyn Tucker Halpern, J. Richard Udry, Benjamin Campbell, Chirayath Suchindran, and George A. Mason, "Testosterone and Religiosity as Predictors of Sexual Attitudes and Activity among Adolescent Males: A Biosocial Model," *Journal of Biosocial Science*, vol. 26, no. 2 (1994), pp. 217–34.

4. Alan Carlson, editor of Family in America, Digital Archive, the Howard Center, Rockford, Ill., commenting on Emogene Fox and Michael Young, "Religiosity, Sex Guilt, and Sexual Behavior among College Students," *Health Values*, vol. 13, no. 2 (1989), pp. 32–37.

5. Arland Thornton and Donald Camburn, "Religious Participation and Adolescent Sexual Behavior and Attitudes," *Journal of Marriage and the Family*, vol. 51 (August 1989), pp. 641–53.

6. S. N. Seidman, W. D. Mosher, and S. O. Aral, "Women with Multiple Sexual Partners: United States," *American Journal of Public Health*, vol. 82, no. 10 (1988), pp. 1388–94. Larson and others, "The Faith Factor," pp. 133–34.

7. Thomas P. Eng and William T. Butler, "The Hidden Epidemic: Confronting Sexually Transmitted Diseases" (Washington, D.C.: Institute of Medicine, National Academy Press, 1997).

8. J. K. Cochran and Leonard Beeghley, "The Influence of Religion on Attitudes towards Non-Marital Sexuality: A Preliminary Assessment of Reference Group Theory," *Journal for the Scientific Study of Religion*, vol. 30, no. 1 (1991), pp. 45–62; Larson and others, "The Faith Factor."

9. Resnick and others, "Protecting Adolescents from Harm."

10. E. Jeffrey Hill and others, "Religiosity and Adolescent Sexual Intercourse: Reciprocal Effects," unpublished manuscript (Utah State University, 1999).

11. Sara B. Kinsman, Daniel Romer, Frank F. Furstenberg, and Donald F. Schwarz, "Early Sexual Initiation: The Role of Peer Norms," *Pediatrics*, vol. 102, no. 5 (November 1998), pp. 1185–92.

12. S. V. Brown, "Premarital Sexual Permissiveness among Black Adolescent Females," *Social Psychology Quarterly*, vol. 48, no. 4 (1985), pp. 381–87.

13. "1998 True Love Waits Report on Sexual Abstinence," available from True Love Waits, 127 Ninth Avenue North, Nashville, Tenn. 37234-0152.

14. Resnick and others, "Protecting Adolescents from Harm."

15. Ibid.

16. Personal communication.

17. Brent C. Miller, "Families Matter: A Research Synthesis of Family Influences on Adolescent Pregnancy Research" (Washington, D.C.: National Campaign to Prevent Teen Pregnancy, 1998).

18. In the National Longitudinal Study of Adolescent Health, the only question for father's worship is whether he had worshipped in the last four weeks. Given the pattern already discernible between the level of parental worship and other outcomes, it seems safe to predict that the father who worships weekly will have a still greater protective impact on the virginity of his children.

19. This study, "Fertility Appreciation for Families," involved a matched control design. It is an unpublished, but peer-reviewed, paper available from Family of the Americas, P.O. Box 1170, Dunkirk, MD 20754.

20. Resnick and others, "Protecting Adolescents from Harm," p. 830.

21. E. S. Herold and M. S. Goodwin, "Adamant Virgins, Potential Non-Virgins, and Non-Virgins," *Journal of Sex Research*, vol. 17, no.1 (1981), pp. 97–113. Reported in Larson and others, "The Faith Factor." p. 68.

22. Resnick and others, "Protecting Adolescents from Harm."

23. Brent C. Miller and others, "The Timing of Sexual Intercourse among Adolescents: Family, Peer, and Other Antecedents," *Youth and Society*, vol. 29, no. 1 (1997), pp. 54–83.

24. R. A. Hunt and M. B. King, "Religiosity and Marriage," *Journal for the Scientific Study of Religion*, vol. 17, no. 4 (1978), pp. 399–406; Larson and others, "The Faith Factor," pp. 49–50.

25. Lee G. Burchinal, "Marital Satisfaction and Religious Behavior," *American Sociological Review*, vol. 22, vol. 2 (January 1957), pp. 306–10; M. J. Sporakowski and G. A. Hughston, "Prescriptions for Happy Marriage: Adjustments and Satisfaction of Couples Married for Fifty Years or More," *Family Coordinator*, vol. 27, no. 3 (1978), pp. 321–28; Larson and others, "The Faith Factor," pp. 73–74.

26. Nick Stinnet, Greg Saunders, John DeFrain, and Anne Parkhurst, "A Nationwide Study of Families Who Perceive Themselves as Strong," *Family Perspective*, vol. 16, no.1 (1982), pp. 15–22.

27. David B. Larson, Susan S. Larson, and John Gartner, "Families, Relationships, and Health," in *Behavior and Medicine*, edited by Danny Wedding (Baltimore, Md.: Mosby Year Book, 1990).

28. Wesley Shrum, "Religion and Marital Instability: Change in the 1970s?" *Review of Religious Research*, vol. 21, no. 2 (1980), pp. 135–47.

29. David B. Larson: "Religious Involvement," in *Family Building*, edited by G. E. Rekers (Ventura, Calif.: Regal, 1985), pp. 121–47.

30. J. S. Moneker and R. P. Rankin, "Religious Homogamy and Marital Duration among Those Who File for Divorce in California 1966–1971," *Journal of Divorce and Remarriage*, vol. 19, no. 2/3, pp. 233–46.

31. Howard M. Bahr and Bruce A. Chadwick, "Religion and Family in Middletown, USA," *Journal of Marriage and Family*, vol. 47, no. 2 (May 1985), pp. 407–14.

32. Arland Thornton, and Donald Camburn, "Religious Participation and Adolescent Sexual Behavior and Attitudes," *Journal of Marriage and the Family*, vol. 51, no. 3 (August 1989), pp. 641–53.

33. Scott M. Myers, "An Interactive Model of Religiosity Inheritance: The Importance of Family Context," *American Sociological Review*, vol. 61, no. 5 (1996), pp. 858–66.

34. Lawerence L. Wu, "Effects of Family Instability, Income, and Income Instability on the Risk of a Premarital Birth," *American Sociological Review*, vol. 61, no. 3 (1996), pp. 386–406.

35. Close to 25 percent now lose their virginity before age fifteen.

36. Deborah M. Capaldi, Lynn Crosby, and Mike Stoolmiller, "Predicting the Timing of First Sexual Intercourse for At-Risk Adolescent Males," *Child Development*, vol. 67, no. 2 (1996), 344–59.

37. Miller and others, "The Timing of Sexual Intercourse among Adolescents."

Teen Pregnancy, Faith, and Social Science

WILLIAM A. GALSTON

Despite a welcome and unexpected decline during recent years, the teen pregnancy rate remains far higher in the United States than in any other advanced industrial country. Roughly four in ten young women will become pregnant before their twentieth birthday, the vast majority out of wedlock. The costs for the children, for the young women and their partners, for communities, and for society as a whole are very high. In this context, it makes sense to mobilize all the forces in our society that can help to keep the recent progress going. I am not alone in believing that faith communities represent a vital, and thus far underused, element of this social movement.

FAITH COMMUNITIES IN U.S. CIVIL SOCIETY

The potential and actual role of faith communities in reducing teen pregnancy is absolutely critical because faith communities are at the heart of America's civil society—not of every country's, but certainly of ours. If you examine international statistical comparisons and ask what keeps us in the lead as a "nation of joiners," the answer is our distinctive propensity to band together in faith-based communities. Some European nations have more secular communities and organizations per capita than we do. What gives America the edge overall is the extraordinary diversity pervading our faith-based communities.

To the extent that America's leaders and citizens are now focusing on civil society as a vital complement to public sector activity and individual self-help, therefore, we must focus on religion. In some neighborhoods, especially in our cities, faith communities are the dominant institutions, the true center of community-based action. Not to look at this carefully would be to ignore the greatest reservoir of energy and commitment and hope in many parts of America today.

WHY FAITH COMMUNITIES CAN HELP

If we ask why faith communities are potentially important in helping us to reduce teen pregnancy, some answers (or at least suggestions) emerge not only from common sense but also from the social science literature.

In the first place, faith communities are an important part of the process of cultural change in the United States, and cultural change is an important part of social change. Since the early 1990s, there has been a significant (some would say providential) reduction in early teen sexual activity and in teen pregnancy, startling the pessimists of the late 1980s and early 1990s. I do not think we can say that all the successful pregnancy reduction programs put together could account for more than a small percentage of the total change. Something larger is happening—a perceptible shift in public opinion—and faith communities, historically and up to the present day, have played a very important role in changing the climate of opinion.

Faith communities are also very important as centers of care, connection, and community. A lot of the social science literature suggests that young people who are connected to something outside themselves are more likely to grow up positively. Similarly, a growing body of social science evidence suggests that there is a connection between serving others and caring for one's self. Faith-based communities are in a distinctive (although not entirely unique) position to forge and strengthen that connection. I also would argue that faith-based communities are in a distinctively strong position to engage the whole person in the process of growth and renewal, rather than treating young persons as clients and addressing a single dimension of their lives in isolation from the rest. A study recently published by the National Campaign to Prevent Teen Pregnancy includes essays by Barbara Whitehead and a research team headed by Brian Wilcox and Sharon Scales Rostosky summarizing the historical, qualitative, and quantitative knowledge of these issues.[1]

As we consider the role of faith-based communities in reducing teen pregnancy, we must distinguish between faith-based programs, on the one hand, and religious belief and observance, on the other. The correlation between deep, family-reinforced belief, regular worship, and sexual restraint and self-control is strong and well established. There is good reason to believe that if more teens were "churched," teen sexual intercourse, pregnancy, and out-of-wedlock births all would decline significantly, even if faith communities did nothing to enhance their programs directed explicitly toward these ends.

Having said this, there is also reason to believe that faith-based programs to reduce teen pregnancy are also helpful and that faith communities could be far more energetic in promoting them. While many religious denominations have issued impressive statements on teen sexuality and some have devised specific curricula and programs of action, these steps at the national level have trickled down only sporadically to local practice. Some congregations are held back by the scarcity of resources and multiple responsibilities, others by the delicacy of the topic and the inherent difficulty of engaging it. Not surprisingly, a recent survey conducted by the National Campaign to Prevent Teen Pregnancy has found that only 5 percent of teens say that they learned the most about preventing teen pregnancy from religious organizations and only 9 percent cite religious organizations as "most influential" in shaping their sexual decisions. If we are to sustain the progress of recent years in reducing teen pregnancy, these numbers must rise substantially. That will not happen unless local faith communities become much more engaged in the fight.

One thing is clear: if faith communities do become more engaged, the American public will be supportive. A recent survey of American views on religion, politics, and public policy conducted by the Pew Research Center for the People and the Press and the Pew Forum on Religion and Public Life shows that 39 percent of Americans believe that religious organizations could do the "best job" of addressing teen pregnancy.

FAITH AND SOCIAL SCIENCE

In my judgment, we need to think through carefully the complex relationship between faith communities and social science. Social scientists in general (and program evaluators in particular) tend to think in ways that philosophers call "consequentialist," and they tend to focus on the results of particular interventions rather than on the nature of those interventions themselves. But from the standpoint of faith communities, the issue is only in part the effectiveness of particular programs. They also are concerned about the consistency of programs with their specific faith traditions. It is entirely possible that, from the perspective of a particular faith community, a program will be effective as measured by the canons of social science, but nonetheless inappropriate when examined in light of the specific commitments of their faith. One would expect that the extraordinary religious diversity in the United States would be—and I would argue from the faith perspective should be—mirrored in the variety of approaches to teen pregnancy reduction that they adopt. Accordingly, the National Campaign to Prevent Teen Pregnancy has used the slogan "Unity of Ends, Diversity of Means" to characterize the contribution of faith communities in this area.

By the very definition and meaning of faith, faith-based social action will (and ought to) get out in front of social science. Some traditions teach us that faith is the evidence of things unseen. That is a distinctive kind of evidence. It may be that, over time, this distinctive kind of evidence will influence the kinds of evidence that social scientists typically measure.

Can this sequence of events be justified from a secular point of view as well? I think it can be, because our demonstrable knowledge of program effectiveness frequently lags behind the actual effectiveness of individual programs. A faith community may be doing something that works, even though from a social science perspective we cannot tell the rest of the social science community that we know it is working.

For this reason, among others, I believe that society at large should invest (in constitutionally appropriate ways) in expanded efforts by faith communities to address teen pregnancy. It would be unreasonable to demand rigorous social scientific demonstrations of effectiveness as a prior condition of public support. It would be entirely reasonable, however, for the public to require evidence of effectiveness after programs have been up and running for a few years. And it would be reasonable for responsible public entities to spell out the basic features that make such evidence credible.

NOTE

1. National Campaign to Prevent Teen Pregnancy, *Keeping the Faith: The Role of Religion and Faith Communities in Preventing Teen Pregnancy* (Washington: 2001).

The Why's behind Reducing Teen Pregnancy

MARY ROSE McGEADY

Despite wide agreement that efforts should be made to reduce teenage pregnancy in the United States, the response to the question of *why* such efforts are needed differs according to who is offering it. Some replies concentrate on social considerations of such pregnancies and usually are accompanied by research emphasizing the negative impact of adolescent childbearing on both child and mother, including poor prognoses for the social future of the child. Other responses emphasize medical considerations. Many moms are physically immature and not ready for childbearing. Many teenage pregnancies end in miscarriages, and many more lead to babies with low birth weights. Still other responses emphasize economic reasons, noting the high impact on our culture and the public responsibility for funding and caring for these teenage mothers. They cite the high costs of delivery, of prenatal and postnatal care, of caring for premature or handicapped babies, or of day care for mothers who are forced to work.

Lastly, answers to the question of why we should work to prevent teenage pregnancy frequently deal with moral or religious considerations. This is the most complicated area, with responses coming from both positive and negative positions. While some view teen pregnancy as a violation of morality or judge such pregnancies as behaviors contrary to religious teachings about sex, marriage, and family, others concentrate on the child and its future rather than on the sex act itself. Traditional attitudes and cultural considerations differ on the issue of out-of-wedlock births. In some cultures, out-of-wedlock pregnancy is not as stigmatized as it is in the United States. Although these cultures host various religious traditions that still may consider such pregnancies as sinful or undesirable, their acceptance of the child creates a much more welcoming atmosphere.

All of these considerations are part of the dialogue that we must engage in if our efforts to reduce teen pregnancy are to succeed. A member of the Religion and Values Task Force of the National Campaign to Prevent Teen Pregnancy said at one meeting, "You know, we have to be very careful not to throw the baby out with the bath water. We have to be very careful as a society that we don't begin to look upon the baby as a bad result of a bad action by a teenager. Instead, we have to continue as a culture to love and care for those babies and love and care for the mothers of those babies."

Because I deal directly with troubled children, I would like to talk a little about the why from the viewpoint of the teenagers themselves. First of all, we now have fifteen Covenant Houses in the United States, two in Canada, and four in Mexico and Central America. In every one of those cultures, teenage pregnancy and birth are a growing reality. Unfortunately, the number of pregnant teens and teen mothers is growing. I was recently at our Covenant House in New Orleans. I met a nineteen-year-old girl who was on the verge of delivering her fourth baby. To give this teen mother hope and to help her to plan a healthy future for herself and her four children are tremendous challenges for us.

These kids have very few satisfactions in their lives. I think that this is one of the reasons that some of them turn to sex. Sex is one area where they can find satisfaction. Several papers have examined the characteristics of teenagers who get pregnant. I see in the lives of these kids very few experiences that build self-esteem. Often they come from families characterized by internal conflict and breakdown. A lot of them have been passed around all their lives.

For these reasons, it is very important for churches to become a significant presence in the lives of these kids. They need more than religious education, more than worship, more than a religious identity. They need a relationship with God. They need to hear that there is a God who loves them, who created them, to whom they can pray, who really cares about them.

We need to care for youth in a holistic way, not by addressing a single dimension of their lives in isolation from the rest. We need to make them happy when they are with us and to help them to plan for a future of happiness. These kids are starving for relationships. So many of the significant others in their lives have let them down. Often they have had conflictual or temporary relationships with their parents. Many have a history of relationships filled with disaster. So, we need to model positive relationships and then begin to say, "You can develop a relationship with God." They are not used to having relationships with people that are positive and caring. Attempts to deal effectively with the sexuality issues must come in the context of total caring.

It is very rare that we have a second pregnancy among those girls. We attribute that to the fact that we embrace the whole of their lives in a caring atmosphere. We teach them the morality of sexuality—that it is very much part of their relationship with God—and we teach them that they need to care for themselves because God expects that from them, too. But morality and hard realities have to be part of a whole, integrated package.

More than the questions about *why* we should prevent teen pregnancy is the question of *how*. The best answer to that question is "with great love and care for the individual young woman and her baby!"

Faith-Based Sexuality Education
Breaks the Silence in Black Churches

CARLTON W. VEAZEY

In 1996 the Religious Coalition for Reproductive Choice began the Black Church Initiative to identify and address sexuality issues with African American clergy and laity. The black community was ravaged by teen pregnancy, dangerously strained family relations, domestic violence, homicide, and HIV/AIDS. We faced a crisis of staggering proportions: more than 60 percent of black children were born into single-parent homes, and 22 percent were born to teenagers. An unmarried teenager who becomes pregnant and has not finished high school has an 80 percent likelihood of being poor, and her child is more likely to be hungry and lack health care. Yet the Black Church—the sanctuary of freedom and progress—was silent. Some even claimed the silence of the church had contributed to these tragedies.

Clearly, the government has the main role in reducing poverty, but the government cannot provide the religious teachings and spiritual guidance that instill the values and build the moral fiber so critical in bettering our lives.

As a pastor for more than thirty years, I felt that black clergy, myself included, did not know how to talk about sexuality prayerfully and realistically. If sex was mentioned at all, it was in a shaming, negative way. It seemed that talking about teen pregnancy and AIDS meant we were doing something morally wrong.

I set about bringing together black religious leaders from across the country to the Howard University School of Divinity for what we called the Black Religious Summit on Sexuality. As Kelly Brown Douglas wrote in *Sexuality and the Black Church*, this conference represented a monumental stride toward breaking the silence about sexuality.[1] When we began to talk about the most serious problem we faced—the health and lives of our young people—we had to admit that most were already sexually active and that we could not help them, or others, with abstinence education. We faced another problem, reaching young people who had left the church. We realized that we could not win them back simply by saying "Jesus saves."

We developed a faith-based sexuality education curriculum called "Keeping It Real!", which is one of the first organized efforts in African American faith communities to address sex and sexuality in both a biblical and secular context. The typical response of teens to moral platitudes and scare tactics about sex is "Get real!" "Keeping It Real!" speaks to youth with respect and honesty. Teens meet in small groups of twelve to fifteen to talk about their feelings and experiences with the support and guidance of trained facilitators from their church. For many teens, this is the first time they have spoken openly, positively, and comfortably about sexuality with a caring, nonjudgmental adult and with members of the opposite sex. We teach young people to be responsible stewards of all God's gifts and prepare them to make healthy, responsible decisions as spiritual and sexual beings. This teaching takes sexuality out of the "do and don't" school, which we know is not effective, and makes it a spiritual principle.

To those who charge that we are promoting sexual activity by teaching about it, we respond that we place abstinence first but recognize that churches have a responsibility, consistent with Christian values, to assist those who are sexually active by providing information that can make the difference between life and death in this age of HIV/AIDS. In the same spirit of living our Christian values, we provide information on family planning and contraception because many young people already have children and need this knowledge to improve their future. And we live our faith by developing serious dialogue about sexual orientation—an issue that has torn apart too many African American families that deny a son's or daughter's sexual preference.

As the Black Church Initiative has found, religious institutions can effectively provide sexuality education because they offer accurate, comprehensive information (including abstinence) in a community that truly cares about the individual. In my own work with African American churches, I have learned that young people are more likely to postpone sexual activity if they can discuss sexuality openly, without fear and judgment, in a setting that reinforces their faith and self-worth.

The Bush administration's promotion of abstinence-only education through charitable choice and welfare reform must be carefully considered. We cannot allow government to dictate how we teach our children to be responsible spiritual and sexual beings. This is clearly the work of the church, not of the government.

NOTE

1. Kelly Brown Douglas, *Sexuality and the Black Church* (Orbis Books, 1999).

Religious Sins: Churches Dealing (Or Not Dealing) with Human Sexuality

JOHN BUEHRENS

I write as a religious leader who must make moral calls about the personal and public issues that social scientists in this volume get to study. I also write as a parent, having raised two daughters with my wife, Gwen (an Episcopal priest), while serving parishes in Knoxville, Tennessee; Dallas, Texas; and New York City. When I was in Knoxville, at the Clergy Consultation Service for Problem Pregnancy, my wife and I had a steady series of young women in our living room, with our two daughters in their cribs upstairs. Gwen preached the gospel and served the poor as a caseworker for young women placing their children up for adoption.

I think both of my daughters would agree with me that the field of religion and sexual justice is replete with sin, but not of the sort popularly associated with sex. Rather it is sin of the spiritual sort, steeped in self-righteousness: temptations to point fingers, project anger, and misconstrue the ideal and the real. Few escape this, and I have no doubt had my own share of faults in this regard.

Religion was dominant in the culture of East Tennessee, and I became angry with the failure of most churches to deal openly with issues of human sexuality. Thirty years later, I am less angry, but I remain afraid of the polarization that is possible in this field. I am glad that many of the more conservative churches are beginning to offer programs of sexuality education that arise out of their own values. Yet I worry that they focus on the single goal of abstinence before marriage instead of dealing with a multiplicity of potential goals, including reducing the early onset of sexual activity and the number of partners, but also increasing the use of available contraceptives and reducing the fear and hatred concerning homosexuality. When religious leaders shy away from such matters, they threaten to let fear prevail over love, which is another form of spiritual sin.

It would be a mistake to expect the church to provide a complete solution in this highly secularized society where media penetrates every aspect of our young people's lives. The sex education and HIV education programs that the Unitarian Universalist Association (UUA) has championed for the last thirty years have made a positive difference, but they have not reached much beyond our own churches. The conservatively oriented abstinence-only programs now so in vogue will not solve the problem either. Nor will leaving the matter to parents and churches.

My feelings on these matters arise on both the pastoral and the prophetic sides of my ministry. Over the years, I have conducted at least twenty funerals for people with AIDS. I have done almost a dozen funerals for young people who took their own lives, a distressing number of them because they were confused about their sexuality and feeling rejected. Nearly all of these funerals were not for my own church members, but for people who were rejected by their own faith communities and families.

What I bring to the table as a progressive religious leader is a concern for the spirit in which we have our discussions and hope for the possibility of the churches making an impact. Over the past five years the UUA has worked with the United Church of Christ (UCC) to develop a new comprehensive sexuality education program called Our Whole Lives. The UUA and UCC have tried to design this comprehensive sexuality education curriculum so that it can be used not only in the voluntary setting of the church, where we can get fairly explicit and talk about *all* of the sexual feelings and relational issues and dilemmas that people have, but also in more public settings.

More parents want comprehensive sexuality education for their children than is currently recognized in today's polarized debate. Our experience suggests that religious communities can help: we can develop good materials to help fill the gap, we can promote the discussion of values, and we can help identify common ground—or at least middle ground—on which more comprehensive, realistic public policies can be built.

PART TWO

THE ROLE OF FAITH-BASED
ORGANIZATIONS IN FIGHTING

*Crime and
Substance Abuse*

CHAPTER FIVE

Defining the Terms of Collaboration: Faith-Based Organizations and Government in Criminal Justice

GEORGE L. KELLING

There was a time when the role of the Christian church in the community was of particular interest to me. After graduating from St. Olaf College—a Lutheran college—I spent two years in a Lutheran seminary. That was a long time ago, during the 1950s. Crime was not yet a widespread issue. World War II was still vivid in our memories, as was the role of the church in pre-war Germany and during the war itself. Clearly, my fellow students and I had not achieved professional maturity, yet we debated the moral and ethical issues associated with church involvement in civic life vehemently. For Lutherans who were fastidious about doctrinal and theological issues, the debate had special meaning. Martin Luther's theology of vocation fed the debate: "A cobbler, a smith, a farmer, each has the work and office of his trade, and yet they are all alike consecrated priests and bishops, and everyone by means of his own work or office must benefit and serve every other, that in this way many kinds of work may be done for the bodily and spiritual welfare of the community, even as all the members of the body serve one another."[1] Nonetheless, one professor loved to taunt us with being advocates of the "social gospel," "more concerned about sewer systems," as he disparaged it, "than the Word of God." But for us, many of German descent, the evils of the holocaust and war kept our attention on the church in the world. (Besides, sewer systems were not to be dismissed.)

That was long ago, and while whatever insights I may or may not have had certainly have shaped my world view, they are long lost to recollection. But two aspects of my training remain with me: homiletics (preaching) and hermeneutics (managing texts). I am not merely a detached academic; I am also an advocate, trying to improve public policy. So, alas, I still preach at times.

What every practical preacher knows is that despite the variety of Gospel and Epistle lessons that are read each Sunday, it is tough to get up every week with a fresh and stirring homily based on the day's lesson. Hence, since one cannot keep up with scholarship on all the lessons and since at times one wants to preach about a topic that is neither explicit nor implicit in the lessons, one "twists the text" to meet his or her message for the day. If readers are attentive they will find both in what follows—preaching and twisting the text to meet my message.

Let me first put forward several assumptions. I have written extensively about each, so I will be brief.[2] The first is that crime control is achieved primarily by what Jane Jacobs, in her classic book *The Death and Life of Great American Cities*, calls "the small change" of life.[3] By that, she is referring to the expression of all those intricate but routine obligations, controls, sanctions, and expectations that shape daily life in communities: the glances, gestures, body positions, actions, and facial casts that communicate approval, wariness, concern, or condemnation. Probably the key concept here is civility: citizens behaving, and expecting others to behave, in ways that are culturally understood to be predictable, reassuring, and respectful. The view that the small change is basic to crime control does not mean that police and criminal justice agencies are unimportant; it means that they are secondary, or ancillary, to the routine controls of communities. That is why the ideas of *community* policing and, more recently, community justice are so important.

The second assumption is that the extraordinary crime wave that occurred from 1970 to 1990 was the result of the erosion of the authority of the institutions that develop and maintain the small change: the family, schools, religious institutions, neighborhoods, and communities. Certainly major social, economic, and cultural changes attended the weakening of these institutions; however, public policies and judicial decisions played a major role as well. Think, for example, of what has been done to neighborhoods and communities by urban renewal programs, expressway construction, conceiving of public housing as housing of last resort, building tower block public housing, instituting school busing, withdrawing police from neighborhoods and communities and isolating them in cars, deinstitutionalizing the emotionally ill, and decriminalizing (or virtually decriminalizing) minor offenses. The list could go on. The intent of such programs and policies was benevolent, but they have eviscerated many urban areas, especially in inner cities. Police and criminal justice agencies, locked into a reactive law enforcement mode, simply were overwhelmed by the breakdown in public order that resulted from such policies.

My third assumption is that the current major reductions in crime are the result of communities organizing themselves to regain the control of public spaces and young people that they had in the past. Neighborhood organizations, religious institutions, developers, business associations, schools, transportation systems, housing authorities, and others, including police and criminal justice agencies, not only are striving to regain control of public spaces and youth on their own, they also have formed, and are forming, powerful working relationships that increase their impact. Those working relationships, the central theme of this chapter, are surprisingly vigorous and enduring.

Note that these three assertions—that crime is controlled by "the small change" of life, that the recent crime wave was the result of the weakening of social institutions, and that the current reduction in crime is the result of communities organizing to regain control of public spaces and youth—are *assumptions*. Evidence for them is anecdotal, inferential, and historical, not empirical. Nor can they be proven empirically in the near future. Hence, the criminological debate—often rancorous and sometimes silly, both about why crime increased during past decades and why it is declining now—is likely to go on for a long time.[4]

It also is important to note that these assumptions are at odds with the view of crime control that has reigned since the 1960s. Since the publication of the report of President Lyndon B. Johnson's crime commission in 1967, "root cause" theories of crime have dominated criminological and criminal justice thinking and practice. In that model, police and criminal justice agencies are primarily "case processors," police being the front end of a criminal justice "system" that focuses almost exclusively on responding to serious crimes once they occur. Such "crime fighting" is a professional responsibility, best left to police and prosecutors, with the role of citizens limited to reporting crime to professionals and serving as good witnesses. Crime *prevention* can be achieved only through broad social change; "minor" problems like drunkenness, prostitution, and other "victimless" crimes are the responsibility of social agencies. While both the political left and right have their variations on this theme, most criminologists and practitioners have subscribed to the left's version. Their thinking went so far that many of them "de-policed" the crime problem—that is, they put forward the idea that police and criminal justice agencies could have only minimal, if any, impact on serious crime. After all, those agencies had nothing to do with crime's root causes, ergo, they could do little about it.

Finally, these assumptions make clear that I believe that the faith institutions can contribute enormously to community order and safety. Having personally accepted that as a given, I will make two basic points in this chapter. The first is that we must come to a clearer understanding of the interorganizational relationships that develop under the rubric of "partnership," "collaboration," and other such terms if the relationships are to thrive. The second is that if faith institutions are to be true to themselves and their values, if they are to live up to their potential to contribute to the quality of civic and community life, they must be prepared to enter into rigorous problem-solving exercises that have as their starting point the awareness that most often the real problems are not what they appear to be. In other words, "doing good" is both hard and thoughtful work. My comments will be based on the evaluation of two federal programs, research into community prosecution (a shift in prosecutorial strategy that is akin to the shift toward community policing), and my current work in Newark, New Jersey, where I have become the "neutral convener" of an interorganizational anticrime collaboration that includes representatives of the faith community. Also, I will give special attention to work that I did for the New York State Metropolitan Transportation Authority, which is important because it illustrates both the points I want to emphasize.

In early 1989, I was asked by Robert Kiley, chairman of New York's Metropolitan Transportation Authority, to confer on problems in the New York City subway. It was out of control. Despite the recent investment of $8 billion in infrastructure, ridership was in steep decline.

Kiley consulted me because of my article with James Q. Wilson, "Broken Windows," which was published in the *Atlantic Monthly* in 1982. The article argued that small things, incivilities, matter a lot in urban life, and that disorderly behavior, fear of crime, serious crime, and urban decay are sequentially linked. Moreover, it implied that taking care of minor offenses could help reduce fear of crime, serious crime, and urban decay.

Those arguments flew in the face of the predominating sociological, criminological, and criminal justice theories. More or less explicitly, they re-raised the issues of the decriminalization of minor offenses and the deinstitutionalization of the mentally ill, and they challenged the idea that the proper use of criminal justice institutions was almost solely for reactive case processing. Finally, the article suggested that crime could be prevented without massive social change.

The main problem that I faced in New York was that virtually everyone "understood" the city's subway problem: the media, the transit police, civil libertarians, advocates, the faith community, and the New York City Transit Authority itself. For virtually everyone, the problem was "homelessness." And, of course, everybody knew how to deal with homelessness: provide emergency care, jobs, apartments, and welfare. That is where the faith community came in. Homeless people obviously need food and clothing; thus a role for churches, many of them suburban, in confronting the problem was to provide food and clothing. And where better than in the subway? Lots of "homeless" people congregated there, especially in stations. So suburban Christians came into subway stations on a regular basis to hand out food and clothing with the promise that next week— same time, same place—they would return with more.

Framing the problem as one of homelessness was not only wrong, at least in my reasoning, it also made whatever the problem was virtually unsolvable. Clearly, the New York Transportation Authority could make minimal contributions to solving the city's homeless problem. But 250,000 people a day going over, under, and around the turnstiles to avoid paying fares was not a *homeless* problem. Certainly, some farebeaters were homeless, but only a small percentage of the total. The problem was *unlawful behavior.* To be sure, most of the farebeaters were harmless: some really did not have money but needed to travel; others were so irritated by the quality of service that they felt justified in not paying; others wanted to catch an incoming train and did not want to wait in a line for a token; and others had simply gotten into a bad habit, rationalizing it by demanding, "Why should I have to pay when nobody else does?" But farebeating, when combined with graffiti, predatory panhandling, youths loitering around the toll booths obviously casing them *and* the passengers, public urination and defecation, open sexual activity, and fare scams (including blocking the turnstiles, holding gates open, and extorting fares from passengers)—with the police, all along, *doing absolutely nothing*—sent a powerful message. To ordinary citizens it said "Enter the subway at your own risk"; to predators, "This is a good place to operate."

Moreover, even the tag "homelessness" was a misnomer that masked a tragic amalgam of personal and social problems and their interaction: alcohol and drug abuse, mental illness, criminality, and social policies ranging from decriminalization to deinstitutionalization that virtually ensured a permanent street population. The idea that such a population should receive even the slightest encouragement to camp or hang out in the subway was a terrible one, indeed an immoral one. It not only jeopardized the viability of the subway, it exposed the "homeless" population to very real dangers. We knew, for example, that up to twelve people a month who did not have identifiable addresses lost their lives in the subway, where they were found murdered by other "homeless" people, accidentally electrocuted or killed by trains, or dead from hypothermia, exposure, and other "natural" causes.

We redefined the problem. New leadership energized the police department, which began to curtail unlawful disorderly behavior. The transit authority expanded efforts to link the genuinely needy with social and emergency services. We successfully defended our policies in court. Within months, order was restored. Crime began to decline immediately; currently it is down about 80 percent.

It is not too strong to say that fear and crime are no longer problems in New York City's subways.

My interest here, however, is in the role of the church in all of this. For those of us trying to restore order, churches were an integral part of the problem. Their involvement complicated the problem in several ways: first, their physical presence contributed to the chaos in the subway; second, their treatment of the problem, bringing food and clothing into the subway, put them into a practical alliance with "homeless" advocates who had a clear political agenda; and, finally, they claimed the high moral ground and, in their practical alliance with advocates, gave the advocates high moral credence as well. We faced the dilemma of having to confront the moral authority of the faith community. (We even had to figure out how to deal with a panhandling "nun." To this day we do not know whether she was legitimate or not.)

The transportation authority was able to capitalize on public indignation about conditions in the subway, and the argument was turned. We uncoupled "homelessness" and disorder, and instead linked disorder to serious crime. Moreover, we countered the moral and legal argument that restoring order was a "war on the homeless" that protected the interests of the rich at the cost of the poor with evidence that the "homeless" were dying in the dangerous environment of the subway and that subway users were not rich—they were primarily workers and students who deserved decent, hassle-free transportation.

The relationship of some churches to the state transportation authority clearly could be described best as one of defiance. Despite the transportation authority's request that they not conduct charitable work in the subways, those churches did as they saw fit. I am certain that they believed that they were fulfilling their moral obligation to feed the hungry and clothe the poor, seeing themselves as their defenders. Despite my belief that the actions of the churches were shortsighted and misguided, they highlight the complex nature of the relationship between the faith community and other organizations, especially government organizations. This example extends the range of possibilities of how, for simplicity's sake, two organizations—say, a faith institution and a police department—relate. As we shall see, properly understanding the terms of a relationship is critical to establishing and maintaining a long-term relationship. I have had the opportunity to observe attempts to develop and sustain such relationships more systematically in my research.

UNDERSTANDING THE TERMS OF THE RELATIONSHIP

In the past two decades I evaluated two federal programs that provided funding for attempts to coordinate crime control activities among organizations under the assumption that the synergy that results from a coordinated effort produces a greater impact than that produced when each organization acts independently and continues with business as usual. The first was the Urban Initiatives Anti-Crime Program of the early 1980s, which was funded by a variety of federal agencies but operated through the U.S. Department of Housing and Urban Development. The second, the Comprehensive Communities Program (CCP), was funded during the mid- and late 1990s by the Bureau of Justice Administration. The first initiative was an unmitigated disaster, primarily because nothing happened. Relationships never were formed; money went unspent; and virtually all programs turned into cash transfer mechanisms, giving people jobs whether they performed work or not. Furthermore, almost every site had bitter feelings toward the "feds" who administered the program.

CCP was another story. At virtually all of the sites, strong relationships had developed among citizen groups, service agencies (including faith institutions), public and private sector organizations, and police and criminal justice agencies, although the mix of participants was particular to each site.[5] In at least three sites—Baltimore, Boston, and Columbia, South Carolina—faith institutions were major players. At a fourth site, in Salt Lake City, the enormous impact of the Mormon Church on the city's culture and values always was felt, although the church was not formally at the table.

Observing the sixteen sites and studying community prosecution in four sites with my wife and colleague, Catherine M. Coles, forced me to try to think about how to characterize relationships among groups, organizations, individuals, and entities.[6] At each site an extensive set of relationships developed. Terms like "coalition-building," "collaboration," "coordination," and "partnership" were used to describe those relationships, and in my own writings about them I have used those terms rather indiscriminately. But the range of relationships that I observed was characterized by considerable variety, and the differences were of consequence. The consequences were evident in a conversation that I had with the head of a chamber of commerce that had formed a business improvement district (BID) in a southern city.

A business improvement district is formed by an organization of businesses that arrange to tax themselves to provide ancillary services within the district. They often start with holiday and other street decorations, move on to street maintenance, and ultimately move into providing security and other services. The chamber representative indicated that he had just concluded a rather nasty political fight with the newly appointed chief of police. Some years ago, the chamber, the city, and the police department had negotiated an understanding. The chamber would provide certain kinds of downtown maintenance services and employ guides who would patrol the district, providing information to the public but, most important, intervening if aggressive panhandlers hassled shoppers or other people on the street. They had no arrest powers, but they did have direct radio contact with the police department. The police department, for its part, agreed to permanent deployment of a foot patrol in the district. The new chief, exercising what he believed to be his sole prerogative, decided in the name of efficiency to end the foot beats. He was stunned by the ensuing brouhaha. After all, who but the chief of police should have final say about the allocation of patrol officers and the use of particular police tactics? Yet the city was confronted with a major political crisis: the BID, of course, challenged the chief before both the mayor and city council.

The *collaboration* that the department had entered into had administrative and tactical consequences; it limited the *internal* discretionary authority of the police chief. While the conflict ultimately was resolved, a partnership had turned sour and contentious because at least one party had not really thought through the implications of being a partner.

Just as some churches had established a relationship of defiance with subway officials, so the BID had established a relationship of collaboration with a police department. But there are many other forms of relationships as well. Figure 5-1 organizes different types of relationships on a continuum from collaboration, the closest and most complex type of relationship, to active opposition, the most remote and conflictual.

While these categories and definitions are arbitrary, they help to demonstrate the range of possibilities, and consequences, of interorganizational activity. Some examples will, perhaps, elucidate in more detail the differences among categories. The anecdote about the business improvement district and the police department is an example of a *collaboration*—clearly one that went awry, but a collaboration nonetheless: boundaries were permeated, and each organization departed from its traditional ways of conducting business. Conflict resulted because the police chief did not understand that the department essentially had agreed to limit its discretion in deciding how to police a particular neighborhood. Ongoing church activity in the subway is an example of *defiance*. Churches, feeling a moral imperative, defied public policy. In many communities, school systems have shown relative *indifference* to attempts to establish some form of working relationship with other parties. Court litigation—for example, by the New York Civil Liberties Union to stop efforts to maintain order in the subway—is a type of *active opposition*. In New Jersey, despite their *passive protest* against racial profiling by the New Jersey State Police, African American church leaders appeared at a press conference giving *consent* to a collaboration of Essex County, the city of Newark, and state and federal criminal justice agencies that planned aggressive action to prevent violence.

Figure 5-1. *Continuum of Interorganizational Relationships*

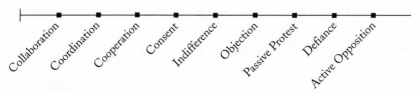

Definitions

Collaboration: an implicit or explicit contract between two entities in which each agrees to implement, conduct, or refrain from certain activities in ways that depart from each entity's traditional business and that permeate traditional boundaries.

Coordination: two entities identify a common problem, adjusting and aligning their activities in light of it and each other; traditional organizational boundaries, however, remain intact.

Cooperation: two entities conduct their respective traditional activities while agreeing to support each other and ensure that their programs do not overlap, conflict, or cross jurisdictional or professional boundaries.

Consent: an ongoing public declaration that one entity approves of the activities of another.

Indifference: Two entities that, if they are aware of each other's activities, do not believe them to be significant to each other.

Objection: an ongoing public declaration that one entity disapproves of the activities of another.

Passive Protest: one entity attempts to stop the activities of another through public declarations and dissemination of information.

Defiance: one entity attempts to block implementation or maintenance of another's program by advocating, implementing, and maintaining conflicting programs.

Active Opposition: active hostility between two entities enacted through political, legal, or violent attempts to stop each other's activities.

Source: Developed by the author in collaboration with Catherine M. Coles.

Moreover, such relationships need not be static; they may change over time. Winship and Berrien, for example, have offered us a fascinating account of the interaction of the Boston Police Department and the Ten Point Coalition, an association of African American clergy.[7] In it, they describe the evolution of the relationship from one of objection to one of consent—describing consent metaphorically as the "umbrella of legitimacy." They also provide an interesting account of one of the forms that consent can take: the Police Youth Leadership Award, a public award to "good cops." Clearly, even since Winship and Berrien wrote their article, the relationship between police and the Ten Point Coalition has moved beyond being one that merely offers an "umbrella of legitimacy" to police. Clergy and police are patrolling and making home visits together.[8]

Developing such categories is more than an academic exercise. The terms of the relationship, as demonstrated by the BID example, influence the quality of the relationship of agencies and contribute to their success or failure. They also have enormous consequences for participating organizations and staff. Let me give an example.

In both of my current areas of research, CCP (still ongoing at most sites) and community prosecution, I have observed staff burnout in innovative partnerships. The common interpretation of burnout is that it occurs when highly motivated and talented people succumb to the pressures of hard work, intensity, great demand, and long hours and leave the project, often frustrated and bitter. My own impression is that this interpretation is wrong. With rare exceptions, most participants love the hard work and intensity that go with interorganizational problem solving. Burnout usually occurs when an individual becomes caught between conflicting demands. On one hand, staff are "captured" by their projects: working with citizens and new colleagues and doing the research associated with problem solving turn into exciting, satisfying activities. I have seen police officers, for example, "cheat" and violate union rules by working more overtime than they can claim for reimbursement. The problem comes when staff find themselves caught between the routine ways that their parent organization does things and the need for innovative problem solving that is associated with interorganizational activities. In other words, such staff come to the table with others from a variety of organizations, come to understand the problem at hand in new ways, see the need for new approaches, but then find themselves unable to "play" because their parent organization wants them to continue to respond to problems in traditional ways. Caught in the middle as they are, they find that they lose both ways: they cannot deliver to their new colleagues and their organizational peers, and superiors view them as disloyal and untrustworthy.

Managing the terms of the relationship can be exceedingly difficult. Most collaborations have support at the top level—no collaboration would last long without it. And it is not hard to buy in at the operating level, at least for those individuals at the table; most recognize that the collaboration enriches their job and affords them new and interesting experiences. It is not the top executive who makes life hell for the involved staff person; it is the immediate supervisor or mid-manager. Attempts to manage difficulties by making end runs around supervisors or mid-managers to top managers often exacerbate, rather than alleviate, problems. Consequently, those who sponsor or coordinate interorganizational activities must help top managers to understand that they have to invest significant time and energy in preparing their organization for collaborative efforts—although doing so often is a difficult sell to executives who are under constant pressure to achieve quick results.

For some staffs and organizations, that is an exciting challenge. The Boston Police Department (BPD), both in ways described by Winship and Berrien and in a variety of other ways, is an example of a department that finds opportunities in such challenges. Indeed, it is so committed to the collaborative approach that it simultaneously maintains multiple relationships with the same organization. For example, as intense and genuine as is the collaboration between the BPD and Reverend Eugene Rivers's Ten Point Coalition in their attempts to prevent gang violence, the Ten Point Coalition can still publicly object to other practices of the BPD without jeopardizing the collaboration.

It is impossible to exaggerate the importance of getting the terms of the relationship right. The political, social, and organizational world in which institutions, organizations, and individuals operate is so complex—and often their business overlaps enough, as with police and prosecutors—that some conflict is unavoidable. In my own experience as the neutral convener of police and criminal justice agencies, service providers, and the faith community in a collaborative effort to reduce violence in Newark, New Jersey, the group often has found itself in a situation in which participants are fighting at one level while skillfully collaborating on another. While a variety of factors keep players at the table, the group's intense awareness of the severity of the problem probably is the most important in compelling the participating agencies to surmount their conflicts. The reality that young people are killing each other and that terror reigns in many neighborhoods, combined with the increasing certainty that only through collaboration can the killing be stopped, makes it hard to back away from or to interfere with what goes on at the table, even for those participants who are the most resistant to change or protective of their agency's domain.

Getting the terms of the relationship right is one matter; getting the *problem* right is another. That is the first step in developing and maintaining any partnership.

GETTING THE PROBLEM RIGHT

The defiant relationship that suburban churches established with the New York Transportation Authority was based on their understanding of both the problem and the means by which the problem should be approached. In a sense, the church members were right. There were desperate homeless people in the subway. Feeding and clothing the homeless is a merciful act.

At least two questions can be raised, however, about the churches' behavior. First, did they consider the possibility that their behavior could have negative consequences for the very people they were trying to help? Second, did they consider the impact of their activities on other subway users? I do not know the answers to those questions. The churches might well have considered them and decided to proceed; I suspect, however, that they did not. I suspect that they had only the most superficial understanding of the nature of the problem—that they were responding to a pop, media-driven understanding of the problem rather than a careful analysis to ensure, first, that they understood the nature of the problem; second, that the means they used to solve the problem were appropriate; and third, that they were in a position to lend their moral authority to any particular side in the ideological, legal, and policy conflicts that were being acted out.

Getting the problem right is a research issue, more or less formal.[9] For anyone thinking outside the box of conventional wisdom about the subway and New York City, only the most cursory "research" was required to understand that labeling the subway's problem as one of homelessness was at best a gross trivialization of a complex issue; at worst, a deliberate misrepresentation of the problems for ideological and partisan reasons. If one defined the major problem as homelessness, the solution was obvious: provide housing and jobs. If one defined the problem as lawlessness, the solution also was obvious: enforce the law. Yet one had only to go into the subway and look to see what the problem was. To be sure, more formal research was required for several reasons. First, we had to be sure that we had gotten the problem right. Second, we had to convince others—the media, the courts, and significant leaders—many of whom were confident that they fully understood the problem already. Finally, we had to make sure that we understood the nature of any sub-problems. To give an example from another site: in studying Boston's violent gang problem, police and researchers discovered the disturbing fact that "good kids"—youths without a history of violence—were starting to carry guns and join gangs in order to protect themselves.[10] That finding was important because the best way to deal with such youths is very different from the best way to deal with hard-core, violent repeat offenders. Indeed, mishandling the youths probably would have worsened the problem. Likewise, to return to the subway example, we knew that on occasion homeless families, including children, sought shelter in the subway. They had fallen through community and family safety nets and, for one reason or another, had drifted into New York City and its subways. They needed help and they needed it quickly; they were extraordinarily vulnerable and often were targeted by predators. Such genuinely homeless people needed to be located, contacted, gotten out of the subway, and linked to social services as quickly as possible.

Also, we identified another population of people, "couchies," who, almost literally, had gone into the subway to die. Couchies were burned out drug dealers/users who had no place to go; they were so desperate that they had stolen from their families to such an extent that their families had kicked them out. They wound up on friends' couches, from which they got their name, but soon, because they stole from their friends as well, they were kicked out again. They ended up in small colonies in the depths of the subways. Many died of hypothermia; others were murdered, electrocuted, or, in one case, burned to death while trying to keep warm near an electric hotplate. Identifying and contacting these people in the warren-like subway tunnels was grim and dangerous work. Every attempt was made to talk them out of the subway and to get them social and medical services. On several occasions when police had convinced one or more couchies to come out of the tunnels and accept a sandwich while being transported to a shelter or service agency, homeless advocates would attempt to dissuade them from entering the buses or talk them off the buses after they had boarded. Keeping the "homeless" in the subway, regardless of the personal cost to homeless individuals, furthered the political agenda of many advocates by keeping the homeless "under the noses" of citizens. Where better to do that than in the subway, with its captive audience of passengers? But, again, the main point is that research is required to fully understand the nature of the problem.

Remembering that problems often are not what they seem and that they have many dimensions is especially important in the context of this discussion, because the framing of the problem ought to determine the terms of the relationship of collaborating organizations. The fact that in Boston good kids as well as hard-core, violent repeat offenders were carrying weapons was more than just a warning sign about how *not* to treat them, it also suggested specific roles for the police, service providers, and the faith community.

For a faith institution, with its special mandate and role in society—often that of moral arbiter—getting the problem right ought to be the sine qua non of any effort to decide how to position itself on any problem. That suggests to me that first, faith institutions must come to the table early on as players in any community problem-solving effort if they are going to be active in dealing with the problem. They must be convinced—in a rigorous sense—that their understanding of the problem is correct.

Second, once the problem is understood, the means or tactics proposed to solve it must stand up to moral, legal, and constitutional scrutiny. Faith institutions are very good at scrutinizing, or, at least, they ought to be. They are trained in considering values and morality. While disagreements will arise about the moral legitimacy of specific tactics, at least faith institutions will (or should) make certain that the *right questions* are asked about any proposed solution to a community problem.

Moreover, the morality of the proposed solution as well as the nature of the problem should determine how a faith institution positions itself on the continuum of relationships. The methods ultimately used to solve a problem may not be acceptable to a faith institution, and therefore it will oppose the program.

And depending how deeply those methods conflict with its core values, the faith institution might position itself farther out on the continuum, toward active opposition.

For example, in Newark, the faith community has become an active part of an ongoing effort to prevent violence. As in Boston's Operation Cease Fire, young violent repeat offenders who are on probation or parole are required to attend a "notification session," a group meeting in which representatives of both the criminal justice and service/faith communities speak to the youths. The faith/service members assure the youth of a wide range of services, from jobs to mentoring to drug treatment. The criminal justice agencies make it clear that any further violence will result in a swift and severe reaction. While the faith community understood that that policy could result in prolonged incarceration for some offenders and did not object to that fact, members insisted, with the backing of the service community, that no arrests be made during the notification session, even if probationers or parolees with a warrant out for their arrest came to the session. (The faith/service representatives understood that if someone who was wanted for a serious violent offense came to the session that he or she would have to be arrested, but they believed that that was very unlikely. As far as they knew, the only warrants outstanding for the population in question were for minor offenses.)

The rationale of the faith community was that the central message should be optimistic and hopeful—delivered with a strong "or else" message if youth do not respond—but positive nonetheless. Representatives made it clear that they would object and withdraw if any arrests were made at the notification sessions. The criminal justice agencies agreed. The clergy understood, however, that some youths might be arrested at subsequent "accountability sessions"—post–notification session meetings of groups of youths with the chief judge or head of the parole board to discuss how they were doing—if they had committed offenses or were not meeting the conditions of their probation or parole.

While a faith institution may share a common understanding of a problem and agree that the tactics proposed to handle it are acceptable, it may lack the capacity to do more than offer consent. Or, like any organization, a faith institution may decide to increase its capacity. That approach was most graphically described to me by an African American minister in Columbia, South Carolina: "We have lost touch with our male youths. I don't want to be in the recreation business, but my new church will have a gymnasium—a good one. I've got to get at these youths."

Finally, as the faith community becomes more involved in partnerships, it has to become keenly aware of the consequences of its ministry to communities, as well as to individuals. The suburban churches that fed and clothed "homeless" people in the New York subway gave little thought to the impact of their activities on the subway environment and other riders—the litter and discarded food and clothes, not to mention the concentration of troubled individuals in a small area of the subway and how their presence affected a station and passengers. Likewise, faith institutions that attract troubled or troublesome persons to their facilities have to understand that their responsibility goes beyond what happens inside their buildings. Many programs are run in communities that already are unstable and overwhelmed with troubles; attracting more troubled individuals to such neighborhoods can further destabilize them. Many community groups, for example, have complained about the concentration of food programs in some neighborhoods, especially when those running the program do not ensure that their clients not litter the neighborhood or create other difficulties. And I am not referring to middle-class or suburban neighborhoods; I am referring to struggling inner-city areas. That by no means should discourage faith institutions from providing services, but their obligations go beyond their own doors. They have to ensure that they and their clients are good neighbors, strengthening their neighborhoods rather than creating additional difficulties. Again, this is the type of issue that ought to be considered in a thorough problem-solving exercise.

CONCLUSION

We are in an exciting era. Communities are reasserting control of public spaces and the behavior of young people. In most communities, streets are safer, and citizens know it and appreciate it. The community policing movement is spreading throughout law enforcement agencies, and relationships have been formed among groups and agencies that are surprisingly strong and enduring. I am optimistic about their ability to continue to reduce crime.

But I am not a Pollyanna. We have much to worry about: the generation of African American youths that have been or are imprisoned; the militarism that persists in law enforcement agencies; the fear that police feel in many neighborhoods; the persistence of domestic violence—the list could go on. But we have made progress, and there is reason to hope that success will build on success.

Many observers have offered what I consider to be oversimplified explanations of why people are committing fewer crimes. They attribute the decrease to police tactics, to demographics, to the economy. Aside from taking credit from those in neighborhoods and communities, including police and criminal justice professionals, who have worked so hard to regain control of public spaces and young people, such explanations reduce our ability to learn from history. Bad public policy and practice got us into the crime mess, and improved public policy and practice is getting us out of it. Economic and demographic determinism allows us to avoid our personal, social, professional, and political responsibility for what happened. That is just too easy.

NOTES

1. Martin Luther, "An Open Letter to the Christian Nobility on the German Nation," in *Three Treatises* (Philadelphia: Muhlenberg Press, 1943), p. 17. This treatise was originally published in 1520 (a record for my professional citations).

2. George L. Kelling and Catherine M. Coles, *Fixing Broken Windows: Restoring Order and Reducing Crime in Our Communities* (New York: Free Press, 1996).

3. Jane Jacobs, *The Death and Life of Great American Cities* (New York: Vintage Books, 1961).

4. For a discussion of these issues, see George L. Kelling and William J. Bratton, "Declining Crime Rates: Insiders' Views of the New York City Story," *Journal of Criminal Law and Criminology,* vol. 88, no. 4 (Summer 1998), pp. 1217–31.

5. Although it is not central to this chapter, the differences between the early 1980s' Urban Initiative program and CCP seemed to include the maturing of citizen groups, a belief that no organization could go it alone, a sense of despair about youth violence in the late 1980s and early 1990s, and a willingness on the part of the "feds" to "let good things happen." Regarding the latter, CCP essentially bought into ongoing agendas and relationships in each site. The major contributions of the Bureau of Justice Administration seemed to be three: the provision of some funds, which in turn made some outside expertise available, and an insistence on careful but time-bound planning.

6. Dr. Coles studied community prosecution in Austin, Texas; Boston; Indianapolis; and Kansas City, Kansas. All of those sites emphasized the importance of working closely with other organizations and neighborhood groups.

7. Christopher Winship and Jenny Berrien, "Boston Cops and Black Churches," *Public Interest,* no. 136 (Summer 1999), pp. 52–68.

8. Personal conversation with Commissioner Paul Evans, April 27, 2001.

9. University of Wisconsin professor emeritus Herman Goldstein introduced the idea of problem-oriented policing to criminal justice and described the method. See Herman Goldstein, *Problem-Oriented Policing* (Philadelphia: Temple University Press, 1990).

10. Personal conversations with David Kennedy, research fellow, Kennedy School of Government, Harvard University.

CHAPTER SIX

Not by Faith Alone:
Religion, Crime, and Substance Abuse

JOHN J. DiIULIO JR.

Under what, if any, conditions can the communities and life prospects of America's most disadvantaged children, youth, and families be improved? How, if at all, can religion in general or faith-based organizations in particular foster those conditions? How should the rest of us, whether as tax-paying citizens or concerned neighbors or in other civic and social capacities, support fellow citizens who, partly or totally out of religious conviction, help "the least of these" among us and "promote the welfare of the city"? To the extent that we deploy government authority or dollars to support community-serving religious individuals and institutions, how can we do so in a way that bears witness to common sense, social compassion, and respect for our constitutional laws and civic traditions? Regardless of how much public or private support faith-based organizations receive, how much should we reasonably expect them to achieve in solving tough social problems such as violent crime and drug abuse?

Those are not academic or abstract legal questions, nor will the usual answers now suffice. The sacred and the secular already are quite mixed, not only in literally scores of organizations like Catholic Charities and the Salvation Army, but also throughout entire social service "industries" in the civic sector.

For example, University of Pennsylvania social work professor Ram A. Cnaan has found that fully one-third of all daycare services in America today are provided through churches and other religious nonprofit or faith-based organizations. Through systematic surveys in six cities and a virtual census of religious social service organizations and community-serving ministries of all faiths (big

This piece is adapted from a paper written and presented at the Sacred Places, Civic Purposes Conference at the Brookings Institution in September 1999.

and small, old and new) in Philadelphia, Cnaan has documented beyond a reasonable empirical doubt that poor children, youth, and families in urban areas of the United States remain critically dependent on "the churches." Even by conservative estimates, in Philadelphia alone it would cost about 1 billion dollars a year to replace what faith-based organizations do for the city's needy, including many people who are receiving public assistance. The single biggest beneficiary of the city's faith-based organizations are poor children and young adults who are neither church members themselves nor from families that are "churched."[1]

Religious organizations that are not necessarily churches make many civic contributions. In just six months of research in the poorest neighborhoods of Washington, D.C., two young Princeton University graduates, Jeremy White and Mary de Marcellus, documented the existence of 129 small faith-based organizations that together served some 3,500 poor neighborhood children and young adults each week. Only a few of them received any public money—no surprise when only about 3 percent of all larger, more traditional religious congregations and ministries nationwide receive public money.[2]

To the civic contributions of grassroots faith-based organizations documented in both systematic surveys and ethnographic studies, add the tens of billions of dollars that traditional religious congregations raise and spend each year on charitable and community-serving good works. Who, we must begin to ask, is subsidizing whom?

That question is not any easier to answer empirically when it comes to specific corners of the civic square where faith-based organizations have long been a major and socially beneficial, if unheralded, presence. It is difficult, for example, to imagine the daily operation of the U.S. criminal justice system and its programs without the contributions of communities of faith.

As Public/Private Ventures vice president Harold Dean Trulear has documented through his work on how faith-based organizations serve high-risk youth in nine cities, throughout urban areas of the United States a large but hard-to-quantify fraction of all community-based crime prevention mentoring programs, including those funded in whole or in part by government, are, in fact, ministering programs. Likewise, many victim services agencies, like many aftercare programs for ex-prisoners and their families, depend almost exclusively on volunteers drawn directly from religious organizations and operate rent free out of "sacred places."

Father Andrew Greely, a sociologist, has aptly summarized the evidence on godly people in the civic square: "People who attend services once a week or more are approximately twice as likely to volunteer as those who attend rarely if ever," and even a third of persons who do not volunteer for specifically religious activities relate their civic service "to the influence of a relationship based in their religion."[3] Much of the data behind Greely's conclusion are derived from surveys of religion in American life by pollster George H. Gallup Jr.[4] Although one often hears journalists doubt that most Americans truly believe in God, the data make plain that they in fact do, and no Americans more than African Americans. Neither can there be the slightest rational doubt that, as Gallup has observed, "churches and other religious bodies are the major supporters of voluntary services for neighborhoods and communities."

So, how should we begin to understand and answer the policy-related and other questions about godly people in the civic square with which I began?

THE TEN POINT COALITION MODEL

One can begin with the community-serving ministry founded by Boston's Reverend Eugene F. Rivers III, a Pentecostal preacher and ordained minister of the Church of God in Christ, the country's single largest black church denomination.

The Rivers ministry began in the mid-1980s, distributing food and clothing from its quarters on the campus of Harvard University, then relocated to the poorest streets of Boston's Dorchester neighborhood. The tiny Dorchester row home of Reverend Rivers and his wife, Jacqueline, a Harvard *summa cum laude* graduate and education specialist, was sprayed with gunfire twice. Once the bullets barely missed their three-year-old son, asleep in his bed. But they stayed and built a prototypical small-budget, inner-city, preschool-to-prison ministry. Since 1990, their ministry has helped thousands of poor minority children, youth, and young adults to achieve literacy, obtain jobs, and avoid drugs.

The Rivers ministry is best known, however, for its role in assisting local police and probation officials in community-oriented crime-control efforts that arguably contributed to Boston's dramatic post-1993 drop in gun-related youth homicides and violence. Through its National Ten Point Leadership Foundation, the ministry has seeded kindred antiviolence "police-preacher" partnerships in Philadelphia, Indianapolis, and other cities since 1996.

Reverend Rivers, Jacqueline Rivers, and their dedicated Dorchester cadre of co-ministers and volunteers, many of them young black professionals with advanced degrees in the sciences from top colleges and universities, are unmistakably and unapologetically evangelical Christians. Or, as the Reverend puts it in his inimitable phrasing, "We're saved like the Bible says. Up on Jesus, love Jesus, walk among and serve the poor like Jesus. No winking or blinking on Christ. We're committed for real to these kids unto death. That's why we're willing to forsake the money thing, the nine-to-five thing, the big church thing . . . and even die ourselves in the name of Jesus. Die that they might live and make it."

Yet not one among the eclectic bunch of writers, analysts, and private funders who have witnessed what the Rivers ministry does on a daily basis has concluded either that it features no "God talk" or that it features nothing but such talk, except during Sunday morning services. Not one has reported either that Rivers and company are not interested in spiritual deliverance or that they are so obsessed with spiritual deliverance that it colors or conditions their every act of social service delivery.

Indeed, no one has found even a single beneficiary of the ministry who was either told explicitly or subtly made to feel or understand that the price of entering the ministry's buildings, receiving its services, eating its food, enjoying its gifts, participating in its programs, or otherwise getting its help was immediate or eventual profession of faith, attendance at Sunday services, or any type of expressly religious commitment: not a single child in the literacy program, in the summer recreation program, or at a Christmas party; not a single drug addict, gang member, accused killer, prisoner, or member of the fatherhood program; and not one welfare mother seeking help finding work.

How does a minister who has received so much local and national media attention gladly preach each Sunday to fewer than thirty people, most of them adults who have been with him for years? "The kids and the others get Christ by our example of prayerful daily service to them. They know I'm the minister, but they have no idea with what denomination or such. If more would go to some church, any church, great. If some become professing Christians, amen. But reaching and teaching is not only or even mainly about preaching. Their hearts and the 'hood will bear our Christian witness to them regardless," says the preacher.

The good news is that, like the Rivers ministry, few of America's thousands of preschool-to-prison ministries are simply or solely about spreading the Good News. There are, to be sure, community-serving ministries that focus on transforming troubled individual lives and that manifest the faith in "faith-based" in ways that rightly make them strictly ineligible for public funding. That would hold even if there were hard empirical data that the services of such ministries were far more cost-effective and rehabilitative than anything anyone had ever seen. But most community-serving ministries, including most inner-city preschool-to-prison ministries, do not do all or most of what they do exclusively in a religious fashion. Even the strictly faith-based programs that succeed often do so in partnership with other individuals and organizations, religious and secular, public and private.

Thus, whether we focus narrowly on what "sacred places" can contribute to specific "civic purposes" such as reducing rates of crime and substance abuse or whether we focus more broadly on all the many good, community-serving works that they indisputably do, *the key to making rational policy judgments will be to make rational, empirically grounded, socially compassionate, public-spirited distinctions.* We need to move beyond—and stay beyond—the strawman arguments, catch-all categorizations, exaggerated fears, and exaggerated hopes that still dominate much church-state discourse and policy debate.

On one extreme is anyone who is so reflexively hostile to religion in the public square—and so intellectually dishonest or devoid of true historical and legal knowledge—that he or she stands ready to act as an inquisitor in *any* effort to deploy government in support of fellow citizens who serve the poor if they do so in the vicinity of a religious symbol or say "God bless you" when nobody has sneezed.

On the other extreme is anyone who is so reflexively devoted to religion as faith alone—and so intellectually dishonest or devoid of true historical and legal knowledge—that he or she stands ready to damn *any* effort to deploy religion in support of fellow citizens who serve the poor if they accept even a nickel of Caesar's coin, partner with people of other faiths, or work with secular social services bureaucrats or other public employees who rarely say "God bless you" even when someone *has* sneezed.

Fortunately, there are very few such extremists on either side, and they deserve not our scorn but our fraternal correction: the former so that they stop viewing all faith-based organizations as social toxins, the latter so that they stop viewing only faith-alone organizations as social tonics.

So, how can we best keep faith with political leaders? How willing and able are we, whatever our religious and political leaning, to be compassionate yet dispassionate when it comes to the "how" of helping those who help the disadvantaged, their communities, their cities, and, by turns, our one nation—which is still, for most Americans, "one nation under God"?

CIVIC "VALUE INVESTING" IN FBOS

After five years of studying and assisting faith-based organizations in cities across the country, with a special eye on ministries that have special promise as agents for reducing crime and substance abuse, I would suggest that government, business, and the rest of the civic sector should approach the utility of the sacred places sector of the nonprofit "market" in achieving civic purposes much the way so-called value investors approach the stock market to achieve financial gains. Let me briefly elaborate upon the analogy.[5]

Basically, value investing is predicated on the view that a company does not need to be outstanding for its stock to outperform the market or to yield big profits; it only needs to be better than investors think it is. Any stock that is viewed with undue pessimism or rejected irrationally by investors is a likely bargain. Value investors buy stocks of sound, if not sensational, companies that research reveals to be undervalued because they represent an industry that has long been out of favor, because they once experienced management or other problems to which investors overreacted, because they have an erratic history of earnings, or for other reasons.

Value investors buy stocks that are priced low in relation to company assets, sales, earning power, and management ability; changes in commercial environments; and other factors that history proves matter economically. Value investors thus profit by paying close attention to economic fundamentals and trading against the economically unwarranted emotions of others. So, rather than picking or riding high-priced hot stocks, they make lots and lots of small bets on cheap stocks. Rather than courting sudden growth in hot sectors, they court steady growth in cheap sectors. Value investing beats its opposite number, so-called growth investing.

By analogy, faith-based organizations (FBOs) are the value stocks of the community-serving nonprofit sector. From the 1960s until quite recently, they were out of favor, not only because of the irrational exuberance that the policy elite expressed in strictly secular, government-centered solutions to social problems, but also because of widespread doubts about their future assets—since religion was supposedly on the wane in the United States—and their management fundamentals, given corruption scandals, charges of politicization, and an innocent yet debilitating lack of administrative competence.

The FBO sector's volatile hot stocks were big-church, big-name ministries that promised much but delivered little. Today's FBO "industry," however, has begun to regain public and "consumer" trust and confidence in a country that turns out to be stubbornly religious. Many of its new "CEOs" are quite willing to open themselves and their organizations to outside scrutiny by skeptical secular researchers and professional foundation auditors, and they are quite eager to engage in interdenominational and interfaith partnerships and program "mergers."

There are various kinds of community-serving FBOs, and only recently have we begun to identify the common characteristics and best practices of those FBOs that seem especially effective in achieving various civic purposes among disadvantaged residents of poor urban neighborhoods. Nevertheless, people of quite different faiths, traditions, partisan leanings, and ideological orientations have developed strikingly similar lists of those characteristics and practices.

One common characteristic is that the community-serving FBO is community-based, not just in rhetoric, but in reality: the ministers and religious volunteers have the same zip code as the people they serve, and they subject themselves to all or some of the same hardships that neighborhood residents suffer. They do not "live large" either within the neighborhood or outside of it. They walk the same crime- and drug-infested streets.

Another characteristic is that the FBO came into existence before anyone—government agencies, foundations, parent churches, or others—offered its leaders financial or other support. Once the FBO was established, its leaders might well respond to government or foundation requests for proposals (RFPs), *but only to strengthen some effort that already was part of their core mission or to expand some program that they already offered.* Said a veteran community-serving minister in Washington, D.C., "Anybody that's got time or staff enough to mess with all them government forms or fill out thirty, forty pages of what the foundation wants you to say, they ain't got no real heart for [these children] and they ain't about doing no real work [in this school or] on those ugly streets."

One FBO best practice that follows naturally from the two common characteristics mentioned above—and appears on absolutely everyone's list—might be labeled "keeping the 'faith' in faith-based, but not by faith alone." Think of the Rivers ministry.[6]

It is increasingly apparent that the biggest civic purposes bang for the sacred places buck is to be found among small religious congregations, para-church groups, and grassroots inner-city outreach ministries. To be worthwhile to government, business, and nonprofit "investors," civic value investing in FBOs does not need to produce daily miracles of individual or social transformation; it needs only to outperform its nonprofit market competition over time, even if only by producing the same civic results at a smaller human and financial cost. As we shall see below, given the record of big-budget, nonreligious, arid crime-reduction and substance abuse programs, that should not be terribly hard to achieve.

Some small grassroots FBOs are widely credited with yielding tremendous social "profits," seemingly overnight. That would appear to be the story of, for example, the Rivers ministry and of FBOs like Washington, D.C.'s Alliance of Concerned Men. Led by Tyrone Parker, the alliance's five principals brokered a truce among rival gangs in a D.C. neighborhood that had witnessed more than fifty murders in five square blocks within two years. The murders ceased, and the press noticed. But even though, as Tyrone Parker says, the alliance has unquestionably helped to "stop the noise" in its neighborhood, and even though its crime-reduction "stock" was "advertised" through stories in the local and national media, this tiny FBO remains radically undervalued. Funds to help monitor, mentor, and minister to ex-gangbangers and their younger brothers and sisters remain scarce, and no one has yet supplied any civic "venture capital" to determine whether the alliance could cut gang violence in other neighborhoods. "If we were McDonald's," says one of Parker's compatriots, "we'd already be franchised." "Amen to that!" chimes in Rivers.

Civic value investing in FBOs should be relatively easy for corporate, philanthropic, and other private institutions and individuals. After all, they can pick their favorite "sacred places" by religious affiliation, location, civic purpose focus, or just about any other organizational characteristics and performance criteria that they choose. They can provide selected FBOs money, technical assistance, or both. They can identify themselves closely with an FBO's religious mission and character or remain detached from all except the FBO's secular dealings and achievements. And they can rather flexibly fund, defund, or increase funding and other support to FBOs as their resources and preferences dictate.

Civic value investing in FBOs by government, however, is a much taller and trickier order. There are all of the usual church-state issues, and there is all of the resulting red tape. That probably is a good thing. As Yale and Brookings political scientist Herbert Kaufman once memorably reminded bureaucracy bashers, "one person's government red tape is another person's treasured procedural safeguard."

The extant survey data suggest that the leaders of the larger and least evangelical Protestant denominations, plus urban Roman Catholic and Jewish congregations, are most willing to seek public funds for their community programs. Even they, however, have been slow to explore, let alone to tap, the charitable choice program authorized by Congress in 1996. Most congregation leaders simply do not know it exists. Some who do and might want to take advantage of it fear having to contend with assorted legal threats to their religious autonomy, employment practices, and more. As a supporter of charitable choice and expanded efforts to bolster the faith-based sector, I am tempted to say, "Let the litigation begin!" But, then again, who really wants to witness any public law intended to assist worthy community-serving FBOs turn into a full-employment policy for analysts, activists, journalists, judges, lobbyists, and lawyers?

Besides, even if every religious congregation in the United States were willing to break bread with federal funding agencies, and even if nobody sued or countersued anybody, would the federal government be any better at civic value investing in FBOs than it would be at picking stocks?

The real church-state policy challenge is the moral, strategic, and spiritual challenge of civic value investing in FBOs, not as directed by Washington, but as led by state and local governments and their governors, mayors, agency chiefs, and other subnational leaders and public employees. How should we understand and meet that challenge? Let us examine two separate but related areas, FBOs and crime and FBOs and substance abuse,[7] through case studies of fellow citizens who, out of religious conviction and through FBOs, are struggling to promote public safety and enhance individual well-being in our poorest urban neighborhoods.

FBOs, CRIME, AND "UNCHURCHED YOUTH"

Inspired in part by Boston's renowned police-preacher partnerships, Philadelphia's district attorney, probation officials, recreation department chiefs, and other city leaders joined together in May 1999 with then Mayor Edward G. Rendell to launch an innovative youth violence reduction initiative involving local FBOs. It came not a moment too soon.

Unlike Boston and many other cities, in the 1990s Philadelphia had little good news about youth violence. The number of young homicide victims dropped from 164 in 1995 to only 157 in 1998, and the number of young gunshot victims "fell" from 137 to 136 over the same period. Philadelphia has the highest rate of gun-related homicide in big-city America—more than 80 percent of total homicides. Philadelphia's youth violence reduction project targets the 100 juveniles in each police district who, based on data shared by city law enforcement and social services agencies, have an extreme probability of "killing or being killed." Each targeted youth is given access to a combination of community-oriented, community-anchored prevention, intervention, or enforcement resources deemed likely to prevent the youth from harming others or being harmed.

The project's leaders aspire to repeat the pilot in each of at least a dozen police districts. "It is a bit like painting a bridge," says John Delaney, the deputy district attorney who chairs the project, "in that once you do the first 100 in each of twelve districts, you start all over again with another coat of prevention, intervention, and enforcement services for another 1,200. God willing, before the youth bulge we're seeing in the elementary school reaches its teens, there won't be a single kid in the city who prosecutors, social welfare street workers or ministers, or others think is in real danger and needs real help fast but gets none."

In conjunction with the project, the city's police commissioner, John F. Timoney, revived a once-vibrant police-clergy training program. So far, about 200 local clergy of different denominations and faiths have joined. Eventually, they will be relied upon as quasi-official counselors, conciliators, and high-profile presences on the streets. Already, many clergy have participated in probation officer-preacher ride-alongs in police patrol cars.

Lest anyone should begin to entertain unfounded fears, or hopes, about the city's youth violence reduction project and police-clergy program, it should be understood that no youth is required to interact with any member of the clergy, religious volunteer, or FBO. And, as probably goes without saying, no youths are directly or indirectly pressured to go to church or to "get religion."

James Q. Wilson stated in "Two Nations," his December 1997 Francis Boyer lecture for the American Enterprise Institute, "Religion, independent of social class, reduces deviance," but added that there are "church programs that work and ones that do not." The only minor amendment I would make to Wilson's statement is that, church-anchored or not, there are FBOs that work and ones that do not in reducing crime and delinquency and that, as Wilson stated, we still "have no way of finding out which is which, save by intense personal inquiry."

I have committed myself to such intense inquiry in the cause of finding, funding, or partnering with the right sacred places for those civic purposes. I believe that faith works, at least under some conditions. But let us back up a bit.

Violent crime has dropped about 26 percent across the nation since 1993, while youth crime has fallen from its horrific 1994 peak. True, we are by no means out of the woods, despite decades of massive public spending on both prevention programs and prison building, massive private spending on security devices and systems, massive suburbanization, and the individual efforts we all reflexively make to avoid crime where we live, work, attend school, recreate, and shop.[8] Still, the happy post-1993 fact is that crime is down almost everywhere. Abortions, births to unwed teens, number of welfare recipients, and many other indexes of social distress are down, too.

But the empirical reality is that almost none of that can yet be systematically related to an undercurrent of national religious revival, the churching of formerly unchurched youth, or specific local faith-based anticrime programs.

But what about Boston? I am second to none in my admiration of and support for the Rivers ministry and cognate anticrime, community-serving ministries in Boston. I also am second to none in my respect for Operation Ceasefire and other law enforcement–led programs that partnered with clergy to help reduce the number of homicides—from 153 in 1990 to "only" seventeen in 1999. And I believe Christopher Winship when he credits Rivers and company with deracializing aggressive police-probation tactics.

But I also am second to none in my view that we live in a multivariate world in which things that happen at time T cannot logically be attributed to things that happen at T plus one year and in which there are many competing theories and conflicting data. No one, including Harvard University economist Anne Morrison Piehl, a researcher trained in econometrics who has written seriously about the "Boston miracle," claims that we can determine with certainty the degree to which those initiatives have been responsible for Boston's good news. It would have been nice if New York City, in the course of its dramatic, ostensibly police-driven, post-1993 reduction in crime, had pursued more community-clergy partnerships, but that was not the case. Nevertheless, the big drops in crime came during the same years in New York as they did in Boston, but without the deracializing, just as they did in other cities with varying degrees of racial tension.

We need to remind ourselves that, as Berkeley political scientist Raymond Wolfinger once quipped, "the plural of anecdote is not data." There are good, published empirical studies suggesting that—across the nation and independent of any changes in policing and of any efforts of religious denominations or FBOs—a sizable fraction of the post-1993 crime drop can be attributed to each of the following factors: abortion; incarceration; laws that restrict gun ownership; laws that relax gun ownership; demographic dips in the number of young males; improved economic conditions; and others. Without reference to policing or preaching, one could scientifically explain all of the post-1993 crime decline. Indeed, if all the crime analysts were somehow right, we would now be free of crime, living in a society of saints. As you may notice, however, we are not living in such a society, so they cannot all be right. Thus we reopen the door to common sense and to such systematic evidence as exists of the effects of the "faith factor" on crime and delinquency.

And we also open the door to criminologist Byron Johnson, who, on his own and with faith factor research pioneer David Larson of the National Institute of Healthcare Research, has catalogued some of the best empirically credible evidence on the relationship of religion and crime. The evidence, as Johnson has carefully scored it, is generally quite positive. In his December 1998 report with Larson for the Manhattan Institute's Jeremiah Project, for example, Johnson concludes that the most rigorous scientific studies to date are nearly unanimous in their finding (consistent with James Q. Wilson's verdict cited earlier) that "religiosity is inversely related to delinquency"—that is, religiosity has "an inverse, or beneficial, impact on delinquency."[9]

But the relevant scientific literature remains thin, and, in most studies, religion is a poorly measured or omitted variable—"the forgotten factor," as Johnson writes. And what counts as "religiosity"? In much of the more advanced research on religion's relationship to a variety of outcomes, religiosity normally has been measured by whether an individual does or does not go to church. There was a great deal of excitement surrounding Harvard University economist Richard Freeman's 1985 working paper that reported that churched low-income young black men were more resilient—for example, less likely to use drugs, commit crimes, or remain unemployed—than otherwise comparable young black men who were not churched. But, as a radio humorist said, "if you think going to church makes you religious, you must think sitting in your garage will make you a car." "Churched" or "not churched" is not only a crude measure of religiosity, it is a largely irrelevant one in community-serving FBO anticrime programs in which many high-risk youth and adults are unchurched.[10]

Research by Johnson and others indicates that prisoners who participate in Bible studies are considerably less likely to recidivate than otherwise comparable prisoners who do not. But, as Johnson himself would likely agree, even in the best study recidivism was measured by whether an individual had been rearrested only one year out. Thus, the research design was sturdy, but not experimental; the measures of statistical significance were suggestive, but not robust. Johnson's ongoing study of a Bible-based low-security prison program will be rich in inmate survey and related ethnographic data, employ a sophisticated multidimensional measure of religiosity, and use a matched design to test for postrelease effects of the program. Whatever the findings, few prisoners of any faith will ever experience anything like the "total immersion" program he is expertly analyzing.

So, what do we know about the influence of faith on prisoners? What might be the impact if Operation Starting Line, a new multimillion-dollar effort by a coalition of the nation's leading Christian para-church ministries, were successful in its mission to evangelize every prisoner in America before the year 2010? It would no doubt depend in part on what "evangelize" turned out to mean—a few extra visits from an outside minister, Bible studies, prisoner aftercare programs? Meaningful estimates of impact are impossible at this stage of our knowledge.

But suppose reliable empirical knowledge were no obstacle. Suppose that getting unchurched youth churched, getting prisoners into Bible studies, or employing other expressly religious means of cutting crime and delinquency were invariably successful. What would that mean for public policy? Public officials must be supremely careful not to coerce individuals under any form of custodial supervision into accepting or participating in any expressly faith-alone religious activity, and they must ensure that whether those individuals participate has no bearing on the legal disposition of their case.

So, let's get back down to basics. Does anyone really *not* want Philadelphia to involve clergy and community-serving FBOs in its youth violence reduction initiatives? Does anyone really want the godly people of the city's sacred places to stop serving low-income children and youth, families of prisoners, ex-prisoners, and crime victims in partnership with the city's justice system and social welfare agencies? Does anybody really *not* want crucifix-bedangled religious volunteers manning job-placement programs for young offenders or contributing disproportionately to community-based government programs that divert first-time delinquents from possible jail terms?

Or, to go back to the case of Boston's Rivers ministry, would anyone actually prefer that the Dorchester clergy had *not* helped Boston's police and probation officers to deracialize or otherwise cut crime? Would anyone like the Rivers ministry *not* to serve as ombudsman for juveniles in the court system or to visit local jails? Would anyone really feel safer in Dorchester if the ministry's summer recreation and other "idle hands" faith-based, but not faith-alone, programs were not in session sunrise to sundown last July? Does anyone really need to seek comfort, constitutional or any other, in the fact that the ministry's single best veteran youth outreach worker is not a card-carrying Christian, but is instead Jewish?

Finally, would anyone really prefer it if local police had dialed 1-800-S-E-P-A-R-A-T-E when instead, on June 27, 1999, Reverend Rivers was called to talk—and, if necessary, to "God talk"—an armed juvenile murderer into surrendering peacefully, and succeeded? On exiting the boy's hideout, should he first have taken off his collar, put on a police hat, and pretended for the cameras that he was "Officer Rivers"?

Most Americans would answer no to most of those questions, thank God for how much sacred places contribute to public safety and all phases of crime prevention, and pray for more and better partnerships between well-supported community-serving FBOs and their government.

FBOs, Substance Abuse, and Transformation

In 1999, past presidents of the nation's two leading professional associations of probation executives and officers issued a powerful, if disturbing, report on the state of their field. Probation, they argued, was failing not only to protect the public, but to enforce court orders and help offenders. "The probation discipline," they noted, "has long argued that probationers need to obtain community-based substance abuse treatment."[11] In Massachusetts, at least 80 percent of all probationers have significant substance abuse problems. But only 37 percent of all probationers nationwide participate in any type of drug treatment program during their sentence, and only 32.5 percent are tested for drug use once they receive treatment.

On any given day, there are more than 3 million people on probation in the United States, 52 percent of them convicted of one or more felony crimes yet under "community supervision." The nation's top probation experts concur that most felony probationers have some substance abuse history and are not getting any substance abuse treatment, public or private, religious or secular.

Likewise, if you think that the social costs of substance abuse have been exaggerated, guess again—the costs are huge. For example, substance abuse consistently has been found to increase, or to have a multiplier effect on, an individual's marginal propensity to commit violent crimes. By "substance abuse," I mean not just use of certain presently illegal drugs, but also alcohol consumption.

In fact, I have argued that the alcohol-crime nexus is at least as potent, and undoubtedly more destructive, than the illegal drugs-crime nexus.[12]

James Q. Wilson has noted that religion "lies at the heart of programs such as Alcoholics Anonymous (A.A.), an extraordinary success that no government could have produced and no business could have sold." As usual, Wilson is right. But do most scientific studies of religion, spirituality, and faith-based substance abuse programs indicate that, others things being equal, "religion" varies inversely with substance abuse? I have been studying the drug treatment literature on and off for more than a decade, and my answer is a qualified yes.

"Qualified" because there is not yet expert consensus about what works best in the way of treatment. There are two basic approaches. One is the "medical model," the twenty-eight-day, short-term approach exemplified by A.A. and kindred "higher power" 12-step programs. The other is the long-term (usually six to twenty-four months), residential, "therapeutic community" approach. Both have their respective academic, practitioner, political, and other champions. Neither works consistently. Nevertheless, both tend to generate successful outcomes, whether with multiple-problem populations like older probationers or otherwise well populations like older professors, but only with individuals who have tried treatment before and failed.

One confounding factor in assessing the efficacy of any type of faith-based substance abuse treatment program—and there many different types—is that many troubled people tend to seek God only after they have tried everything else. Call this "spiritual selection bias," for it is not uncommon for faith-based programs to get clients who may be new to religion but are old to treatment. Someone on his or her fifth or sixth try might have a higher probability of succeeding at whatever the next mode of treatment is, whether secular or religious or both.

Good science sorts and controls for such data biases. David Larson has produced numerous good scientific studies that find that faith works in preventing, coping with, or kicking substance abuse. Aaron Todd Bicknese's June 1999 political science dissertation on the much-discussed Christian drug treatment program known as Teen Challenge presents similar findings. Teen Challenge is at least as successful in checking substance abuse as most secular antidrug programs. More generally, the exhortation to stay drug free embodied in Teen Challenge, Fellowship of Christian Athletes "campus huddles," and other faith-based programs is at least as efficacious as that of many government drug education programs like the much-maligned D.A.R.E.

Why do faith-based substance abuse programs seem to work at least as well as many or most of the secular or purely public alternatives? The answer is buried in a finding from a 1995 evaluation by Public/Private Ventures of the Big Brothers Big Sisters of America mentoring program. The strongly experimental study found that, in addition to generating a host of other social benefits, low-income minority youth who had a Big Brother or Big Sister were 52 percent less likely to initiate drug use than otherwise comparable youth who did not. The "Bigs," if only for a few hours a week, put a caring, responsible, nonparental adult presence directly in the lives of poor children who were in many cases without any other positive, one-on-one, up-close and personal adult presence, parental or nonparental. If, as some seem sure, faith-based antidrug programs on average outperform secular ones, I would speculate that is because *ministering is the original species of mentoring.* Like many others who study and assist preschool-to-prison ministries, I have witnessed ex-prisoners who had been addicted to drugs for years, both in prison and out, get and stay straight and sober in faith-based programs run by unassuming clergy and religious volunteers. Why? Because, in the words of a Jamaica, Queens, youth and former drug dealer I once interviewed, "I know the man loves me, and that God loved me even when I was doing all that evil to myself and others. He's always here for me. Even when he's not, I know God is."

Byron Johnson could fill volumes about how just one prison ministry program has changed the lives of prisoners who were previously untreated, drug-addicted, problem-drinking probationers. Maybe, as the eminent University of Pennsylvania psychologist Martin E.P. Seligman suggests, "religion" as manifest in such programs is a particularly powerful instance of the applied "psychology of the positive." Or, maybe, as Penn's Pastor William Gibson would suggest, it has something to do with God.

For whatever reason, it is an empirically documentable reality that programs that attempt not so much to "treat" as to "transform" the self-concept of substance-abusing individuals—that attempt to get drug-addicted youth to understand themselves not as problem children but as children of God or to get binge-drinking ex-convicts to forgive themselves as God has forgiven them— are often passably effective *and* do not cost lots to administer. Civic value investors, take heed.

Besides, would anyone truly prefer that hundreds of thousands of probationers go untreated when there are good faith-based, but not faith-alone, anti–substance abuse ministries that could help? Does anyone really want to prohibit a probation officer who has read a prisoner's file and noticed that he identified himself as a Christian from encouraging that prisoner to look up Victory Fellowship or a kindred program as he leaves the jail detox center? Does anyone really want to keep even a penny of government money from, in effect, providing vouchers for probationers who voluntarily seek faith-based treatment for drug or alcohol problems? I sure don't.

A Great Compromise?

Those Americans who serve God with gladness by serving their needy and neglected neighbors deserve our praise. We should mobilize more support, both public and private, for faith-based organizations that help to achieve civic purposes. But I would gladly forsake the push for federal funding if I could be assured that henceforth even strict separationists, whether secular or religious, would join those of us who work and pray for private value investing in faith-based, but not faith-alone, FBOs. To wit: James Wilson has suggested that what we really need is not a generation of conflict over church-state issues, but in each and every city "privately funded groups that would evaluate the fiscal soundness and programmatic intensity of church efforts . . . and help raise money for ones that pass this initial screening."

Amen. Any takers? Or must it be "See you in court"?

NOTES

1. Ram A. Cnaan and Stephanie Boddie, *Black Church Outreach*, CRRUCS Report 2001-1 (Center for Research on Religion and Urban Civil Society, University of Pennsylvania, 2001).

2. Jeremy White and Mary de Marcellus, *Faith-Based Outreach to At-Risk Youth in Washington, D.C.*, Jeremiah Project Report 98-1 (New York: Manhattan Institute, 1998).

3. Andrew Greeley, "The Other Civic America: Religion and Social Capital," *American Prospect* (May-June 1997), pp. 70, 72.

4. Gallup's bedrock studies on religiosity in America merit citation: George H. Gallup Jr., *Religion in America* (Princeton, N.J.: Princeton Religious Research Center, 1996) and *The Spiritual Life of Young Americans* (Princeton, N.J.: George H. Gallup International Institute, 1996).

5. The next four paragraphs are based largely on Sanford C. Bernstein & Co., Inc., *Global Investment Strategies* (New York: September 1999).

6. And to get a sense of how such an approach to community-serving good works is mandated and justified theologically in the Judeo-Christian tradition, read, for example, the recently revised Catechism of the Roman Catholic Church (no kidding!), specifically the sections that deal with "human community" in God's plan. To get a sense of how it is now being justified, even among "by faith alone" Protestant evangelicals, read two new books by steadfast Christians, one by the politically liberal Ronald J. Sider, *Just Generosity: A New Vision for Overcoming Poverty in America* (Grand Rapids, Mich.: Baker Books, 1999), the other by politically conservative Charles W. Colson, *Now How Shall We Live?* (Wheaton, Ill.: Tyndale House Publishers, September 1999). Even the most unmistakably and unfailingly Christ-centered voices in the field of community-serving ministry today are exhorting their fellow Christians to revitalize their faith commitment, not just through intercessory prayers for the poor, not just by preaching and proselytizing, and not just by getting more people directly into church pews, but by bearing religiously motivated "witness" on the model of Christ's everyday love for and "walk" among "the least of these."

7. Readers who wish to violate their own Eighth (if not anyone else's First) Amendment rights (that is, "no cruel and unusual punishments") may follow up with my chapters in two Brookings volumes: "Black Churches and the Inner-City Poor," in Christopher H. Foreman,

ed., *The African American Predicament*, and "Federal Crime Policy: Declare a Moratorium," in Henry J. Aaron and Robert D. Reischauer, eds., *Setting National Priorities*.

8. For more detailed party pooping on crime, see my "How Goes the Battle?" *The New Democrat* (July/August 1999).

9. David B. Larson and Byron R. Johnson, *Religion: The Forgotten Factor in Cutting Youth Crime and Saving At-Risk Youth* (Manhattan Institute, Center for Civic Innovation, 1998).

10. Richard B. Freeman, "Who Escapes? The Relation of Church-Going and Other Background Factors to the Socio-Economic Performance of Black Male Youths from Inner-City Poverty Tracts," Working Paper 1656 (Cambridge, Mass.: National Bureau of Economic Research, 1985), as cited in *What's God Got to Do with the American Experiment?* (Brookings, 2000).

11. Reinventing Probation Council, *Transforming Probation through Leadership: The "Broken-Windows" Model* (Center for Civic Innovation, Manhattan Institute and the Robert A. Fox Leadership Program, University of Pennsylvania, July 2000).

12. For a brief but sobering analysis, see my "Broken Bottles: Alcohol, Disorder, and Crime," *Brookings Review* (Spring 1996).

Effectiveness over Ideology:
Church-Based Partnerships in Crime Prevention

EUGENE F. RIVERS III

I am glad that the faith community, policymakers, and academics are starting to come together to address important issues such as crime and substance abuse. Indeed, one of the things that has made the Ten Point Coalition in Boston unique—and many would say uniquely successful—is the interface between the clergy and academics and policymakers. My colleagues—Jeffrey Brown, Ray Hammond, and a group of other members of the clergy—and I were in regular communication with scholars like Christopher Winship as we developed our strategies and carried out our work in Boston. We invited and encouraged systematic evaluation of our work so that we would not be deluded into smoking our own press clips. We also invited the social science community in to help us analyze our efforts so that we could distinguish rhetoric from reality.

As a result, the "academic" issues of how we researched, tested, replicated, analyzed, and evaluated our work were more easily resolved and our work was more successful. But that kind of interface is still pretty unique to our experience; often academics and community members don't work together that well.

George Kelling's chapter is right on target and helpful in a number of ways. First, he talks about churches getting and doing things wrong. Up until 1988, there was a fairly traditional black church model in which cops were considered racists and the black community was considered a victimized community. What was significantly different in my work in Dorchester through the Azusa Christian Community and the Ten Point Coalition—and this relates to Kelling's broken-window thesis—is that we were forced to deal with what happened on the street, not just our preconceived ideas or theories. We learned that the discourse changes when you are confronted with reality: it is one thing to go to meetings and do the dog-and-pony show and talk about racism; it's another when you are forced to confront the criminal elements of your own community.

Being forced to confront the criminal activity in Boston through the first-person testimonials of young men who reported to us what they were doing complicated life. But for the better. George Kelling's and Christopher Winship's work suggests that once someone gets on the ground and really deals with what's going on, it is inevitable that the ideological nonsense will collapse. I've found that to be true in my own experience. I have been on the left side of most things for thirty years, and I could have used that position to come to quick and easy conclusions. However, once I was forced to deal with criminal activity at the street level, all of my left-leaning rhetoric and ideology collapsed. The same is true of proselytizing. In thirty years, never have I come across a person on the ground who was committed to saving lives who said to a kid that if he didn't accept the ideological party line or religious dogma, he'd go to hell. It has never happened.

The debate about church and state becomes stupid once you arrive on the scene and you deal with people where they actually live and come to understand their real problems. When it is a matter of life or death, certain debates quickly become irrelevant. But when you live safely removed from the problem, your priorities change, because you do not have to worry about who's on the other side of the door. In that case, you can be as philosophically elegant and interesting and abstract as you like.

Increasingly, the thinking of many of us across the country who come out of the black community is that at the end of the day we want to see sacred spaces empowered to serve secular needs and purposes. For us, at the end of the day, serving the needs of the poor is the priority. And that's not about religion, it's about results. It's not about proselytizing, it's about performance. And we want sacred institutions to be judged on the basis of their performance and results, not by the fact that they are religious.

Now, if it is a crime that our religion can produce a strong result, then we plead guilty. Our argument is that people should not be discriminated against on the basis of religion. If, in fact, the most effective model for reducing violence and shootings among black youths is a faith-based model, we don't think that we should be discriminated against by the Department of Justice just because we happen to follow Jesus. If people who happen to pray to Allah or Yahweh are the ones who are close to the problem, produce measurable results, and demonstrate disinterested concern, they also should be evaluated on the basis of their performance, not their religious beliefs. So the question is not about religion, but about results.

We are simply attempting to get those sacred institutions sufficiently strengthened to serve the secular needs of millions of very poor people whose needs must be met if society is to be fair or compassionate or rational. There needs to be philosophical debate, but we can't let that debate keep us from serving the needs of kids who are too frequently ignored by the elite, on both sides of the political aisle, for different ideological reasons.

Maintaining Legitimacy: Church-Based Criticism as a Force for Change

CHRISTOPHER WINSHIP

Churches are not always on the side of progress, a fact verified by George Kelling's chapter and my own experience. I lived for a period on the South Side of Chicago during the early 1970s, when many of the major African American churches were very closely allied with the Daley machine. During that time community activists made a concerted effort to desegregate Chicago's trade schools; it was a particularly important goal because it was necessary to attend a trade school in order to get into a trade union. The churches, however, supported the Daley machine indirectly by refusing to openly support the desegregation effort.

The dangers of church involvement in reform are not limited to Chicago. In the book *The Color of School Reform,* Jeffrey Henig and others discuss the role of black churches in school reform in four cities—Atlanta, Baltimore, Washington, D.C., and Detroit—from 1960 to 1980.[1] They point out that in earlier periods, when whites controlled the public school system in those cities and teachers were predominantly white, black churches were strong supporters of reform efforts. Over time, however, those school systems became increasingly important sources of jobs for blacks. As a result, large black middle-class churches, many of whose parishioners were teachers or, more generally, government employees, often sided with the teachers' unions in strongly opposing reform.

Even in Boston, the home of one of the most highly acclaimed examples of a successful partnership of religious and community leaders to reduce youth violence, the role of the church is not as unqualifiedly positive as one might initially think. Reverend Eugene Rivers's work with the Ten Point Coalition focuses on a small neighborhood with twenty-eight churches, many of which are storefront churches. The vast majority do not serve people who live there; the churches are there because the rent is cheap. As a result, disagreement has arisen among the churches and others in the community about the direction the community should take. Because the churches enjoy the low rents, they sometimes have opposed economic development initiatives that would bring new businesses into the neighborhood and thereby raise rents.[2]

Churches are complicated institutions with multiple goals and varied interests. At times their goals may conflict with the public good. I say that as a strong *proponent* of church and religious community involvement in society's problems. We need to expand the policy options available, and the story of the Ten Point Coalition and many others demonstrate that the churches, despite their necessarily complicated agendas, can act as a force for needed change.

We have not made a lot of progress in dealing with poverty over the last decade in this country. We have not made a lot of progress in dealing with single-parent households. We have not made a lot of progress in dealing with inner-city schools. Those are the factors that the political left typically has pointed to as the root causes of crime. Yet we *have* made enormous progress in reducing crime. The subway example offered by Kelling suggests how important it is to look outside the box and think about solutions that may not necessarily be associated with root causes.

At the moment everybody is aglow with the need to partner with everybody else, as if partnering alone can solve the world's problems or single-handedly reduce youth violence. The Ten Point Coalition's partnership with the police in Boston often has been held up a model. But there is very little discussion in the research literature about the nature of such partnerships, what their purpose is, and what their limits are.

What the Ten Point Coalition, along with others, has accomplished in Boston is to get the police to focus on the small number of youths who truly are a problem and to stop harassing the large numbers of inner-city minority young people who are not. When the police act in a way that is consistent with the community's interests, the coalition publicly supports them. When the police do not, the coalition is more than willing to expose them to a rain of public criticism.

So it is a peculiar partnership, one that has changed the way the police (and other elements of the criminal justice system) and the inner-city community relate to each other. In its role as intermediary between the two parties, the Ten Point Coalition strives for balance between the community's desire for safe streets and its reluctance to see its children put in jail, and it does so in a way that offers an "umbrella of legitimacy" to the police in exchange for the fair and just exercise of their power. They support the police when the police act appropriately. But the coalition's very effectiveness rests on its willingness to criticize any police behavior that falls outside the bounds. Indeed, members of Boston's religious community—led by Rivers, who always is willing to exercise a prophetic voice and to speak truth to power—have at times been among the most vocal and publicized critics of the police department, even after the two parties became strong and long-standing partners in the battle against youth violence.

For example, a Boston street minister of color was arrested in the middle of a fight that he was trying to break up. He was out of collar, and the police did not realize that he was a minister and ignored him when he said that he was. Rivers was vocal in the press about the importance of investigating the matter and holding the police accountable for the minister's unfounded arrest. His statements were essential to maintaining his credibility. Had he not openly criticized the police, many in his community would have assumed that he had been bought off, that his silence was repayment of a debt.

The lesson of the Boston experience, along with that of other cities, is this: in the struggle against crime, the police cannot go it alone; they need the cooperation of community leaders. Such partnerships help reduce youth violence and, equally important, delineate what constitutes legitimate police behavior. Police strategies can acquire legitimacy within inner-city communities only if the community harshly criticizes inappropriate police tactics while supporting appropriate tactics. Under those circumstances, ministers and police are ideal partners, because the clergy can maintain a prophetic voice even while actively partnering with the police. At the very least, the possibility that faith-based organizations in Boston have found an effective strategy for reducing youth violence, without severely and broadly compromising the civil liberties of inner-city residents, certainly is promising. But further research on and rigorous analysis of the complex nature of church-state partnerships in all cities is necessary if we are to truly understand the potential of faith-based organizations in reducing crime.

NOTES

1. Jeffrey R. Henig and others, *The Color of School Reform: Race, Politics, and the Challenge of Urban Education* (Princeton University Press, 2001).

2. Omar M. McRoberts, *Saving Four Corners: Religion and Revitalization in a Depressed Neighborhood,* Ph.D. dissertation, Department of Sociology, Harvard University, 2000.

The Enforcer: The Role of Churches in Maintaining Social Control

JOYCE A. LADNER

George Kelling discusses the destruction of the social institutions and relationships that have maintained social control by meting out negative sanctions to punish misbehavior and positive sanctions to reinforce conforming behavior. My firsthand experience with the function of sanctions to reinforce conforming values and behavior occurred during my coming of age in a small community called Palmers Crossing, near the town of Hattiesburg, Mississippi. My mother, Annie Ruth, who was also known as Miss Annie, was one of the reinforcers of the social norms in our tiny community.

For example, two young adults in the community who dated each other appeared drunk in public on a regular basis. The woman's nickname was Slingshot, and her boyfriend's nickname was Sa Poe. I think his name was Sam Poe, but his neighbors gave him the nickname Sa Poe. Whenever they passed our house drunk, they walked hurriedly to avoid Mother's sermonizing. More often than not, Mother saw them. "Oh, you're not going to slip past me. I see how drunk you are. Come here." Mother invited them to sit at our kitchen table, where she had them drink loads of black coffee; no sugar was allowed. Then she gave her standard lecture about how they should change their deviant ways and how they needed to make something of themselves and how "your mama is very disappointed in you and you don't want to hurt her by continuing to misbehave this way. You know this is not the way you were raised."

However, the small tightly knit communities that existed then have declined across the nation and with them the informal relationships and mores that exert control. Moreover, there is less consensus among community residents on what constitutes appropriate norms and who should enforce them. Kelling understands that it is not the big events that define an era or that are the most important underlying phenomena. Instead, it is the cumulative impact of the little events—the day-to-day sanctions of "Miss Annies" who remind individuals and groups of the traditional boundaries that the community has established for them. The informal mediators and enforcers of societal norms are critical to maintaining social control.

How does society maintain informal social control in an era when the formal institutions have declined and there are fewer informal arbiters of behavior? Those changes have come with massive changes in the way we relate to each other: we are less likely to know our neighbors; we do not dare to discipline a neighbor's children; teachers are hesitant to discipline students for fear that parents will object or file formal complaints against them. There has been a rapid deterioration of community values and with it decreased interest in participating in the reciprocal relationships—with their implicit obligations—that reflect shared values and responsibilities. That, indeed, is what constitutes the most serious problem in our communities.

My view is that we no longer have a uniform set of norms and values, no agreed-upon definitions of appropriate informal conduct. Nor is there a common language, a common understanding of concepts such as that evident in the 1960s when Americans collectively said that to deny some Americans the right to vote constituted a national problem. That is how Martin Luther King Jr. was able to organize citizens across racial, religious, and ethnic boundaries—by using agreed-upon standards of what was morally, legally, and socially right and proper.

An underlying theme of this discussion is the decline of the patterned behavior that both reflects and imposes social order, or the weakening of civility and its disappearance in large part from American life. With the decline of civility has come the emergence of deviant behavior. Kelling's discussion made me ponder the reasons why we embrace community policing. Is it because it is a way to recreate a sense of community among people for whom the community no longer exists? When members of Boston's Ten Point Coalition, including Eugene Rivers, Jeffrey Brown, and other members of the clergy, walked the streets in territory controlled by gangs and talked to the young men, they were successful, in part, because the young men were responding to face-to-face interaction and the restoration of community.

There are countless examples of communities in which the tide is turning and community norms are being restored. A recent Public Broadcasting Service program featured the dismantling of warring drug gangs in Washington, D.C.'s Benning Terrace, where members of the Alliance of Concerned Black Men convinced gang members to stop the killing that helped Washington earn its notoriety as the "murder capital" of the nation a decade ago. All of the gang members put down their weapons, and there has not been a murder in Benning Terrace since then.

Another question raised by Kelling is that of how to practice a social gospel today, how to apply the rules and norms of the faith community to solve today's social problems. A model may be the community-based organizing efforts led by churches in the 1960s, when civil rights activists were welcomed by many church leaders and members and when a social gospel that fought for equal rights for all was an indispensable part of faith-based initiatives. Which of today's problems demand the application of a social gospel? How do we merge the secular and the sacred—or the sacred and the profane? How is it that so many religious institutions continue to exist in the middle of the most crime-riddled communities? How is it that they open on Sundays and Wednesday nights for prayer meeting and but feel no obligation to become a safe haven for the young and the elderly?

How can we provide more incentives for faith-based institutions to remain open? How can community be strengthened when church members move to suburban communities and return only for Sunday services? More important, as more churches follow their members to the suburbs, who and what will fill the void in urban neighborhoods?

John DiIulio states that only a small percentage of churches, synagogues, temples, and mosques apply for available government grants. How can technical expertise be provided to the smaller congregations that exist amid the worst kinds of social problems? What type of assistance can help them? Can crime be prevented without recapturing public space?

The issue of how to develop more effective partnerships already has been dealt with. But how do we approach the problem through the re-creation of community and uniform values? How can consensus be built around which values are most important? How do we socialize young people to become law-abiding and respectful of authority if those values are not taught in the home and if the traditional institutions have abdicated the responsibility for teaching them? How can we decide which are the most important problems to tackle?

I am concerned about how to diminish or eliminate those problems on the front end, at the prevention stage, so that we do not have to deal with them at the criminal justice level. How can churches get law enforcement agencies to parole some of the people who have committed lesser offenses to their congregation instead of continuing to lock them up? I do not reject the importance of dealing with root causes—and rejecting it lets the government off the hook. But how can we develop an approach to crime prevention that combines immediate measures to reduce crime with long-term measures to deal with root causes?

The most important question that has been raised is how faith-based organizations that are designed to solve problems can be made more effective. How can we empirically validate the effectiveness of the work that faith-based organizations carry out? Allow me to use the Nation of Islam as an example of a faith-based organization that has a proven track record of getting men off drugs and engaged in productive activities so that they can be assimilated back into the mainstream of society. What is the role of faith in the treatment of drug addicts? How is that Chuck Colson, a former White House staff member under President Richard Nixon, can take his ministry behind prison walls and help turn people's lives around? How do we design rational, empirical studies and make socially compassionate, public-spirited policy judgments based on that research?

I do not think that the successes we have observed in solving individual manifestations of social problems are due solely to the influence of faith-based organizations. I would like to see a form of multivariate analysis used to examine the effect of different factors, including that of faith-based organizations. We *must* also examine root causes; the role of government; and the role of the individual in his or her own rehabilitation.

I think it is time for us to become advocates for the replication or dissemination of models that have proven effectiveness, especially those that are cost effective. There are many, such as Sandtown, a faith-based, community program in Baltimore that has successfully provided a variety of services with little funding.

The final question I would like to raise is how relevant charitable choice can be when according to Dilulio only a small number of clergy are even aware of its existence. How can charitable choice become more widely used? How can those in the field make sure that all individuals who are eligible to take advantage of it in fact do so?

Fighting Crime: Overcoming the Arguments of Church-State Separationists

KEITH PAVLISCHEK

We should not be so naïve as to think that the heated opposition to the White House Office of Faith-Based and Community Initiatives or to public funding of faith-based organizations has all that much to do with empirical or social science data on the effectiveness of such funding. Whether faith-based organizations are in fact more effective than non–faith-based organizations in addressing the problems of the poor and disadvantaged is open to debate. But even if they are proven to be more effective, it would not matter to the church-state separationists. They oppose the funding of FBOs, or at least those "pervasively sectarian" ones that refuse to secularize, because they believe that it violates the First Amendment prohibition against the establishment of religion. They reason that just as government would not violate other First Amendment rights—freedom of speech or freedom of the press, for example—in the interest of "social effectiveness," so it should not violate the establishment clause.

But what if you reject the radical separationist views of Americans United for the Separation of Church and State, the American Civil Liberties Union (ACLU), and People for the American Way as historically and jurisprudentially preposterous? What if you were committed to a social policy that would help establish a healthier relationship between government and the institutions of civil society? Certainly a primary goal of such a policy would be to nourish and sustain the integrity and identity of a wide array of nongovernment institutions and organizations and to end discrimination against institutions that currently are discriminated against. That is the best way to view charitable choice. It should not be seen first as a funding mechanism for faith-based institutions. Rather, it is an important attempt to restore a healthy relationship between government and the institutions of civil society.

The ideology embraced by the separationists, however, can only produce an unhealthy and dysfunctional relationship between government and civil society because it is inherently discriminatory against one very important class of institutions of civil society. It inevitably excludes organizations and institutions from fair and equitable funding simply because of their most basic beliefs and convictions. To see why, take the not-so-hypothetical example of a nonprofit drug treatment organization that might be eligible for a government fee-for-service or voucher arrangement. What is masked by the simplistic distinction between "religious" and "nonreligious" (or "faith-based" and "non–faith-based") drug treatment organizations is that those that labor under the nonreligious or secular label hold highly contentious views about the nature of human beings, no less than those that are labeled "religious." How they implicitly or explicitly think about the "big issues" will profoundly influence their methodology. You might have a drug treatment program that is Freudian in methodology. Another might be modeled on a behaviorist approach. Another might be radically feminist or influenced by your favorite French post-modern philosopher. Justice dictates that all are and should be eligible to compete for public funds.

But what about a drug treatment organization that is theistic in its orientation, philosophy, and methodology? According to the separationists, the theistic approach must be treated differently from that of the Freudians, behaviorists, feminists, and French philosophers. In fact, the separationist insists that theistic organizations may not receive funding *even if* they can be shown to be more effective than the others in treating drug addicts, because their particular responses to the big questions are religious or faith-based, while the others purportedly are not. According to the separationists, when it comes to funding, the Establishment Clause requires the government to discriminate against those organizations *because* they are theistic.

But in truth, the answers to the big questions given by nontheists are no less faith-based that those given by theists. The choice is thus not really between faith-based and non-faith-based approaches to drug treatment, homelessness, job training, and other social problems, but among a variety of perspectives and methodologies. All of those perspectives are faith-based when it comes to the really big questions that orient, direct, and motivate their organizations: What is the nature of human beings? What is their place in the world? What is the ultimate solution to human pathologies? For that reason, it is simply unjust for the government to favor nontheistic over theistic providers of literacy and job training, drug treatment and counseling, care for the homeless, juvenile crime

prevention programs, and so forth. To the extent that charitable choice legislation and the new White House Office of Faith-Based and Community Initiatives seek to remedy that injustice, they should be applauded and supported.

Even Church-State Separationists
Care about Serving the Poor

JULIE A. SEGAL

Everyone agrees that religious organizations play an important role in efforts to
solve society's ills. In fact, even strict church-state separationists believe that government may cooperate with faith-based organizations in providing many social service programs. The disagreement over government funding of religious
organizations is not about *whether* faith-based groups may form partnerships
with government but about *how* those partnerships are structured. Among all
the proposals for government collaboration with religious organizations in
George Kelling's and John DiIulio's chapters, as well as the proposals that make
up President George W. Bush's Faith-Based Initiative, charitable choice is the
only one that fails upon closer inspection.

Although, at first glance, charitable choice appears benign, it violates the constitutional requirement of church-state separation by inadequately protecting
social service beneficiaries from proselytization; by allowing discrimination on
the basis of religion in hiring for positions funded with taxpayer dollars; and by
leading churches and other houses of worship down the primrose path without
alerting them to all the possible pitfalls associated with government funding.
Further, while purporting simply to expand the good work of many faith-based
social service programs, charitable choice will cause great damage to religious
liberty—a price that some may not agree is worth the benefit. While many religious organizations may provide beneficial services in their communities, that
does not negate the requirement that collaboration between those groups and
government withstand legal and ethical scrutiny. The U.S. Constitution is not
an obstacle to effective public policy or a pesky detail, and serving the poor and
protecting religious freedom are not mutually exclusive. Because charitable
choice has eclipsed the myriad appropriate ways in which religious groups can
form partnerships with government to serve those in need, it is necessary to discuss the law and to elucidate the pitfalls.

The separation of church and state is one of the least understood and most maligned concepts in current political discourse. Created by the Establishment Clause and the Free Exercise Clause of the First Amendment, the separation of church and state simultaneously prohibits the government from advancing religion and protects religious organizations from government intrusion. Government funding of religious organizations therefore must be carefully examined. When the government funds faith-based social service programs, taxpayers will rightfully demand an accounting of how the money is spent, possibly compromising the autonomy of religious organizations and hindering religious programs by regulating them. Financial support also is problematic because few things could advance a religious mission more than paying for it. As a result, all nine justices of the current Supreme Court have consistently held that "special Establishment Clause dangers" exist when money is given directly to religious organizations.[1]

Many religious organizations provided government-funded social services long before charitable choice legislation was passed. For years, those organizations—among them Catholic Charities, Lutheran Services in America, and United Jewish Communities—have received billions of dollars from governments to provide faith-based social services, but without conveying a religious message and with other appropriate constitutional safeguards in place. Charitable choice obviously is not intended to apply to those programs.

Instead, charitable choice purports to end the so-called discrimination against religious organizations by permitting them to receive government money for their social service programs while allowing them to proselytize social service beneficiaries with private funds. It also allows them to discriminate on the basis of religion in hiring employees who are paid with taxpayer money. For some reason, charitable choice proponents claim that it merely "levels the playing field" by treating religious and secular organizations equally with respect to their ability to obtain government grants and contracts for social service programs. That is not so.

First, there is not pervasive discrimination against religious groups in government programs. As mentioned, religious organizations receive billions of taxpayer dollars to feed the hungry, care for the aging, house the homeless, and teach job skills to the unemployed. Second, charitable choice proponents want equal treatment only with respect to funding, not program implementation. Charitable choice does not require religious organizations to play by the same rules as all other social service providers. No other government contractor would be granted the privilege of discriminating on the basis of religion in hiring employees who are paid with tax funds.

It is important to note that, although religious organizations are permitted to discriminate on the basis of religion in hiring employees paid with private funds, charitable choice extends that concession, allowing them to discriminate in hiring employees who work on or who are paid through public grants and contracts. Accordingly, charitable choice allows religious organizations to exclude nonbelievers from government-funded positions and thereby to advance their religious doctrine with taxpayer money. This aspect of charitable choice is unconstitutional and amounts to federally funded employment discrimination.

Furthermore, in the context of employment, the term *religion* includes adherence to religious tenets and teachings. For example, if a church receives a government grant to provide welfare services on behalf of the government and it requires its employees to adhere to a religious tenet requiring sexual abstinence before marriage, it could fire an unmarried female social worker if she were to become pregnant and thereby violate that religious tenet.[2] Although religious organizations should retain that right in private employment, such discrimination should not be permitted with taxpayer dollars.

Finally, charitable choice threatens our country's religious liberty and jeopardizes the autonomy of religious programs. Religious organizations may feel compelled to compete for political favor and lobby for scarce government appropriations. Churches and other houses of worship also may be reluctant to continue their traditional and important role as critic of government conduct out of fear of losing a government contract. Furthermore, despite its goals, government money will lead to government regulation of faith-based organizations—a threat that has led many would-be supporters, such as Pat Robertson and Marvin Olasky, to question the wisdom of government grants to churches.

In addition to charitable choice, the new White House Office of Faith-Based and Community Initiatives is cause for concern. Although no federal agency has a prohibition against contracting with religious organizations, President Bush has ordered an audit of five federal agencies' rules and regulations to determine whether they "discriminate" against faith-based organizations. Regrettably, what the president considers a discriminatory barrier to entry may be another person's neutral, generally applicable safeguard. Only time will tell whether religious organizations will be granted an exemption from the rules and regulations that apply to all other government contractors.

Although there are no empirical or social science data on the effectiveness of faith-based social service programs, many observers, including strict church-state separationists, believe that religious organizations provide some of the best social services available. But enhancing those organizations' resources is a goal that can be achieved without charitable choice. The chapter entitled "In Good Faith: A Dialogue on Government Funding of Faith-Based Social Services," with an introduction by Melissa Rogers, aptly details the ways all of us—government, religious and community organizations, and the for-profit sector—can serve the poor together. If we direct our energies to increasing private funding, we could serve those in need with the Constitution's blessing.

NOTES

1. *Mitchell* v. *Helms*, 530 U.S. 793 (2000).

2. See *Boyd* v. *Harding Academy of Memphis, Inc.*, 88 F.3d 410 (6th Cir. 1996).

PART THREE

THE ROLE OF FAITH-BASED ORGANIZATIONS IN

Community Development

CHAPTER SEVEN

Community Development and Religious Institutions

JEREMY NOWAK

Over the past thirty years many of the poorest communities in American cities have become headquarters for nongovernmental organizations dedicated to neighborhood revitalization. At the center of that effort are community development corporations (CDCs): private, largely nonprofit, citizen-led organizations that use public and private resources to support programs to maintain and develop real estate, social services, and business.[1] The growth of CDCs has been accompanied by that of other service, civic, and finance organizations pursuing related goals. Together, these organizations constitute the field of community development.

While many community development organizations are the direct offspring of government-funded community action programs and philanthropic demonstration projects, they also are heirs to a rich tradition of community-based efforts that include immigrant mutual-aid associations, settlement houses, congregational outreach programs, cooperative business enterprises, and union-related programs.

This chapter focuses primarily on the work of community development corporations as a whole, not simply on that of faith-based institutions. Yet in many cases religious congregations are crucial catalysts, allowing CDCs to organize, win public support and financial backing, and develop roots in the community.

The role of faith-based organizations in building CDCs often falls outside the raucous debate on public funding of faith-based social service programs—partly because their role has, on the whole, not been controversial and partly because the congregations often serve as organizing and vouching forces for their community rather than themselves. It would be a great mistake to interpret the relative lack of controversy over the role of religious institutions in community development as an indication that their role is unimportant. Quite the opposite is true: their role is noncontroversial because so many of the key actors see it as essential.

Like all institutions that serve public purposes, community development organizations have complex histories. Their existence is the result of more than grassroots initiatives, although that is the view commonly held by the press. Instead, they are the product of the interaction of social activism and social isolation. Their existence says as much about what public policy and private markets do not do as it does about development mediated by civic groups.

Scratch the surface and you discover the activism generated by the1960s' war on poverty legislation, the role of national philanthropic organizations in funding antipoverty programs, ethnic identity politics, and community organizing efforts.[2] Look more deeply and you discover the institutional vacuum created by the reduction in federal support for cities, the transformation of settlement patterns in U.S. metropolitan regions, the persistence of a high degree of racial segregation, and a private sector that is less involved in local politics and civic affairs than before.

Community-based revitalization efforts in U.S. cities arrive as both symptom and cure, reflections of a historical renegotiation of power, capacity, and role. They assert the power of local institutions to act as a catalyst for social change, while also serving as an implicit reminder of the limited public investment in low-income populations and the economic gap between poor and mainstream America. Community development corporations emerge in the space left to them by changing market patterns and public policy. They can be defined, in part, by three characteristics. First, they are *local* institutions, in a society in which commitment to maintaining local identity is less important. A sense of local rootedness looms large in the CDC movement. Most urban CDCs define their territory of operation in terms of relatively small areas, through the affective ties of neighborhood or the administrative logic of service districts. In many instances, race and social class play an important role in defining place or locality. Strictly speaking, CDC interventions do not begin with the logic of markets or the logic of a poverty reduction strategy, but rather with the logic of communities, reinforced as it is through social and spatial boundaries.

Second, CDCs have excelled largely in the areas of residential real estate development and provision of place-based social services. While the earliest CDCs placed a heavy emphasis on job training and economic development, many of those efforts failed. There are important exceptions to that rule, and some important innovations in those areas are taking place today. The role of CDCs as drivers of affordable housing production from the late 1970s onward was heightened by public policy and the limits of private market incentives. They became housing and service providers to a constituency that suffered from lack of housing, for a product that had limited market profitability, and for projects that required access to multiple sources of public and private investment.

Third, despite their nongovernmental status and their entrepreneurial quality, most CDCs maintain a significant dependence on public or private subsidy, provided principally by government and private philanthropy. While they certainly are more market-driven than most public agencies and more entrepreneurial than traditional social service institutions, most CDCs require substantial subsidy to sustain operations. That need follows from the nonmarket role that they play, the high transaction costs of their services and products, and an organizational culture defined by a deep sense of civic responsibility and public purpose.

Community development corporations evolved from a variety of institutional contexts and experiences. If you search for the historical roots of the local neighborhood development organization in any city in the United States you will find links with schools, civic groups, block associations, business groups, unions, political organizations, and corporations. You also will find the persistent presence of religious institutions at almost every turn.

While often it is unrecognized or understated, the role of religious institutions in facilitating community development is fundamental. Religious institutions always have functioned as the most significant source of community development organizations and projects, serving as *institutional incubator, organizer, investor*, and *civic leader*. That is particularly true in the African American community, in which historically the role of the congregation in public life has been central.

Acting as incubator is among the more common functions of urban religious congregations. As one of the primary centers of civic life, churches, either alone or in coalition with other institutions, have launched a significant percentage of development organizations and projects in cities. That is as true today as it was when the late Reverend Leon Sullivan created one of the first CDCs in the country through Zion Baptist Church in North Philadelphia in the early 1960s. The structure of congregation-based development organizations varies widely— some are held tightly within the leadership and organizational culture of the congregation, some spin off into a more independent identity. But no matter what the nature of the ongoing connection, the historical relationship exists.

In addition to their role as incubator of CDCs, religious congregations throughout the country have been at the forefront of neighborhood organizing efforts from Los Angeles to Baltimore, creating a public space for citizen education and advocacy. Many of their efforts have been associated with national networks such as the Industrial Areas Foundation. Here it is important to recognize that congregations, operating as they do within an institutional framework that conveys a sense of permanence and discipline, often serve as the most important place within low-income communities for building secular public relationships. Congregations become a locus of citizen participation and interaction, which leads to longer-term civic change.

The faith-based community also has been among the most active investors in community development. Many of the earliest investors in community development financial institutions came from Catholic religious orders and several mainline Protestant denominations. In many instances it has been neighborhood congregations themselves that have taken the lead in making direct equity investments in their own projects or in incubating credit unions and microenterprises. More than most institutions, religious institutions have been able to bring not only organized members to the task of neighborhood renewal, but organized money and leadership as well.

Finally, the enormous social structure that religious institutions represent through their involvement in a variety of social welfare agencies and private sector relationships has been one of the principal sources of leadership for community development organizations. The presence of that leadership can be felt from the smallest homeless shelter to national efforts such as Habitat for Humanity. Even among the most secular community development institutions it is common to find leaders who are rooted in the ministry or financial and civic support that comes from local and regional religious bodies.

GROWTH AND ACCOMPLISHMENTS

Reports on CDCs during the past decade note their prominence in the production of affordable housing, their increasing numbers (2,500 to 3,500, depending on how they are defined), their more limited success in commercial development, their reentry into work-force development activity, and the breadth of their political support.[3]

CDC involvement in urban housing has produced some remarkable successes, in many instances priming the pump for non-CDC market involvement. At least four CDC strategies have influenced public and private sector investment in housing. First, community development organizations and development finance intermediaries not only have been responsible for the production of tens of thousands of new, low-income rental housing units during the past two decades but also have quietly championed a style of property management that incorporates delivery of social services.

Second, community development organizations have demonstrated the existence of a market for the sale of newly constructed low- and moderate-income units in a number of cities. East Brooklyn Congregations, for example, has constructed more than 3,000 townhouses in one of New York City's poorest neighborhoods, drawing almost 50 percent of its buyers from local public housing projects. Market values in the area have risen dramatically.

Third, working with banks, public agencies, and private sector institutions such as Fannie Mae, community development groups and many of the nation's best community development financial institutions (for example, Center for Community Self-Help in North Carolina) have helped lower the barriers to homeownership for low-income buyers through mortgage counseling programs, savings and downpayment support, and specialized lending programs.

Fourth, largely through the leadership of organizations such as Neighborhood Housing Services, community development organizations have instituted programs to combat the deterioration of relatively strong neighborhoods before they deteriorate further. Such projects have shown real success in both cities and inner-ring suburbs.

In the area of commercial real estate development, CDCs in cities such as Oakland, Denver, Kansas City, and Cleveland have been among the first investors in and developers of new inner-city shopping centers. They usually have performed best when functioning as the bridge institution (as planners, investors, managers, and builders) that makes it possible for private investors and commercial operators to enter an area.

In the nonretail end of commercial real estate, a few community development groups have successfully managed business incubators and light-industrial properties. Such organizations are led by people with industry-specific skills. WireNet in Cleveland is one of the most interesting examples of a community-based nonprofit with the business-related expertise necessary to add value to geographically clustered enterprises.

Commercial real estate linked to social service provision is an increasingly important product for community development. Spurred, in part, by changes in the health care system, school reform, and demand for daycare, community development groups have become builders and sometimes managers of clinics, schools, and child-care centers. Of the first half-dozen charter schools that the Reinvestment Fund in Philadelphia financed, for example, three were sponsored and built by community development organizations.

A number of community-based institutions play significant roles in workforce development. The major successes come from organizations that have specialized job skills training capacity and industry knowledge, such as Project Strive in New York City, Quest in San Antonio, Focus: HOPE in Detroit, or CET in San Jose, California.[4] None of those organizations would view itself as a CDC, although all have historical roots in some form of community-based service delivery and some of them have CDCs as partners. While few development organizations play a direct role in job training, hundreds offer job recruitment services and postplacement counseling, functioning as intermediaries between residents and employers.

In some urban neighborhoods the success of CDC housing developments and other services and relationships has achieved a significant scale, helping middle-class housing take root. In Newark, New Jersey's Central Ward, for example, the New Community Corporation has built several thousand units of housing as well as participated in the rehabilitation and management of commercial space, daycare centers, and business incubators. Today New Community is a major engine of economic development in the city. In the Bronx, CDC housing and services have been highlighted by the national media as one of the factors behind the physical revitalization of one of America's best-known symbols of decline.

The endurance of the CDC movement is aided by its ability to capture support across ideological lines. Liberal Democrats view community development through the lens of social equity while conservative Democrats and Republicans view it through the lens of volunteerism and self-help. The nongovernment, grassroots character of CDCs makes them ideologically malleable.

As community development organizations become part of the social structure of urban communities, they become integrated into the local political structure. In some instances they have become an important source of political leadership, with mayors, aldermen, and legislators from low-income neighborhoods coming through their ranks. As they become integrated into the culture of wards and political parties, they also become objects of political competition and patronage. Strong community development organizations learn to navigate turbulent political waters with their development capacity and programs intact.

Today a national community development movement has emerged through the activities of individual CDCs as well as trade associations, banking and philanthropic supporters, training programs, research institutes, and financial intermediaries. That movement has had an impact on public policy. Its lobbying efforts have been effective in maintaining some affordable housing subsidies, supporting bank reinvestment legislation, and shaping aspects of legislation regarding public housing reform, federal empowerment zones, and community development financial institutions. In many states, CDCs have created a broad range of state-sponsored development programs.

Community development financial institutions (CDFIs) have played an increasingly important role, during the past ten years in particular. The establishment of the Community Development Financial Institutions Fund within the U.S. Treasury Department in 1994 gave a name and national credibility to the financial services niche in the community development field.

CDFIs flourished and became particularly active and numerous in the 1980s and 1990s. Some were established to provide direct financing and technical assistance to CDCs, others to finance a broader base of low-income neighborhood institutions and borrowers: retail, service, and manufacturing businesses; household consumers; private developers; nonprofit facilities managers; and others. Unlike most urban CDCs, community development financial institutions are usually structured as intermediaries for multiple neighborhoods throughout a city, region, or state.

Rooted in both the early CDC movement as well as the social investment movement of the 1980s and 1990s, today's network of CDFIs includes regulated development banks, credit unions that serve low-income areas, unregulated loan funds that finance housing projects and businesses, microfinance funds that concentrate on small-scale entrepreneurs, and community development venture funds that provide growth capital to businesses unable to obtain equity from conventional lenders. Collectively they manage somewhere in the neighborhood of $5 billion, and they have demonstrated a strong portfolio management and lending record.[5]

The capital management role of CDFIs and their ability to establish regional and national relationships with public and private sector institutions allows them to build specialized capital access and real estate or business development networks among private capital sources, the public sector, and neighborhood-based institutions and borrowers. Citywide housing partnerships have done so in a dozen cities or more by combining public subsidy and bank capital into one-stop housing production systems for developers of affordable housing. National intermediaries such as Local Initiatives Support Corporation (LISC) and the Enterprise Foundation have done so on a national level by being syndicators of the low-income housing tax credit. And scores of other capital-led community development programs have been instituted by CDFIs such as the Illinois Facilities Fund, the Low-Income Housing Fund, and Boston Community Capital.

ASSESSMENT AND CRITIQUE

The community development field underwent an internal and external reassessment throughout the 1990s. From the perspective of community development practitioners and supporters, that reassessment revolved largely around the issue of the relevance, or impact, of CDCs. The relatively small scale of community development efforts stood in stark contrast to the extent of inner-city decline. Moreover, in an age of rapidly changing institutions and economic relationships, CDCs appeared to be removed from the mainstream. While some in the field were beginning to achieve some scale in real estate development, practitioners and supporters began to confront four challenges to long-term viability and legitimacy: the challenge of scale and public visibility, the challenge of comprehensive service delivery, the challenge of social capital, and the challenge of inner-city economic growth.

First, examples of significant impact by the best CDCs are not as numerous as most practitioners and supporters would like, particularly in areas not related to housing. There are too many examples of institutional marginality—small-scale organizations with limited track records searching for limited public subsidy. One promising route toward greater scale and visibility involves developing partnerships with some of the core institutions with which community development groups have some common interests—hospitals, universities, cultural institutions, and others.

Second, to balance physical development with human development, increased attention is now being paid to forming multiorganizational alliances to deliver a range of social services, from family counseling to job training. This approach has been linked, in part, to the self-sufficiency demands of welfare reform legislation.

Third, as high levels of unemployment, substance abuse, and crime continue to affect the quality of neighborhoods, the importance of building stronger social capital has become a more prominent issue. Community development groups are finding it increasingly important to identify ways to strengthen social networks through everything from block clubs to citizen crime patrols.

Fourth, aware of the inherent limitations of providing housing and human services, most large CDCs continue to identify ways to stimulate economic development in their neighborhoods, usually through involvement in work-force development and commercial real estate development. For most CDCs, however, undertaking a more substantial role in stimulating general business and minority enterprises remains relatively elusive.

The dialogue within the community development field about capacity and direction was further influenced by new thinking in the areas of regional development and market-oriented social policy. Both are firmly rooted in a sober assessment of the competitive disadvantages of many urban environments given the rapid rate of suburbanization and the accompanying loss of urban middle-class residents and jobs that has left impoverished minorities concentrated in the central cities.

While it was apparent to many observers in the 1960s and 1970s, the significance to cities, and inner-city neighborhoods in particular, of the geography of segregation by socioeconomic class became politically and economically stronger in the 1980s and 1990s. Regional approaches to inner-city decline and poverty are associated with the work of Myron Orfield and David Rusk,[6] as well as with the literature of housing programs and transportation-related development projects. Regional development arguments have several common characteristics. They assert that the dominant characteristics of regional growth are concentrated poverty and suburban sprawl; high levels of central city poverty, which drives away middle-class users, isolates low-income residents, and creates pressure on cities (and later inner-ring suburbs) to either raise taxes or reduce services; sprawl-like development that is caused not only by market and life-style choices but by public policies that provide subsidy and incentives for new infrastructure, outer-ring transportation, and single-family, large-lot housing; a continual process of outer-ring suburbanization that represents income or subsidy transfers from older central cities and inner-ring suburbs to newly developing areas; and an impaired capacity to address regional growth and urban poverty issues that results from the fragmented administration of metropolitan regions by multiple jurisdictions.

The regional perspective places the problems of inner-city neighborhoods in a more systemic framework than is found in most analyses of neighborhood development. Urban decline and renewal is viewed as a product of the self-reinforcing dynamics of multiple policy and market decisions, and the renewal of inner cities is seen to depend on the renegotiation of their structural disadvantages within the regional system. If those disadvantages are not redressed, current social and spatial processes will continue, increasing and concentrating poverty in the inner city, repelling middle-income residents, limiting the potential of public investment in older cities and towns, and transferring subsidy to new development in outlying areas.

Regional systems can help turn the tide by redirecting public incentives for development back to cities and towns through everything from growth boundaries to targeted subsidy allocation; creating more tax equity through regional or statewide systems of distribution that balance the playing field when it comes to paying for public goods and services; providing both incentives and requirements for deconcentrating affordable housing, distributing it throughout the regional area; and making better use of transportation subsidies to support the growth of central cities and multiple-income, multifunctional town-like developments.

Orfield and Rusk challenge traditional notions of community development in favor of metropolitan policy interventions that would spur neighborhood revitalization. In *Metropolitics*, Orfield views traditional approaches to community development as an inadequate response to a growth logic that cannot be changed through interventions at the neighborhood level. His six-part strategy—fair housing, tax-base sharing, reinvestment, land planning and growth management, welfare reform and public works, and transportation reform—requires metro-politanwide reforms to shift growth back to the urban core.

In *Cities without Suburbs* and *Inside Game, Outside Game,* David Rusk provides a similar analysis of regional growth and a similar critique of community development. While much of Rusk's work deals with the comparative impact of urban-suburban political connections on income and racial segregation, he undertakes a direct review of thirty-four of the best CDCs in the country. While he recognizes the quality of their work, judged by the reduction of poverty in their neighborhoods over time, nevertheless they appear lacking.[7] While improvements can be observed in several areas, most CDC target neighborhoods follow the same general trajectory of urban decline exhibited in non-CDC areas. The analysis is not an indictment of CDC activity per se; it demonstrates instead the overwhelming tide of market forces, policy decisions, and demographic changes against which an *inside game* is powerless.

Like Orfield, Rusk favors an approach that works simultaneously on the issues of urban reform and investment while also pursuing tax-base sharing, containment of sprawl, and the scattering of affordable housing throughout a region. The potential of the regional coalition politics that Rusk and Orfield propose is being tested throughout the nation through alliances of urban equity advocates, suburban environmental activists, and business interests concerned with economic competitiveness.[8]

The work of both Orfield and Rusk has much in common with the housing opportunity movement, a tradition of fair housing legislation and litigation as well as affordable housing policies and programs that promote opening suburban and other middle-income neighborhoods to affordable housing in an effort to increase racial and economic integration.[9] In contrast to community development, which has concentrated on rebuilding low-income and affordable housing in the inner city, the housing opportunity movement concentrates on increasing low-income individuals' choice of housing in order to link them to social networks and institutions that promote mainstream integration. Like community development practitioners, housing opportunity advocates note the differential access of low-income people to public goods (schools, jobs) and they argue for equity. They simply seek a different solution to the problem.

Research on the Gautreaux housing program in Chicago, the best-known and oldest of the housing opportunity programs, gives some cause for optimism about the effects of moving low-income residents to the suburbs, where better schools and public amenities can have a significant impact on everything from school performance to employment.[10] Information on housing opportunity replication programs across the country sponsored by the U.S. Department of Housing and Urban Development paints a more uneven picture of the potential scale, management, and acceptance of such efforts. At the same time, many new smart growth, inclusive zoning, and tax-base sharing efforts in states as diverse as Minnesota, Maryland, California, Oregon, and New Jersey include suburban affordable housing programs. It will be important to pay attention to the results of those efforts over time.

The housing opportunity movement has been reinforced by a number of efforts that use transportation planning and investment as a way to promote urban development and connect low-income people with regional job opportunities.[11] Demonstration projects sponsored by the federal and state governments have been accompanied by countless others—sponsored by chambers of commerce, local transportation authorities, business office parks, and welfare-reform programs—to promote ride sharing, new bus routes, and workplace shuttle services.

While the regional approach to development has gathered momentum, public policymakers increasingly have focused on the role of economic markets and private sector investment in revitalizing low-income communities. Michael Porter's work on the market positioning of inner-city economies played a significant role in this regard, given the importance of his classic study on national competitive advantages.[12] Porter's analysis of the inner city asserts the need to encourage inner-city revival through the logic of self-interested, profit-making business investors and entrepreneurs rather than the logic of social programs and social investment. In addition, it asserts the need for government and civic groups to concentrate on lowering the barriers to entry and cost of operations for new businesses, not through direct subsidy but through investment in infrastructure, work-force development, and business-friendly regulatory policies. It also asserts the need to concentrate on the competitive advantages of inner cities, particularly their willing labor force and proximity to regional economic growth clusters, geographically bound groups of similar firms that have a variety of horizontal and vertical links, including common infrastructure and work-force needs.

The Porter analysis was criticized by some community development activists and academics for being too dismissive of the history and role of community-based institutions in urban economic development. Others welcomed the attention it focused on the inner city as an asset whose market potential has been unrealized. Like that of the regional development analysts, Porter's work looks at systemic links between regional growth and urban decline—but not in order to intervene with equity-oriented social policies. Porter views the links in terms of economic opportunity: urban places and people, although they are strategically located, suffer from underinvestment; investors have a ready-made work force and network of firms and industries to build on; regional growth is the substance of inner-city growth possibilities, not a cause of urban decline. The challenge is to use the same economic principles in the inner city as in other areas, to build value through existing regional growth clusters, not to reorganize growth through policy interventions.

While Porter's work achieved some notoriety for its more market-focused approach to inner-city social problems, it was only one of many factors that have moved urban policy and some aspects of community development in that direction. At least three trends have played an important role in promoting market-oriented policy. First, the combined effects of a strong economy and welfare reform have caused policymakers and private investors to emphasize work-force development—both job training and mechanisms for connecting workers to the labor market.

Second, both policymakers and private investors have increased their attention to market-based strategies. There has been a significant, bipartisan shift in national public policies designed to assist cities since the push in the mid-1980s for enterprise and empowerment zones. For example, the most recent anti-poverty package, the New Markets Initiative, includes tax credits and regulatory changes that reflect a market orientation.[13] That shift in public emphasis had its correlate in private philanthropy. Before the 1980s major philanthropic organizations rarely directed their attention beyond traditional concerns such as education, health care, environmental issues, and the like. While that focus prevails, a new willingness to use philanthropic resources to support economic growth efforts has emerged. The Ford Foundation, Annie E. Casey Foundation, and Mott Foundation, for example, no longer think about their grants only in terms of social services; they also consider their wealth-building potential.

Third, the 1980s and 1990s witnessed the emergence of a new breed of entrepreneurial mayors who had to be more fiscally disciplined, friendlier to small business investment, and more willing to pursue market-oriented approaches to service delivery than their predecessors. New York City's Rudolph Giuliani, Richard Daley of Chicago, Philadelphia's Ed Rendell, Stephen Goldsmith of Indianapolis, John Norquist of Milwaukee, and others differ in many ways, but all became mayors at a time when residents, investors, and consumers were dissatisfied with public goods and services and were leaving.[14] Their political success—and the success of their cities—required a new package of public goods.

THE REPOSITIONING OF COMMUNITY DEVELOPMENT AND THE IMPORTANCE OF FAITH-BASED SOCIAL NETWORKS

Changes in metropolitan social structure and the market orientation of urban policymakers reflect fundamental changes: the frictionless nature of capital flows, the use of new telecommunications technologies in the workplace and home, the difficulty public institutions have in accommodating rapid change, the increasing dominance of market exchange in new areas of civic life, and the geographical disconnection between areas of poverty and of growth.

The increasing absence of institutional mechanisms for connecting low-income people with economic opportunities provides the community development field with a framework that can make it more economically relevant. In an era when the public sector has lost some of its capacity to keep up with change and when private sector institutions exhibit less loyalty to any one place, CDCs can play the intermediary. Just as the settlement houses of a century ago viewed themselves as midwives delivering new urban citizens, community development institutions can assume a similar role.

To do so requires changes in how CDCs are organized and how they operate, and it is more than a matter of adding a new product or function within the existing organization. It requires making changes in the relationships and positioning of organizations that are not too dissimilar from the changes that have occurred in the private sector in recent years. Community development organizations must move from narrowly local, single-organization program building to maintaining a market-oriented network of relationships that allows them to exert influence across a broader social geography. Many of the strongest and most agile community development organizations already have begun to make those shifts in structure and strategy. There are three aspects to their change in positioning.

First, it involves the need to expand the geography of influence of urban-based CDCs through institutional expansion, organizational consolidation, and the formation of strategic alliances between neighborhood and regional institutions. Overreliance on small-scale, neighborhood-based civic infrastructure limits CDCs' capacity to participate in and influence an ever-evolving market. The organization of regional and community development financial institutions and the formation of alliances between local and regional institutions create opportunities for CDCs to engage in the civic and market arenas across a regional trade area.

That is not to say that small-scale neighborhood civic groups have no important role to play; they do, within both low- and middle-income neighborhoods, in community organizing and planning. And locally oriented CDCs will continue to play an important role in residential and commercial development and in delivery of social services. Rebuilding urban areas requires the catalytic leadership that community development corporations sometimes are able to offer; moreover, the strength of regional connections relies on the knowledge and credibility of people and institutions at the local level.

But community development as a field cannot be overly defined by the aggregation of small parts; it needs to do business within the broader civic and economic market. That means that neighborhood development institutions must collaborate in substantive ways across the region. It also means that new regional institutions are needed—some with specialized development and investment capacity and others that are able to organize citizens or provide policy support.

Second, a repositioned CDC must organize its mission and activities as much as possible around the core issues of poverty—the need to increase low wages and employment rates and the need to build housing values, quality public services, and savings for low-income households. Place-based human service activities must be viewed as tools to support the core mission, which is to alleviate poverty; accomplishing that mission requires, in part, facilitating connections between low-income people and opportunities. That includes building affordable housing across the widest possible geographic area, providing the most convenient and high-quality child care, and making investments in transportation that facilitate access to jobs and in work-force training that lead to career growth and better wages. Such links and investments facilitate connections among neighborhoods, residents, employers, and a variety of public and private institutions and services.

The third attribute follows directly from a broadened geographical sphere of influence, a focus on poverty alleviation, and an organizational structure able to influence the environment by managing a variety of relationships and products. It is critical in the twenty-first century for the community development field to engage in a broader range of public policy issues. The traditional policy concerns of the field have been limited to subsidies and regulations that support the real estate activities of CDCs, such as the low-income housing tax credit or the Community Reinvestment Act. They are, of course, important. But they represent a very narrow response to the universe of policy that relates to poverty: employment opportunity, fair housing, child care, transportation, local tax policy, and building and investment incentives.

There is new opportunity today for CDCs to broaden their policy horizons. On one hand, the emergence of suburban antisprawl sentiment creates an opening for regional partnerships to promote reinvestment in cities and towns. At the same time, if labor markets remain tight, CDCs can forge a connection between a business community that promotes regional competitiveness and an urban constituency working to alleviate poverty. The so-called three E's of regional policy—economy, equity, and environment—form a natural field of new relationships and allies.

How does broadening the concept of community development and the agenda of community development organizations relate to religious institutions?

Just as religious institutions have been critical in forming community development organizations, they are in many ways even more critical to organizing regional civic networks that link low-income households with economic opportunities. More than any other nongovernment institution in the United States, religious institutions cross boundaries of race, class, and geography. And they are critical hubs of networks that can be deployed for broader purposes than serving their own congregations. Moreover, religious institutions often have a structure that includes both local (congregational) and regional (judicatory) bodies. They are accustomed to thinking about and planning within a framework of institutional diversity and place-based distinctions.

The judicatories (administrative bodies similar to a diocese), congregations, social networks, and para-church organizations of faith-based institutions are indispensable participants in any effort to build regional consensus on how, given the nature of regional growth, to give low-income people and places the best possible advantages. If the neighborhood organizing efforts that animated much of community development thirty and forty years ago—and still do—could make effective use of religious institutions as one foundation of neighborhood stability and civic care, a new regional community development strategy can do so today.

At the Reinvestment Fund in Philadelphia, religious community investors have played a fundamental role. They represent not only a source of capital but a source of social and institutional networks as well, with connections to colleges, hospitals, boardrooms, and political offices. A Catholic religious order may be the parent corporation of a group of urban hospitals with connections to insurance companies and business trade groups. The investment committee of a suburban church may be composed of some of the most important corporate leaders in the city. An inner-city church may have historical links to suburban voters. The challenge is to use those relationships to forge a connection between faith and everyday institutional interests. That requires a commitment that is more complex than volunteering to do weekend duty at an affordable housing site in the inner city, although that certainly is helpful and admirable. It involves claiming the alleviation of poverty—and community development—as a civic as well as religious value and employing religious institutions and their networks to help create and influence policies made in a new regional public sphere.

NOTES

1. This section draws on concepts and ideas from my experience in the field, as well as a variety of books, articles, and evaluation reports. References include the Ford Foundation, *Corrective Capitalism* (New York: 1989); Avis Vidal, *Rebuilding Communities: A National Study of Urban Community Development Corporations* (New York: Community Development Research Center, New School for Social Research, 1992); and Robert Halpern, *Rebuilding the Inner City* (New York: Colombia University Press, 1995).

2. For a good background on organizing see Sanford Horwitt, *Let Them Call Me Rebel* (New York: Knopf Press, 1989).

3. The problem of obtaining good numbers is fundamentally a problem of definition. The higher-end numbers tend to include a broader range of nonprofit institutions than some would use.

4. See the study by Bennett Harrison, Marcus Weiss, and Jon Gant, *Building Bridges* (New York: Ford Foundation, 1994).

5. Early work on CDFIs includes Richard Taub, *Community Capitalism* (Boston: Harvard Business Press, 1988) and Julian Parzen and Michael Hall Kieschnick (Philadelphia: Temple University Press, 1992). Currently the best data on the CDFI field are published by the National Community Capital Association in Philadelphia.

6. Myron Orfield, *Metropolitics* (Brookings, 1997); David Rusk, *Cities without Suburbs* (Washington: Woodrow Wilson Center Press, 1993); and David Rusk, *Inside Game, Outside Game* (Brookings, 1999).

7. Rusk, *Inside Game*, pp. 17–61.

8. Bruce Katz's Center on Urban and Metropolitan Policy at Brookings has done much to stimulate public debate on these issues.

9. A review of the issues can be found in Alexander Polikoff, ed., *Housing Mobility: Promise or Illusion?* (Washington: The Urban Institute, 1995).

10. See James Rosenbaum, "Expanding the Geography of Opportunity by Expanding Residential Choice: Lessons from the Gautreaux Program," *Housing Policy Debate*, vol. 6, no.1 (1995).

11. See Mark Alan Hughes, "A Mobility Strategy for Improving Opportunity," *Housing Policy Debate*, vol. 6, no.1 (1995).

12. Michael E. Porter, "The Competitive Advantages of the Inner City," *Harvard Business Review*, vol. 73 (1995).

13. See Roy Green, ed., *Enterprise Zones* (Newbury Park, Calif.: Sage Press, 1991) and Tamar Jacoby and Fred Siegel, "Growing the Inner City," *New Republic*, August 23, 1999.

14. A quick summary of many of the new governance ideas from these mayors can be found in Center for Civic Innovation, *The Entrepreneurial City: A How-To Handbook for Urban Innovators* (New York: Manhattan Institute, 1999).

CHAPTER EIGHT

Many Are Called, but Few Are Chosen: Faith-Based Organizations and Community Development

AVIS C. VIDAL

The interest generated by President George W. Bush's initiatives to encourage greater participation of faith-based organizations in government-financed social action programs relates primarily to the role of religious organizations in the direct delivery of social services. From one perspective, that is understandable: those initiatives build on the foundation laid by the charitable choice provisions of the 1996 welfare reform law and highlight activities in which religious organizations are believed—albeit without real evidence—to have been successful. But from another perspective, that focus is anomalous. It ignores numerous highly visible examples of investments in more fundamental neighborhood change by congregations determined to make a lasting difference in their communities—investments in new and rebuilt housing, improved retail facilities, new child-care centers, and other durable community improvements.

It is true that congregational commitments to community development are as poorly documented and understood as congregational participation in the delivery of human services. Indeed, they are among the least well researched aspects of the community development field. This field, brought to maturity by the community development corporation (CDC) movement, understands community development to be "asset building that improves the quality of life among

The author thanks the Office of Policy Development and Research in the U.S. Department of Housing and Urban Development (HUD) for its support of the research on which this chapter is based. The views expressed and any errors are her own and should not be attributed either to HUD or to the Urban Institute or its trustees.

residents of low- to moderate-income communities."[1] In that context, community development centers on housing and community economic development (both real estate development and business development) but also includes efforts, including job-training programs, to build human capital. In short, community development helps communities and their members to get ahead, not simply to get by.[2]

This chapter seeks to remedy the gap in public understanding by presenting a review, primarily an analytical literature review, of the current state of knowledge about the role of congregations in community development. Critical empirical analysis on community development is scarce; most works focus only on congregations' work in human services. There are no analyses of the outcomes of congregational activities, no assessments of the factors influencing the scale or quality of outcomes, and no comparisons of similar activities conducted by secular and faith-based organizations. For that reason, I interviewed twenty-seven leading practitioners and researchers in the field of community development to supplement the literature review.

CONGREGATIONAL ENGAGEMENT IN SOCIAL SERVICES AND COMMUNITY DEVELOPMENT

Mark Chaves finds in his National Congregations Study that 57 percent of congregations engage in some kind of service activity.[3] Those activities vary enormously, but most of them fall under the broad umbrella of health and human services. Youth programs, marriage and family counseling, and food services are the most typical human services; visitation and other assistance to sick individuals are the most common health-related services.[4]

As Chaves reports in his chapter in this volume, the community development activities of congregations are much more limited, and they are heavily concentrated in housing. While 18 percent of congregations support some type of housing or shelter activity, only 1 percent engage in employment activities.

Even those modest numbers overstate direct congregational participation in community development, because most congregations support development only indirectly. The most common form of congregational support for housing is providing volunteers for Habitat for Humanity, an ecumenical Christian housing ministry that produces primarily new single-family homes, many built with some sweat equity from the purchasing family. Congregations are a major source of volunteers, but most Habitat affiliates build a relatively small number of homes each year.[5]

Nevertheless, some faith-based organizations have been active housing developers. They have sponsored more Section 202 projects (which provide federally subsidized housing for the elderly) than any other type of organization, and a survey of all Section 202 projects in service in 1988 found that 49.7 percent of them had religious sponsors. Those projects included an estimated total of 161,000 housing units.[6] Anecdotal evidence indicates that many sponsors were congregations, but denominational organizations and their affiliates, particularly Catholic Charities and the Jewish Federations, have been active providers as well.

Faith-based organizations also were important participants in the Section 236 program, which provided subsidized housing for families. Here, the history is less positive. Congregational sponsors experienced high default rates in the Section 236 program, and nonprofit sponsors had higher default rates than for-profit ones.[7] No hard data are available about how faith-based groups performed compared with other nonprofit sponsors, but one HUD evaluation surveyed "several troubled nonprofit projects" and found that "church groups often looked upon the projects they sponsored as a form of charity, kept rents artificially low, and were willing to overlook rent delinquencies."[8] No information is available about the participation of faith-based sponsors in the more recent project-based Section 8 program, nor about their current use of low-income housing tax credits.

Congregational support for community economic development programs—most of which comes from African American churches—is much less common than support for housing. The best-known examples of commercial real estate development projects sponsored by faith-based CDCs include a strip mall anchored by a Pathmark supermarket in central Newark, New Jersey, developed by New Community Corporation; a similar development by Abyssinian Development Corporation in Harlem; and a smaller-scale retail development done by Allen African Methodist Episcopal Church in Jamaica, Queens, on the block that includes its school.

New business development, widely known as one of the most difficult and risky components of community development, is quite rare. One example is Greater Christ Temple Church in Meridian, Mississippi, which pulled together 35 members, 96 percent of whom were on welfare, to pool their food stamps in order to purchase groceries wholesale. That initial self-help activity (often known in faith communities as mutual aid) ultimately led participants to build a supermarket and subsequently led to the formation of several other nonprofit corporations.

Congregational support for community development financial institutions (CDFIs) appears to be more common than support for other types of community economic development.[9] Those institutions include microloan and other loan funds, but credit unions appear to be more common—perhaps the most common form of support for community development other than housing.[10] For example, Concord Baptist Church in Brooklyn follows a tradition in the African American church of serving community residents in areas in which society at large has failed to serve them. After eight members of the congregation were refused credit by conventional banks, the church established Concord Federal Credit Union (CFCU), a separately incorporated nonprofit organization accountable to the church through its 14-member board of directors. They manage the credit union with the help of a part-time paid manager. According to Pamela Ann Toussaint in *Signs of Hope in the City*, "CFCU offers a number of services, from payroll deductions to auto loans, and boasts almost 1,000 members and just under \$3 million in assets."[11]

Some CDFIs benefit from social investments by denominational and related organizations in addition to the credit union deposits made by congregants, and they also receive funds from secular sources such as foundations. Like CDCs and other community-based organizations that have been spun off by congregations, some receive in-kind support from the sponsoring congregation, such as free office space. Some CDFIs are tied into familiar community development trade associations and membership groups, such as the National Federation of Community Development Credit Unions, but many are not, so their numbers are almost certainly underestimated. Much less common than support for credit unions is support for microloan funds like the one managed by First African Methodist Episcopal Church (FAME) in Los Angeles. After the violence in South Central Los Angeles that followed the announcement of the verdict in the Rodney King case, FAME's Reverend Cecil Murray became a prominent spokesperson for the African American community in South Central and played an important role in coalition building and social reconciliation efforts. When rebuilding began, FAME competed for and received a \$1 million grant from the Walt Disney Company that led to establishment of a microloan program that supplies low-interest loans of \$2,000 to \$20,000 to minority entrepreneurs in the area.[12]

THE MOST ACTIVE TYPES OF CONGREGATIONS

According to Chaves's chapter, six factors appear to influence the likelihood that a congregation will engage in some type of social ministry: size, income, racial composition, need in the congregation's neighborhood, theological and political orientation, and leadership. Specifically, congregations that are large, wealthy, African American, located in high-poverty neighborhoods, liberal, and led by clergy who support community service tend to be more heavily engaged in social service activities.[13] It appears that the same broad features also are associated with participation in community development activities. However, qualitative evidence suggests that some kinds of congregations, including African American churches and Catholic churches, may find community development more consistent with their beliefs and outlook than others.

There was widespread agreement among those interviewed that involvement in community life comes most naturally to black churches, a legacy of the history of racial discrimination and segregation in the United States and the historic responsiveness of black churches to the exclusionary practices of mainstream secular institutions. The church was a vehicle through which African Americans organized alternative institutions, such as fraternities and sororities, burial societies, insurance companies, and banks. Until relatively recently, racial segregation ensured that the church's focus remained on the local community. The black church historically has been the only strong community institution controlled by the black community. Black churches are overwhelmingly congregation centered, a focus that gives them great flexibility in choosing the activities they wish to pursue. But it also means that generally they do not have access to the denominational resources available to Roman Catholic and some mainstream Protestant congregations.

The mainstream denominations vary greatly in how they view and relate to the community, and their service orientation affects the ease with which they move into community development and the technical assistance they require. The Roman Catholic church is most commonly cited as having a strong, clear orientation toward serving the local neighborhood. Roman Catholic parishes are defined geographically, and traditionally Catholics have been expected to attend the church closest to their residence. When parishioners move, they normally join a parish near their new home. If the composition of a neighborhood changes, the parish's mandate is to serve the new population. Such an orientation, combined with Roman Catholic teachings on social justice, lends itself philosophically to participation in community development.

In contrast, some denominations consider the members of the church to be the community. These churches seek to play an important role in the lives of their members, and while they may be drawn to social ministry to help the poor—caring "for the least of these"—historically they have had no institutional impetus to engage in, or assume responsibility for, the surrounding neighborhood. Moving into community development would require many such congregations to develop a new rationale to encompass this form of ministry, and it would affect the way they work. They would, for example, have to be willing and able to participate with nonmembers in setting a neighborhood development agenda and in speaking on the community's behalf when seeking funds or taking a stand on local policy issues.

THE NEED TO ADOPT DIFFERENT APPROACHES

The way congregations support community development differs considerably from the approach that most of them use to deliver health-related and other social services. Whereas a substantial majority of community development activities sponsored by congregations are undertaken in collaboration with others, only the most intensive social service activities are conducted that way and only if suitable partners are available. Reliance on collaborative activity is a response to the technical and financial demands of community development, which make it difficult for congregations to engage in it effectively on their own. Direct congregational participation in development—especially real estate development—

Table 8-1. *Percentage of Congregations Engaged in Activity by Program Type*[a]

Activity	All congregations	All programs	Program run within congregation	Program separately incorporated	Participates in, supports, or is affiliated with programs in other organizations or in denomination
Human services					
Visitation or support for sick and shut-ins	84.7	116.1	72.5	3.7	23.8
Youth programs	72.6	101.8	44.4	8.9	47.2
Marriage counseling	70.5	89.3	68.5	5.4	26.1
Family counseling	61.8	78.8	57.4	6.0	36.7
Meal services/food kitchens	50.1	59.6	26.0	8.6	65.4
Community development					
Homeless housing/shelter programs	38.7	43.6	9.9	6.9	83.3
Affordable housing development or programs	19.7	22.5	13.8	12.9	73.3
Senior housing programs	19.2	20.8	3.4	10.6	86.1
Community programs, including economic development, job training, etc.	20.2	24.0	16.7	11.3	72.1

a. Number of congregations = 257,648. Congregations could give multiple responses.
Source: Author's calculations based on figures in Virginia A. Hodgkinson and others, *From Belief to Commitment* (Independent Sector, 1993).

is relatively rare. It also is legally and financially unwise, since it can leave the project sponsor and its assets at risk if the development falls into legal or financial difficulty.

Rather than run programs themselves, most congregations collaborate on community development by donating money or supplying volunteers for programs run by denominations. However, congregations may participate directly in community development in three ways: directly sponsoring a community development corporation; joining a coalition that forms a CDC (or similar entity); or participating in a joint venture with an experienced developer.

The most common way for congregations to enter community development on their own is to establish and spin off an affiliated nonprofit organization—typically a CDC. The Abyssinian Development Corporation (ADC), established by Abyssinian Baptist Church in Central Harlem, is a prominent example. During its early years, the church provided ADC with significant in-kind support, including rent-free office space, free telephone and telephone answering service, access to photocopy and fax machines, help from church volunteers, and financial management services provided by the church's financial manager. ADC's first project was a twenty-five-unit transitional housing development that included on-site services for formerly homeless families. ADC since has developed more than 400 units of housing and a variety of economic development projects.[14] Another widely publicized example is Allen African Methodist Episcopal (AME) Church in Jamaica, pastored by Reverend Floyd Flake. The development corporation started by the church began its work by developing a $13 million, 300-unit senior citizens center—one of the largest faith-based elderly housing developments ever constructed—with funding from the Section 8 and Section 202 programs.[15] As in the ADC example, housing production marked the beginning of a steady stream of community development activity.

Although congregations commonly act alone in establishing CDCs, they sometimes take joint action. A prominent example is New Community Corporation (NCC) in Newark's Central Ward, by far the largest faith-based CDC. It has developed more than 3,300 units of permanent housing for both families and seniors, plus transitional units for formerly homeless families. It also has sponsored economic development projects, and it provides a variety of social services through affiliates. Although associated in the public's mind with St. Rose of Lima Church, where NCC's leader, Monsignor William Linder, is a priest, NCC's true origin lies in a coalition of urban and suburban churches formed in response to the Newark riots in 1968.[16]

The Nehemiah Project mounted by East Brooklyn Churches (EBC) is a coalition of congregations brought together after several years of discussion and exploration assisted by the Industrial Areas Foundation (IAF). The partnership was formed in 1981 to recreate livable neighborhoods in devastated parts of East Brooklyn by providing opportunities for homeownership. The Nehemiah Project built two- and three-bedroom rowhouses that it sold to families with average annual incomes of $15,000 to $25,000 for less than the actual cost of construction; by 1996 the partnership had built and sold 2,300 single-family rowhouse units.[17] Other well-known examples with a similar sponsorship structure include South Bronx Churches Nehemiah Homes and Harlem Churches for Community Improvement (HCCI), which spurred the redevelopment of Bradhurst, a forty-block neighborhood in upper-central Harlem.

A less familiar example is the Resurrection Project (TRP) in the Pilsen and Little Village neighborhoods of Chicago. It began with the collaboration of six Catholic parishes that later affiliated with the IAF and grew within about five years into a nationally acclaimed CDC involved in housing production; in homeownership, child-care, and community safety programs; and in promotion of minority enterprises.[18] Because Roman Catholic churches commonly have stayed in urban neighborhoods rather than following their parishioners to the suburbs and because the Catholic Campaign for Human Development has provided modest but steady financial support for IAF, TRP could be another model with real promise.

The nation now has approximately 3,600 community-based development organizations. Of those, about 500 (14 percent) report that they consider their organization to be faith-based.[19] My unpublished preliminary analysis indicates that as a group, faith-based CDCs (excluding groups whose only development work is done through Habitat for Humanity) have developed about 109,000 housing units. On average, the faith-based groups are younger and smaller than their secular counterparts, appear to have significantly smaller full-time staffs, and are more than twice as likely to have annual operating budgets of less than $500,000. They also are much less likely to be involved in development activities such as job training and placement than in housing development, commercial/industrial real estate development, or business enterprise development. However, nationally well-known examples, such as New Community Corporation and Abyssinian Development Corporation, make it clear that some do a great deal.

A third, less common approach is for a congregation to partner with a well-established community developer. Religious Institutions as Partners in Community-Based Development, a demonstration program launched by the Lilly Endowment in 1989, employed that approach. The program invited congregations to form partnerships with experienced community development groups and to propose an initial development project. It funded twenty-eight competitively chosen partnerships, the majority of which were in urban areas and served low-income communities of people of color. Although such partnerships appear to be infrequent outside the context of the Lilly initiative, they are instructive.

An evaluation of that initiative found that most partnerships accomplished all or most of what they set out to achieve.[20] At the end of the project period, 900 units of various types of housing had been built, rehabilitated, or repaired or were under construction; another 400 units were in the planning or design phase. In addition, eight businesses were started or strengthened; eleven new revolving loan funds with nearly $6 million in assets were established; and there was a total increase of $500,000 in the funds held by seven faith-based credit unions. The evaluation also found evidence that "bringing religious institutions and community development groups together opens up the possibility for building bridges across racial and class lines."

Those positive results no doubt rest on the important fact that many of the partnerships included very strong community development organizations. The congregations learned a great deal about community development, including which aspects fit—or did not fit—well with their organizational culture. They did not, however, shoulder the full burden and responsibility of development on their own. Their experience thus represents only one possible strategy for entering the field. Although they had strong partners and expressed great satisfaction with their accomplishments, the congregations' participants reported:

> The cautious or balky behavior of financiers and government officials was "frustrating"; the required technical knowledge of design, construction, finance, marketing, and property management was sometimes "overwhelming"; the persistence and attention to detail was "tedious"; and the tendency of secular partners to value religious partners' financial or property contributions more than their spiritual and interpersonal contributions was "irritating."

What Congregations Can Bring to Community Development

Community development that has a meaningful impact on the community is difficult to accomplish because it depends on conducting a set of specialized and complex activites over a considerable period of time. Successful CDCs secure resources from multiple sources, plan effectively, exercise strong and stable management and governance, and ensure community representation on their boards.

Given the difficulty of effective community development, affiliation with a congregation offers community developers advantages and disadvantages. As

Jeremy Nowak argues, "The most effective church-affiliated developers are able to maximize the advantages and minimize the disadvantages."[21] Nowak lists four possible advantages of congregational engagement in community development: The congregation can serve as an incubator and organizer. It can provide volunteers. It can provide access to financial resources. And it can engender public trust. Each of those advantages is countered by potential disadvantages and risks. Communities might perceive development activities as church rather than neighborhood initiatives. Church leaders and staff may lack the time and skills to undertake community development activities consistently and effectively. Religious values may conflict with the demands of the marketplace, especially since community development is unique among the charitable activities of most congregations. And there is always the risk that funds for secular community development services and funds for religious activities may be commingled. (See also Nowak's chapter in this volume.)

Those factors suggest that entering community development without partners is likely to be attractive to only a small fraction of congregations. Those congregations, however, could make significant contributions to community development.

CONGREGATIONS ARE NOT THE WHOLE STORY

Although this chapter has focused on the activities of congregations, the universe of faith-based organizations is substantially larger and more diverse. It includes national denominations; their social service arms, such as Catholic Charities and Lutheran Social Services; networks of related organizations, such as the YMCA and the YWCA; associations of clergy or other religious leaders; and a wide variety of nonprofit organizations and social service organizations that have a religious origin or basis.

Those groups have received even less research attention than congregations, but they are clearly significant forces in community development. A number of large denominational service organizations develop housing, including Catholic Charities, Lutheran Social Services, the Salvation Army, the Jewish Federations (United Jewish Communities), and B'nai B'rith. They also get involved in other ways—from social investing to start-up assistance and emergency financing for individual CDCs. Examples include providing a CDC with seed capital or in-kind contributions; donating staff time; and assisting affordable housing developments that get into financial trouble.

Many more denominational organizations, religious orders, pension funds, hospitals, and other religious institutions are engaged in social investing than are engaged in developing housing. The Interfaith Center for Corporate Responsibility (ICCR), an affiliate of the National Council of Churches, oversees more than $1 billion in social investments on behalf of 270 such investors. Of that amount, between $5 and $6 million dollars is invested in community economic development. Typical investments are deposits in minority banks, credit unions, various types of loan funds, and cooperative businesses. ICCR participants also make similar investments through a multitude of local and regional social investment vehicles. In addition, pension funds of various denominations and religious orders participating in ICCR have approximately $300 million invested in low-income housing.[22]

In short, congregations are the most familiar component of the faith-based universe, but they work in a rich institutional context. Denominational organizations, religious orders, and others control significant financial, technical, and, in some cases, political resources that they can bring to bear, either as independent actors or in support of congregational efforts. In some faiths they play a powerful role in encouraging and shaping the choice and conduct of the congregational ministry.

CONCLUSION: COMPASSION OR SOCIAL JUSTICE?

There is still much to learn about what it takes for congregations to succeed at community development and what their advantages and disadvantages are compared with those of secular agents. But we do know some things. It appears that only a small fraction of congregations currently are well positioned to become independent community development agents in communities where development is needed. An equally small proportion are able to attract the necessary financial and technical resources. The strongest candidates are those that are located in poor neighborhoods and have large congregations but are not themselves poor. Many of those are African American churches.

Enough good examples exist to make it clear that well-positioned congregations can make significant contributions to community development. To succeed, they need a professionally staffed, independent, nonprofit development organization, which can be supported by one or more congregations. They need a long time horizon. They also need to be committed to staying in the community. And they need to understand that development is a demanding, time-consuming process.

Capitalizing on the potential of congregations requires investing in the organizational capacity of both congregations and newly incorporated development organizations. They need technical assistance—above all to decide whether they want to become involved in community development in the first place. They need to understand their comparative advantages and capitalize on them.

Many also need specialized technical assistance to work through the issues involved in establishing a new nonprofit corporation. A better understanding of what has enabled existing faith-based CDCs to emerge and grow—and what distinctive problems they have faced—should inform that effort.

Finally, there are many other ways for a wide variety of congregations— including those in middle-income communities—to contribute to community development. They could adopt sound social investment practices in managing their bank deposits and other assets. They could provide mentors to participants in job-training programs and provide financial assistance to emerging faith-based CDCs in low-income neighborhoods. They could collaborate with others to create a supportive climate for local development of affordable housing. Coalitions of congregations are potentially significant allies for community developers in building local and regional coalitions to promote supportive local, state, national, and corporate policies.[23] Most important, all congregations could contribute by working to create a political climate that promotes social justice, rather than charity, as a national priority.

NOTES

1. Ronald F. Ferguson and William T. Dickens, eds., *Urban Problems and Community Development* (Brookings, 1999), p. 5.

2. This distinction is adapted from Xavier De Souza Briggs, "Brown Kids in White Suburbs: Housing Mobility and the Many Faces of Social Capital," *Housing Policy Debate*, vol. 9 (1998), p. 178.

3. Mark Chaves, *Congregations' Social Service Activities,* Charting Civil Society, no. 6 (Washington: The Urban Institute, December 1999).

4. Virginia A. Hodgkinson and others, *From Belief to Commitment: The Community Service Activities and Finances of Religious Congregations in the United States* (Independent Sector, 1993).

5. Applied Real Estate Analysis, *Making Homeownership a Reality: Survey of Habitat for Humanity, Inc. Homeowners and Affiliates* (U.S. Department of Housing and Urban Development, 1998).

6. Select Committee on Aging, Subcommittee on Housing and Consumer Interests of the House of Representatives, *The 1988 National Survey of Section 202 Housing for the Elderly and Handicapped* (Government Printing Office, 1989).

7. Comptroller General of the United States, *Section 236 Rental Housing: An Evaluation with Lessons for the Future* (U.S. General Accounting Office, 1978); Charles Calhoun and Christopher Walker, *Loan Performance of Management Cooperatives* (Washington: The Urban Institute, 1994).

8. Comptroller General, *Section 236 Rental Housing.*

9. The term CDFIs is used generically here, referring to all such organizations, not just those officially designated as CDFIs under federal legislation.

10. Jeremy Nowak and others, *Religious Institutions and Community Renewal* (Philadelphia: Delaware Valley Community Reinvestment Fund, 1989).

11. Pamela Ann Toussaint, "Concord Baptist Church: Taking Care of Business in Bed-Stuy," in Robert D. Carle and Louis A. Decaro, eds., *Signs of Hope in the City: Ministries of Community Renewal* (Valley Forge, Penn.: Judson Press, 1997).

12. Lloyd Gite, "The New Agenda of the Black Church: Economic Development for Black America," *Black Enterprise,* December 1993.

13. Mark Chaves and William Tsitos, "Congregations and Social Services: What They Do, How They Do It, and with Whom," paper presented at the annual meeting of the Association for Research on Nonprofit Organizations and Voluntary Action, December 2000.

14. Avis Vidal, "Abyssinian Development Corporation," in *Sustained Excellence Awards: Profiles of the Awardees* (Washington: Fannie Mae Foundation, 1998).

15. Louis A. Decaro Jr., "Bethel Gospel Assembly: Ministry to Harlem and Beyond," in Carle and Decaro, eds., *Signs of Hope in the City,* pp. 70–81.

16. Xavier De Souza Briggs and Elizabeth J. Mueller with Mercer L. Sullivan, *From Neighborhood to Community: Evidence on the Social Effects of Community Development* (New York: Community Development Research Center, New School for Social Research, 1997).

17. June Manning Thomas and Reynard N. Blake, "Faith-Based Community Development and African American Neighborhoods," in W. Dennis Keating, Norman Krumholz, and Phillip Star, eds., *Revitalizing Urban Neighborhoods* (Lawrence: University of Kansas Press, 1996), p. 131–43.

18. Avis Vidal, "The Resurrection Project," in *Sustained Excellence Awards.*

19. National Congress for Community Economic Development, *Coming of Age: Trends and Achievements of Community-Based Development Organizations* (Washington: 1999).

20. David Scheie and others, *Better Together: Religious Institutions as Partners in Community-Based Development.* Final Evaluation Report on the Lilly Endowment Program (Minneapolis, Minn.: Rainbow Research, Inc., 1991).

21. Nowak and others, *Religious Institutions and Community Renewal,* vol. I, p. 56.

22. Interview with Timothy Smith, executive director of Interfaith Center on Corporate Responsibility, June 7, 1999.

23. Michael W. Foley and John D. McCarthy as reported in Foley and others, "Social Capital, Religious Institutions, and Poor Communities"; Scheie and others, *Better Together;* Nowak and others, *Religious Institutions and Community Renewal.*

Faith-Based Community Partnerships: Toward Justice and Empowerment

JOSEPH R. HACALA

Much recent discussion surrounding partnerships between the federal govern-ment and the faith-based community to implement social service and commu-nity development programs has treated such partnerships as a creative and radical new initiative of the current administration. While President George W. Bush's new White House Office of Faith-Based and Community Initiatives has focused renewed attention on them, these partnerships have a long and rich his-tory. Indeed, through the years, faith-based groups as various as Habitat for Humanity International, Lutheran Services in America, the Catholic Campaign for Human Development, and B'nai B'rith have engaged in community organ-izing and community development strategies that have produced housing, cre-ated jobs and, most important, provided hope for millions. A recent study by the National Congress for Community Economic Development, for example, re-ported that in its survey of 3,000 community development groups, at least 15 percent were faith-based.

The U.S. Department of Housing and Urban Development's Center for Community and Interfaith Partnerships, which I directed for four years, has been deeply involved in partnerships between government and faith-based or-ganizations. Initiated in 1997 by Secretary Andrew Cuomo, and building on earlier efforts by Secretary Henry Cisneros, HUD's Center for Community and Interfaith Partnerships grew out of Cuomo's experience in providing housing for the poor and homeless in the New York City area. The mission of the inno-vative center was "to focus, integrate, and intensify HUD's involvement with faith- and community-based organizations in an effort to maximize the use and impact of mutual resources in building community."

The center's objectives were to listen to community and faith-based groups, educate them about HUD and its resources, coordinate activities with them, and build new partnerships at the national level. The center's activities and successes

This essay is a revised version of an article that appeared in *America* magazine. Reprinted with permission.

were grounded in a multifaceted approach that involved building awareness, providing outreach and education services, and publicizing successful efforts and models. By responding to requests from faith-based groups, troubleshooting, promoting new and better partnerships, facilitating participation of community and faith-based groups in HUD initiatives, and shaping policy, among other efforts, the center worked to empower neighborhoods across the United States.

HUD administered nearly $1 billion in assistance to community and faith-based organizations in fiscal year 2000; made 230 grants to faith-based organizations specifically to provide homeless services and a similar number of grants to groups to serve individuals with HIV/AIDS; provided nearly 40 percent of the funds for Section 202 senior citizen housing programs; and set aside 40 percent of new technical assistance grant funds for previously unfunded faith-based and nonprofit groups. In addition, the center sponsored eight regional faith-based conferences that engaged some 4,000 churches or individuals; a resource guide highlighting best practices and sources of funds; and several nationwide educational satellite broadcasts.

It is against this long-standing backdrop of vibrant and varied activity that President Bush proposes his "new initiative," which, in fact, includes expanded cooperation with faith-based groups. The administration's objectives to "enlist, enable, empower, and expand the work of faith-based and other community organizations" are largely in the form of "social service initiatives" and, as such, are not entirely new, but they are important.

I find encouragement in some particular features of Bush's White House Office of Faith-Based and Community Initiatives: tax breaks to assist communities, perhaps along the model of the recent bipartisan New Markets legislation of the Clinton administration, whose goal is to empower communities left behind in the new economy; the embrace by the new administration of the Corporation for National Service, which could engage a significant force of deeply committed participants in faith-based community development efforts; and the extension of opportunities to form working relationships with the federal government. These should build on HUD's positive community and faith-based model, the Center for Community and Interfaith Initiatives, and lead to new initiatives in the Departments of Education, Health and Human Services, Justice, and Labor.

However, a variety of cautions and potential pitfalls have surfaced that need further investigation. As many have noted, there is a need to consider the legal tradition, history, and realities of the separation of church and state. And it is necessary to monitor religious proselytizing in the context of providing assistance to the needy and to adhere to local and state employment and discrimination practices. We must also avoid mere expansion of charitable choice, whose success in the implementation of the 1996 welfare reform initiatives has been mixed. Furthermore, it is imperative that this effort not promote charity at the expense of justice by underfunding real structural needs. When we merely provide more water for soup or additional cots for church basements, *we are only attempting to alleviate symptomatic problems while ignoring the cycles of disadvantage and persistent needs* for affordable housing and jobs for the unemployed and underemployed. One can question the effectiveness of the new White House proposals in view of the Bush administration's early budget cuts, which included the elimination of a rural housing program and a reduction in technical assistance funds for those faith-based groups most in need. Early efforts of the new administration's faith-based proposals have been further hindered by challenges and criticism from both far-right and religious conservatives and the threat of excessive legal challenges from the left.

My hope is that the Bush administration's plan will become substantive by building on a variety of ongoing and successful efforts, including the positive recent experience of HUD's Center for Community and Interfaith Initiatives. I believe this serves as a good model for meeting our nation's serious social needs. But the ultimate solution to poverty for the poor of Appalachia, the Mississippi Delta, the border colonias, Indian reservations, and rural and inner-city areas necessarily involves a combination of methods that *directly engage and empower the poor; provide increased and adequate government funding for housing, food programs, and social problems at all levels; and promote many kinds of collaborative partnerships between faith-based, community, and government entities.* Those partnerships should include and build on past models of collaboration between government and congregations that involved direct funding of religiously related nonprofit organizations with tax-exempt status.

As our nation continues to meet the challenges and opportunities of the new century under new political leadership, the issue of building stronger, more sustaining communities remains central to our future. The role of community and faith-based organizations in this process is particularly relevant in light of the history, success, and moral credibility of these groups. At this threshold in our history, recent experience has renewed hope that faith-based community participation may continue to lead neighborhoods and communities toward much-needed social change and authentic empowerment. If the Office of Faith-Based Initiatives, with its renewed public consciousness, also leads to a commitment of additional resources to fight domestic poverty, there will be cause for celebration, especially among the poor.

Comparative Advantages of Faith–Based Organizations in Community Development

WILLIAM T. DICKENS

Avis Vidal has looked at the contribution of faith-based organizations to community development as it typically is practiced; Jeremy Nowak has suggested a much more ambitious agenda. Rather than ask what FBOs can contribute to the current practice of community development, I would like to ask what they can do to contribute under a more expansive model: asset building that promotes the welfare of community residents. That model, for which Ron Ferguson and I have argued, considers social and organizational capital as well as physical capital as assets, so that organizing a tenant association or lobbying local businesses to provide more jobs for neighborhood residents is as much community development as refurbishing an apartment building.

As I see it, faith-based organizations have four unique advantages: they have particular experience, expertise, and legitimacy in dealing with issues of individual identity and human needs; they can engage highly and specially motivated people in their activities; they can claim to speak for the interests of the disadvantaged in public disputes more credibly than can most secular political leaders; and many have longer institutional histories and more stability than secular community-based organizations.

Building housing, the most common community development activity, draws on at most one of those four advantages. Houses cannot occupy the moral high ground, bricks do not care about the motivation of the bricklayer, and apartment buildings do not require ministry. Even the management of housing may not be the forte of religious groups, if as Vidal suggests, solid business practices are more important than compassion in the success of that activity.

The list of advantages indicates that faith-based organizations wishing to contribute to community development would be most effective at community organizing and delivering social services—particularly the treatment of substance abuse. Certainly churches have been active in both types of activities. However, as Vidal documents, a very large part of what congregations have done is to build and manage housing. Some of their biggest success stories involve those activities. Why is that?

I can think of three explanations for why churches engaged in community development would fail to fully employ their comparative advantages. First, the

CDC model of housing development is well known; a congregation that wants to aid a community has examples to follow, and institutional support is available for the CDC approach. There also are successful examples of faith-based community organizing and service programs, but they are fewer in number and they are not supported by as large and effective an institutional network. But saying that congregations adopt the CDC model because it is a common, well-supported approach just explains the success of the CDC model as a product of its own success. We have to look deeper for a prime mover.

Perhaps the explanation is that whatever the community development potential of faith-based oganizations, their allocation of effort is determined by the demands of the communities they wish to serve. In some sense, housing is where demand is greatest. Of all the needs of disadvantaged communities, housing is the biggest one for which there is an acknowledged gap between need and what is supplied by existing programs. Everyone who qualifies for food stamps can receive them; only a small fraction of people who qualify for public housing assistance receive it. Further, if a neighborhood is physically run down, the obvious and most direct way to address the problem is to refurbish or rebuild the buildings that constitute the neighborhood. Thus faith-based organizations are drawn into filling a need because other systems have failed or have proven inadequate.

Finally, it may be their disadvantages and not the advantages of faith-based groups that lead them to become involved in housing development. Faith-based groups can organize enthusiastic volunteers, but they seldom are sufficiently skilled to deliver specialized social services. However, they can help build or refurbish housing. That is how Habitat for Humanity works.

But when inner-city congregations get into the housing business it is not primarily to employ volunteer labor in construction. As Vidal has described, the people from the congregation end up doing the work of a housing developer: securing land, securing funding, securing financing, and negotiating with contractors, subcontractors, city authorities, and other development organizations. Volunteers sometimes go away feeling that their unique contribution—their faith—is not appreciated by those with whom they work.

That last consideration, more than anything else, convinces me that the energy of faith-based groups could be more effectively used if their housing activities were deemphasized and other sorts of activities expanded. If these organizations can become adept at building housing, then they can become adept at working to expand job opportunities, providing individual counseling, developing recreational activities, and helping prevent crime. Such activities are likely to be much more rewarding to church workers than negotiating with bankers.

What can government do to help congregations find their niche in community development? First, it can do more to remove the burden of providing housing from the private nonprofit sector. To date, I have seen no evidence to suggest that this sector has any advantage over the for-profit sector in building or managing housing; on the contrary, there is evidence that the for-profit sector is better at it. There are two primary impediments that keep the private sector from filling the housing needs of distressed communities: residents' low incomes and zoning and building regulations that make it difficult to provide housing that people with low incomes can afford. Simply setting building standards is not enough. If we truly believe that no U.S. resident should have to live in housing that is below a certain standard, then we need to ensure that everyone has the resources to afford housing of that standard; otherwise, government should lower standards enough that the private sector can provide affordable housing. In an era of trillion-dollar tax cuts, clearly the resources to fill the need are there, if we have the will.

What else can government do to promote the participation of faith-based organizations in community organizing and service delivery? The development of a substantial infrastructure of national and regional organizations that help local CDCs by providing information and access to resources has been essential to the success of the CDC movement. Government organizations could foster the development of such an infrastructure to support a wider range of activities by faith-based organizations, in part by funding research to determine what models and methods would be successful.

President Bush has initiated a major effort to promote the work of faith-based charitable organizations by establishing government organizations to promote their interests, eliminating federal barriers to their work, and promoting private giving. I suspect that good things will come of this initiative in several areas, but I fear that it will do little to promote the more effective deployment of the resources of faith-based organization in community development.

It will be good to have federal offices in high places that are charged with tapping faith-based resources and acting as ombudsmen for faith-based oganizations. But I see only one way in which congregational development activities are seriously constrained by federal regulation, and that is not discussed in the Bush proposal. Nearly all the problems created by the constitutional requirements for separation of church and state can be dealt with by having churches work through secular nonprofit spin-offs. Such organizations are restricted from proselytizing, but that is not a problem in most social service work. In the few cases in which it may be (for example, drug treatment, pregnancy prevention, and crisis counseling programs), direct government funding would likely be judged unconstitutional because it would have the effect of promoting specific religious beliefs. However, the government can provide vouchers to individuals so that those who want to can participate in faith-based programs.

As Vidal makes clear, the financial contributions of faith-based organizations to community development are dwarfed by government and foundation contributions. The effects of a small change in government funding for development activities would be vastly greater than any effect of changes of the sort that President Bush has proposed to promote more giving.

But again, charitable giving to faith-based community service organizations is a minor issue compared with the two major things that government could do to support faith-based community development: removing the burden of supplying low-income housing from the private nonprofit sector and facilitating the work of that sector in doing things that it can do better than the for-profit sector.

Eyes on the Prize

JIM WALLIS

As faith-based organizations become more deeply involved in partnerships with government, the fundamental question that must be raised is that of our vocation. Are we service providers or prophetic interrogators? And, if we are both, how do the two relate?

Those in power usually prefer that faith communities run service programs than raise our prophetic voice for social justice. Government will invite faith-based organizations into program partnerships because many faith-based programs work very well, but it will not so easily invite the same organizations to act as advocates. As the Bush administration proposes new partnerships with faith-based organizations, the most important issue is safeguarding our prophetic integrity. Our mission is to overcome poverty, not simply to service it, so we must constantly ask why so many people remain poor in the midst of amazing prosperity.

Practically speaking, that means evaluating all the administration's policies by how well they reduce poverty and challenging those that do not. We must continue working for a health care policy that includes the 10 million children who have no coverage. We must act as advocates for poor working families that need a living wage and affordable housing. When the debate on reauthorizing welfare reform begins, we must make sure that there is funding for the critical supports needed to help families move out of poverty's deadly cycle. We must challenge excessive tax cuts and misguided budget priorities that benefit the wealthy and leave few resources to invest in effective antipoverty strategies.

For many community development organizations—even for the model projects that are working best—the most significant issue is lack of resources. How can government help to mobilize new multisector partnerships and allocate its resources in the most effective, strategic way? The idea of new partnerships suggests that we can link problem-solving ability at the lower levels with resources at the higher levels. We need not only to recognize the work of both community groups and faith-based organizations but also to provide them the resources to do what needs to be done. Government must determine what already is working and then figure out how to apply those solutions on a broader scale.

We know that grassroots organizations cannot, and should not, be expected to provide a safety net for the entire society. The government still is responsible for handling fundamental issues such as Medicaid for poor kids, health care for the uninsured, education, and housing policy. We cannot allow government to abdicate its responsibilities, leaving hopelessly underfunded churches and charities to fight poverty on the cheap by forcing them to make bricks without straw. In all policy discussions, our voice must be heard.

And I would suggest that the larger issue involves more than questions of policy. Sometimes the policy choices that we need are not on the table. When what we need most is not even being discussed, it is not a lobbying issue, because there is no justice to lobby for. A deeper prophetic agenda then emerges, about how we can change society's sensibilities and the way we think about poor and homeless people. How do we think of our poorest children? Are all of them ours or just some of them? If we do not raise the fundamental religious and moral questions, then the right policy questions do not enter the conversation either.

Now that the administration is talking about new partnerships, we should seize the moment as a prophetic opportunity. If faith-based organizations and the government are to become partners, we must make clear that our role is not simply to make the government more efficient but also to make U.S. society more just. It is not simply to clean up the mess created by bad social policy or to assume what are legitimate responsibilities of the government, but to raise a morally prophetic voice for new policies. With all the attention on faith-based organizations, now may be the best time to speak the language of both love and justice. While doing our works of love in neighborhoods across the country, we can and must also make the demands of justice known to those in power.

We must not allow ourselves to be sidetracked into intellectual debates that leave our poorest children behind. We should keep our eyes on the prize, as the civil rights anthem says, and focus our energies on the most effective models for overcoming the poverty that imprisons our youngest and most vulnerable citizens. And we must ensure that those models have sufficient resources to do the work they do best in overcoming poverty.

Redefining the Mission of Faith-Based Organizations in Community Development

PIETRO NIVOLA

What is the purpose of community development? Should community development organizations redefine their missions? Jeremy Nowak's central point is that community development needs to move beyond its parochial focus on the provision and management of affordable housing to what he calls a broadened geography, one that includes not only the issue of access to housing but also of economic development and a better interface with emerging labor markets. I think his delineation of the challenges that face community development corporations is very much on target.

In my opinion (and I think it is also his), the continuing concentration and isolation of an urban underclass in U.S. cities and the relentless dispersion of everyone and everything else to sprawling suburbs is a problem. And I think we all agree that CDCs can make some difference—no one really knows how much—in relieving the concentration of poverty at the urban core and thereby persuading economically viable households and businesses to reinvest in cities.

But how? Nowak's point is that what is needed are regionally oriented housing, job placement, and networking strategies. Back in the 1960s that approach was called ghetto dispersal—not a pretty designation. What are my criticisms of his analysis? My only quibble is that I think Nowak may be too optimistic about the ability of CDCs to pull off the rather formidable paradigm shift that is implicit in his recommendation, which is to switch from a place-based orientation to become organizations with a wider geographic reach and a regional, market-oriented mission. That switch is difficult probably because, at the end of a day, most faith-based organizations have a vested interest in limiting their activities to the community.

FBOs, it seems to me, are intrinsically uninterested in acting as passport agencies, issuing exit visas to their members and clients. That would seem to be particularly true if they are congregations or parishes. To put it another way, there is an inherent contradiction, or at least a tension, between implementing programs that facilitate access of the inner-city poor to jobs and residences in regional markets and, on the other hand, undertaking community development, with its emphasis on improving existing inner-city neighborhoods. One approach says "We want you to stay put"; the other says "We want you to join the millions of other Americans who move every year." CDCs naturally are inclined to prefer the stay-put approach rather than the mobility-enhancement approach because mobility implies eventually disbanding one's membership, one's constituency. Regrettably, the place-based focus, which is trying to arrest the decline of inner-city neighborhoods without changing their demographics, may well prove futile.

For the most part, Avis Vidal's chapter conforms with my assessment: there is not much hard or measurable evidence that the CDCs that Vidal examines have had a large, visible impact in helping their members get ahead, as opposed to simply running in place, so to speak.

That is beginning to change; many of these organizations are beginning to develop asset-creation strategies. The chapter stresses that faith-based CDCs do, in fact, bring some unique assets to the game that they are trying to play. They bring, for example, a natural base of members. Members—better still, volunteers—are needed to get things done. A membership base is a significant plus.

Faith-based organizations also enjoy greater public confidence in their credentials. Put another way, they reputedly hold the moral high ground: they have moral authority to do their work, since churches generally are perceived as legitimate institutions, as distinct from fly-by-night operations that might abscond with funds. That is very important.

The chapter also notes, however, that the organizations carry their share of liabilities. They often have little sense of how to operate as entrepreneurs in the urban marketplace. They often have a cultural preference for performing acts of charity, as opposed to devising self-help strategies for the indigent, and so on.

To the list of liabilities, I would add at least two more. One is fairly obvious. Although I think it is true that faith-based institutions enjoy a good deal of public trust, that trust has its limits. A substantial part of the public does worry about church-state separation issues, especially when public funds are involved. The second concern, as mentioned, is that some of these organizations may not really want their members to get ahead if getting ahead means leaving the community. Helping one's members get out, after all, implies losing them.

Now, there are major differences among faith-based institutions. My guess is that the Catholic Church, for example, might play a distinctive role in disadvantaged communities. Because the church has a global reach, perhaps Catholic organizations may be in the habit of thinking beyond parochial confines more than are some other kinds of faith-based groups.

We have to ask a fundamental question: What do we want so-called community development to *do*? Do we want it to enhance the mobility of the nation's urban have-nots or to invoke in them and other community residents a greater sense of place, which sometimes means less rather than more mobility?

My own view is that national urban policy must make it a priority to raise the living standards of the urban poor, to make it easier for them to obtain employment, housing, and essential services—particularly better schools—anywhere in the metropolitan region. That cannot be accomplished by force-feeding or socially engineering inner-city revitalization projects that propose to keep the poor where they are.

Faith in Harlem: Community Development and the Black Church

DARREN WALKER

I have the privilege of living and working in an extraordinary place called Harlem and having a connection to a church—the Abyssinian Baptist Church— that has a rich history and tradition of activism on behalf of people of African descent. The Abyssinian Development Corporation (ADC) is an outgrowth of the ministry of the church, founded by Reverend Dr. Calvin O. Butts III and a group of local residents who were appalled by the conditions that existed in Harlem in the 1980s.

We proudly trumpet the many accomplishments of our organization: more than 2,000 children and families served annually through our programs in child care, education, human services, and civic engagement; more than 1,000 units of affordable housing; 300,000 square feet of commercial construction. Those achievements have not come easily, and we know that were it not for the institutional strength of the Abyssinian Baptist Church, our success would be more modest and muted. Yet while we have so much to be proud of and to share with others, we are a bit uneasy about just where we are going. It is most regrettable that we find ourselves caught in the current quagmire of hysteria and hyperbole around the role of faith-based organizations in ameliorating poverty, reducing teenage pregnancy, and building neighborhoods.

THE BLACK CHURCH TRADITION

It is our faith that inspires us to do our work; it is our belief that people and neighborhoods can be transformed. But especially now, we must be mindful of the fact that black churches were engaged in faith-based community development long before the term was popularized by highly credentialed urban planners and foundation executives. In fact, microenterprise lending, building housing, operating schools, running food pantries, and community organizing were staple activities of churches—especially black churches—since the nineteenth century. So it is only an extension of our historical role that brings us to this critical juncture. Much has been gained and much could be lost if we do not proceed adroitly as we consider the prospects under the current faith-based framework. We are grateful that President Bush affirms and exalts the contributions that black churches and other religious institutions have made to our society. However, that attention, coupled with the mistaken belief on the part of many congregations (especially small black churches), that money soon will begin falling from the sky into church coffers, compels me to offer some unsolicited rules of engagement to those who are considering embarking on community development in the name of faith.

Rule One: Always protect the integrity and independence of the church. Unfortunately, some have simply thrown any pretense of church-state separation out the window in pursuit of government grants. As some congregations have found out the hard way, when a church accepts direct grants from government, it places itself under the direct *supervision* of government. In some parts of the world, that is not unusual. In the United States, however, the last time a government placed organized religion under its supervision, a revolution was fought, thousands of people lost their lives, and a constitution establishing the strict separation of church and state was adopted.

Rule Two: Can you say transparency? No entity—government or private—currently requires religious institutions in this country to operate with transparency. That is true of the black church, which is characterized by a detached management style, with governance and power limited to a core group of church leaders. However, running a 501(c)(3) nonprofit organization, which any church with a marginally competent lawyer will be advised to do in order to separate its worship and social services, requires a complete change in disclosure and accountability. Church leaders running a CDC must be prepared to submit the organization's financial statements to public scrutiny and review. Contracting, salaries, procurement policies, and personnel standards become part of the public domain, easily accessed on the Internet and subject to misinterpretation and legal action if administration is not based on sound principles and practices and taken seriously.

Rule Three: The founding church is not the primary constituency of a faith-based CDC—the general community is the primary constituency. Service must be provided without preference or discrimination. Recently, a local church asked whether we would help it secure nominally priced, city-owned land and a housing subsidy that it wanted to use for a housing development exclusively for church members. The church's leaders were offended when we declined. But the city of New York's housing agency would not have supported such an action, and any attempt to circumvent agency policy would have required us to break laws designed to ensure fairness and nondiscrimination in publicly funded programs.

Rule Four: Most of the time, especially in the beginning stages of organizational growth, community development is a money-losing proposal. The church therefore needs deep enough pockets to withstand the drain on its financial resources. In addition, it must be willing to accept the undeniable fact that church staff will spend an increasing amount of their time working with consultants, researchers, evaluators, bankers, brokers, and a whole host of other nonchurch folks. Although it can be argued that such work is an extension of the ministry, it does put pressure on staff capacity, hindering the progress of other church-related objectives. Finally, those government contracts that appear so enticing often are performance based: the church does not collect a fee until specific outcomes are achieved—for example, a client obtains employment *and* spends six months on the job. Therefore, the church must finance a government-sponsored job-training program for six months. If the final objective is not met, the church could end up paying to train folks for the government and getting no financial compensation in return.

The debate over faith-based development has been framed in a way that creates a phony dichotomy between good and bad choices. Proponents of President Bush's faith-based initiative say that it should be obvious that religious institutions are better positioned than secular ones to deliver social services and a host of other programs and that not to accept that as fact minimizes the historic significance of faith in this country. The most regrettable aspect of the debate is that it has distracted us from public discourse about a much more fundamental question: Is it defensible in times of relative peace and prosperity to invest so little in housing the poor and feeding the hungry? The pie isn't getting any larger—we have just shifted our focus to the less important question of who gets to pass the pieces around the table.

Housing Needs and Housing Resources: A Mismatch

CUSHING DOLBEARE

The resources that churches and others have to address housing are tiny in comparison to the need. The stark fact is that of all households, half of renters and one-quarter of owners—a total of 35.6 million households—have a significant housing problem. They pay more than they can afford for housing, they occupy dilapidated units, or they live in overcrowded conditions. Some 15.9 million of those households pay more than half of their income for housing or live in severely substandard units, and 5.3 million, those with the so-called worst case housing needs, live in unsubsidized very low-income rental properties. The others are very low-income owners (5.4 million), renters who live in subsidized housing but still pay more than half of their income for rent (1.9 million), or unsubsidized renters with incomes above 50 percent of median income (0.9 million).

Since 1937, the federal government has had a variety of programs and approaches to provide housing for low-income people and has added, bit by bit over most of those years, to the stock of federally assisted low-income housing. But the number of assisted households peaked at 5 million in the mid-1990s and has been dropping ever since.

In 1949, Congress adopted a national goal of ensuring "a decent home and suitable living environment for every American family." In 1968, Congress authorized construction or rehabilitation of 6 million low-income units—600,000 a year for ten years. If all of those units had become available and if Congress had continued to provide housing assistance at that level, 20 million subsidized units would have been ready for occupancy—more than enough, if properly located, to house all low-income households with critical housing needs.

Just before leaving office, the Ford administration submitted a proposed budget for fiscal year 1978 to Congress that would have provided 500,000 additional low-income housing units, including 100,000 for-sale units. If that level of production had been achieved and maintained, about 14 million families would now be living in federally assisted low-income housing.

Since 1981, when extremely low-income housing production programs were terminated except to replace some demolished public housing, the United States has not had a program capable of providing affordable housing for extremely low-income families. The low-income housing tax credit and mortgage revenue bond programs, both of which have substantial roles in expanding the stock of affordable rental housing, require additional subsidies—including ongoing operating subsidies—to provide affordable units for those households. Yet federal spending for maintaining and expanding low-income housing assistance has dropped by two-thirds since 1976, the last full year of the Ford administration.

Because resources are inadequate under current law, two major dilemmas have emerged that have to be addressed in order to serve people with incomes below 30 percent of the median income, many of whom are working households. First, CDCs, whether faith-based or not, face the dilemma of whom to serve. How do they meet the urgent needs of extremely low-income people, who constitute more than 60 percent of all households with severe housing problems, when the resources provided—public and private—are so inadequate? Many CDCs choose to assist families that have somewhat higher incomes and thus require less subsidy. As a result, they are able to provide more housing but they serve few extremely low-income people. Instead, they serve families with incomes of 50 or 60 percent of the median—families with genuine, but less critical, housing problems.

The second dilemma is the relationship between church-based CDCs' provision of housing and other social services and churches' advocacy for justice. Since 1980, a majority of the members of Congress have not represented districts where poverty is a significant problem. We will not be able to meet the nation's most critical housing needs until we solve the political problem of how to get voters in more affluent congressional districts to approve the necessary federal expenditures. In 1999, the gap between 30 percent of household income and housing costs capped at the relevant fair-market rent (which determines the amount of housing assistance for those lucky enough to receive it) was $67 billion. Neither the private sector nor state and local governments have the resources to close a gap of that magnitude, even if they make it a major priority. Also in 1999, the federal government spent a total of $29 billion for low-income housing assistance. In contrast, the cost to the federal treasury of homeowner deductions from federal income tax was $100 billion, with more than 95 percent of those benefits going to households in the top 40 percent of the income distribution. If an equal amount had been spent on addressing the housing needs of the bottom 60 percent, there would be no major housing problems.

Churches and church-based organizations are uniquely situated to overcome the economic gap between the inner city and rural areas and the more affluent suburbs. Most church members live in suburban areas, as does most of the rest of the U.S. population. It is critical that churches and church-based organizations not get so wrapped up in daily operations that they fail to address the all-important question of how to translate their faith and their experiences into advocacy of effective public policies. Members of Congress, including those who do not represent districts where poverty is a burning problem, must be made to feel a responsibility for solving the problems of poverty and for providing the resources essential to the undertaking.

Faith as the Foundation for the New Community Corporation

WILLIAM J. LINDER

It was the winter of 1963, and I was a newly ordained priest just a few months into my first assignment at a parish in Newark, New Jersey. I had been asked to take food to an impoverished mother and child who were living in a decrepit building in the Central Ward. The unheated apartment was freezing. In that stark unit, I found a baby deathly ill with pneumonia, lying motionless in a crib that had been covered with wire mesh to protect the child from rats.

When I returned two days later with more food, the mother told me that her child had died. I was stunned but also frustrated, for although I had brought them food, I could provide neither medical help nor a warm home. I had cared, but I had failed in the face of larger societal problems such as the racial hatred and class distinctions that left the city's low-income communities at a severe disadvantage. I was devastated by my inability to give the family the help it needed. Despite my goodwill, I was powerless to overcome the larger forces of evil on my own.

The discovery of my own limitations gave birth to the concept of the New Community Corporation—a community development corporation that would bring together and empower the very people in need of assistance. Together, with adequate support and training, they would work to overcome the inequities that faced them all. The death of that baby nearly forty years ago thus served as a catalyst in my life, compelling me to reflect on the essential elements of the community development model and eventually to put them into action after continuing inequities resulted in the riots of 1967.

New Community Corporation (NCC) serves low-income areas by developing and implementing a neighborhood development agenda that reflects local values—for example, by keeping money within the neighborhood rather than pushing out existing residents. Its first business venture was the conversion of a 120-year-old church into an office building housing NCC's offices, restaurants, shops, a banquet center, and an atrium that doubles as visual and performing arts venue. The building attracted members of the nearby university, medical center, and business community to come to enjoy and subsequently invest in the immediate neighborhood. Other business ventures include establishing a major supermarket that makes affordable food available while showing a profit; building a components plant that brought manufacturing jobs to the city; and providing affordable homes for more than 7,000 existing and new residents in safe and secure neighborhoods. NCC's coordinated ventures provide local residents quality job training, including training in new technologies; daycare; health care; charter schools and adult education programs; transportation services; community arts and recreation programs; and other much-needed services. Today, NCC is the nation's largest community development corporation, with a network of programs and services that affect more than 50,000 people every day, either through tangible improvements in their daily life or through a spirit of mutual understanding and respect that values the dignity and capacities of *all* people and especially those with low incomes.

NCC credits its successes to various factors, including strong leadership, personal strength, financial and strategic skills, and political acumen, but its mission and wide-ranging activities are rooted primarily in faith: a historically based and persevering faith on the part of its constituent population and a prophetic and challenging faith on the part of its agents for change. Without its religious center, NCC would not exist.

At least three interrelated and indispensable dimensions of religion are at work in the community development process: religion as a source of community, vision, and empowerment. As a source of community, religion answers the question "Who are we?" NCC's answer is that we are God's people. We find our identity not merely in our separate selves, but in the fact that we belong to one another and to God. As a source of vision, religion answers the question "Where are we going?" NCC's answer is that we are on a prophetic journey in a direction that God's design has revealed. As a source of empowerment, religion answers the question "How is God's design to be fulfilled?" NCC believes that the way to reach our goals is to struggle for justice and reconciliation in ways that strengthen and call upon those who most need God's love and His gifts. Our organizational mission and strategy thus combines all three elements and articulates the centrality of religion to our work: "To help residents of inner cities improve the quality of their lives so that they reflect their God-given dignity and personal achievements."

After more than thirty years of effort, it is fair to say that NCC belongs in and to Newark. Our mission is an indispensable, long-term strategy to bringing about the transformation that must take place in the inner city if justice is to be served.

Charitable choice legislation begins a new era in the community development movement, with a new set of problems. One major challenge is political identification: we must always identify with the poor, using our power and money to work for the betterment of the poor and not for our own glory. We must find new and creative ways to make the powerful listen. We also must juxtapose our desire for social justice with the concrete reality of our individual situation: if a church is not ready—if it does not have adequate resources or is not prepared to make a commitment to working with others—it should not attempt to take on what then will be an unbearable burden. Finally, though partnerships between congregations and the government offer several new opportunities, we must begin to exploit the possibilities of partnerships of congregations and private businesses. Although the New Community Corporation identified the need for a supermarket in a nearby neighborhood, no major chain would open a store there. So we raised $2.5 million and then negotiated a deal with Pathmark: we now receive two-thirds of the profits from what has become one of the most profitable stores in the Pathmark chain.

In entering this new era, we must recognize that ours is a project for the long term. Short-term solutions do not work. When we founded New Community, we asked board members to make a twenty-year commitment, believing that it would take that long to see results. Some of those board members have been with us now for thirty-two years. When performance determines funding, we must be careful not to judge too soon. Results in the world of community development take time, but CDCs like the New Community Corporation are committed for the long haul.

PART FOUR

THE ROLE OF FAITH-BASED
ORGANIZATIONS IN

Education

CHAPTER NINE

Partnerships of Schools and Faith-Based Organizations

MAVIS G. SANDERS

Educational practitioners, policymakers, parents, and other key stakeholders in the current school reform environment are discussing, planning, and implementing school-community partnerships to improve schools and educational opportunities for students. Because of the influential role that faith-based organizations play in family and community life, they are seen as natural participants in those partnerships. The interest in a larger role for faith-based organizations in schools is becoming stronger as the public school population grows in its diversity and needs.

Statistics show that currently one in five children enrolled in U.S. public schools is poor and that about 40 percent of U.S. public school students come from racial and ethnic minority groups.[1] Many of those students are immigrants or members of immigrant families whose first language is not English.[2] An estimated 6 million children in U.S. public schools have learning disabilities that require special educational approaches.[3] To educate those and all students effectively, public schools require greater human and material resources. Community organizations, including faith-based organizations, possess such resources.

This chapter discusses the role of faith-based organizations in school-community partnerships, which are defined as the connections between schools and individuals, organizations, and businesses in the community that are forged to promote, directly or indirectly, students' social, emotional, physical, and intellectual development. Within this definition, community is not constrained by the geographic boundaries of neighborhoods but refers more to the social interactions that may occur within or transcend local boundaries.[4]

Faith-based organizations are defined as self-identified religious groups or institutions from a wide variety of traditions that include but are not limited to various Christian, Jewish, Islamic, Buddhist, and Hindu groups. This definition is not meant to ignore the existence or importance of other faith-based organizations, but simply to narrow the focus on what is a very broad topic. Discussion also is limited to community partnerships with state-funded public schools.

I first draw on the theoretical literature on school-community partnerships to describe their importance in school reform. Then I review literature on the role of faith-based organizations in youth development and on the effect of youth involvement in religious organizations on school outcomes. Next I discuss the role of faith-based organizations in school-community partnerships and the factors that influence the development of effective partnerships. In conclusion, I explore the limitations of these partnerships, contending that the nation's children, families, and communities are best served through both separate and collaborative practices among faith-based organizations and schools.

THE ROLE OF COMMUNITY PARTNERSHIPS IN SCHOOL REFORM

The family and the school traditionally have been viewed as the institutions that have the greatest effect on the development of children. The community, however, has received increasing attention for its role in socializing youth and ensuring students' success in a variety of societal domains. Epstein's theory of overlapping spheres of influence, for example, identifies schools, families, and communities as major forces in the socialization and education of children.[5] A central principle of the theory is that certain goals, such as student academic success, are of interest to each of those institutions and are best achieved through their cooperative action and support.

Similarly, Heath and McLaughlin argue that community involvement is important because "the problems of educational achievement and academic success demand resources beyond the scope of the school and of most families."[6] They identified changing family demographics, demands of the workplace, and growing diversity among students as some of the reasons that schools and families alone cannot provide sufficient resources to ensure that all children receive the experiences and support they need to succeed in the larger society.

Describing the importance of community involvement in educational reform, Shore focused on the mounting responsibilities placed on schools by a nation whose student population is increasingly at risk. She states: "Too many schools and school systems are failing to carry out their basic educational mission. Many of them—both in urban and rural settings—are overwhelmed by the social and emotional needs of children who are growing up in poverty."[7] She contends that schools need additional resources to successfully educate all students and that those resources, both human and material, can be found in students' communities. Waddock agrees. She explains that good schools are part of a system of interactive forces, individuals, institutions, goals, and expectations that are inextricably linked together.[8]

School-community partnerships take a variety of forms, the most common being partnerships with businesses, which can differ significantly in content and scope. Others involve universities and educational institutions; government and military agencies; health care organizations; national service and volunteer organizations; senior citizen organizations; cultural and recreational institutions; other community-based organizations; community volunteers; and faith-based organizations.[9]

Partnerships also focus on a variety of activities, which may be student centered; family centered; school centered; or community centered. Student-centered activities include those that provide direct services or goods to students—for example, mentoring, tutoring, contextual learning, and job-shadowing programs—as well as awards, incentives, and scholarships. Family-centered activities are those whose primary focus is on parents or the entire family; they include parenting workshops, GED and other adult education classes, family counseling, and family fun and learning programs. School-centered activities are those that benefit the school as a whole, such as beautification projects or the donation of school equipment and materials, or activities that benefit the faculty, such as staff development opportunities and classroom assistance. Community-centered activities focus primarily on the community and its citizens through, for example, charitable outreach programs, art and science exhibits, and community revitalization and beautification projects.[10]

Research suggests that partnership activities can lead to measurable outcomes for students and schools. Mentoring programs have been found to have a significant positive effect on students' grades, school attendance, and exposure to career opportunities.[11] School-community collaborations that focus on academic subjects have been shown to enhance teachers'and parents' as well as students' attitudes toward those subjects.[12] Documented benefits of initiatives among schools, health providers, and social service agencies to integrate services include behavioral and academic gains for students who received intensive services.[13] Research also has shown improved student attendance, immunization rates, and conduct at schools providing coordinated services.[14] Nettles reported positive effects on students' grades and attendance of school-community collaborations that had an instructional component.[15] Finally, partnerships with businesses and other community organizations have provided schools with needed equipment, materials, and technical assistance and support for student instruction.[16] School-community partnerships, then, can be an important element in programs to reform and improve schools.

The Role of Faith-Based Organizations in Education and Youth Development

Faith-based organizations often are effective partners in school-community collaborations because of their long history of involvement in the social and educational development of children and youth. For example, during the colonial period in U.S. history, religious or sectarian schools were the order of the day. According to Bryk, Lee, and Holland, "education was viewed as a fundamentally moral enterprise, and Protestants and Catholics alike sought to ground the education of their children in their particular beliefs."[17] Religious organizations also became involved in the education of youth in order to effect social change. Before the Civil War, members of the Quaker religion were instrumental not only in the abolitionist movement, but also in providing educational opportunities to African American youth when other religious denominations had little interest in doing so.[18] After the Civil War, both black and white churches played an important role in establishing schools for previously enslaved African American youth.[19] Moreover, during the mass immigration of the early nineteenth century, the Catholic Church played a significant role in educating and facilitating the assimilation of children from diverse European ethnic groups.[20]

After 1830, publicly funded common schools became increasingly secularized. By that time, most states had included in their constitutions clauses that prevented any kind of state-supported religious activity, thereby officially adopting the First Amendment principle of separation of church and state. The involvement of religious institutions in public schools continued to decline throughout the second half of the nineteenth century and into the beginning of the twentieth century as states passed compulsory school attendance laws that required students of various religious backgrounds to attend public educational institutions together.[21]

Religious institutions in the twentieth century, however, continued to be involved in the educational development of youth outside the public schools. For example, in a study of 216 churches, Billingsley and Caldwell found that 11 percent sponsored formal educational programs for children and older youth, including college preparatory and support programs as well as preschool programs, after-school academic programs, and full-scale elementary and secondary schools. A number of the churches also provided college scholarships.[22]

Faith-based organizations also have played a more subtle role in the educational development and socialization of youth. The intergenerational membership of such institutions has provided children and youth opportunities to develop warm, nurturing, and supportive relationships with caring adults.[23] Within those relationships, young people acquire social capital—information, attitudinal and behavioral norms, and skills that can improve their chances for success in societal institutions such as schools.[24]

The involvement of faith-based organizations in the socialization and development of youth has yielded measurable educational outcomes. In their seminal work, Argyle and Beit-Hallahmi reported that formal church membership and regular church attendance were positively related to educational attainment. About a decade later, Hansen and Ginsburg found that there was a link between religious values and success in school. They found that religious values affected school outcomes both directly and indirectly through out-of-school behavior. The effect of religious values as a whole was consistently greater than the effect of socioeconomic status in predicting both level of school performance and change in student performance.[25]

The relationship between student involvement in faith-based organizations and school success is particularly significant among African Americans.[26] Adding religious involvement to measures of socioeconomic status increased the variance explained in black children's IQ scores from 14 percent to 16 percent.[27] Brown and Gary also found that religious socialization was positively related to both educational achievement and attainment among African Americans under the age of forty-six.[28]

In a study designed to explain these documented effects, Freeman found that participation in church events and activities affected allocation of time out of school, school attendance, employment, and frequency of socially deviant activity—variables that were found to affect the achievement of inner-city African American male adolescents. More recently, my colleague and I found that religious involvement indirectly affected the achievement of African American adolescents through its direct effect on their academic self-concept. During interviews, students indicated that the church provided them the opportunity to engage—in a supportive environment—in a number of activities that required skills that also were required in school, such as public speaking and reading and analyzing texts.[29]

Such findings are not limited to African American youth. In a study of educational success among Chicanos, Galindo and Escamilla found that the church "was not just about spiritual matters, but also served as a support system to do well in school."[30] The study also found that church events designed to promote literacy—for example, reading and discussing biblical stories—had a positive impact on students' language skills and academic success.

Thus, in both their traditional and contemporary roles, faith-based organizations have provided educational opportunities and support to children and youth. Nevertheless, in our changing times—when the demands of the workplace have created greater stress on the family, neighborhoods and communities have become less cohesive, and schools have become increasingly overburdened—the need has increased for schools and faith-based organizations to provide a more comprehensive and coordinated system of support to promote students' success in school. Greater collaboration between faith-based organizations and public schools can provide the human and material resources needed to make a difference in the quality of schooling and in the academic and social assistance provided to children and young people.

ROLE OF FAITH-BASED ORGANIZATIONS IN SCHOOL-COMMUNITY PARTNERSHIPS

The relationship between U.S. public schools and faith-based organizations has not been without conflict. Both groups have engaged in heated legal and philosophical battles over issues such as school prayer and other forms of religious expression, school vouchers, the place of creationism in the teaching of science, government funding, and the role of religious values in public schooling. With the growth of Christian fundamentalism, many of those conflicts have intensified over the last decade. Christian fundamentalist organizations such as the Christian Coalition and Citizens for Excellence in Education (CEE) have risen in national prominence and have been active in shaping the content and outcome of educational debates and reform efforts.[31]

In 1994, for example, the CEE waged a campaign in Pennsylvania to stop a statewide educational reform that would have required students to master fifty-five academic and nonacademic goals in ten subjects before they could graduate from high school. The CEE disputed the nonacademic goals dealing with personal living, family values, and racial and cultural diversity and harmony. Other Christian fundamentalist groups have sought to influence public education reform, especially around issues of sex education, gay rights, and school prayer, through membership and activism on public school boards. Still others have established private schools, often as an expression of their discontent with the secular teachings of public schools.[32]

In contrast to this rising tide of conflict and divisiveness has been an equally prominent movement toward collaboration, coordination, and cooperation.[33] The spirit of this movement is reflected in a guide jointly published by the American Jewish Congress, the Christian Legal Society, and the First Amendment Center at Vanderbilt University and endorsed by national educational and faith-based groups. The introduction to the guide states: "By working together in ways that are permissible under the First Amendment, as interpreted by the

U.S. Supreme Court, schools and religious communities can do much to enhance the mission of public education."[34] Since the mid-1990s, various attempts have been made to clarify the appropriate, or constitutionally permissible, relationship between religious organizations and schools.[35] Those guidelines have helped many educational, religious, and other community leaders craft a role for faith-based organizations in public education that both upholds the establishment clause of the First Amendment and allows religious organizations to fulfill their service mission.

Although constitutionally prohibited from proselytizing, recruiting, or imposing religious views and doctrines on students, faith-based organizations, as social institutions, can participate in public school reform in a variety of ways.[36] They can partner with public schools and school districts in efforts to improve educational environments, processes, and outcomes.

For example, religious leaders can play an important role in educational reform and improvement in the United States by promoting greater understanding of and dialogue on educational issues among their congregants. Dryfoos contends that "church leaders definitely have 'bully pulpits' from which they are in a position to influence the thinking of their parishioners and congregants. They can help people understand the importance of assisting all children to overcome social, economic, racial, and other gender barriers to success."[37]

Faith-based organizations also can influence educational reform by working directly with schools to provide educational information to families. For example, many schools conduct workshops to promote families' understanding of the educational and socioemotional needs of their children at different stages of development. Family attendance at such workshops, however, often is low. Faith-based organizations and schools can create partnerships to ensure broader dissemination of the information provided at school workshops. The information can be summarized for families before, during, or after worship services, or videotapes of parenting workshops can be shown and discussed before or after services. Through such efforts, faith-based organizations and schools could provide larger numbers of parents and caretakers with valuable information on how to help their children become more successful in and out of school.

Faith-based organizations can affect students and public schools in other ways—for example, by providing college scholarships or recognizing the accomplishments of students, teachers, and school volunteers through award programs. Members of faith-based organizations also can act as volunteers in schools. Possible activities include phoning or visiting the homes of chronically absent students, participating on school improvement teams or committees, assisting with before- and after-school tutoring or enrichment activities, and volunteering labor and materials to renovate the school interior or exterior.

Faith-based organizations also can "adopt" schools or classrooms, providing supplies to students or books, computer software, science equipment, and other supplies to teachers.

In addition, faith-based organizations can contribute to educational reform by promoting their members' political awareness of legislation and policies that affect schools. They can do so by holding public forums in which school officials, state legislators, and school board members discuss their position and actions in regard to educational improvement. Faith-based organizations also can be "good neighbors" to schools by providing free space for school events and activities or simply by advertising and encouraging community participation in school meetings and events.

These partnership possibilities focus on secular educational goals and maintain religious neutrality, thereby complying with the establishment clause of the First Amendment of the U.S. Constitution. As further illustrated in the examples that follow, adherence to the principle of separation of church and state does not minimize the impact that such partnerships can have on educational reform and improvement.

EXAMPLES OF PARTNERSHIPS OF SCHOOLS AND FAITH-BASED ORGANIZATIONS

There is no "one size fits all" formula for school-community partnerships; the resources and objectives of the partners must guide the development of such collaborations. Descriptions of eight partnerships of schools and faith-based organizations are given below. The descriptions are not intended to be representative or exhaustive but simply to show the range of partnerships that currently exist in the United States.[38]

Alexandria, Virginia. The faith-based community and public elementary schools in Alexandria work together to tutor children in reading. A congregation-based coordinator recruits volunteer tutors and assists with scheduling; a school-based coordinator acts as the point of contact at the school. Classroom teachers identify children who need tutoring and assist coordinators with scheduling sessions. Tutoring materials and training for tutors is provided by the public schools. Tutors and students meet for three thirty-minute sessions per week.

Phoenix, Arizona. A coalition of faith-based communities and education associations in Phoenix uses America Goes Back to School, an initiative to encourage family and community involvement in schools, as a focal point each year to honor both current and retired teachers for their work on behalf of children and youth. Each participating religious community honors the teachers at its worship service; award certificates are presented later during a ceremony held at a central location.

Chicago, Illinois. The Chicago Public Schools Interfaith Community Partnership, a multicultural group of religious leaders, assists local schools in addressing issues such as student discipline, truancy and low attendance rates, school safety, and student and staff attitudes and interactions. The partnership provides crisis intervention services and workshops for parents, undertakes curriculum development in the area of character and values, and sponsors radio and television interviews with public school staff to promote Chicago public school initiatives.

Washington, D.C. Shiloh Baptist Church in Washington, D.C., established a learning center to teach critical thinking and problem-solving skills to children in grades four through eight by using a math-, science-, and computer-based curriculum. The center, which is staffed by both paid employees and volunteers, is open after school and during the evening. During the daytime, the center is used to teach adults job skills in a welfare-to-work program. The church also has established a reading tutorial program for children attending Seaton Elementary School and a program called the Male and Female Youth Enhancement Project. The project is designed to encourage healthy life-styles in African American youth between the ages of eight and fifteen by providing them with positive role models and educational and social activities.

The National Council of Churches. Each year, the National Council of Churches disseminates materials related to public education to its member denominations and congregations. The materials highlight education initiatives of the Partnership for Family Involvement in Education, urge local churches to participate in national educational projects such as the America Reads Challenge and America Goes Back to School, and list published resources available to local communities of faith.

Jackson, Tennessee. Ten churches in Jackson have designed a tutoring program in cooperation with the local school system to serve children residing in public housing. Three nights a week, church buses provide transportation to church facilities where 250 volunteers work with 350 children, helping them in reading and math. Volunteers from the tutoring program also raise funds to purchase school supplies and then operate a "store" where students can get school supplies.

The National Council of Jewish Women (NCJW) Center for the Child. The NCJW Center for the Child conducted the Parents as School Partners campaign, which included focus groups with parents, teachers, and principals to hear what parent involvement means to them and what they need to make school-parent partnerships work; surveys of school district superintendents regarding parent involvement policies and programs; a critical review of the research on parent involvement; and a compilation of material on promising school-based programs for enhancing parent involvement. They included the results of their efforts in a kit and disseminated the kits to school districts, teachers, parents, and advocates of parent involvement across the country.

Baltimore, Maryland. The Child First Authority (CFA) in Baltimore is a communitywide after-school program that seeks to improve the quality of life in low-income communities. The CFA, which is funded by the local government and coordinated by Baltimoreans United in Leadership Development (BUILD), established after-school programs in ten schools during its first year of operation. The schools become hubs of activity in which parents, staff, administrators, students, and church members work together to promote student achievement and socioemotional well-being.[39]

PROMOTING THE SUCCESS OF SCHOOL PARTNERSHIPS WITH FAITH-BASED ORGANIZATIONS

Because school-community partnerships are still in the emergent stage, comprehensive research on processes and outcomes of specific partnerships is relatively limited. However, available studies and descriptions suggest that at least three factors influence the effectiveness of school-community partnerships in general and partnerships between schools and faith-based organizations in particular. Those factors are a shared vision, clearly defined roles and responsibilities, and open communication.

Shared Vision

Research suggests that in order for successful partnerships to develop, participants must have a common vision.[40] When a shared vision exists, partnerships are more likely to develop in a manner that is satisfactory to all parties and to meet their stated goals. The need for a common vision is especially important in partnerships between schools and faith-based organizations because of the constitutional restrictions with which these organizations must comply.

For partnerships between public schools and faith-based organizations to thrive, participants on both sides must understand and accept the following principles:

—Under the First Amendment, public schools must be neutral concerning religion in all of their activities.

—Students have the right to engage in religious activities as long as they do not interfere with the rights of others, and they have the right not to engage in those activities.

—Cooperative programs between religious institutions and public schools are permissible only if participation in programs is not limited to religious groups and if students' grades, class ranking, or participation in any school program is not affected by their decision to participate or not participate in a cooperative program with a religious institution.

—Student participation in any cooperative program is not conditioned on membership in any religious group, acceptance or rejection of any religious belief, or participation (or refusal to participate) in any religious activity.[41]

Mutual understanding and acceptance of those principles helps to ensure that all stakeholders' rights are protected, especially those of the students for whom school-community partnerships are designed.

Clearly Defined Roles and Responsibilities

The literature on school-community partnerships also emphasizes the importance of clearly defined roles and responsibilities in successful collaborations.[42] All partners should understand what they are expected to contribute; without clearly defined expectations, misunderstandings can ensue that jeopardize the partnership's effectiveness. The need for clearly defined roles and responsibilities is not limited to but may be more pronounced in partnerships between faith-based organizations and public schools.

For example, in any community partnership in which privately owned facilities are used, it is critical to clarify the roles and responsibilities of individual parties regarding the preparation, use, maintenance, and supervision of the facilities. However, special arrangements may be required when schools use sanctuaries, playgrounds, libraries, or other facilities owned by religious groups, such as the removal of religious symbols or messages.[43] Successful partnerships between public schools and faith-based organizations must be aware of such requirements and determine who will be responsible for meeting them.

Open Communication

Open communication—the process through which shared visions are created and roles and responsibilities are articulated—is the foundation for any successful partnership.[44] It also is critical to carrying out other collaborative processes, including shared decisionmaking, conflict management, and reflection and evaluation.

Open communication also allows educational leaders and other community partners to express any concerns they may have about the motives and intentions of volunteers from religious organizations. According to one such volunteer, school officials often are afraid that volunteers from faith-based organizations seek involvement in public schools in order to proselytize. She commented that several public schools rejected overtures that her group made to volunteer time and resources to students because of their fears of blurring the separation of church and state.[45] If such concerns are to be dealt with effectively and fairly, open communication among all partners is necessary.

The success of partnerships between school and faith-based organizations rests on careful planning and implementation. In addition, all parties must have a common vision informed by a shared understanding of the principle of separation of church and state, and roles and responsibilities, especially as they relate to the use of religious facilities, must be clearly defined. Finally, educational and religious leaders must facilitate and engage in open communication to ensure that the perspectives, ideas, and concerns of all collaborative partners are heard and addressed.

CONCLUSION

Partnerships between public schools and faith-based organizations have tremendous potential to improve educational opportunities and outcomes for all students. However, as religious leaders work to identify common ground with public educators, they also must consider areas where their goals for children and youth are distinct and should remain distinct. In her theory of overlapping spheres of influence, Epstein argues that some goals for children and youth are best achieved through the collaborative efforts of adults in their families, schools, and communities.[46] The theory, however, also acknowledges the separate responsibilities to youth of each of these spheres.

Faith-based organizations, then, must identify when collaboration with public schools best meets their educational goals for youth and when strategies that do not include public schools would be more appropriate. For example, knowledge of religious tenets and texts contributes to the moral and intellectual development of youth. However, transmission of that knowledge by members of faith-based organizations may not be permissible or desirable in after-school or summer programs implemented in partnership with public schools. Religious organizations, however, can independently sponsor programs to provide children and youth with spiritual and moral instruction. Thus a major challenge for faith-based organizations committed to collaborating with public schools is to determine how to allocate time and resources in order to act both collaboratively and independently.

The nation is sure to face new and continuing challenges in extending equal educational opportunities to all children, irrespective of race, socioeconomic status, and linguistic background. Schools alone cannot adequately address all those challenges—families and communities also have an important role to play. Thoughtful collaboration among all parties is vital to ensure that schools are able to meet their fundamental obligation to provide all students with the tools necessary to be self-determining and productive citizens.

NOTES

1. National Center for Educational Statistics (NCES), *Digest of Education Statistics: 1999* (U.S. Department of Education, 1999).

2. Children's Defense Fund, "Comprehensive Immigrant Outreach through Building Community Partnerships," *Sign Them Up: A Quarterly Newsletter on the Children's Health Insurance Program*, Fall 2000.

3. NCES, *Digest of Education Statistics: 1999*.

4. S. M. Nettles, "Community Involvement and Disadvanaged Students: A Review," *Review of Educational Research*, vol. 61, no. 3 (1991), p. 380.

5. J. Epstein, "Toward a Theory of Family-School Connections: Teacher Practices and Parent Involvement," in K. Hurrelmann, F. Kaufmann,and F. Losel, eds., *Social Intervention: Potential and Constraints* (New York: DeGruyter, 1987), pp. 121–36.

6. S. B. Heath and M. W. McLaughlin, "A Child Resource Policy: Moving beyond Dependence on School and Family," *Phi Delta Kappan*, vol. 68 (April 1987), p. 579.

7. R. Shore, *Moving the Ladder: Toward a New Community Vision* (Aspen, Colo.: Aspen Institute, 1994), p. 2.

8. S. A. Waddock, *Not by Schools Alone: Sharing Responsibility for America's Education Reform* (Westport, Conn.: Praeger, 1995).

9. See C. Ascher, Urban School-Community Alliances (New York: ERIC Clearinghouse on Urban Education, 1988); M. Sanders, "A Study of the Role of 'Community' in Comprehensive School, Family, and Community Partnership Programs," *Elementary School Journal* (forthcoming).

10. Sanders, "A Study of the Role of 'Community.'"

11. J. M. McPartland and S. M. Nettles, "Using Community Adults as Advocates or Mentors for At-Risk Middle School Students: A Two-Year Evaluation of Project RAISE," *American Journal of Education*, vol. 99 (1991), pp. 568–86; S. Yonezawa, T. Thornton, and S. Stringfield, *Dunbar-Hopkins Health Partnership Phase II Evaluation: Preliminary Report—Year One* (Baltimore: Center for Social Organization of Schools, 1998).

12. B. A. Beyerbach and others, "A School/Business/University Partnership for Professional Development," *School Community Journal*, vol. 6, no. 1 (1996), pp. 101–12.

13. L. Newman, "School-Agency-Community Partnerships: What Is the Early Impact on Students' School Performance?" paper presented at the annual meeting of the American Educational Research Association (AERA), San Francisco, April 1995; M. Wagner, "What Is the Evidence of Effectiveness of School-Linked Services?" *The Evaluation Exchange: Emerging Strategies in Evaluating Child and Family Services*, vol. 1, no. 2 (1995), pp. 1–2.

14. C. Amato, "Freedom Elementary School and Its Community: An Approach to School-Linked Service Integration," *Remedial and Special Education*, vol. 17, no. 5 (1996), pp. 303–09.

15. S. M. Nettles, "Community Contributions to School Outcomes of African-American Students," *Education and Urban Society*, vol. 24, no. 1 (1991), pp. 132–47.

16. T. Longoria Jr., "School Politics in Houston: The Impact of Business Involvement," in C. Stone, ed., *Changing Urban Education* (University Press of Kansas, 1998), pp. 184–98; T. Mickelson, "International Business Machinations: A Case Study of Corporate Involvement in Local Educational Reform," *Teachers College Record*, vol. 100, no. 3 (1999), pp. 476–512; M. G. Sanders and A. Harvey, "Developing Comprehensive Programs of School, Family, and Community Partnerships: The Community Perspective," paper presented at the annual meeting of the AERA, New Orleans, April 2000.

17. A. Bryk, V. Lee, and P. Holland, *Catholic Schools and the Common Good* (Harvard University Press, 1993), p. 18.

18. W. Jordan, *White over Black: American Attitudes toward the Negro, 1550–1812* (Penguin Books, 1968).

19. A. Billingsley, *Climbing Jacob's Ladder: The Enduring Legacy of African-American Families* (Simon and Schuster, 1992).

20. Bryk, Lee, and Holland, *Catholic Schools.*

21. R. Pounds and J. Bryner, *The School in American Society* (Macmillan, 1967).

22. A. Billingsley and C. Caldwell, "The Church, the Family, and the School in the African American Community," *Journal of Negro Education,* vol. 60, no. 2 (1991), 427–40.

23. C. E. Lincoln and L. H. Mamiya, *The Black Church in the African American Experience* (Duke University Press, 1990).

24. J. Coleman, "Families and Schools," *Educational Researcher,* vol. 16, no. 6 (1987), pp. 32–38.

25. M. Argyle and B. Beit-Hallahmi, *The Social Psychology of Religion* (Boston: Routledge and Kegan Paul, 1975); S. L. Hansen and A. L. Ginsburg, "Gaining Ground: Values and High School Success," *American Educational Research Journal,* vol. 25 (1988), 334–65.

26. Nettles, "Community Contributions to School Outcomes of African-American Students"; V. Lapoint, "Accepting Community Responsibility for African American Youth Education and Socialization," *Journal of Negro Education,* vol. 61, no. 4 (1992), 451–54.

27. F. S. Blau, *Black Children/White Children: Competence, Socialization, and Social Structure* (Free Press, 1981).

28. D. Brown and L. Gary, "Religious Socialization and Educational Attainment among African Americans: An Empirical Assessment," *Journal of Negro Education,* vol. 60, no. 3 (1991), pp.411–26.

29. R. B. Freeman, "Who Escapes? The Relation of Church-Going and Other Background Factors to the Socio-Economic Performance of Black Male Youths from Inner-City Tracts," in R. B. Freeman and H. J. Holzer, eds., *The Black Youth Employment Crisis* (University of Chicago Press, 1986); M. Sanders, "The Effects of School, Family, and Community Support on the Academic Achievement of African-American Adolescents," *Urban Education,* vol. 33, no. 3, pp. 384–409; M. Sanders and J. Herting, "Gender and the Effects of School, Family, and Church Support on the Academic Achievement of African-American Urban Adolescents," in M. Sanders, ed., *Schooling, Students Placed at Risk: Research, Policy, and Practice in the Education of Poor and Minority Adolescents* (Mahwah, N.J.: Lawrence Erlbaum, 2000).

30. R. Galindo and K. Escamilla, "A Biographical Perspective on Chicano Educational Success," *Urban Review,* vol. 27, no. 1 (1995), p. 11.

31. W. Smith, "Religious Diversity in the Schools: Christian Fundamentalism, Educational Reform, and the Schools," paper presented at the Management Institute, Hilton Head, S.C., February 1994.

32. Smith, "Religious Diversity in the Schools"; G. Michel, "Religious Diversity in the Schools—The Overview," paper presented at the Management Institute, Hilton Head, S.C., February 1994.

33. Waddock, *Not by Schools Alone*; J. Epstein, "School/Family/Community Partnerships: Caring for the Children We Share," *Phi Delta Kappan,* vol. 79, no. 9 (1995), pp. 701–12.

34. *Public Schools and Religious Communities: A First Amendment Guide* (Annandale, Va.: American Jewish Congress, Christian Legal Society, and the First Amendment Center, Vanderbilt University, 1999), p. 1.

35. Partnership for Family Involvement in Education, *Faith Communities Joining with Local Communities to Support Children's Learning: Good Ideas* (U.S. Department of Education, 1999); American Jewish Congress and others, *Public Schools and Religious Communities.*

36. Partnership for Family Involvement in Education, *Faith Communities Joining with Local Communities*; D. Shirley, *Community Organizing for Urban School Reform* (University of Texas Press, 1997); Waddock, *Not by Schools Alone*.

37. J. Dryfoos, *Safe Passage: Making It through Adolescence in a Risky Society* (New York: Oxford University Press, 1998).

38. Unless otherwise indicated, the partnership examples described are taken from Partnership for Family Involvement in Education, *Faith Communities Joining with Local Communities*.

39. O. Fashola, *The Child First Authority After-School Program,* Report 38 (Baltimore: Center for Research on the Education of Students Placed at Risk, 1999).

40. B. Hopkins and F. Wendel, *Creating School-Community-Business Partnerships* (Bloomington, Ind.: Phi Delta Kappan Educational Foundation, 1997); M. Walsh, D. Andersson, and M. Smyer, "A School-Community-University Partnership," in T. Chibucos and R. Lerner, eds., *Serving Children and Families through Community-University Partnerships: Success Stories* (Norwell, Mass.: Kluwer Academic, 1999), pp. 183–90.

41. American Jewish Congress and others, *Public Schools and Religious Communities.*

42. Epstein, "School/Family/Community Partnerships"; J. L. Epstein and others, *School, Family, Community Partnerships: Your Handbook for Action* (Thousand Oaks, Calif.: Corwin, 1997).

43. American Jewish Congress and others, *Public Schools and Religious Communities.*

44. B. Gray, *Collaborating: Finding Common Ground for Multiparty Systems* (San Francisco: Jossy-Bass, 1991); C. Nasworthy and M. Rood, *Bridging the Gap between Business and Education; Reconciling Expectations for Student Achievement* (Washington: Office of Educational Reseach and Improvement, 1990).

45. Sanders and Harvey, "Developing Comprehensive Programs of School, Family, and Community Partnerships."

46. Epstein, "School/Family/Community Partnerships."

CHAPTER TEN

Faith-Based Organizations and Public Education Reform

DENNIS SHIRLEY

If you like paradoxes, you'll love the ones you'll find in an analysis of church-state relations in the United States. This country generally upholds the strictest separation of church and state among western democracies, with the possible exception of France. Yet it is here in the United States that citizens are most religious, in terms of their expressed beliefs, and most observant, in terms of their participation in religious institutions. Research consistently documents the socially beneficial effects of religious belief and practice, particularly for children, but strategies derived from those findings are handicapped because of the manner in which the First Amendment has been interpreted to erect a "wall" between church and state. Research indicates that some programs that have a clear evangelical mission and are run by community members (such as Teen Challenge) result in more positive outcomes than secular programs run by experts. And in spite of the Supreme Court's consistent rulings on "no aid to religion" since 1947 in *Everson* v. *Board of Education*, one recent survey found that 63 percent of religiously affiliated nonprofits receive more than 20 percent of their budgets from public funds.[1]

What is different about President Bush's new undertaking? The Bush administration has offered much more financial backing for faith-based initiatives than did the Clinton administration; further, by creating the White House Office of Faith-Based and Community Initiatives within the first fortnight of his term in his office, Bush sent a clear signal that the office forms an important part of his social policy. Can the federal government enhance the valuable resources that religious institutions have to offer schools and communities while minimizing possible negative consequences? How might we go about designing policies to enable faith-based organizations to play a powerful role in addressing social problems without trampling on the rights of religious minorities, atheists, or agnostics?

My focus in this chapter is on faith-based organizations and public schools. The U.S. Department of Education is one of five cabinet agencies that will have a center for faith-based and community initiatives. In the president's public statement defining the mandate of the Office of Faith-Based and Community Initiatives, the brief reference to the public schools is enigmatic. According to the text, "the Center in the Department of Education will be concerned with the agency's social programs, such as after-school programs and efforts to link public schools with community partners, including neighborhood faith-based groups. It will not work on K–12 or higher education policy as such." Yet as is clear to all parties, increasing department of education collaboration with and funding for faith-based groups will have policy ramifications. One of the major challenges for the new office will be to clarify those ramifications, including the likelihood of litigation on issues pertaining to the separation of church and state.[2]

I will comment briefly on the actual wording of the establishment clause of the First Amendment, note some historical realities pertaining to American public education, and suggest some reasons that faith-based groups should be given real opportunities to work with public schools. To ground the discussion in the real world, I turn to two examples of collaborations that demonstrate the capacity of churches to improve public schools. With those cases in mind, I then articulate some caveats pertaining to such collaborations.

My conclusion is one of cautious optimism. One must recognize from the very outset that there *are* dangers in collaboration between public schools and faith-based organizations. Concerns about proselytizing or coercion are legitimate and must be heard. However, it is my impression that there is a capacious middle way that has worked well in the past and can continue to serve us well in the future. Religious institutions have received resources in the past to provide social services—for example, through Head Start and after-school programs in urban churches—and there is no compelling reason why such efforts should not be continued and expanded when they reach populations in need and contribute to the public good. As much as possible, however, resources should not be provided directly to religious institutions but should be channeled through schools and affiliated nonprofit organizations that have a history of working successfully with government agencies and achieving desirable social outcomes.

The First Amendment and the
History of American Education

A primary value of the study of history is that it awakens one to the relativity of contemporary attitudes by revealing widely varying assumptions from previous eras. If one looks at the wording of the First Amendment to the Constitution, one discovers an important demarcation: "*Congress* shall make no law respecting an establishment of religion, or prohibiting the free exercise thereof. . . ." The emphasis is my own, and it is intended to highlight a critical and often overlooked feature of the amendment. The wording was chosen to delimit the role of the *federal* government in establishing a national religion. There was universal agreement at the time that individual states could establish their own state religions if they so elected, and only Virginia and Rhode Island declined to do so at the time of the founding of the republic.[3]

One should note that the Constitution articulates no role for the federal government in education. Responsibilities for educating citizens are specified in each state constitution. It was not until 1947 that the Supreme Court determined that the establishment clause applied not only to the federal government but also to state and local governments, thereby broadening the First Amendment.[4]

A brief review of the history of American education reveals a tremendous interplay between religious groups and the schools. All of the first schools in British North America had religious origins, whether they were founded in Puritan Massachusetts, Quaker Pennsylvania, Catholic Maryland, or Anglican Virginia. New York City's earliest public schools were funded through a mix of public and private revenues and run by Protestant church groups. In a recent essay in the *History of Education Quarterly*, Siobhan Moroney contrasts twentieth-century historians' celebration of the separation of church and state in American educational history with a close reading of numerous primary documents from the late eighteenth and early nineteenth century. She found that modern historians have distorted the past by emphasizing the innovation entailed in Jefferson and Madison's articulations of a separation between church and state and neglecting the many statements in the popular press throughout the early republic that held religious education in the schools to be an integral part of a proper upbringing.[5]

The United States has, of course, undergone multiple revolutions since the framing of the Constitution and since the public schools were established. The nation is in many ways far more complex today, and there should be little doubt that Jefferson's language about "a wall of separation between Church and State" has often helped to protect the rights of religious minorities, agnostics, and atheists. Nonetheless, given current assumptions, it is important to recall that the separation of church and state is not an absolute value but a relative one that has undergone many revisions throughout U.S. history and that might experience further revision in the current context.[6]

President Bush's recent policy initiative made no reference to public support of private schools, and opposition to his proposed legislation concerning vouchers appears to have defeated that part of his platform. We are left, then, with a fairly simple truth: Americans like public schools, and they want their public schools to be as good as they can make them. Hence, the focus of discussions of faith-based organizations working with schools should be exactly where the President has placed it: on public schools.[7]

Are there ways out of these conundrums—strategies that can be used to engage faith-based organizations in improving public schools and promoting desired student outcomes while respecting the First Amendment? I submit that there are—that there is a balanced, middle-ground approach to improving public education through collaboration with faith-based organizations.

ORGANIZING FAITH-BASED GROUPS TO IMPROVE PUBLIC SCHOOLS

There is an extensive base of research on family and community partnerships that promote high levels of student achievement, especially in schools and neighborhoods that lack adequate resources.[8] The research on faith-based organizations' participation in efforts to improve public schools, however, is meager. We know that there are broad-based coalitions of churches, synagogues, and mosques throughout the country, such as the Chicago Public Schools Interfaith Community Partnership, the Ten Point Coalition in Boston, and the Interdenominational Ministerial Alliance in St. Petersburg, Florida, that have come together to establish innovative after-school, literacy, and youth-mentoring programs. We do not know whether there is a "faith factor" that makes the above-named initiatives any more successful than more orthodox strategies of school improvement, which might focus on the professional development of teachers or collaborations with the business community.

We do know that collaboration in and of itself is no magic bullet. Collaborations often break down because of rigidity on the part of one or more participants, differences of temperament among community leaders, and unclear goals. We have little reason to believe that collaborations of faith-based organizations and schools escape those problems, any more than collaborations with business partners or parent groups.

There is, nevertheless, evidence that congregations can be powerful allies with schools in the struggle to create a safe environment for urban youth and to provide them with a high-quality education. I would like to turn to my own research, which has followed a number of schools in low-income communities in Texas over the last decade, to present two case studies of schools that have worked productively with faith-based organizations allied with the Industrial Areas Foundation (IAF) to improve academic achievement in low-income communities serving children of color. These case studies are intended to whet the appetite of readers who suspect that much *could* be done to develop powerful collaborations between religious institutions and schools, but who have few real-world examples to verify that hunch.

It is important to note that the IAF construes itself primarily as a *political* organization that works to mobilize a broad base of stakeholders. Each IAF organization relies primarily on dues paid by congregations to support community organizers, staff, and overhead. Since the 1970s, the IAF has focused on organizing congregations, as the names of its individual groups suggest: the El Paso Interreligious Sponsoring Organization, Valley Interfaith, Dallas Area Interfaith, and so forth. The IAF consists of organizers, who are paid staff, and leaders, who are drawn from congregations and other IAF-affiliated institutions, such as unions or schools, and are not paid.[9]

The first case study concerns Morningside Middle School in Fort Worth, Texas. In the mid-1980s, Morningside was in a state of crisis. The principal of the school had his jaw broken in a playground scuffle, and when he resigned and a new principal came in, her office was firebombed on the first day of classes. Morningside ranked twentieth of the twenty middle schools in Fort Worth on the state standardized test of achievement in 1985.

The new principal, Odessa Ravin, recognized that she would have to do something dramatic if she was going to turn Morningside around. On her own initiative she began a campaign in the African American churches of South Fort Worth, introducing herself to congregations on Sunday mornings and stating frankly that she was frightened of her new responsibility and needed help. At the same time, the local IAF group, the Allied Communities of Tarrant (ACT), was exploring the possibility of improving an urban school. When ACT organizers and leaders heard about Ravin's outreach efforts, a partnership seemed imminent. One of ACT's primary leaders, Reverend Nehemiah Davis of Mount Pisgah Missionary Baptist Church, recalled that "not only did Mrs. Ravin have a very positive attitude toward parental involvement, but she had already been out visiting churches in the community and beating on our doors, *asking* us to get involved. I don't know anyone else who was such a pathbreaker in this area as she was."

Reverend Davis, Ravin, ACT organizers Mignonne Konecny and Perry Perkins, and clergy and lay leaders from ACT congregations such as the First

Missionary Baptist Church and the Community Baptist Church then began making home visits to the parents of all of the students in Morningside Middle School. During the visits, ACT leaders and organizers urged parents to attend upcoming school assemblies to discuss ways in which they could engage with the middle school. "People were incensed by the firebombing, and they wanted to react," Reverend C. M. Singleton of First Missionary Baptist recalled. ACT was careful not to dictate the terms of engagement, however. "We told our leaders not to attempt to answer the parents' questions," Reverend Davis said, "but just to keep them talking. We wanted them to answer their own questions."

The home visits and subsequent assemblies gradually transformed Morningside from a school with no ties to the community to a fulcrum of parental engagement. Many parents had never understood their children's actual course of study or how their children were assessed. ACT leaders held sessions to teach parents about the structure of the school and to advise them of ways that they could reinforce school activities at home. Parents contributed by volunteering to provide extra attention to children with special needs and to read aloud to small groups in the library, and they shared their concerns at staff development workshops. "Just being able to talk to a teacher, when they had never done that before, meant a lot to the parents," Reverend Singleton recalled, "and it meant even more when the teachers made an effort to reach out to talk with them." Teresa Chaney, who had taught at Morningside for nine years, was amazed at the transformation. "Parental involvement was almost nonexistent before," she said. "I've seen more parents this year than in all the years I've taught."

ACT and Morningside Middle School received the first major indication that home visits, training sessions, and parental engagement were paying off in December 1988. At that time Ravin, Reverend Davis, Reverend Singleton, and all of the parents and teachers who had been involved in shaping the new school climate learned that the middle school had moved from last place to third among Fort Worth's twenty middle schools on the state standardized achievement test. The percentage of students who passed the reading, writing, and math sections of the test had climbed from 34 to 71 percent from 1986 to 1988. Previously, 50 percent of the students were failing one subject; in 1988 only 6 percent were in that category.

A similar story can be told of Sam Houston Elementary School in McAllen, Texas, in the early 1990s. Like Morningside, Sam Houston served a low-income community; also like Morningside, the school suffered from low test scores on state standardized tests. Unlike Morningside, Sam Houston served predominantly Mexican American rather than African American students, and the town was close to the border with Mexico, which made it a natural point of entry for immigrants crossing the Rio Grande. Whereas black Baptist churches predominated in South Fort Worth, most McAllen residents attended the one large Catholic Church, Saint Joseph the Worker, on the south side of town.

If the transformation of Morningside Middle School began with Odessa Ravin's unprecedented outreach to faith-based organizations in Fort Worth, the revitalization of Sam Houston can truly be said to have been sparked by the leaders at Saint Joseph the Worker. Father Bart Flaat assumed leadership of Saint Joseph's in 1991 after working closely with an IAF group in San Antonio, Communities Organized for Public Services (COPS), and learning about congregation-based community organizing strategies. At that time Saint Joseph's was considered a "sleeping member" of the IAF group in the lower border region, Valley Interfaith. Yet Father Bart sensed a hunger for change among many individuals with whom he had his first contacts in the parish, and he began a series of meetings in the homes of parishioners in the barrios of La Paloma, Hermosa, Balboa, Alta Linda, and Los Encinos. "Basically, I asked them to tell me two things," Father Bart said, "first their stories, and second, their dreams. I wanted to know what they hoped for and what they dreamed for. And once they had told me that, I had a pretty good agenda."

The parishioners of Saint Joseph's wanted a lively religious community that enriched their Catholicism, so Father Bart began to establish *comunidades de base*, or base communities, throughout his parish where they could engage in Bible study, relating scripture to their own lives. In addition to having religious yearnings, parishioners wanted improved public schools.

Through his previous work with the IAF, Father Bart knew of several successful efforts to turn around struggling schools in Texas. After Morningside's transformation in the 1980s, IAF organizations throughout Texas had begun to nurture collaborations with schools. By 1992 twenty-one schools throughout the state were ready to form a network of "Alliance schools" with the Texas Education Agency (TEA) and the IAF's community organizations. The Alliance schools received a limited amount of funding directly from the TEA to promote parent participation in the schools, and they also received waivers of a number of mandates that stifled innovation.[10]

Father Bart was intrigued with the development of the Alliance schools. He and Sister Maria Sanchez began to meet with all school principals in south McAllen and all school board members to identify schools that could join the new network. When the Texas IAF organized a large statewide conference for prospective Alliance schools in Houston in January 1994, representatives of six of the eight public schools in south McAllen attended.

One of the principals in south McAllen was Connie Maheshwari. Married to an Indian immigrant, Maheshwari is the daughter of Carmen Anaya, one of the most powerful leaders in Valley Interfaith and a major force in bringing infrastucture improvements to unincorporated rural communities called *colonias* in the 1980s. Maheshwari was the principal of Sam Houston, and she instantly saw the Alliance school network as an opportunity for her school.

Unlike at Morningside, however, some of the teachers at Sam Houston expressed reluctance to work with the Texas IAF. Morningside teachers had been so traumatized by the school's low test scores, the chaos in the hallways, and the firebombing of the principal's office that they were desperate for help from any quarter to regain control of the school. While Sam Houston had low test scores and a fatal shoot-out between a youth and the police in South McAllen in the summer of 1993 had frightened families throughout the barrios, they were not sure that Valley Interfaith would help them solve their problems. Part of the teachers' hesitation was caused by fear of losing their professional autonomy. "Teachers are afraid that Valley Interfaith is going to come in and tell them what to do," Maheshwari said. "This is a real fear." Some teachers worried also about the religious dimension of Valley Interfaith, while others were anxious about its political nature.

It took Maheshwari several months to persuade her faculty that the Alliance school concept represented a calculated risk; the upside was that it could benefit their students by improving the relationship between the home and the school. Sam Houston became the first Alliance school in McAllen in April 1994. Valley Interfaith organizers then began working closely with faculty and parents to develop leadership in the community. Mentored by Sister Pearl Ceasar and Estela Sosa-Garza of Valley Interfaith, teachers and staff at Sam Houston began learning the nuts and bolts of organizing in the summer and fall of 1994. They learned how to conduct "one-on-ones"—an IAF term for individual meetings that quickly but respectfully identify individuals' major political issues. They learned how to do "power analyses" of the community in order to understand issues of accountability and control. Finally, they learned how to conduct "research actions" with public officials to identify latent resources, such as money or human resources, that could be used to attack the problems that confronted their community.

Throughout the fall and winter of 1994 Valley Interfaith organizers, Sam Houston teachers, and community residents conducted scores of house meetings in the neighborhood surrounding Sam Houston. A host of issues was brought to the table. Parents complained about poor lighting and lack of supervision in the numerous back alleys that students took to and from school. Others worried about abandoned houses close to Sam Houston where teenagers met to sell and use drugs. Many parents, especially single mothers, were concerned because they had to work full time and had no way to supervise their children in the late afternoon. Other parents were worried simply about the abundance of trash—old tires, broken glass, rain-soaked mattresses—that littered the streets and alleys around the school and seemed to escape the attention of city sanitation workers. Teachers who attended the house meetings and parents who were active in the school shared their concerns about the crumbling physical infrastructure of the school and the persistent presence of rats in the classrooms and cafeteria, and they expressed their hope for a new building.

Working closely with Valley Interfaith, Sam Houston teachers and parents established task forces to research and address each of the issues presented. Valley Interfaith organizers suggested that parents might be able to acquire the funds needed for an after-school program from McAllen's Department of Parks and Recreation. They helped parents to understand that it was important to initiate a relationship with the police and to work together to target high-crime areas if they wanted greater security in the neighborhood. The organizers also helped parents and teachers to comprehend that they could develop the political clout necessary to redirect city and school revenues to improve their school and community in each area of concern.

The momentum that was being generated by all of the "one-on-ones," house meetings, and task-force undertakings began to build to a peak in January 1995, when the community worked with Valley Interfaith to prepare a large public assembly—which participants called the Kids' Action Assembly—to create a climate of greater community accountability for the children. Sosa-Garza worked closely with parents and teachers as they engaged in role-playing to rehearse the statements they wanted to make and the questions they wished to address to public officials. According to IAF community organizing traditions, even if public officials have agreed to work with the community, those agreements must be made public. Large gatherings such as the Kids' Action Assembly demonstrate to the community the progress that it has made through months of political organizing, and they also demonstrate the leadership abilities that community residents have developed.

Parents, teachers, and Valley Interfaith organizers invited numerous public officials to come to the assembly, which was scheduled for February 1995, to commit themselves to improving educational conditions. Officials such as the chief of police, the director of the department of parks and recreation, the city manager, city commissioners, the superintendent of schools, and school board members were informed in advance of the nature of the assembly and the kinds of questions that they would be asked. When the evening of the Kids' Action Assembly finally arrived, more than 300 parents from the school attended—a theretofore unprecedented gathering of the community on behalf of its children. Entertainment was provided by the McAllen High School mariachi band, creating a festive atmosphere in the school cafeteria. Then Raquel Guzman, a teacher, gave the introduction in English, and David Gomez, a parent, repeated it in Spanish. Public officials heard parent leaders such as Delia Villarreal, Christina Fuentes, and David Gomez, as well as teachers such as Leticia Casas, Raquel Guzman, and Mary Vela describe the problems in the neighborhood. Speaking in both Spanish and English, the parents and teachers committed themselves to working together and to demanding accountability from their civic leaders.

The Kids' Action Assembly played a pivotal role in the history of Sam Houston Elementary School. For the first time, members of the community saw a host of leaders made up of their friends and neighbors seeking a new relationship with public officials and getting results. As a consequence of the meeting, the city department of parks and recreation agreed to fund an after-school program, which enrolled more than 200 children in its first year. A police substation was opened closer to the school, and additional officers were assigned to patrol the area. City commissioners made sure that the trash in the alleys near the school was cleaned up, and additional lighting was installed. And to make sure that the community developed its own capacity to improve its children's education, parents at Sam Houston signed a "parent contract" in which they agreed to ask their children over dinner about their day in school and to insist that homework be done punctually.

Valley Interfaith's efforts in Sam Houston paid off in the spring of 1998, when the South McAllen community learned that students' academic achievement on the state's standardized test was so high that the school would be rated "exemplary"—the highest designation the state school system conferred. In the following years, Sam Houston teachers and parents worked together to develop an innovative curriculum, to engage students in a "mini-society" program to learn everyday citizenship skills, and to focus on academic achievement. As with Morningside Middle School, the collaboration with the IAF paid off handsomely, and it led to an increase in the number of Alliance schools in the Rio Grande Valley in ensuing years.

PROMISES

One promising facet of collaboration between faith-based organizations and public schools relates to the use of religious assets in poor communities, which orthodox school improvement strategies entirely exclude. Poor people in urban neighborhoods tend not to view schools as community resources. Everything from the warning signs on the front doors to the sign-in sheets at the front desk tells parents that the school's relationship with the community is ambivalent. Consider the very different relationship of a religious institution in a poor community, which must earn the community's trust if it is to survive. It should not be surprising that the Bush initiative generally has been received more favorably by low-income Americans than their more affluent counterparts or that African Americans and Hispanics have been more responsive than whites.[11]

The second promising facet is that religious institutions offer a concentration of people who do not have to be recruited individually, who already have some cohesion based on their faith and its rituals. When schools go about recruiting parents to assist in their child's learning, the almost-universal strategy tends to be restricted to using students as conveyors of messages. Students bring home slips of paper inviting parents to PTA meetings, school dinners, sports events, and cultural activities. Yet the message of the importance of parental participation is much more powerful when it is reinforced by religious leaders. Individuals such as Reverend Davis in Forth Wort and Father Flaat in McAllen became community organizers as well as preachers of the gospel.

A third promising facet of partnerships of faith-based organizations and public schools is the element of faith itself. Disagreeable as it may be to many secular Americans, the notion of civic engagement as a good in its own right lacks meaning for many Americans who are looking for deeper beliefs to guide their lives and imbue them with them moral purpose. When Morningside religious leaders established the practice of praising during church services students whose school work had improved, or when Father Bart established base communities that reflected on the challenges in McAllen's barrios in light of Christian ethics, individuals were able to transcend purely political motivations to tap the deeper wellsprings of faith, which in turn served as a catalyst for civic engagement.

PERILS

The most common peril facing collaborations of faith-based organizations and schools involves trepidation that laity or clergy will use the occasion to proselytize. In the cases elaborated above, that problem did not surface. The clergy and laity who worked in Morningside and Sam Houston respected the civic mission of the public schools and were more concerned with helping the schools to succeed than they were with evangelical activities. Alliance schools draw on the social capital of a community to improve learning; although clergy and laity may be driven by their faith to work in schools, that faith becomes channeled into educational activities that do not have an overt religious content, easily avoiding the courts' concern with government funding of pervasively sectarian organizations.

Having said that, I also should say that I have observed departures from that general respect for avoiding any religious references in working with public schools. For example, I was a presenter at an Alliance school conference held in Houston in February 2000. In a remarkable acknowledgment of the contribution of the Alliance schools to public education, the district had turned over an entire day of obligatory professional development for teachers to the Metropolitan Organization, the IAF group in Houston. The day's activities began with a prayer by a minister who concluded with the statement "in Jesus' name we pray." No one protested. If a teacher had protested—objecting either to the specifically Christian nature of the prayer or prayer itself as part of teachers' professional development activities—then the district would have had to acknowledge the legitimacy of the teacher's objections. At issue here is the specifically Christian nature of the prayer, along with the fact that attendance was mandatory—public school teachers could opt out only with a loss of pay. One should keep in mind also that Texas is a "right to work"—that is, largely nonunionized—state, so that dissident teachers do not have the same protections as teachers in northern cities with strong union contracts.

A second kind of peril relates to teachers' concerns at Sam Houston that their professional autonomy could be compromised through collaboration with a faith-based group like Valley Interfaith. I observed little of that effect during my field studies in Alliance schools. However, there were some noteworthy cases. In one middle school, after an assistant principal urged teachers to support Valley Interfaith's agenda during a team meeting, the teachers later expressed resentment. "This really isn't part of our job," one seasoned teacher complained. Members of faith-based organizations and their allies will need to be sensitive to teachers' concerns if they are to convince them that they are not subtly undermining their professional autonomy.

A third peril relates to goal displacement, in the sense of losing focus on the issues that relate directly to children's learning. The civic activism involved in meeting with city council members, attending school board meetings, and gaining media publicity can be thrilling for parents and teachers who had felt excluded from the political process before. Yet teachers and parents have to make sure that those activities are kept in balance with the daily challenges of teaching children to read, do mathematical problems accurately, and learn critical thinking skills. Without a constant return to the core activities of their profession, teachers can be viewed by their colleagues as having a wavering commitment to the central tasks of their educational mission.

Faith-based organizations have their own concerns about working in schools. One sad outcome of the Morningside story is that once the school had turned around and achieved public recognition, Allied Communities of Tarrant was edged to the margins. The principal placed more emphasis on orthodox strategies of teacher professional development than on community engagement, and

ACT leaders and organizers began withdrawing from the school. Some of the clergy and laity who had been most engaged in the transformation of Morningside felt that their work was completed and were ready to pass leadership of the school to the principal and teachers, but others felt that they had earned a right to continue to shape Morningside's culture, and they were disappointed as their influence waned. When I last visited Morningside in 1999, the new principal and her colleagues in ACT said that the school's collaboration with faith-based institutions had collapsed and would need to be revived again, almost from scratch. Clearly if schools would like to collaborate with faith-based institutions, they will need to commit to long-term relationships rather than call on churches only when they are most desperate for short-term assistance.

I regret that I am not in a better position to comment on one prevalent fear: many religious leaders worry that collaboration with public schools and other government agencies may undermine their autonomy. That is part of the grand "civil society" debate, with some (such as Theda Skocpol) arguing that government traditionally has worked well with voluntary associations and others (such as Melissa Rogers) suggesting that collaboration between faith-based organizations and government is "the wrong way to do right" because it will "diminish religion's prophetic witness, which sometimes includes the obligation to criticize those in power."[12]

Perhaps one way to circumvent the problem would be to channel government resources not to faith-based organizations, but to public schools and nonprofit organizations that maintain partnerships with faith-based organizations.

CONCLUSION

Religious institutions have tremendous potential to help improve public schools, and I greet the growing interest in exploring that potential with enthusiasm. I write this as a thoroughly secular person who was convinced through my research on Alliance schools that faith-based institutions provide a remarkable resource not only for school and community improvement, but also for moral uplift and inspiration. There must be real guidance and reflection about these matters so that the collaborative efforts made possible by the White House Office of Faith-Based and Community Initiatives will not be misdirected.

What is needed? First of all, it is time to establish a kind of national clearinghouse to help schools and congregations determine optimal ways to work together as well as identify potentially destructive kinds of relationships to be avoided. The First Amendment Center at Vanderbilt University provides an important public service by producing clear guidelines to help teachers understand how they can teach about religion in school while respecting the diversity of religious traditions. A similar center could be established to help public schools and congregations identify the best ways to work together to support student learning.

To establish guidelines, practitioners need examples to help them understand the possibilities for fruitful collaborations with schools. Hence a research base should be established to document the kind of work that is now going on between faith-based institutions and schools. The information should be expressed in a reader-friendly format that avoids social science jargon and resonates with teachers, parents, congregations, and clergy. Most of the work is local, and little is documented. Here is a field of inquiry that is relatively open and that should be supported through grants from philanthropic organizations and government agencies.

There is an extensive literature relating to school and community partnerships that can be drawn on in conducting this research. Collaborations break down or fail to reach their potential for a multitude of reasons. Teachers' preservice professional training typically neglects the theme of community collaboration. While administrators usually have some academic preparation in this area, it almost always excludes the kinds of relationships that can be forged with religious institutions. Clergy and congregations, for their part, are likely to be mystified by the bureaucratic mandates imposed on schools, which do so much to shape the schools'culture. Hence, technical assistance on a wide variety of levels is called for.[13]

My own preference is to fund faith-based and community initiatives as much as possible through entities like public schools and nonprofit organizations that have a history of working with government agencies and are not faith-based organizations themselves. Not only does that circumvent litigation, which can easily cripple innovative social policies, it also ensures that faith-based and community initiatives remain connected to the schools. Finally, it also should reassure those clergy and congregations that are eager to contribute additional resources to their communities but also want to maintain a mediated rather than a direct relationship with the federal government.

NOTES

1. Barry A. Kosmin and Seymour P. Lachman, *One Nation Under God: Religion in Contemporary American Society* (New York: Harmony, 1993), p. 280; Norman Garmezy, "Stressors of Childhood," in Norman Garmezy and Micahel Rutter, eds., *Stress, Coping, and Development in Children* (New York: McGraw-Hill, 1983), pp. 43–84; Charles L. Glenn, *The Ambiguous Embrace: Government and Faith-Based Schools and Social Agencies* (Princeton University Press, 2000); Stephen Monsma, *When Sacred and Secular Mix* (Lanham, Md.: Rowman and Littlefield, 1996), p. 68.

2. George W. Bush, "Rallying the Armies of Compassion" (www.whitehouse.org [February 2001]). The four other agencies to have a Center for Faith-Based and Community

Initiatives are the Department of Health and Human Services, the Department of Housing and Urban Development, the Department of Labor, and the Department of Justice.

3. James W. Fraser, *Between Church and State: Religion and Public Education in a Multicultural America* (New York: St. Martin's Griffin, 1999), pp. 9–13.

4. Ibid., p. 143.

5. Siobhan Moroney, "Birth of a Canon: The Historiography of Early Republican Educational Thought," *History of Education Quarterly*, vol. 39, no. 4 (Winter 1999), pp. 476–91; Diane Ravitch, *The Great School Wars: New York City, 1805–1973* (New York: Basic, 1974); Carl F. Kaestle, *Pillars of the Republic: Common Schools and American Society, 1780–1860* (New York: Hill and Wang, 1983), pp. 182–217.

6. Fraser, *Between Church and State*, p. 20.

7. One recent survey asked respondents "Which one of these two plans would you prefer—involving and strengthening the existing public schools or providing vouchers for parents to use in selecting and paying for private and/or church-related schools?" 75 percent of the respondents preferred to improve the public schools, and 22 percent preferred the provision of vouchers. See Lowell C. Rose and Alec M. Gallup, "The 32nd Annual Phi Delta Kappa/Gallup Poll of the Public's Attitudes toward the Public Schools," www.pdkintl.org/kappan/kpoll0009.html (September 2000), p. 6.

8. Partnership for Family Involvement in Education, "Faith Communities Joining with Local Communities to Support Children's Learning: Good Ideas." (U.S. Department of Education, 2000).

9. For fuller treatment of the Texas IAF and its politics of education, see Dennis Shirley, *Community Organizing for Urban School Reform* (University of Texas Press, 1997) and *Organizing the Valley: Community Empowerment and School Reform in South Texas* (University of Texas Press, 2001).

10. On the origins of the Alliance Schools see Shirley, *Community Organizing*, pp. 200–20.

11. Pew Research Center for the People and the Press, "2001 Religion and Public Life Survey," http:www.people-press.org. The Pew survey contains a host of intriguing data on public response to the Bush initiative; regrettably, it did not include reference to the potential relationship between Bush's initiative and public school reform. According to the Pew survey, "fully 81 percent of blacks and Hispanics support the proposal, compared to 68 percent of whites."

12. Theda Skocpol, *Protecting Soldiers and Mothers: The Political Origins of Social Policy in the United States* (Harvard University Press, 1992) and "Don't Blame Big Government: America's Voluntary Groups Thrive in a National Network," in E.J. Dionne Jr., ed., *Community Works: The Revival of Civil Society in America* (Brookings, 1998), pp. 37–43; Melissa Rogers, "The Wrong Way to Do Right: A Challenge to Charitable Choice," in E.J. Dionne Jr. and John J. DiIulio Jr., eds., *What's God Got to Do with the American Experiment?* (Brookings, 2000), pp. 138–45.

13. One survey revealed that only 15 percent of teacher education programs dedicate even part of one course to community involvement and only 4 percent devote an entire course to the subject. Another survey revealed that of the more than eight hundred skills, competencies, and objectives measured in state teacher certification tests, less than 2 percent had anything to do with influences on education outside of the classroom. See Gordon E. Greenwood and Catherine W. Hickman, "Research and Practice in Parent Involvement: Implications for Teacher Education," *Elementary School Journal*, vol. 91, no. 3 (1991), pp. 279–88; Nancy Feyl Chavkin, *Teacher/Parent Partnerships: Guidelines and Strategies to Train Elementary School Teachers for Parent Involvement* (Austin, Tex.: Southwest Educational Development Laboratory, 1987).

CHAPTER ELEVEN

Faith Communities and Public Education: The View from the Superintendent's Office

DAVID HORNBECK

I enter this discussion as one who has been a professional educator for more than twenty-five years, although my degrees are in law and theology, not education. My observations in this chapter grew not out of research but out of my six years as superintendent of the School District of Philadelphia from 1994 to 2000. A typical large urban school district, the Philadelphia district has more than 200,000 students, 80 percent of whom are minorities. Eighty percent also are eligible for free or reduced-price lunches. When we established baseline performance data in 1996, 40.6 percent of the students could read at the basic level or above on the ninth edition of the Stanford Achievement Test; by 2000 that number had grown to 52.3 percent, an increase of nearly 29 percent in four years. Forty-eight percent of the students entering the ninth grade in 1992 were graduated on time in 1996; in 2000, that rate had improved to 56 percent of the students entering the ninth grade in 1996. Faith communities were part of the effort that led to that dramatic growth.

The Philadelphia school district is critically and chronically underresourced, and the situation gets worse every year. About $2,000 less is spent on each Philadelphia student than is spent on average on each student in the sixty-one surrounding school districts.[1] Those sixty-one districts constitute the primary market within which Philadelphia competes for teachers and principals. The

The author wishes to acknowledge the generous support of his work by the Otto Haas Charitable Trust Number Two and the Pew Charitable Trusts. The opinions expressed in this chapter are those of the author and do not necessarily reflect the views of either trust.

paucity of resources, both financial and human, results in daily struggles throughout the district to educate the children in its charge.

The home of the typical Philadelphia student is less stable than the norm. A substantial proportion of the students are from financially struggling single-parent homes. The average education level of the parents, many of whom had poor educational experiences as children, is low. Violence, fear, abuse, and death are realities in the communities where many, if not most, of Philadelphia's children live. Safety and security—physical, economic, and emotional—are problematic for many students. The facts of daily existence in urban, poor America—young people planning their funerals, not their futures; the absence of a social safety net; no place to go after school—characterize the lives of a large number of public school students in Philadelphia.

During my tenure we considered those realities to be challenges that we needed to help the students overcome, not insurmountable barriers. As we struggled with the state of Pennsylvania's historic unwillingness to provide adequately for its poorest students, we turned to our communities of faith for help on two fronts that correspond to important religious traditions: the pastoral/service tradition and the prophetic tradition.

PASTORAL SERVICE TRADITION

In Matthew 25:35 and following, Jesus, drawing on the prophet Isaiah,[2] admonishes us to feed the hungry, give drink to the thirsty, welcome the stranger, and clothe the naked—that is, to provide everyone with the essentials of daily living. It is not a stretch to imagine a litany of commandments today that includes the admonition to ensure that every child has the skills and knowledge to get a good job, graduate from a four-year college, and practice the art of good citizenship. Today, those goals are essential to living effectively as an adult. Helping the "least of these" children to attain those goals is rooted in the great faith traditions. The first partnership between public schools and faith communities that I examine demonstrates how faith communities render service to schools.

Project 10,000, one of our early initiatives, was implemented to recruit 10,000 new school volunteers within five years; as it happened, we recruited 15,000 in less than three years. That extraordinary success arose from a very ordinary tactic: we simply asked people whether they would help us, and they did. We provided new volunteers with a modest amount of training to give them confidence that they were up to the task. In addition, we tried to greet them when they arrived at the school the first time and to offer them a meaningful task, sending the signal that they were valued. Each year, we found ways to thank them.

Faith communities were a central recruiting ground for Project 10,000. Of course, many congregations had taken the initiative long before Project 10,000 to partner with the schools; we simply built on that history. Congregants tutored, provided after-school programs, created and staffed computer labs in churches, monitored hallways and lunchrooms, and performed various administrative tasks in the school office. Our imagination proved to be the only limitation.

One interesting example of successful collaboration was the Safety Corridors program. As in most urban settings, a school in Philadelphia, while facing potential disruption and even violence during the school day, remains one of the safest places for a young person. However, the same cannot always be said of the route to and from school. Students are subjected to harassment, violence, shakedowns, theft of clothes and lunches, and other fearful experiences. To reduce such encounters, we established Safety Corridors en route to nearly sixty schools, partnering largely with churches. Parishioners were given orange vests and walkie-talkies, and they were posted on street corners along a corridor leading to the school. Parents were responsible for getting their young children to the corridor from the side streets. The parishioners then took over and kept a protective eye on the students as they continued their journey. That was done in the morning on the way to school and again on the way home at the end of the day.

Another wonderful example of a school-congregation partnership is the Reading Buddies program of the First Presbyterian Church in downtown Philadelphia, which works with Presbyterian Homes to match primary classrooms with senior citizen residences. Eight schools and eight residences are involved. Students travel to the senior residences weekly to work with their Reading Buddy, who helps them develop their language skills. The First United Methodist Church of Germantown is unusual in that it works with high-school students, providing an after-school program for ninth graders to help the young people make a successful transition to high school. It continues with academic assistance and other support in the upper grades.

The Philadelphia school district found these partnerships very useful. In 1997, I directed each of the district's more than 260 principals to establish at least one partnership with a faith institution located in the school's immediate neighborhood.

Another opportunity for a pastoral/service partnership arose when the school district imposed a new service-learning requirement for promotion and graduation. While we placed high value on the role of public education in preparing students for productive work and successful postsecondary education, we also believed that public schools have a duty to prepare students for effective citizenship. In 1998 the board of education raised the standards for promotion and graduation in the academic disciplines and at the same time enacted a service-learning requirement for promotion from grades 4 and 8 and for graduation from high school. During the 2000–2001 school year, about 35,000 students will participate in service learning as the capacity of the system to support the requirement is tested. When the requirement is fully implemented, 70,000 students per year will engage in service learning.

Since service is a tradition among faith communities, the question arose of whether students could receive credit for service performed within their congregation or whether such service would cross the constitutional line between church and state. We thought that it was clearly acceptable if the service was sponsored by a church, synagogue, or mosque and was unrelated to religious practice. The more difficult question was posed by activities such as serving as a junior teacher in a vacation Bible school, where part of the activity was directly religious. The district's general counsel concluded that the First Amendment prohibited a service-learning project with religious content. Since then, the district has abided by that interpretation.

In retrospect, I am not certain that we made the right decision. It can be argued that it is acceptable for a student to perform a service that includes religious content if the project meets three criteria: the choice of the activity is entirely voluntary; the student has membership in, or prior significant involvement with, the congregation (to avoid, for example, a teacher or fellow students suggesting service in their congregation as a subtle form of proselytization); and the service occurs in a context wholly separate from fellow students who are nonreligious or of another faith and might feel pressure, discomfort, or embarrassment.

One also might ask whether the practice would give religious students an unfair advantage by creating more opportunities for service than would be available to nonreligious students. That is possible, though unlikely. Service opportunities are determined by many factors, including a student's special interests, family contacts, available transportation, and individual initiative. A student's connection to a congregation is one of many parts of the student's life. If we prohibit service in congregations, it may put religious students at a disadvantage by withdrawing opportunities in a place that constitutes the central non-school interest in their lives.

In order to illustrate the breadth of possibilities, I want to mention a few other ways that our schools integrated faith and faith communities into their mission. During my tenure as superintendent, we began to treat religious institutions as community institutions, allowing them to use school facilities outside of school hours; to recognize the significant way that participation in faith communities shapes students' behavior;[3] and to acknowledge the Muslim student population by excusing their absence on Islamic holidays and providing an appropriate place in school where they could perform their daily prayers.

THE PROPHETIC ROLE

Both the Old and New Testaments are filled with admonitions—from the prophets in the former and from Jesus and the disciples in the latter—to beware of service to false gods. Indeed, God destroys virtually his entire creation in the flood because he is unhappy with human behavior, while prophets such as Jeremiah and Isaiah berate the children of Israel for not following the instructions of the Lord. In the New Testament, Jesus commands that we feed the hungry, house the homeless, heal the sick, and free the prisoners. We are warned of false prophets and of the principalities and powers that lurk among us doing evil.

Children and the poor are central themes of the Scriptures, which make clear that it is the duty of the faithful to nurture, serve, and protect children and the poor. Whether we look to the Beatitudes, where the last are declared first, or to Jesus' observation that it would be better for anyone harming a child "if a great millstone were fastened around your neck and you were drowned in the depth of the sea,"[4] those who believe are instructed "to do justice, and to love kindness, and to walk humbly with your God."[5]

My purpose is not to offer a scriptural exegesis but to emphasize that the Judeo-Christian tradition leaves no doubt about our responsibility to children and poor people or about our duty to act morally and to seek justice. We can predict the correlation of the following variables with unwavering accuracy: academic performance and income level; dropout rates and race; truancy rates and primary language; employment rate of high school graduates and disability; and college completion and incarceration rates and the zip codes of children when they were in elementary school. How can communities of faithful respond?

The question for faith communities is whether the dramatic disparities brought to light by those correlations reflect God's will or political choices. If faith communities decide that the disparities are God's will, then they probably should do little more than pray for understanding. If, however, they decide that the conditions under which our children are educated are fundamentally the consequence of political choices, not God's will, then they are called to prophetic action.

What must faith communities do? To paraphrase the late Rabbi Abraham Heschel, philosopher, theologian, and a member of the faculty of the Jewish Theological Seminary for many years: to speak about God and not protest gross unfairness to our children is blasphemous! Faith communities are called to speak and act courageously in response to the historic mistreatment of children in public education. Fighting for public education that is adequate and equitable should be the next great civil rights battle in our nation.

The prophetic voice of faith communities is needed because those people in positions of power and influence who make the decisions about public education policy attained their positions, at least in part, by accommodating the status quo. They are not likely, at their own initiative, to exercise their power in ways that will radically change the status quo. The large majority of elected officials dance, as the saying goes, "with them that brung them." Since ordinary people in general and poor people in particular did not finance their campaigns and do not wield much power, school districts with significant concentrations of poor children will exercise little influence at the traditional tables where the pie of opportunity is divided up.

The anti-child/anti–poor child policies of the commonwealth of Pennsylvania are bipartisan. While the present governor and legislature have been significantly less friendly to public education than any others during the last thirty-five years, the basic policies were created and sustained by both Republicans and Democrats. Something much more fundamental must be changed than either the party or the incumbents, although it may be necessary to change them as well.[6]

In the PBS documentary *A Force More Powerful*, which describes the most successful nonviolent movements of the twentieth century, Mahatma Gandhi is reported to have said that Great Britain did not dominate India by virtue of greater armed power—Great Britain dominated India because the people of India gave Great Britain permission to do so. When that permission was withdrawn, Great Britain withdrew. And so it is in Pennsylvania. We have given those who determine education policy permission to impose unjust conditions on our children. Sometimes that permission has been explicitly given; more often, however, it has arisen from the deafening silence of the vast majority of people. When polled, the people support fairness, including equity of funding.[7] But they have not found a way to speak powerfully to their leaders about issues of justice and fairness in public education. Faith communities are called to provide that prophetic leadership, to create the opportunity for their congregants to send a different message to Harrisburg.

But why faith communities? First, prophetic leadership is central to their mission, as I have described above. Second, as a factual matter, most, if not all, successful movements have had significant faith community leadership: the abolitionist movement; the fight to enact child labor laws; the civil rights movement; and the protests surrounding the Vietnam war come to mind. The second point is true because in the most difficult moments of every campaign against injustice, when the perpetrators seem to be winning again, faith sustains hope and reinforces commitment to moral values. Political, educational, legal, and economic concerns bring many allies to the cause, but too often their commitment flags. Often, they are too easily bought for the price of their narrower interest. In contrast, if a political, educational, legal, or economic concern is coupled with faith or moral standards, their price is less easily negotiated.

While I was superintendent, there were two collaborations of the school district and communities of faith that fit within the prophetic role. The first was the creation of the Alliance Organizing Project (AOP), a coalition of advocacy groups, many of which are related to faith institutions. We raised more than $3 million for the AOP with virtually no strings attached. Their organizing philosophy parallels that of the Industrial Areas Foundation. The AOP worked with parents to identify the issues that concerned them most and helped them develop the skills, knowledge, and other tools they needed to act as advocates. They worked with principals and other leaders, including me, and confronted us, when necessary, with demands for changes in school practices that they felt were required.

Many principals and other members of my staff were angered or mystified by my support of the AOP, because its members often were confrontational. It was difficult for many district leaders to understand that a real partnership with parents and faith institutions, which they professed to want, could develop only if the community was in a position to add value to the partnership. That is not possible when one partner in a collaborative effort is utterly subordinate to the other.

The second example of the school district's collaboration with faith communities in their prophetic role arose when the district asked the Black Clergy of Philadelphia and Vicinity to join a school district–initiated federal civil rights lawsuit as a co-plaintiff.[8] We alleged that under Title VI the commonwealth racially discriminates against poor, African American children because of the impact of its system of funding public education. For example, in districts where a majority of the students are poor and minority, for every 1 percent increase in the proportion of the minority population the district received $52.88 less in state aid per pupil per year. The lawsuit is presently in the federal district court.

Neither of these initiatives nor any other advocacy effort, with or without faith communities, has resulted in a fundamental change in the system. Advocacy has tended to consist of a few busloads of people from Philadelphia, with a scattering of people from other places, going to Harrisburg once a year. We listen to a few speeches and hold up a few placards; a small number of friendly legislators come out to press the flesh. Then we all go away for another year. The legislators have become very adept at enduring what little annoyance these annual treks cause, knowing that it will be short lived and that they will not have to respond. Between the annual treks, there are intermittent letter or postcard campaigns and other initiatives that also have failed to alter the basic structure of the system.

Conditions have gotten steadily worse over the years. In 1974–75, the commonwealth paid 55 percent of the state's educational costs. Today, it pays less than 35 percent. Expenditures per pupil across the state range from a low of $4,396 to a high of more than $13,500. The average expenditure on each student in the 100 highest-spending districts (20 percent of the total) in 1997–98 was $9,386. More than one-half of the state's 501 school districts had at least $2,000 less to spend per pupil than the wealthy districts. That amounts to at least $50,000 less for each classroom of 25 pupils in those districts.

Between 1994 and 2000, the achievement and graduation rates in Philadelphia improved dramatically, while the financial situation worsened from year to year. In 1998, we made it clear that we could improve performance for a few years by harder, smarter work without increased financial assistance, but that by 2000, significant additional resources would be necessary to maintain and increase the annual growth in student achievement. It is impossible for huge concentrations of disadvantaged children to reach the same level of achievement as their more wealthy counterparts with 25 percent fewer resources.

When we then faced a projected cumulative deficit of as much as $200 million for school year 2000–01, we were reduced to two choices: We could cut programs and make a bargain with the state to bail us out or fight the injustice that the commonwealth imposed on our children and all poor children across the state. For a variety of reasons, the new mayor and board of education chose the former route. The "deal" even included the suspension of the civil rights lawsuit. They bought a year's continued "normal" operation of the district, and the governor bought peace during the Republican National Convention and the ensuing general election for president. Unable to live with that strategy, I was effectively forced out as superintendent at the end of my sixth year in August 2000.

Frustrated by the absence of the will and courage in political and corporate communities to support the children despite what they and their teachers and administrators had accomplished, I spent several months probing the depth of appetite for a serious campaign by the citizens of the state on behalf of all children. There was considerable interest, particularly among leaders in the faith community.

A new activist advocacy campaign, Good Schools Pennsylvania: Every Kid Counts, is taking shape. As of May 2001, we had designed six strategies that will result in a dramatically different public education system in Pennsylvania, one that has adequate funds, equitably distributed. The overriding theme of all the strategies is to send a new message to state leaders in Harrisburg, making clear the commitment of ordinary people to a quality public education for all the children of the commonwealth. The prophetic voice of faith communities is central to the effort. The six strategies are as follows:

—Establish 1,000 groups of ten people (10,000 total) who meet monthly and engage in a variety of advocacy activities, including writing letters to elected officials and newspaper editors, appearing on talk shows, and speaking to groups. Faith community congregants and parents are the primary sources of the 10,000 participants.

—Organize networks of college students to act as advocates for quality public education for all students. The first cadre of college students was drawn from seven Pennsylvania colleges through their chaplains or evangelical organizations. After they were trained, their first activity was to engage fellow students in making nearly 400 calls one Wednesday to targeted legislators, urging them to support public education. With two full-time campus organizers on board, this network will be expanded dramatically over the months ahead. Campus faith communities will continue to play a central role, but we also will look to other student organizations that provide service, have aspiring teachers as members, or indicate interest in social justice issues.

—Organize networks of high school students to act as advocates for quality public education for all students. Our initial outreach will be through the Internet; in the beginning we will focus on editors and writers on hundreds of high school newspapers and students involved in their local faith community youth groups. We believe that if high school students know the facts about the disparities in opportunity they will raise serious questions and engage in creative activism to change the system.

—Hold rallies in different parts of the state to give all those involved the opportunity to see how many fellow citizens are concerned about the issues. We foresee these rallies as a cross between a pep rally and a revival.

—Witness through monthly interfaith vigils. Ten faith leaders, including several bishops and other heads of communion, went to Harrisburg in June 2001 and stood in silent vigil, framing fair opportunity in public education as a moral issue. Twenty went in July. Our plan is to double the number of faith-based participants each month for several months, thereby increasing the number to thousands of witnesses. On the same day each month, we will have a three-person interfaith vigil in front of a number of strategically chosen legislative offices in communities throughout the state.

—Make public education the number-one issue in the 2002 elections. A new governor will be elected, as will a new legislature. The primaries of both parties will be hotly contested, providing the opportunity to challenge the several candidates to compete with one another in demonstrating their commitment to quality education for all children and adequate, equitably distributed funds for public education.

To date, we have raised nearly $5 million, hired nine of fourteen full-time staff members, and established the first of what will be seven offices throughout the state. We have pledges of more than 550 of the 1,000 groups of ten (more than 360 of those pledges come from faith institutions). Five heads of communion have signed on to help with the groups of ten and to participate in the vigils.

The early support suggests that there is broad-based concern about the quality and fairness of public education that cuts across party, income, racial, and geographic lines. There is initial evidence that the silence of decades is rooted in the absence of a vehicle that allows people to raise their voices in witness and protest in a manner that gives them some hope for success. The hard work of sustaining the effort is just beginning across Pennsylvania, a state with almost no experience with large grassroots movements; more people living in rural communities than in any other state in America; the second-largest number of senior citizens; and much distrust between its large rural areas and its sizable urban centers.

But Pennsylvania also is said to be the most "churched" state in the union. We have 1.8 million children, a significant majority of whom go to schools victimized by the unjust system we have created. Nearly all of the parents and grandparents of those children want them to have the very best that is available. Others who enjoy the advantages the present system offers nevertheless recognize that they and their children also are victims of an unfair education system. Many of them are prepared to help.

The most important chapters of this story of collaboration between faith communities and public education will be written in the months ahead, but the prologue is promising. The epilogue will depend largely on the depth, breadth, and strength of the prophetic voices and actions of those who profess faith in a just God as revealed in the Scriptures of Jews and Christians, in the Koran, and in the holy books of other faiths.

NOTES

1. The import of that gap is particularly dramatic when it is translated into $60,000 for each class of thirty students, of which there are about 7,000 in Philadelphia.

2. New Revised Standard Version, Isaiah 58:7

3. There is not a principal or teacher who would not acknowledge the behavior-changing impact of serious involvement of students in the faith community. When I preached on weekends, as I often did, I always raised the issue of the faith community's responsibility to give direction to its young people, to teach right from wrong. In addition to provoking better behavior generally, one unusual example was the respect accorded young women who converted to Islam by young men when they began to wear clothes reflecting their new faith.

4. Matthew 18:6, New Revised Standard Version.

5. Micah 6:8, New Revised Standard Version.

6. In addition to my years as superintendent, since 1966 I have observed Pennsylvania's treatment of its children from several vantage points, including the positions of community education organizer and the commonwealth's executive deputy secretary of education.

7. For example, the annual poll of the Greater Philadelphia First Committee, an organization of Philadelphia's largest businesses, has supported this conclusion each year for at least the last five years.

8. Two previous equity/adequacy lawsuits much like ones decided by state courts in about three dozen others states had been dismissed by the Pennsylvania Supreme Court on the basis that they raised political questions and thus belonged in the legislature, not the court. The state judiciary thus placed itself beyond the reach of children in the some 275 school districts in rural, suburban, and urban Pennsylvania on whose behalf those suits were brought.

Mobilizing Communities
to Improve Public Schools

ERNESTO CORTES JR.

My experiences working with the Industrial Areas Foundation (IAF) and the Alliance schools in Texas demonstrate how faith-based institutions can organize to improve public institutions. One of the troublesome things about the debate on participation of faith-based organizations in public programs is that the government and churches, synagogues, and mosques often are cast as enemies or competitors. In fact, the successful working of public institutions depends on the successful working of civil society, including religious institutions.

The vision of the Alliance schools is to increase the capacity of kids to achieve a high level of learning by developing rigorous standards of inquiry and accountability in public education. But we also think that public education has a larger role: the responsibility to teach all of us what it means to be an American and what it means to be involved in civic culture. I happen to believe that public schools are public institutions. And by "public," I do not necessarily mean "governmental." Public schools ought to be institutions that are the public expression of our commitment to the full development and education of our children.

The IAF has accomplished a great deal in its efforts to improve education. We developed a model of collaboration that creates powerful constituencies committed to school reform, a model that takes into account the role of parents, teachers, and principals in the schools and that of religious institutions, teacher organizations, unions, and other groups in the community. That model turned around Zavala Elementary, the worst-performing elementary school in Austin, Texas. At Zavala, if a kid in the fifth grade was performing at the second-grade level, he would get an "A" because his teachers felt that he was doing the best he could. When Al Melton, a new principal at Zavala, discovered that fact and had the temerity to tell parents the truth, there was what our British friends would call a "slaying match" that polarized the school. Melton turned to IAF because he was not sure where else he could turn. We put together the remnants of the faculty and community at Zavala, and as a result of the collaborative relationship that developed between parents and teachers, Zavala went from being last to being a blue-ribbon school. Since then, the Zavala model has spread to other parts of Texas, so that now there are about 120 Alliance schools collaborating for reform.

The collaborative vision at the core of the Alliance model comes from my own experience growing up in San Antonio, where there were 250 adults who felt responsible for me. Going to school in the morning was like going through Checkpoint Charlie: at every street corner I was interrogated by adults about what I was doing, where I was going, what was I going to do when I got there—all kinds of questions. The explicit understanding was that those 250 adults felt that they had the right to intrude in my life because they felt responsible for me. I compare that experience to what I now see in Los Angeles. Instead of 250 adults organized against every kid, you have communities in which fifty or sixty kids are organized against every adult. That adults also are isolated from one another and not connected to communal institutions does not bode well for public education.

What does this have to do with President Bush's faith-based initiatives? Maybe nothing, maybe everything. The kind of work that the IAF does with congregations does not depend on the kinds of government funding arrangements at stake in the current debate. But the Alliance schools are a clear example of how people of faith can draw from the deep reservoir of inspiration, understanding, and meaning that their faith tradition gives them and translate that tradition into understandable and meaningful public policy. Their actions have to be evaluated not on the basis of their individual faith traditions, but on the basis of the common faith that we all share—our civic culture. John Courtney Murray said it best: "We can operate out of the traditions of the Gospel, but we have the responsibility to translate those traditions and those ideas into understandable public conversations, dialogue, and actions."

Congregations can plug into the IAF model of organizing in several ways. First, they can help build the ties that the IAF believes are crucial to sustaining democracy. I have come to the conclusion that whether my wife and I go to church matters less than whether the parents of the kids that my kid hangs out with go to church—that is, whether a dense network of relationships exists that reinforces coherent values in which kids can find meaning and significance. But not all churches have dense networks; some have very sparse networks, and some have no networks at all. In those cases, the question is not how to use the church's networks to promote involvement in public education but how to enable the church to create the networks necessary to promote involvement. For example, most of the parents at Zavala were within the parish's boundaries, but they had a very weak, attenuated relationship with that particular congregation. We pointed out to the pastor that those parents were his parishioners, or potential parishioners. Once pastors recognize that they can build their congregation by becoming engaged, they begin to collaborate.

Second, congregations represent a pool of possible leaders. We teach congregations to identify, develop, train, and mentor leaders who can then relate to the public school. At the same time, we work inside the school to get parents, teachers, principals, and other potential leaders connected to the community. The school draws on the vision and values of a democratic culture in galvanizing the congregation, and the congregation draws on the vision and values of Judaism, Christianity, Islam, or whatever other tradition in agitating for the improvement of the school. The IAF organizations working with the Alliance schools are not faith-based institutions. They are political organizations that are involved in public policy and whose members draw deep inspiration and meaning from their faith traditions. We see our position as playing an engaged and prophetic role that comforts the afflicted and afflicts the comfortable in this business of building the system of public education needed to sustain a democratic society.

Creating Partnerships of Schools and Faith-Based Organizations that Uphold the First Amendment

CHARLES C. HAYNES

Partnerships of public schools and religious communities are proliferating across the nation. From character education classes on the Eastern Shore of Maryland to after-school programs in Southern California, religious groups are working closely with public school teachers and administrators.

If the First Amendment Center's work in hundreds of school districts is any indication, many of those cooperative arrangements are fully constitutional. We can point to a considerable number of schools whose administrators are careful to engage religious communities in ways that are permitted under the First Amendment as interpreted by the U.S. Supreme Court. As Mavis Sanders and Dennis Shirley both point out, partnerships of this kind can greatly enhance the mission of public education.

There also are plenty of bad stories in school districts where the First Amendment is either misunderstood or ignored. We see clergy allowed on campus to proselytize during the school day, school officials who use their position to promote activities at their own church, and other clear violations of current law. At the same time, we are aware of places where school boards and administrators largely ignore religious communities or, worse yet, are actively hostile toward them. Those are the districts with no guidelines or policies, run by administrators who are unclear about what is and is not constitutional.

The widespread confusion about the ground rules for cooperation led to publication of the guidelines discussed by Sanders.[1] The lead drafters were Marc Stern of the American Jewish Congress and Steve McFarland, then of the Christian Legal Society. Twelve other religious and educational organizations—including the Baptist Joint Committee on Public Affairs, the National School Boards Association, the U.S. Catholic Conference, and the Council on Islamic Education—endorsed the document. We crafted, for the first time, the closest thing we could to a constitutional "safe harbor" for schools entering into cooperative arrangements with religious groups.

Not everybody was pleased with the effort. Some separationist groups are concerned that disseminating guidelines, no matter how carefully drafted, risks opening the door to activities that violate the establishment clause of the First Amendment. But I would argue that the greater risk is to ignore the problem, leaving school districts confused and conflicted about how to engage religious communities. Partnerships are here to stay. They were strongly encouraged by the Clinton administration, and they will be even more of a priority under President Bush's faith-based initiative. True, guidelines will not end the abuses. But it is far better to have them than to leave school districts scrambling to figure things out for themselves.

The push for more partnerships between schools and faith groups comes at a time when the nation is rethinking the role of religion in public education. We now have agreement among most educational and religious groups on most of the religious liberty issues that have long divided us. We agree on legal guidelines for many of the religious liberty rights of students, including the right to pray, to express religious views, to distribute religious literature, and to form religious clubs in secondary schools. And we agree on the importance of including study about religion in the curriculum.[2]

Far too many districts still ignore those agreements and continue to violate the First Amendment by either promoting or ignoring religion. But the emergence over the past decade of a shared vision of religious liberty in public schools has begun to change the school culture in many places. When we proactively address the role of religious liberty and religion in the school and the curriculum, we take seriously the worldviews—the deepest commitments—of millions of parents and students. That is the best foundation for creating partnerships that involve religious communities in the mission of public schools while upholding the First Amendment.

What is new under the faith-based initiatives proposed by President Bush—and what is not addressed in our current First Amendment guidelines—is the question of funding. All of the partnerships discussed by Sanders and Shirley are cooperative arrangements that are constitutional under current law. Many are "school-affiliated" programs that may use the facilities of religious institutions but are careful not to afford an actual opportunity for proselytizing of any school children by clergy, school employees, or adult volunteers during the program.

But what happens if—as the current administration proposes—religious groups become eligible to receive direct grants from the government to offer after-school programs? The president has indicated that he does not intend for tax dollars to be used to aid religion. But he also says that he does not want to force religious groups to eliminate the religious character of their programs, which is the dimension that the president believes makes their programs successful.

It remains to be seen whether that paradox will be addressed and if so, how. But it is safe to say that if the president's plan passes Congress, faith-based after-school programs receiving federal grants are likely to have religious content. Whether or not that arrangement violates the Establishment Clause will depend on what (if any) safeguards are in place to ensure that tax money is not used to promote religion. Even with safeguards and guidelines, the question undoubtedly will be the subject of much litigation.

Where does that leave public schools? At the very least, we will need to revisit the guidelines and work out the extent to which public school officials may cooperate with after-school programs that are faith based. Ironically, the partnerships between government and faith groups created by direct grants to religious organizations may discourage partnerships with public schools. School officials will find it difficult, if not impossible, to cooperate with after-school and other programs that are religious in nature. However the funding issue is resolved in the courts, school officials cannot be in the business of promoting religion through cooperative programs or partnerships with religious communities.

None of these uncertainties, however, should keep public schools and religious communities from reaching out to one another within the current guidelines. Public schools and faith communities may have different missions, but each is committed to the well-being of children. The key is for both parties to follow constitutional principles and guidelines that are intended to protect the conscience of all students and parents in the public schools. With the First Amendment as the civic framework, schools and religious communities can and should work together for the common good.

NOTES

1. *Public Schools and Religious Communities: A First Amendment Guide* (Nashville, Tenn.: American Jewish Congress, Christian Legal Society, and the First Amendment Center, 1999).

2. See, for example, *A Teacher's Guide to Religion in the Public Schools* (Nashville, Tenn.: First Amendment Center, 1999), which was endorsed by twenty-one religious and educational organizations.

Balancing Principles and Implementation: Muslim Responses to Charitable Choice

ABDULWAHAB ALKEBSI

In an impetuous effort to legislate the protection of Americans from terrorism, President Clinton signed the Anti-Terrorism and Effective Death Penalty Act of 1996, which overran the constitutional right to due process of law by giving the government broad discretion to use classified evidence in deportation proceedings without giving the accused the right to view the evidence and prepare an adequate defense. The debate among the Muslim community is whether President Bush's attempts to involve religious institutions in the provision of social services will cross that constitutional threshold again.

In a recent survey conducted by the American Muslim Council, three-quarters of the respondents showed support for the faith-based initiative in principle, although they remained concerned over details surrounding its implementation. Some leaders are fearful that in our rush to empower religious institutions to participate in publicly funded social service programs, we would be legislating away the same institutions' guarantee of independence in the First Amendment.

Will charitable choice expose religious institutions to government regulation, including compliance reviews, audits, and perhaps even the subordination of religious principles to government policies and objectives? Will these institutions lose their discretion in hiring practices and be forced to adhere to labor laws that so far they have been exempt from?

On the other hand, skeptics are fearful that in our attempt to protect the independence of religious institutions, Congress will continue to exempt them from Title VII of the Civil Rights Act, thus clearing the way for them to discriminate against prospective employees and recipients of social services on the basis of race or other factors. In the myriad of issues emerging around charitable choice, that one in particular presents an interesting dichotomy. We find ourselves between the anvil of the First Amendment and the hammer of Title VII of the Civil Rights Act. A wrong move in one direction could place the advances that we have gained in civil rights in peril, while an erroneous move in the opposite direction could run afoul of the Establishment Clause of the First Amendment.

The magnitude of the challenges presented by these issues should not be underestimated. Advocates must acknowledge that they are legitimate concerns that need to be seriously addressed. A laissez-faire approach will not work. Discussing difficult issues and devising solutions at this stage—before it is too late—is of paramount importance. This is an initiative that is attempting to gain traction, and either one of these two issues has the potential to slam the brakes on it altogether.

In short, the dialogue among Muslim leaders is not about supporting the initiative. Virtually all of those surveyed stated that religion is an effective source of better personal and community values, and 76 percent felt strongly that the faith-based community could be effective in helping the government address homelessness, job training for welfare recipients, and prevention and treatment of drug addiction. The dialogue is about the need for a concerted effort to clarify the issues and details. In any case, one of the many challenges facing the Bush administration is the need to seek innovative ways to alleviate the concerns of both sides. That would allow the administration to bridge the gap between promising initiative and sustainable practice. In order to meet such challenges, we need to establish a context for productive dialogue that can lead to viable approaches and action.

What Public Schools Might Learn
from the Catholic School Experience

ROBERT MUCCIGROSSO

C. L. Glenn asserts that the major role that faith-based organizations can play in the improvement of private schools is that of an external force that demonstrates through its positive outcomes the superiority of nonpublic schools.[1] I suggest that there is another, less adversarial way to look at how the nonpublic school can contribute to public school improvement. Cast in the role of competitors, "publics" and "privates," often faith based, engage in little in the way of information sharing. There are few open avenues of communication, for instance, between public schools and Catholic schools, two of the largest educational establishments in the United States.

Public schools can learn much from the accumulated experiences, successes, and failures of private secular and faith-based schools, including Catholic schools like the ones I have served as principal.

Perhaps the most critical lesson to emerge from the Catholic school experience is the importance of ensuring a degree of *administrative autonomy* for the administration and teaching staff of individual schools. Simply put, private school principals serve their schools in much the same way that superintendents typically serve a public school district. Budget and personnel recruitment, training, and retention decisions are made at the individual school level. Each school, with accountability to school boards and central offices that function as monitors, is free to respond as it deems fit to curricular and instructional pressures in a manner that is sensitive to its perceptions of the needs of its students. Teachers are afforded great latitude in developing their own strategies and resources in response to the pedagogical challenges they meet. Central offices and school boards generally play the role of guarantor of quality results rather than operational decisionmaker.

The flip side of that issue is *tenure for principals.* Teacher tenure at the elementary and secondary levels is undergoing a dramatic review, and in the next decades the concept of tenure will be radically reconstructed. The lesson of Catholic schools, which typically extend some form of tenure to teachers, is that tenure has no place with respect to administrators. Give principals authority, reward those who succeed, and hold those who fail accountable.

Catholic schools often are constrained by budgetary factors from responding to every curricular innovation that presents itself. Other times, that resistance is born of deeply held convictions about the nature of the educational process. Whatever the source, *sticking to the curricular knitting* has served Catholic schools well. The back-and-forth of the reading wars, the old math/new math/newer math debates, the emergence and disappearance of language labs, and the recent geometric rate of growth in what we call special education all reflect pressures and influences that eventually become distractions from what private school educators have been compelled to recognize as the heart of the matter: allowing skillful, dedicated, and motivated adults to share their experience and knowledge with willing learners in a supportive, structured, and nurturing environment.

The nation's Catholic schools, for example, cannot afford to offer classes in English as a second language. Yet Catholic secondary schools often serve immigrant populations. If Catholic education plays an important cultural role in their native lands, first-generation immigrant families often send their youngsters, with little or no competence in English, to Catholic high schools. After a period of adjustment and with the help of teachers and peers, immigrant children often become competent students without the benefit of specially tailored programs.

As discussed in Bryk and Holland's *Catholic Schools and the Common Good*, one aspect of the success of Catholic schools has been the *preservation of a core curriculum* that students of all ability levels are required to complete.[2] That characteristic has emerged, in the case of Catholic schools, from deeply held religious convictions about the worth of each and every individual and finds its secular expression in a characteristic shared by successful schools of all sorts: the maintenance and communication of high expectations for all students. Catholic secondary school students pursue more demanding academic course work for longer periods of time than do public secondary school students.

The misguided notion that Catholic schools are bastions of exclusivity that indiscriminately toss aside students who fail to measure up flies in the face of the educational and formational mission of Catholic schools, which is based on the gospel's teaching of the value of each and every individual. A recent survey conducted by the National Catholic Education Association documents the openness and inclusivity of the admissions policies of the great majority of U.S. Catholic secondary schools. Let us learn from two of the central tenets of Catholic schools in *sustaining institutional integrity*: first, education is not something that can be *done to* anyone—the primary responsibility for learning resides with the learner; and second, the recalcitrance or outright ill will of one member of the learning community cannot be accepted at the cost of diminishing learning opportunities for the many.

The identity, integrity, and worth of the institution needs nurturing, and the learner needs to be kept cognizant of and sensitive to the privilege of being part of the learning community. Decisions to separate the individual from the community of willing learners need not be permanent, and alternative means of access need to be developed and preserved. But educational institutions, in order to succeed, need to be respected and cherished; full participation in them must again be conceived of as something to be earned, rather than taken for granted.

These aspects of at least one faith-based organization's educational program identify some content for a dialogue in which religiously affiliated schools would be viewed not as an "exit strategy" from inadequate public schools but rather as a powerful tool for public school improvement.

NOTES

1. Charles L. Glenn, Jr., *The Myth of the Common School* (University of Massachusetts Press, 1988).

2. Anthony S. Bryk, Valerie E. Lee, and Peter B. Holland, *Catholic Schools and the Common Good* (Harvard University Press, 1993).

PART FIVE

THE ROLE OF FAITH-BASED
ORGANIZATIONS IN
Child Care

CHAPTER TWELVE

The Child-Care Landscape

JOAN LOMBARDI

The increase in the number of women in the work force is one of the most significant social changes of our times. In the 1940s, fewer than one in five women with children under eighteen worked outside the home, compared with seven in ten women today.[1] Over the years, child care also has changed. Services have become more diverse as more families rely on nonfamilial care while parents are working. Today, child care consists of early care and education for children from birth until they enter school, and after-school services are offered from kindergarten through early adolescence. As indicated in this section, faith-based institutions have played a role in child-care and after-school programs for children of all ages.

According to the latest data from the U.S. Census Bureau, in 1995 there were 19.3 million children under the age of five; three-fourths of those children (14.4 million), were in care on a regular basis during a typical week. That includes care for children of parents who are employed or in school (11 million) and children with nonemployed parents (3.4 million). Young children are in care for an average of 28 hours a week; however, children of working parents are in care for an average of 35 hours a week. About half of the children are cared for by nonrelatives, with 30 percent of those children in center-based care.[2] The diverse delivery system is particularly important given the variation in the schedules of working families.

Again according the Census Bureau, in 1995 there were 38.2 million children five to fourteen years old. The parents of the vast majority of those children (24.7 million) were in school or employed. While many children are in school while their parents are working, care for school-age children during nonschool hours may be provided by relatives, family child-care providers, and center-based programs. A significant number of children, however, are without adult supervision during the nonschool hours. Despite growth in services in recent years, there continues to be a lack of school-age programs, particularly in low-income communities.

Families face the child-care trilemma of trying to find affordable, high-quality, and available child care. The number of hours children spend in care provides an important opportunity to promote education and to support parenting. Yet, there is a continued struggle to keep fees affordable while ensuring the quality of services. Faith-based institutions have played a role in each of these issues.

Over the years, churches and synagogues have been a critical source of facility support for programs and an important source of support for families. If you ask any child-care providers about their experiences, they probably have had some faith-based experience somewhere. It is possible to argue that in the child-care arena, at least, the discussion is less about religious content than about the availability of space. Religious institutions often have the only spaces available, especially for low-income families.

But we need more than free space to operate a good child-care system. In the United States, in contrast to many other countries, the system is paid for primarily by parents. Many leaders in the faith community have been strong advocates for increasing public investments in child care, which is particularly important since child care can take a serious bite out of the budget of low-income working families. Poor families who pay for child care spend 35 percent of their income on it; nonpoor families, on the other hand, spend 7 percent. The largest source of federal support for child care is the Child Care and Development Block Grant, under which the majority of funds are distributed in the form of vouchers (or certificates) that allow parents to choose from a range of options, including faith-based programs. Funding for child care has increased over the past decade, yet the U.S. Department of Health and Human Services reported that in 1999 we were serving only a little more than one in ten families eligible for assistance.[3]

While the history of the involvement of faith-based institutions in child care provides much promise, many challenges remain. The quality of care continues to be a concern, regardless of affiliation. It is very difficult to run a quality program solely on vouchers, particularly when reimbursement rates are so low. We need more direct assistance to programs; the full cost of care cannot be borne by sponsoring organizations alone. Faith-based and non–faith-based organizations alike face severe shortages of support to continue their services for working families. Faith-based institutions may bring in new volunteers, and that would be helpful, but when we are really struggling to staff child-care programs, we cannot pretend that volunteers can make up the difference or take the place of qualified staff.

The issues around after-school programs are even dicier, because public schools are a bigger part of the picture than they are in early care. The core of the debate here is over who should provide services: public schools or community-based groups, including faith-based organizations. I have always felt that there should be partnerships; it should not be an either/or thing. Inevitably, the issue will be joined—there is a new sense of urgency about providing more and better after-school programs. Here again, we cannot get away from the question of cost. There is a peril in thinking that private after-school programs will miraculously meet the demand for after-school services. It still takes money to do that.

Finally, in upcoming years the demand for child care will continue to grow. The United States needs a significant increase in public resources to support high-quality programs that meet the needs of working families and promote the education and overall well-being of children. Viewing faith-based groups simply as service providers ignores the vital role that the faith community plays in advocacy, including advocacy for better care and more public funding. We certainly would not want to lose that voice.

NOTES

1. Committee on Ways and Means, U.S. House of Representatives, *2000 Green Book* (Government Printing Office, 2000), p. 573, table 9-1.

2. Kristin Smith, *Who's Minding the Kids? Child Care Arrangements,* Current Population Reports, P70-70 (U.S. Census Bureau, 2000).

3. U.S. Department of Health and Human Services, "New Statistics Show Only Small Percentage of Eligible Families Receive Child Care," press release, December 6, 2000.

CHAPTER THIRTEEN

A Survey of Congregation-Based Child Care in the United States

MARY M. BOGLE

The provision of child care in sacred places is not a minor phenomenon, nor is it a new one. As a group, churches and synagogues may be the largest of the providers of center-based child care in the United States, including for-profit and secular nonprofit providers, employers, and public schools. In fact, the roots of faith-based child care are so deep that it is possible to ascribe religious motivations to the first daycare program offered in the United States. Even the history of church-state partnerships in providing early childhood education services can be traced back more than thirty years.

This chapter briefly reviews the history of congregation-based child care. It explores congregations' pragmatic and theological purposes for providing care and examines the child-care "trilemma" of availability, affordability, and quality as it relates to congregation-based care. Key church-state issues such as licensing and government funding also are reviewed. The chapter concludes by probing the impact of growing institutional responses from denominations and cross-faith partnerships.

The information is based on an analytic literature review that includes relevant study data where available and in-depth interviews with more than thirty informants. It is important to note that the only source of detailed descriptions of the nation's congregation-based child care is the study *When Churches Mind the Children: A Study of Day Care in Local Parishes* (referred to hence as the NCC study), which collected and analyzed data from member denominations of the National Council of Churches almost twenty years ago. Because of the impor-

The author gratefully acknowledges the support and insights of Joan Lombardi in the development of this chapter.

tance of congregation-based child care to the overall field, the NCC study should be updated and its sample expanded to include providers representing the full range of faiths, denominations, and geographic locations as well as children from various income, ethnic, and racial groups.

The term *congregation-based* child care is used to describe weekday early childhood programs provided in houses of worship. The term does not include, nor does this chapter address, religious organizations whose primary mission is to provide services (for example, Catholic Charities and Jewish Community Centers). Where more specificity is appropriate or necessary, terms like *church-based* to denote Christian institutions and *synagogue-based* to denote Jewish institutions and so on are used.

The term *congregation-operated* child care is used to refer to programs that are directly or indirectly operated by congregations, which relate to the child care provided through their facilities in three ways: direct operation, in which the congregation exercises full financial and programmatic control over the child-care center; indirect operation, in which the congregation incorporates the child-care center as a separate nonprofit but remains closely involved in its operation by seating representatives on the board of directors; and independent operation, in which the congregation rents out space to an independent entity such as a secular nonprofit.

THE HISTORY OF CONGREGATION-BASED CHILD CARE

The religious motivations of a group of Quaker women appear to have been the driving force behind the earliest known child-care facility in the United States, although it was not based in their meeting hall. It took the form of a nursery founded in 1798 as part of the Philadelphia House of Industry, which sought to counteract the breakup of families by offering poor women a way to support themselves and keep their children with them. Social justice was likely the "mission theology" that motivated the founders.[1]

Evidence of congregation-based child care emerges during the Progressive Era, when congregations began to respond to the tide of immigration from Europe by sponsoring day nurseries for immigrant children in settlement and neighborhood houses. For those new to the country, churches and synagogues were a natural place to turn for family support.[2]

It was in the post–World War II era that congregations came of age in their capacity to provide child care. That surge in capacity was not driven by theological or social imperatives but by a postwar boom in building educational wings on churches. Although the new stock of child-friendly physical plants was built to provide Sunday school space for the children of the baby boom, church stewards began to view child care as a natural use of space that was empty during the week.[3]

As the NCC study points out, church-based child care also can be understood as a modern-day grassroots phenomenon. During the 1970s and 1980s, many houses of worship responded to the need for child care that arose when large numbers of women began to leave full-time child rearing for the paid labor market.[4] And in response to that growing ministry, the National Council of Churches established the Child Day Care Project, publishing its landmark study in 1983.[5]

Today, the phenomenon of congregation-based child care has entered a new phase—one characterized by a wide and growing variety of responses from denominational home offices, cross-faith partnerships, and vendors and membership associations that serve the educational component of the religious community. Until the NCC study, "no national church agency even recorded the names or numbers of parishes operating child day care centers."[6] Since the publication of the study's findings in 1983, and perhaps in part because of them, that is no longer the case. The response of the central offices of specific faiths is a critically important component in the growing institutional response to congregation-based child care. This chapter concludes with a discussion of those responses and the potential implications for congregation-based child care and the field at large.

WHY CONGREGATIONS PROVIDE
EARLY CHILD CARE AND EDUCATION

On a practical level, the availability of suitable classroom space and child-sized furnishings continues to be the primary reason that congregations provide child care. In addition, the geographic placement of synagogues and churches at the heart of their communities as well as their tax-exempt status makes them natural venues.[7] Also, it is important to note that many congregations lease classroom space for child care to generate revenue or to offset mortgage costs on their buildings.[8]

Beyond merely practical concerns, congregations often point to theological reasons for providing early childhood services. Among Christian denominations, the most commonly cited theological imperative for providing *high-quality* child care is found in the promises that some make to children at their baptism. For example, in its policy statement on child care, the United Methodist Church expresses its commitment in this way: "Our service of Infant Baptism in The United Methodist Church recognizes the sacredness of each person from birth and our responsibility to nurture each child in faith. . . . Through the particular ministry of child care, we extend the nurturing ministry of the church and proclaim justice to children, families, and communities. . . . The church has important responsibilities in initiating, encouraging and participating in the highest quality of child care for children and families, not only in the local community, but nationwide."[9]

Although no formal written statements could be located, Jewish sources whom I consulted, including a rabbi with the conservative movement, identified deep theological underpinnings for both the outreach and "in reach" expressions of child care within Judaism. Child care that reaches beyond the Jewish community is grounded in the Jewish ideal of Tikkun Olam, which says that when God created the world it remained incomplete and that the Jewish people are partners in assisting God to "fix the world." The dominant theological motivation behind synagogue-based child care, however, is found in the heavy emphasis that the Hebrew Bible places on transmitting the tenets of the Jewish faith to succeeding generations.[10] Thus, as a recent report by the Jewish Council for Public Affairs states, "while hundreds of synagogues throughout the Untied States are engaged in vital social action endeavors . . . most of that work is being carried out in a pervasively sectarian context."[11]

It is possible to break the mission theology of most congregation-based care into component parts. Although the following motivations are borrowed largely from the NCC study,[12] they have been adapted to reflect purposes described by both Jewish and Christian sources. Five purposes apply to both synagogue- and church-based child care. *Pastoral care* is a form of ministry that views child care as a service to families within the congregation. *Community service* is a form of ministry that views congregations as having a responsibility to their neighbors, whether or not they are members of the congregation. *Education* is a form of ministry in which religious instruction is viewed as an integral program component. Although not raised in the NCC study, a closely related purpose is *enculturation*, the process of instilling the norms and beliefs of a cultural or faith group. Finally, *social justice* is a form of ministry that defines child care as an expression of the faith community's outreach to particular populations, such as low-income families or children with special needs.

Though common to church-based child care, two other purposes do not apply to synagogue-based child care.[13] One is *stewardship*, which is a form of ministry that views the effective use of physical resources as a trust placed in the congregation's hands by God. Weekday use of educational facilities is an expression of good stewardship. The second is *evangelism*, which sees child care as a way to proclaim one's faith and recruit new members to the faith community.

Although synagogue-based programs generally welcome children from outside their congregations and from other faiths, Jewish sources indicated that education/enculturation is the foremost reason for the provision of weekday services for children in synagogues.[14] Among church-based programs, the NCC study found that twenty years ago, the prevalent impetus for the provision of church-based care was community service.[15]

CONGREGATION-BASED CHILD CARE AND THE CHILD-CARE "TRILEMMA"

Although congregations' physical assets and theological motivations for providing child care may set them apart, they as well as nonsectarian providers face the child-care "trilemma" of availability, affordability, and quality.

Availability

Throughout the country, demand for child care is outstripping supply. Families of all income levels, from California to Washington, D.C., often remain on waiting lists for up to twelve months or longer.[16] According to the 1997 National Survey of America's Families (NSAF), 32 percent of children nationwide under the age of five whose mothers are employed are placed in child-care centers.[17] Other forms of care include care provided in the home of a private provider, nanny or babysitting services, and care by a relative.

Even the most conservative studies suggest that the availability crisis would be much more severe without congregation-based child care. Back in the early 1980s, the NCC study estimated that church-based programs as a group are the largest provider of center-based child care in the nation.[18] A more recent survey conducted by the trade journal *Child Care Information Exchange* (*CCIE*) estimated that one of every six child-care centers in the United States is housed in a religious facility.[19]

Child care and after-school care are provided by a significant percentage of congregations across the country. According to *From Belief to Commitment: The Community Service Activities and Finances of Religious Congregations in the United States*, a survey of the nation's Buddhist, Catholic, Jewish, Mormon, Muslim, and Protestant congregations, 24.2 percent of congregations provide daycare for very young children and 18.2 percent provide after-school programs.[20] There is some evidence that the availability of center-based child care is expanding more rapidly within congregations than throughout the field in general. The *CCIE* survey estimates that the number of child-care centers operated in religious facilities increased by more than 26 percent from 1997 to 1999, compared with 19 percent for the field overall.[21]

What role inner-city congregations play in the availability of care for low-income urban children is an important question, but one for which little specific data are available. That it may be substantial and deserving of further examination is indicated by a recent study of 100 older religious properties in six cities. According to Diane Cohen and Robert Jaeger in *Sacred Places at Risk*, "at the turn of the century, many urban congregations adopted a 'social gospel' that welcomed poor and immigrant people that had nowhere else to turn. To support that agenda, they hired the era's best architects to design ambitious, imposing facilities, some with gymnasia, theaters, bowling alleys, and meeting rooms adjacent to the main sanctuary. Now, contending with flight, blight, and other adversities, these same inner-city congregations have adapted their properties once again to address their communities' changing needs."[22] Foremost among those adaptations, say the authors, is the provision of services for children, including child care.

It is important also to understand the role that churches may play in making services available to low-income rural children. A primary reason for the establishment of the innovative Church Child Care Initiative of the North Carolina Rural Economic Development Center—the mission of which is to increase the number of church-based child-care centers available to rural children—was the discovery that often churches are the only facilities in rural areas that are appropriate for children and meet building safety codes.[23]

Affordability

A 1998 Census Bureau analysis demonstrated that, regardless of income level, child care is the third-largest expense after housing and food for families with children ages three to five.[24] Even after most parents have been stretched to the limits of their capacity to pay the price of the service, costs remain. Hidden subsidies typically are provided through the low wages offered to caregivers and noncash contributions provided by nonprofits. According to the NCC study, churches may be especially generous in that regard: they provided three-quarters of the centers surveyed with space and utilities free of charge or at below-market value.[25]

According to the *Cost, Quality, and Outcomes Study*, an analysis of center-based child care published in 1995, the fees that church-based providers charge parents are substantially lower than those found in other child-care sectors. The study also found that a higher percentage of total revenue came from parent fees for congregation-based providers than from other types of providers.[26] Both data from the NCC study and the more recent *Cost, Quality, and Outcomes Study* confirm that the use of public subsidies to support slots for low-income children is lower among congregation-based child-care providers than other nonprofit providers.

Quality

The quality of child care is vexingly low throughout the nation. The *Cost, Quality, and Outcomes Study*, which collected data on centers in four states (California, Colorado, Connecticut, and North Carolina),[27] found that the quality of care in most centers is "poor to mediocre" and that "only one in seven centers provides a level of quality that promotes healthy development."[28]

As for congregation-based care, the study's findings indicate that, in North Carolina, "the state with the most lax regulations," child-care centers in the for-profit sector scored lower on indexes of quality (for example, staff-to-child ratio, teacher education) than the nonprofit sector. The study found that in the other states the quality of care in the two sectors was comparably "mediocre." However, when both the for-profit and nonprofit sectors were broken into subsectors, "church-affiliated" centers across the four states were statistically similar to for-profits in scoring lower on indexes of quality than the other nonprofit subsectors. The for-profit subsectors were defined as independent, local chain, and national chain. The three types for nonprofit centers were church-affiliated centers, some operated by churches and some not; public centers operated by municipalities, school districts, or colleges and universities; and independent centers, which include all other nonprofit centers.

The principal investigators concluded that "the nonprofit sector [has] important differences among subsectors, mainly because the performance of church-affiliated centers differed considerably from other nonprofits. Compared with the other two nonprofit sectors, church-affiliated centers had lower staff-to-child ratios, lower levels of trained and educated teachers, a smaller percentage of assistants with at least a CDA, less educated administrators, lower staff wages, and lower labor cost and total expended cost per child hour. More importantly, they had lower overall quality."[29]

In a recent study that used the *Cost, Quality, and Child Outcomes* data set to probe more deeply into differences in quality among child-care centers, John Morris and Suzanne Helburn pin findings of lower quality more specifically on church-operated child care: "Church-operated and community agency–operated centers provided quality levels similar to for-profit centers but significantly lower than the other nonprofit sectors. [Independently-operated] church-affiliated centers provided higher-quality services than the [church-operated and for-profit] subsectors."[30]

Helburn and Morris indicate that findings of lower quality in church-operated care may be linked to the lower fees those centers typically charge: "Church-operated centers, however, may be serving a somewhat different clientele of families with somewhat lower incomes seeking lower-cost services because church-operated centers charged lower fees than most other subsectors."[31]

The isolation of church-based providers from the mainstream early childhood community also seems to be a strong explanatory factor.[32] As Deborah Hampton, director of the Ecumenical Child Care Network, indicates, church-operated centers must answer to their individual congregations and denominations first and then, in the time remaining, network and resource with the larger early childhood community. As anyone who has worked in child care knows, time is a precious and all-too-scarce commodity. The mission of the Ecumenical Child Care Network (ECCN), which began in 1984 in response to the NCC study findings, is to address the isolation experienced by congregation-based child-care providers through publications, technical assistance, special recognition of quality programs, and other program support services, such as an annual conference.[33]

Another frequently cited explanation for why church-operated care may be of lower quality is that the centers often are poorly administered. The skills it takes to run a church are different from those required to manage a high-quality early childhood program. For that reason, cross-faith partnerships like ECCN encourage church-operated providers to incorporate separately from the houses of worship in which they are located; in other words, to adopt the indirect operation model.

CONGREGATION-OPERATED CHILD CARE AND THE GOVERNMENT

Just as the phenomenon of congregation-based child care is not new, neither are the issues it raises concerning church-state relations. The following is a brief overview of the two biggest challenges for congregation-operated programs: licensing and the use of public funds.

Licensing

Most states require congregation-operated child-care programs to meet the same licensing standards applied to secular providers. Although numerous court cases have confirmed the constitutional right of states to regulate congregation-operated services, the U.S. Supreme Court also has held that, consistent with the establishment clause of the First Amendment of the U.S. Constitution, states may exempt congregation-operated facilities from regulatory oversight if they so choose.[34]

Today, about fourteen states exempt or partially exempt child care provided by a religious institution from licensing requirements. Generally, however, states that offer exempt status still require congregation-operated facilities to register with the regulatory agency and certify that they meet minimum health and safety standards. Besides not applying many standards that go beyond health and safety issues to congregation-operated programs, the primary difference between the licensure and registration methods of regulation is the breadth of state monitoring and enforcement. Under the licensure method, the state plays an active role in monitoring and enforcement; under the registration method, the state plays a much more passive role.

For example, in North Carolina religiously sponsored centers that choose not to be licensed must meet minimum standards regarding health, safety, child/staff ratio, and group size. The same child-care centers generally are exempt from standards concerning staff qualifications, training, and the use of developmentally appropriate activities and play materials. Following written certification and a visit from a state inspector, programs that choose not to be licensed receive a notice of compliance from the state department of health and human services.

The issue of corporal punishment is a particular source of church-state tension, especially for some conservative Christian congregations, and it illustrates the delicate balance of church-state relations in child care. North Carolina law specifically allows congregation-operated centers to use corporal punishment if the facility files a notice with the state stipulating that it "is part of the religious training of its program" and issues a written statement of its discipline policy to parents.

Again, however, the courts often are the final arbiters of disputes over such matters. In 1987, the United States District Court of California denied the petition of North Valley Baptist Church to have its preschool exempted from the state ban on corporal punishment in child-care facilities on the grounds that compliance would not burden the exercise of the plaintiff's religious beliefs. The court noted that while the plaintiff's beliefs permitted spanking, they did not require spanking.[35]

Several states, such as Texas, require religiously sponsored child-care centers to be fully licensed or to employ an independent accrediting body to verify their ongoing compliance with all licensing regulations. Currently, the Texas Association of Christian Child Care Agencies, an independent Baptist organization, is the only agency on the list approved to verify compliance by the Texas Department of Protective and Regulatory Services. An application from the Council on Accreditation, a national secular organization, is pending. A host of public policy and other issues raised by alternative accreditation merit further study, including the following: What are the implications for parent understanding of minimum standards in a state that allows multiple agencies to "quasi-regulate" child-care facilities? Are there variations among states in the rigor applied to assessing the expertise and legitimacy of an alternative accreditation agency? How do liability concerns affect the willingness of a private agency to undertake a traditionally public function? What are the implications of allowing one religious organization to monitor the compliance of another?

Most of the faith-based sources I consulted believed that congregation-operated child-care programs should be licensed just as any other provider. And, in fact, armed with data that the majority of church-based providers have no problem with licensing their child-care facilities, the NCC circulates a policy statement that says that licensing is an appropriate responsibility of the state and that it need not interfere with the free exercise of religion. The statement encourages churches to neither seek nor accept exemption from licensing standards.[36]

There is, however, hardly unanimity on this issue among Christian leaders. In response to a complicated debate over the state's authority to regulate any nonprofit child-care provider, the Pennsylvania Catholic Conference (PCC) recently drafted a bill to clarify and ensure the exempt status of congregation-operated child-care providers in that state. As to PCC's reasoning, executive director Robert J. O'Hara Jr. says: "It's the same rationale for why we don't want the department of education coming into our schools. We see this as part of the teaching mission of the church. That means that it's a religious mission, and we don't ask the government for permission to perform our religious mission. People choose to put their children in religious child-care facilities because they expect to have their child taught particular values—that's why they chose a Jewish facility, or a Catholic facility, or Presbyterian, or whatever. They chose a religious child-care facility because it is an extension of the religious teaching of the church. That is different than some of our Catholic Charities facilities, where we offer adoption services or a food bank. In those particular instances, there might be cause for licensing and we might accept that, but that's not the teaching mission of the church."

O'Hara states that his organization does not oppose Pennsylvania's "legitimate, yet limited, supervisory powers" over matters concerning child health and safety in religious child-care facilities but that it does object to any attempts to regulate staffing, curriculum, and general management. He adds: "Our concerns in this regard are not unwarranted; past [state] regulations required, among other things, that child-care programs provide 'appropriate' materials for 'affective development,' which was defined as acquiring proper behavior related to 'attitudes' and 'values.' Were such regulations imposed on religious facilities, government would be authorized to determine whether children in religious programs are obtaining 'appropriate' values and attitudes. If the materials used to instill values and attitudes in children were not deemed 'appropriate' by government, the facility could lose its license and be prevented from operating."

Ultimately, as William Gormley points out in *Everybody's Children: Child Care as a Public Problem*, it is important to move beyond the legal issues to examine the consequences for children. He and a number of other child-care policy experts believe that licensing exemptions play a role in pushing the quality of church-based care lower.[37] The bottom line is that any further study of congregation-based care needs to look carefully at this subsector in relation to the finding of the *Cost, Quality, and Outcomes Study* that states with more demanding licensing standards have fewer poor-quality centers.[38]

Public Funding

Historically, when "pervasively sectarian" institutions have been viewed as serving the public good, they have been permitted to use public funds in achieving the secular goals of their ministries. Although few pieces of legislation set guidelines on church-state relations before the 1990s, the nation's courts generally have held that religious organizations may receive government contracts and grants as long as they refrain from using them for sectarian activities.

And indeed, congregation-based early childhood programs have been supported by taxpayer dollars for at least thirty years. For example, since its establishment in the 1960s, the Head Start program has partnered with congregation-based providers, particularly those housed in predominantly African American churches. And in the 1980s, Title XX block grant funds were made widely available to congregation-based child-care programs.

Following Title XX, the next watershed in federal funding for child care was the Child Care and Development Block Grant (CCDBG), which was included in the Omnibus Budget Reconciliation Act, signed by President George H. W. Bush in 1990. The act represents the first significant legislative effort to define church-state roles in the provision of a social-service program.[39]

In so doing, the legislation was careful to distinguish between certificates or vouchers, which are viewed as aid to the parents, and grants or contracts, which are considered assistance to the provider or organization. Typically, under the certificate system, parents take their voucher directly to the provider, who may or may not be congregation based. The provider fills out the appropriate paperwork, which then is returned by the parents to a state representative. On submission of periodic timesheets verifying provision of care to the parents' child, the provider is reimbursed at the rate allowed by the state. The CCDBG legislation and a subsequent regulation issued in 1992 do not view the state as providing assistance to the child-care provider; the assistance is to the parent, who in turn uses it to exercise an independent choice.

The CCDBG was reauthorized under the Personal Responsibility and Work Opportunity Reconciliation Act of 1996. Although the 1996 version of the act consolidated separate child-care funding streams, including the certificates, into a single fund, no major changes were made to the language on sectarian providers. Table 13-1 sketches the major church-state issues that generally affect sectarian providers and how they are handled for contractors and certificates under both the 1992 and 1996 versions of the CCDBG law and regulations. There have been no court cases alleging violations or asserting constitutional issues with regard to sectarian providers who receive certificates through the CCDBG since its passage in 1990.

Although child-care certificates are widely available to congregation-operated programs as a result of the CCDBG, there are no quantitative data on how many such programs actually access public funding to serve low-income children. Many sources I consulted claim, however, that two factors drive the use of CCDBG funding among sectarian providers: awareness of the parent of the availability of certificates for use for a broad range of options, including congregation-operated care, and the willingness of congregation-operated providers to accept government aid.

Regulations issued in 1998 place greater emphasis on the responsibility of state lead agencies to make parents aware of all their child-care options, including the use of certificates for access to the "full range of providers," a term that encompasses congregation-based providers. There are those who claim, however, that states are generally ineffective in carrying out consumer education because the regulations do not specify how the lead agency is to ensure compliance by its regional or local agents. That represents yet another question for future studies to examine more closely.[40]

Table 13-1. *Sectarian Issues in the CCDBG Legislation*

Issue	Grant/Contracts	Certificates
Display of religious symbols	Not referenced	Not referenced
Religious instruction	Prohibited	Not prohibited
Employment discrimination based on		
Religious beliefs	Prohibited	Not prohibited
Adherence to religious tenets	Not prohibited	Not prohibited
Discrimination in admission of		
children based on religious beliefs	Prohibited	Not prohibited
Capital improvements	Sectarian and nonsectarian providers may apply for capital improvement funds (with a general bar on construction) if their state chooses to make them available. However, sectarian providers may engage in minor remodeling only to meet health and safety requirements.	

Gaining a clear picture of the willingness of congregations to accept child-care vouchers is equally difficult. The Data collected before the advent of CCDBG funding indicate that church-run centers were less likely than secular nonprofits to provide care to subsidized children.[41] The 1995 *Cost, Quality, and Outcomes Study* supported that finding. However, the potentially growing impact of the certificate system, combined with the unknown effect of large increases in funding for child-care subsidies since 1996, underscores the need for new research on congregation-operated child care and the use of public funds.

Although no hard data are available, a number of my sources suggest that resistance to the use of federal funds for child care is most prevalent among congregations of particularly conservative denominations such as the Southern Baptist Convention. The fear generally expressed by conservative evangelicals is that any government money inevitably entails government intrusion into religious activities, curriculums, and hiring practices.

However, an important and largely unanswered question is whether the likelihood that a particular congregation will accept government funding has as much to do with its conservative theology as its history of social progressivism. In his 1998 National Congregations Study, University of Arizona sociologist Mark Chaves found that most of this country's 300,000 congregations engaged in some form of social service but that only 3 percent used public funds to do so. However, 28 percent of predominantly Caucasian congregations and 65 percent of predominantly African American congregations said that they would be interested in applying for federal funds. In addition, Chaves finds that Catholic and liberal/moderate Protestant denominations were significantly more likely to apply for government funds.[42]

Emmet Carson, in his essay "Patterns of Giving in Black Churches," provides a possible explanation for the phenomenon uncovered by Chaves: "American history is filled with examples of how blacks developed the capabilities of their churches to respond to racism and segregation. Black ministers not only gave their parishioners spiritual and material solace for their present conditions; they also instilled them with hope and engaged them in charitable and other activities so that the black church became a catalyst for the very societal changes that the ministers prayed for in their sermons."[43]

In a discussion of his findings, Chaves adds: "There is already a lower barrier—both culturally and institutionally—between church and state in African American religion than in other religious communities in the United States (Patillo-McCoy 1998)."[44] Several of my sources believe that there is greater use of public funds for child care among congregations representing predominantly African American denominations like the National Baptists, a theologically conservative faith, and the African Methodist Episcopal Church.

INSTITUTIONAL RESPONSE TO
CONGREGATION-BASED CHILD CARE

In the NCC study, the authors conclude that "the church is a major provider of child care in this nation. As such, it is a major factor—however unintentional—in any national debate about child care. . . . Our evidence suggests that child care in churches requires more intentionality on the part of national church agencies if the quantity and quality of care offered is to continue and increase."[45] Almost twenty years later, it is clear that many faiths and denominations have taken up that implicit challenge. While the absence of consistent study data makes firm claims about expansion in the quantity of care impossible to make, it is evident that an institutional response to care is influencing the purposes of congregation-based care and may well be having an impact on the quality. The denominational response may also be increasing the number of programs that are directly operated by congregations. Back in the early 1980s, the NCC study found that 53 percent of all centers in churches were operated by the congregation.[46] Neugebauer says that, based on the results of the more recent *CCIE* survey, "in recent years, the trend has been to shift even more dramatically in this direction."[47] (See table 13-2.)

What is most evident is that the purposes of education/enculturation and evangelism (for Christian churches) are rising with the tide of institutional interest. Again, comparing the NCC study data with his own data, Neugebauer states: "In the 1983 National Council of Churches' study, only 13 percent of church-housed centers surveyed listed spiritual development as one of the primary goals of their program. Traditional early childhood goals of fostering 'love and worth,' 'sharing and cooperation,' and 'positive self-image' were the most common program goals cited (Lindner, 1983). This pattern appears to be changing. In a recent survey of the nation's twenty largest denominations, while traditional early childhood goals were still cited most frequently as denominational goals, spiritual development was identified as an increasingly important secondary goal."[48]

Because of the impact of isolation on the quality of congregation-operated centers, the most important institutional responses may be those that come from the headquarters of the various faith traditions. Several brief glimpses at how various national offices are responding to the needs of very young children in their facilities follow.

The Evangelical Lutheran Church in America (ELCA) offers the most highly developed support for early childhood programs within its community of all the denominations profiled. The ELCA promotes religious instruction and high-quality practice in collaboration with the Evangelical Lutheran Education

Table 13-2. *Religious Organizations Housing Early Childhood Facilities in the United States*

Organization	Members	Congregations	Centers
Roman Catholic Church	61,208,000	22,728	5,002[a]
Southern Baptist Convention	15,692,000	40,565	4,100[b]
United Methodist Church	8,495,000	36,361	—
Presbyterian Church (USA)	3,637,000	11,328	1,900[b]
Evangelical Lutheran Church in America	5,181,000	10,936	2,100[b]
Lutheran Church-Missouri Synod	2,601,000	6,099	2,184[b]
Episcopal Church (USA)	2,537,000	7,415	923[b]
Assemblies of God	2,468,000	11,884	888[b]
Jewish Organizations	5,981,000	3,416	951[a]
American Baptist Churches (USA)	1,503,000	5,807	750[b]
Disciples of Christ (Christian Church)	910,000	3,840	480[c]

Sources: Data on numbers of members and churches come from *The Yearbook of American & Canadian Churches 1999*. The estimates on the number of centers were arrived at as indicated in the footnotes.

a. Data supplied by the Wilson Marketing Group, Inc.

b. Count or estimate supplied by national office of the organization.

c. Count of centers reported in *When Churches Mind the Children* and increased by 30 percent to account for growth over past nineteen years.

Table reprinted with permission from *Child Care Information Exchange*, P.O. Box 3249, Redmond, Washington 98037.

Association (ELEA), which offers workshops and conferences, a quarterly newsletter, and geographic networking meetings and leadership retreats to its member early childhood education centers. ELEA recently added a three-phase certification process for early childhood programs that incorporates a self-study process, initiated by the ELCA department of schools, to assist congregations in reviewing and evaluating the relationship of the congregation and the early childhood program; formal certification from the ELEA, which begins with a program of self-study on high standards of quality and culminates in a visit from an ELEA certification team; and accreditation by the National Association for the Education of Young Children. In addition, Augsburg Fortress Publishers, along with the ELCA department of schools and the ELEA, is adapting a Lutheran Church of Australia faith-based curriculum for use among Lutheran and other churches in the United States. Known as Graceways, the curriculum includes an early childhood module and is advertised as providing "a framework for [programs] to develop their own sequence of content and learning ... to suit [their] own needs" and as offering "a resource to enable and encourage Christian teachers to model and witness their own Christian commitment without manipulating students or coercing a similar commitment from them." Finally, the ELCA department of schools offers formal assistance to congregations wishing to open early childhood education programs.

The Roman Catholic Church is the most difficult to access on a national level of all the faith traditions profiled. Although the U.S. Conference of Bishops collects data on preschools operated within parochial schools, more detailed information on the full range of this faith's child-care and early childhood activities must be searched for diocese by diocese. Data from the *National Congregations* study and hard-to-substantiate comments from Catholic sources whom I consulted suggest several questions for further study: Given the Catholic Church's history and teaching on social action, would the social justice purpose in providing child care be particularly pronounced for this faith? Are Catholic churches playing a significant role in providing child care for Latino immigrants?

The Southern Baptist Convention (SBC) has the longest history of providing an institutional response to early childhood issues within its congregations. Because the tradition places a premium on congregational autonomy and independence, each church is considered an independent governing body. However, the SBC historically has provided technical assistance and group cohesion to its member congregations through nine "boards." The Sunday School Board, which was renamed Lifeway Christian Resources in the mid-1990s, is responsible for providing networking services, technical assistance, and curricular materials to the weekday early childhood programs of Southern Baptist churches. Today, Lifeway curricular materials may be the most widely distributed of all the religious early childhood teaching aids. The Lifeway mailing list includes 5,000 church-based directors of centers that span far beyond the congregations of the SBC. In addition to the curriculum, Lifeway holds an annual conference attended by 850 church-based early childhood professionals. All of the early childhood activities of Lifeway are oriented around eight competency areas: God, Jesus, the Bible, church, family, natural world, others, and self. However, the SBC has no official statement of policy or theology on the child care provided within its churches.

The Union of American Hebrew Congregations (UAHC), the central body of Reform Judaism, serves approximately 875 affiliated synagogues.[49] The UAHC supports its approximately 300 preschool programs, most of which are part-day programs, through its early childhood coordinator, a position that was established in 1999. Martha Katz, the current early childhood coordinator, says that her services include phone consultation with center directors on issues like start-up and program content; a semiannual newsletter that features articles on topics such as how to teach Jewish values to children of different ages; an annual networking conference for directors; and consultation with the UAHC publication and music departments on the development of printed materials and musical resources for children that feature Jewish content and themes. In the future, Katz hopes to provide more in-synagogue consultations and workshops.

Katz notes an important distinction between Jewish and Christian congregations on the issue of sharing space with a congregation. Within Judaism, school-age children of the congregation generally attend Hebrew school several times a week, not just on Saturday or Sunday. Thus, programs for preschool children operate on a part-day basis to accommodate synagogues' after-school education programs.

A final example is the United Methodist Church (UMC). All of the children's ministries within the UMC are provided guidance through the denomination's General Board of Discipleship (GBOD). The mission of GBOD, according to Mary Alice Gran, the director of children's ministries, is "to resource leaders in congregations as they work to make disciples of Jesus Christ." Gran's office provides support to leaders in UMC congregations for all children's ministries, including those that take place on Sunday morning, in the evening, after school, and on weekdays. GBOD activities fall into four categories: resource development, events, research, and networking. Although the UMC has not developed a specifically Methodist curriculum for its programs, it refers providers to Cokesbury Press, which produces a quarterly set of lesson plans for Christian preschool weekday ministries. Gran herself has produced a book, *The First Three Years: A Guide for Ministry with Infants, Toddlers, and Two-Year-Olds*, as part of the array of written materials she produces each year. The UMC policy statement on child care grounds the denomination's concern with quality firmly in the theology of infant baptism. The statement goes on to say: "Each congregation of The United Methodist Church that houses or supports any child-care program must intentionally assess its understanding of discipleship as it relates to this program. Child care is a valid expression of the Christian faith. However, too often, programs in local churches exist without much thought to intentional ministry. Concerns often focus on budgeting and facility use instead of viewing the programs as ministry. When this happens, misunderstandings arise between the child-care program and the congregation, and missed opportunities occur for witnessing and mirroring the Christian faith." With regard to licensing, the statement echoes NCC's guidance by saying: "The regulations of basic health and safety conditions in a building/program that serves children are the appropriate responsibility of the state and do not interfere with the free exercise of religion."[50]

These profiles confirm the *Child Care Information Exchange* survey finding that religious institutions may be focusing more on the purposes of evangelism and education in providing child care. In addition, they make clear that national faith offices are taking a greater interest in promoting quality as a theological concern—a welcome trend indeed. According to Deborah Hampton and others, congregation-based caregivers in need of support in dealing with the issues they face tend to call on their faith institutions first. Any further study of congregation-based child care needs to explore the implications for children now that those institutions are answering their call.

NOTES

1. Sonya Michel, *Children's Interest, Mother's Rights: The Shaping of America's Child Care Policy* (Yale University Press, 1999), p. 20.

2. Ibid., p. 53.

3. Eileen W. Lindner, Mary C. Mattis, and June R. Rogers, *When Churches Mind the Children: A Study of Day Care in Local Parishes* (New York: National Council of Churches of Christ in the U.S.A., 1983), p. 17.

4. Ibid., p. 22.

5. Ibid., p. 9.

6. Ibid., p. 7.

7. Ibid., p. 17

8. Ibid., pp. 18–19.

9. www.gbod.org/children/articles/childcarepolicy.html [December 18, 2000].

10. Interviews with Ruth Feldman, director of early childhood services, Jewish Community Centers Association of America (February 14, 2001); Rabbi Mayer Waxman, director of synagogue services, the Union of Orthodox Jewish Congregations of America (February 7, 2001); and Martha Katz, early childhood coordinator, Union of American Hebrew Congregations (February 23, 2001).

11. Guila S. Franklin, Rebecca Wind, and Laura Furmanski, *Pursuing* Tikkun Olam*: A Survey of Jewish Involvement in Family Development and Neighborhood Transformation Initiatives in Selected Sites throughout the United States* (New York: Jewish Council for Public Affairs,1998), p. 7.

12. Lindner and others, *When Churches Mind the Children,* pp. 20–21.

13. Interview with Martha Katz.

14. Interviews with Ruth Feldman, Rabbi Mayer Waxman, and Martha Katz.

15. Lindner and others, *When Churches Mind the Children,* p. 26.

16. *Opening a New Window on Day Care* (New York: National Council of Jewish Women, 1999), p. 6.

17. Jeffrey Capizzano, Gina Adams, and Freya Sonenstein, "Child Care Arrangements for Children under Five: Variation across States," in *New Federalism, National Survey of America's Families,* Series B, no. B-7, March 2000 (Washington: Urban Institute, 2000), p. 2.

18. Lindner and others, *When Churches Mind the Children,* p. 12.

19. Roger Neugebauer, "Religious Organizations Taking Proactive Role in Child Care," *Child Care Information Exchange,* May 2000, p. 19.

20. Virginia A. Hodgkinson and Murray S. Weitzman, *From Belief to Commitment: The Community Service Activities and Finances of Religious Congregations in the United States* (Washington: Independent Sector, 1993), p. 31.

21. Neugebauer, "Religious Organizations Taking Proactive Role," p. 29.

22. Diane Cohen and Robert A. Jaeger, *Sacred Places at Risk* (Philadelphia: Partners for Sacred Places, 1998), pp. 7–8.

23. Interview with Diana Jones Wilson, director workforce development, North Carolina Rural Economic Development Center (February 7, 2001).

24. *Opening a New Window on Day Care*, p. 7.

25. Lindner and others, *When Churches Mind the Children*, p. 74.

26. Cost, Quality, and Child Outcomes Study Team, *Cost, Quality, and Child Outcomes in Child Care Centers*, 2d ed. (University of Colorado at Denver, April, 1995), p. 61.

27. The principal investigators in *Cost, Quality, and Child Outcomes in Child Care Centers* note that "in the research design, we deliberately designed an intensive on-site study of centers in four fairly representative states with varying licensing standards and demographic and economic characteristics. Taken together, our results give a national overview. Individually, the results for given states are representative of other states with similar characteristics" (p. 1).

28. Ibid.

29. Ibid., pp. 60–61.

30. John R. Morris and Suzanne W. Helburn, "Child Care Center Quality Differences: The Role of Profit Status, Client Preferences, and Trust," *Nonprofit and Voluntary Sector Quarterly*, vol. 29, no. 3 (September 2000), p. 387.

31. Ibid.

32. Lindner and others, *When Churches Mind the Children*, p. 102.

33. www.eccn.org [December 14, 2000].

34. William T. Gormley Jr., *Everybody's Children: Child Care as a Public Problem* (Brookings Institution, 1995), p. 143.

35. *North Valley Baptist Church* v. *Linda McMahon* [in her capacity as director of the California State Department of Social Services], No. Civ. S-84-0767 RAR (1987).

36. *Policy Statement on Child Day Care*, adopted by the Governing Board of the National Council of Churches, November 7, 1984.

37. Gormley, *Everybody's Children*, p. 144.

38. *Cost, Quality, and Child Outcomes in Child Care Centers*, p. 1.

39. Elizabeth Samuels, "The Art of Line Drawing: The Establishment Clause and Public Aid to Religiously Affiliated Child Care," *Indiana Law Journal*, vol. 69 (Winter 1993), p. 42.

40. William J. Tobin, *Let the Children Come to Me: A Handbook for Faith-Based Early Childhood Centers/Programs Regarding the Federal Child Care and Development Block Grant* (Falls Church, Va.: William J. Tobin and Associates, 2000), pp. 12–13.

41. Gormley, *Everybody's Children*, p. 144.

42. Mark Chaves, "Religious Congregations and Welfare Reform: Who Will Take Advantage of Charitable Choice?" *American Sociological Review*, vol. 64 (1999), pp. 839–41.

43. Emmett D. Carson, *Faith and Philanthropy in America* (Washington: Independent Sector, 1990), pp. 234–35.

44. Chaves, "Religious Congregations and Welfare Reform," p. 843.

45. Lindner and others, *When Churches Mind the Children*, p. 101.

46. Ibid., pp. 14–15.

47. Neugebauer, "Religious Organizations Taking Proactive Role," p. 20.

48. Ibid.

49. Eileen W. Lindner, ed., *Yearbook of American and Canadian Churches 2000, Religious Pluralism in the New Millennium* (New York: National Council of Churches of Christ in the U.S.A., 2000), p. 22.

50. www.gbod.org/children/articles/childcarepolicy.html [December 18, 2000].

CHAPTER FOURTEEN

Promises and Perils: Faith-Based Involvement in After-School Programs

FRED DAVIE, SUZANNE LE MENESTREL, and RICHARD MURPHY

When we were approached to write this chapter, we were pleased to be able to address such a high-profile issue as the involvement of faith-based organizations in child-care and after-school programs. However, as we began to discuss the issue, we kept returning to two questions: "Why is something that has been going on for so long being viewed by so many people as a brand-new idea?" and "What are the real cost implications of leveling the playing field to include faith-based organizations?"

Faith-based organizations have had a long and rich tradition of providing social services and child care to children, youth, and their families in the United States, longer than government funds have been available at any level—federal, state, or local. From the settlement houses of the 1800s to modern-day Catholic Charities USA, "the largest private network of social service organizations in the United States," faith-based organizations have played an important role.

Fred Davie would like to thank Susan Beresford, president of the Ford Foundation, and Melvin Oliver, vice president for asset-building and community development at the Ford Foundation, for supporting his work on this chapter. Suzanne Le Menestrel and Richard Murphy would like to express their appreciation to the staff of the Center for Youth Development and Policy Research at the Academy for Educational Development, particularly Emmett Gill, Elizabeth Partoyan, and Alexia Zdral, for their useful comments on earlier drafts of this chapter.

Government financial support of faith-based organizations' operations is not a new phenomenon. For instance, Catholic Charities USA reported that in 1999 it received 62 percent of its income from local, state, and federal government grants.[1] What is currently at the heart of the debate is how the separation of church and state will be ensured and whether faith-based organizations have the capacity to provide additional high-quality services.

What makes this issue seem new are the actions of former President Clinton and, even more, of President Bush. Four major actions have been taken in the last five years:

—*1996.* The first charitable choice provision was included in the Personal Responsibility and Work Opportunity Reconciliation Act of 1996 during the Clinton administration. Charitable choice was defined as a "legislative effort to expand the universe of religious organizations that can participate in publicly funded social services programs."[2]

—*1998.* The second charitable choice provision, a modified version of the one included in the 1996 welfare reform legislation, was included in the Community Services Block Grant Program of the Human Services Reauthorization Act of 1998.

—*1999 to the present.* Bush's use of the bully pulpit as governor, presidential candidate, and president to expand the role of faith-based organizations in delivering social services.[3]

—*January 29, 2001.* Establishment of the White House Office of Faith-Based and Community Initiatives to increase charitable giving; level the playing field for community-based groups; and find effective models of public-private partnership.

In this chapter, we discuss the promises and perils of faith-based organizations' involvement in child-care and after-school programs. "Faith-based organization" refers to any organization that is affiliated with a religion or spiritual movement, whether traditional mainline faiths—Christian, Jewish, Muslim—or the growing minority religious groups in this country, such as Buddhists, Hindus, Wiccans, and others.

We describe current demographic and other "realities" of child care in the United States today and how those realities affect the supply of and demand for child-care and after-school programs as well as the programs' quality. We also consider how those realities affect providers' ability to deliver quality services.

We then turn to some of the promises or benefits of faith-based organizations' involvement in the provision of child-care and after-school programs as well as the perils, or potential dangers, of their involvement. Finally, we examine the implications for children, youth, families, service providers, faith-based organizations, and the community at large.

REALITIES OF CHILD CARE IN THE UNITED STATES

First, child-care use is increasing. There were approximately 21 million infants, toddlers, and preschool children under the age of six in the United States in 1995, and more than 12.9 million of them were in child care. Forty-five percent of children under age one were in child care on a regular basis.[4] Nearly two-thirds of school-age children and youth live with a single employed parent or two parents who are both employed.[5] Parents are working more. One study found that the typical married-couple family worked more than six weeks more in 1996 than in 1989 because of a variety of factors, such as increased employment of women, employers' increased expectations, reduction in the number of unionized workers, and falling wages.[6]

Second, many school-age children are spending some time at home alone. A recent study of families with working mothers indicates that 10 percent of six- to nine-year-old children are left alone or with a brother or sister younger than age thirteen on a regular basis each week and that 35 percent of ten- to twelve-year-old children regularly spend time in self-care or with a sibling younger than age thirteen.[7] However, surveys are not the best way to capture information on self-care because of the "social desirability" factor, or parents' propensity to re-port what they believe researchers would like to hear.[8] Estimates from recent time-diary data from the 1997 Panel Study of Income Dynamics indicate that 4 million (14 percent) of five- to twelve-year-old children spent some time at home alone after school.[9]

Third, there are concerns about the safety and well-being of children and youth who spend time unsupervised after school. The hours between 3:00 p.m. and 6:00 p.m. on school days are peak hours for violent juvenile crime. In addi-tion, youth are most likely to become victims of violent crime, be in or cause a car crash, and engage in other high-risk behaviors, such as substance use and unprotected sexual intercourse, during those hours.[10] Spending time in self-care also affects children's social and academic competence. For instance, one study of sixth graders found that those who had spent more time in self-care during first and third grade were less socially competent and received lower academic grades than children who had spent less time on their own. That association is even more evident among children from low-income families.[11]

A fourth important reality is the affordability and availability of high-quality child care. A recent survey of local child-care resource and referral agencies con-ducted by the Children's Defense Fund found that the average annual cost of care for a four-year-old living in an urban area was more than the average an-nual cost of public college tuition in all but one state. The average cost of school-age care in an urban area can be as high as $3,500 per year.[12] Consequently, low-income families often are faced with placing their children in lower-cost, lower-quality care.

Many communities confront often severe shortages of openings in child-care and after-school programs because of a variety of factors, such as the strong economy, the increasing number of mothers in the work force, and the influx of children of former welfare recipients who are now holding jobs. For example, in the three cities (Boston, Chicago, and Seattle) that are taking part in the Making the Most of Out-of-School Time (MOST) Initiative, there are full-time after-school program slots for only between 9 percent and 35 percent of the school-age population.[13] In addition, child-care workers are leaving for better-paying jobs elsewhere, causing many centers to freeze enrollment or close their doors altogether.

One of the fastest-growing federally supported programs for after-school care is the U.S. Department of Education–funded 21st Century Community Learning Centers, which targets rural and inner-city public schools. Most of the programs in rural and urban elementary schools currently are operating at capacity or expanding to meet the demand for care.[14] In addition, in the 2000 competition for 21st Century Community Learning Centers grants, 2,252 communities sought assistance to establish or expand after-school programs, but the U.S. Department of Education had enough funding to provide only 310 grants. The Center for Youth Development and Policy Research estimates that available funding for the 2000 21st Century Community Learning Centers program covered only about 2 percent of the school-age population (ages five to seventeen) in the United States. In sum, in both urban and rural areas, there is a documented, extreme need for after-school programming in schools, especially for low-income families.[15]

REALITIES FOR CHILD-CARE AND AFTER-SCHOOL PROGRAMS

Early childhood programs are faced with turnover rates ranging from 36 percent for center directors to a high of 59 percent for teacher assistants.[16] Average annual salaries for teachers range from $13,125 to $18,988 for full-time employment, and average salaries for assistants are about $6 to $7 per hour.[17] After-school programs have similar problems with staff turnover and low salaries, compounded by the part-time nature of most of the available positions. In addition, rapid expansion of after-school programs and the introduction of new players, such as cultural institutions, religious organizations, and libraries, have led to increased competition for qualified staff.[18]

While both child-care programs and the emerging after-school programs share many of the same challenges, after-school programs are just beginning to establish program standards, curriculums, and staff training and credentialing requirements. As the field expands, all providers should be aware of the unrealistic expectations being attached to after-school care. Both private and public funders of after-school programs are expecting their funding to have a positive effect on academic performance and problem behavior. While there is some evidence of such short-term outcomes, there are too many other variables in young people's lives to expect after-school care to solve all their problems.

THE PROMISES

Involving faith-based organizations in providing child-care and after-school services has some promising aspects, among them increased public support for after-school programs and involvement of religion in daily life, access of faith-based organizations to pools of volunteers, and potential benefits in the socialization of young people.

Increased Public Support and Need for More Providers

Recent polls indicate that there is strong public support for after-school programs. For instance, 92 percent of registered voters polled in the 2000 Mott/JCPenney Nationwide Survey on Afterschool Programs said that children and youth should have some type of organized activity or place to go after school every day. That support cut across partisan lines. In addition, seven of ten voters believed that it is difficult for parents to find after-school programs.[19] In another recent poll conducted for Fight Crime: Invest in Kids, 67 percent of adults said that providing access to after-school programs is a higher priority than a tax cut.[20]

There also is strong support for increased involvement of religion in daily life. In a recent national survey of Americans, 70 percent of those surveyed said that they want religion's influence on American society to grow. Sixty-three percent of the respondents were in favor of giving religious groups and churches government money to fund programs aimed at helping the poor.[21] Thus strong public support may make it easier for faith-based organizations to adopt the role of provider of child-care and after-school programs.

Close Community Connections

Child-care and after-school programs sponsored by faith-based organizations have the potential to address many community needs. In 1997 most of the 353,000 religious congregations in the United States were located in residential neighborhoods within metropolitan areas.[22] Parents might be more comfortable having their children attend programs in their own neighborhoods rather than transporting them across town. Program staff and volunteers are likely to be members of the faith-based organization offering the program and to come from the same communities as the children who attend.

After-school programs often face difficulties obtaining adequate space in school buildings, and they have to compete with school personnel for use of school supplies, utilities, and custodial staff. Physical space limitations affect the type of programming, program size, and children's behavior.[23] Many faith-based organizations have large physical spaces, such as recreation halls, gyms, or outdoor areas that go unused, particularly during after-school hours, and they also may have access to vans or other modes of transportation.

Pools of Volunteers

Faith-based organizations traditionally rely on volunteers to carry out many of their programs. For example, in 1998, Catholic Charities USA reported the participation of nearly 300,000 volunteers (and only 52,000 paid staff) in the administration of its social service programs.[24] A recent study conducted by Independent Sector found that nine of ten religious congregations used volunteers. Fifty-seven percent of total volunteer time in those congregations was devoted to religious worship and education; 15 percent to education; 9 percent to health; and 8 percent to human services and welfare.[25]

In a 1997 study of 113 historic urban congregations that reported providing 449 programs, 338 of the programs used volunteers, for an average of 148 hours each of volunteer time per month. The estimated monthly value of volunteer time for the entire sample was $577,751.[26] Given the shortage of qualified staff in general in the child-care field, faith-based organizations may be well situated to staff programs from already existing pools of volunteers.

Benefits to Child and Youth Development

Youth development can be defined as the "ongoing growth process in which all youth are engaged in attempting to (1) meet their basic personal and social needs to be safe, feel cared for, be valued, be useful, and be spiritually grounded; and (2) to build skills and competencies that allow them to function and contribute in their daily lives."[27] How youth meet those needs depends, in part, on the quality and availability of people, places, and possibilities.

The youth development field has identified a series of psychosocial and competency outcomes that "reflect the goals that adults have for youth and youth have for themselves."[28] Spirituality is one psychosocial outcome that faith-based organizations may have a considerable role in developing. There are within most faith traditions universal values that transcend dogma and doctrine; for example, there is the ethic of love, especially love and respect for oneself and one's neighbors. Coupled with that ethic is the notion of love for those in need, a love that manifests itself in service. A second value, hope, engenders the courage to believe that no matter how dire the circumstance, one should persevere to overcome it; that no matter how bleak things are today, they can always be better tomorrow. Many individuals of faith believe that love and hope are the best inoculation against hate and nihilism, two realities that sometimes characterize the lives of young people from both the barrios and the "burbs."

Additional important psychosocial outcomes include a sense of closeness/ affiliation and belonging.[29] Those outcomes may also be referred to as a sense of "connectedness," feeling close to and cared for by someone, which research has demonstrated to be an important protective factor for youth.[30] In addition to being connected with parents, youth also may benefit from being connected to a community of adults outside their immediate environment, such as those found in faith-based organizations. For example, "resilient" youth, those who display competence in the face of adversity, are more likely to seek support from nonparental adults, especially teachers, ministers, and neighbors.[31]

Another benefit of participation in child-care or after-school programs sponsored by faith-based organizations may be an increased appreciation for human diversity and tolerance of others with different religious backgrounds. Given the scarcity of available child-care and after-school slots, parents may need to place their children in programs sponsored by religious organizations that are different from their own, with corresponding opportunities for children and youth to learn about and appreciate other faith traditions.

Increasing the Pool of Informed Advocates

Leaders in faith-based organizations are strong advocates for programs for children and youth. For example, the Children's Defense Fund has a Children's Sabbath program that involves mobilizing tens of thousand of churches to support issues related to children and youth. On the Children's Sabbath, religious congregations hold worship services, religious education programs, and other congregational activities that focus on supporting long-term commitments to children and families. Another example of faith-based organizations' involvement in advocacy can be found in North Carolina. In early 2001, the Piedmont Interfaith Council of Greensboro hand-delivered a letter signed by interfaith leaders to the Guilford County commissioner demanding the release of funds for the public school budget. The funds were released the next day.

Examples such as those abound, proof of the potential for gathering a substantial pool of informed advocates for the cause of children and youth. Involving community-connected providers in the world of child care and after-school care will provide them with firsthand knowledge of the weak and underfunded infrastructure that exists for developing the community's youngest citizens. Those new providers could become an important voice for improving the quality and quantity of child-care and after-school programs.

THE PERILS

Involvement of faith-based organizations in child-care and after-school programs also entails some potential perils, among them inadequate programs, poorly trained volunteers, and sectarianism.

Program Quality

One of the first potential perils of increased involvement of faith-based organizations in the provision of child-care and after-school programs is their ability to operate quality programs. There is scant empirical evidence at present to demonstrate that private sector service delivery is any more or less effective than public service delivery.[32] Congregations themselves often fail to evaluate the quality of their programs because of lack of expertise, resources, or interest.[33] More important factors may be whether an organization can ensure clear accountability for results, clear public objectives, and clear contracts for services.[34]

Many organizations that traditionally have been involved in providing social services, youth programs, or child care are small and do not have the staff capacity to comply with government regulations. Ironically, the primary factor preventing most organizations from meeting government regulations is government's insufficient funding of quality services. In addition, a recent Charles Stewart Mott Foundation/JCPenney poll of registered voters found that only 7 percent of respondents wanted to see after-school programs take place at churches or temples, whereas 50 percent said that they would like to see daily after-school programs take place in public schools.[35] While it is not certain why the respondents expressed that preference, it suggests that public schools are recognized as providers of after-school programs. Another challenge for congregations that focus on serving high-risk youth is that they often become fragmented and stretched to the limits of their capacity to provide the necessary services. Competing demands for limited resources may lead to weakening of the congregration's service delivery infrastructure and burnout among its leaders.[36]

Results from the National Congregations Study, a nationally representative sample of congregations, indicate that congregations are more likely to be involved in activities that address immediate, short-term needs for food, clothing, and shelter than programs that require a sustained long-term commitment.[37] In addition, only 12 percent of the congregations in the study reported that they ran one of the most common types of programs (food, housing, and homeless services) by themselves. Furthermore, only 12 percent of the congregations that reported some sort of social service provision had a staff person who devoted at least 25 percent of his or her time to social service projects.[38] Those results raise the question of whether the majority of faith-based organizations have the capacity and expertise to run high-quality, larger-scale child-care and after-school programs.

It also is uncertain whether the White House Office of Faith-Based and Community Initiatives will loosen government regulations for faith-based organizations that receive federal funding. President Bush has said that the new office will "clear away the bureaucratic barriers in several important agencies that make private groups hesitate to work with government."[39] He also noted in his education plan that "before- and after-school learning opportunities will be expanded by granting states and school districts freedom to award grants to faith-based and community-based organizations."[40]

John DiIulio, the first director of the Office of Faith-Based and Community Initiatives, remarked in a speech delivered at the conference of the National Association of Evangelicals in March 2001 that the "conversion-centered program that cannot separate out and privately fund its inherently religious activities can still receive government support, but only via individual vouchers."[41] Those vouchers would be given to clients who then could choose from a variety of programs. How the system of awarding grants to some organizations and vouchers to others will be implemented has yet to be determined. At any rate, it has not been specified whether faith-based and other community organizations will face less stringent government regulations, such as those for meeting certain licensing standards and ensuring fiscal accountability.

Finding, Training, and Maintaining a Pool of Volunteers

While many faith-based organizations rely on volunteers to carry out their programs, it is uncertain whether they will have the resources to develop a well-trained and committed staff of volunteers if they expand their programs to provide child-care and after-school services. Data from the National Congregations Study point to the fact that the number of volunteers that congregations can mobilize actually is very small. Of the 80 percent of congregations involved in social service activities, the average congregation mobilized only ten volunteers in 1998.[42] In the Independent Sector study of religious congregations, "personnel issues" was named one of the three most common challenges over the next five years. Specifically, congregations were concerned with staff burnout, training volunteers as opposed to paid staff to carry out the congregation's programs, and being able to retain a large pool of volunteers.[43]

Moreover, recruiting, training, and managing volunteers is costly. In its evaluation of the Big Brothers Big Sisters program, the research firm Public/Private Ventures determined that it cost approximately $1,000 to train a volunteer, develop a match between a child and a volunteer, and supervise a volunteer.[44] In addition, many nonprofit organizations have discovered that it is time-consuming to develop the set of skills required to manage volunteers. Whether most faith-based organizations can devote sufficient resources to recruit, develop, and retain a trained volunteer pool remains to be seen. As a final note, it should be remembered that the child-care and after-school programs are having difficulty finding staff even when they can pay a salary, albeit a low one.

Disadvantages for Child and Youth Development

While youth involvement in programs sponsored by faith-based organizations has many advantages, several potential risks or perils also exist. First, there is a danger in engaging faith-based institutions in values development because they often confound values and doctrine. Doctrines can be judgmental, condemning behaviors without any regard for the political, economic, and social conditions that generate the behaviors. Doctrine often establishes who is saved and who is damned, setting up people outside a particular faith as "other" or "deviant" and thus deserving of their poor status, discrimination, imprisonment, and so forth.[45] Many young people may consider such a doctrinal approach irrelevant in their lives and too rigid to be of any use to them and so turn away from faith-based organizations, as many already have done.

In addition, developmental theorist Erik Erikson noted that during adolescence, young people are faced with a crisis of identity versus role. During that period, a young person is faced with developing a sense of self in relation to others and to his or her own internal thoughts.[46] Thus youth are attempting to establish their own identities, separating from their parents or caregivers. Consequently, they may reject involvement in any type of organization that they identify with their parents or caregivers.

In any partnership of faith-based organizations and government, faith-based organizations should be encouraged by government to teach the importance of acceptance of diversity, rooted in the ethic of love and consistent with contemporary notions of community building. Government must discourage, indeed disallow, the teaching of doctrine and dogma because it violates the Constitution and is extremely inappropriate for when services are supported with public resources. There also is the danger that faith-based organizations may create "provincial worlds" that greatly reduce children's and youths' exposure to the religious, ethnic, and cultural diversity found in the outside world. That exposure is more important than ever to develop the skills and competencies needed to negotiate in an increasingly diverse society.

Faith-Based Organizations as Court Prophets

One of the biggest perils to confront religious institutions that align too closely with government is the loss of their independence and thus their ability to hold government accountable. The United States has had no shortage of religious leaders who provide justification for questionable government policies. Yet we have come to expect our religious leaders and institutions to challenge government when government transgresses the rights of people who live on the margins—the poor, the disenfranchised, racial minorities, and others. The concept of religious leader as a critical or prophetic voice to government is older than the republic itself. The first voices to decry slavery in this country came from the faith community, including Reverend Henry Ward Beecher, a Presbyterian minister and the brother of Harriet Beecher Stowe, who said that "liberty is the soul's right to breathe."[47] The Quakers and the Methodists were some of the earliest religious communities to stand against the institution of slavery. Methodism, for example, has "typically been concerned with ministry to the poor and disadvantaged, expressing its faith in compassion for the human condition."[48]

Among African Americans, resistance to racial discrimination and other forms of social injustice was born in the church. The prophetic voice best known to contemporary Americans is Martin Luther King Jr., but many others preceded him. From the religious leaders who held secret meetings in the bush arbors (known as hush harbors) of the antebellum South to Dr. King's predecessor, Vernon Johns, of the Dexter Avenue Baptist Church in Birmingham, there is a rich tradition of religious leaders challenging government-sanctioned and -supported injustice.

An example of the tradition of prophetic religious leaders speaking to those in power comes directly from the Hebrew scriptures. Isaiah, Amos, Jeremiah, and Micah all inveighed against royal excesses and religious practices that had gone awry. Amos cried, "Instead let justice flow on like a river and righteousness like a never-failing torrent."[49] Micah stated, "The Lord has told you mortals what is good, and what it is that the Lord requires of you: only to act justly, to love loyalty, to walk humbly with your God."[50] Isaiah and Jeremiah accused those in power of forgetting the widow and trampling the poor and the orphaned under foot.[51] Out of this tradition came some of this country's most dynamic prophetic religious voices, men and women who did not depend on the resources of "Caesar" and thus were free to hold "Caesar" accountable.

Nevertheless, there were religious leaders who became much too dependent on the state, and instead of speaking truth to the powerful, they began to say what the powerful wanted them to say. Those leaders often were called court prophets, for they served in the king's court and spoke in support of the king's position or remained silent for fear of falling out of favor. Johannes Lindblom states that "one of the main professional tasks of these cultic [court] prophets was to announce [a message] in the interest of the royal house and of official policy, to encourage the people, and by the power of their prophetic words influence the course of events in a favorable direction [for the king]."[52]

Religious leaders who become too dependent on government will be compelled to speak favorably of the government or risk delay or defunding of their publicly supported projects or programs. An example is provided by the experience of Reverend Calvin O. Butts and the Abyssinian Community Development Corporation (ADC) in New York City, which receives government money and needs public approval for most of its development projects. When Reverend Butts became a vocal critic of Mayor Rudolph Giuliani's policies and actions, several of ADC's projects were delayed, and, in one case, the mayor sought to completely arrest the development of the ADC-sponsored Pathmark Shopping Center, at that time Harlem's first major economic development project in thirty years.

In considering the role of faith-based organizations in child-care and after-school programs, especially programs supported by public dollars, there is a critical need to keep in mind the peril of undermining the power of religious leaders to speak a prophetic word to power on behalf of the young people they serve. Distance must be maintained between government and the sacred place. An intermediary, either a separate organization or a separately incorporated nonprofit affiliate, would help to ensure at least some independence for the religious institution and its leaders.

Maintaining the Focus on Faith-Based Work

Many faith-based organizations are wary of applying for public funds because of the strings attached, including a perceived threat of government control of their programs, increased accountability for positive results, and more red tape.[53] Data from the National Congregations Study indicate that theologically and politically conservative congregations are significantly less likely to express a willingness to apply for public funds, regardless of denominational affiliation and other background characteristics.[54] That finding suggests that those congregations may fear government intrusion and control. Finally, there is the reality of managing time and dual responsibilities. Being both a spiritual and educational leader may be too demanding for many leaders of congregations.

Separation of Church and State

Many questions have arisen about the constitutionality of the charitable choice provisions as well as the intent of the White House Office of Faith-Based and Community Initiatives. The First Amendment to the U.S. Constitution establishes that "Congress shall make no law respecting an establishment of religion or prohibiting the free exercise thereof."However, we defer an in-depth consideration of this complex issue to the legal scholars who currently are involved in the debate.

IMPLICATIONS

Implications for families. If faith-based organizations were to become increasingly involved in providing child-care and after-school programs under the auspices of the White House Office of Faith-Based and Community Initiatives, families, especially low-income families, may have increased options, particularly in their own neighborhoods. However, parents and caregivers might also be faced with increased "homework" when selecting a program, such as ascertaining whether a program is licensed by the city, county, or state; whether it meets quality standards established by organizations such as the National Association for the Education of Young Children and the National School-Age Care Alliance; and whether the staff (volunteers and paid staff) are well-trained and experienced. The stability of the program (that is, whether the program will exist in another year or two) and the staff, especially for those programs that rely on volunteers, also are significant considerations.

Moreover, parents and caregivers may need to know whether a program is secular or incorporates a particular religious philosophy. If a program focuses on a religious ideology that is different from their own, parents and caregivers need to decide whether they are comfortable with having their children spend a considerable amount of time exposed to teachings that may or may not be compatible with their own religious beliefs. In any case, it is important to educate parents and caregivers about their options, and they must know how to determine whether a particular program will meet their children's needs.

Implications for service providers. Removing regulatory barriers could be beneficial for old and new providers, with or without a faith-based connection. However, many practitioners would argue that the field of child care and after-school care needs additional regulation in the form of uniformly adopted standards that translate into quality programming. Likewise, they could easily say that the biggest barrier to providing quality services is the fact that the government does not fund programs on a real-cost basis to allow for hiring qualified staff who are paid a living wage. Both President Bush and John DiIulio have used the phrase "level the playing field" to allow new providers onto the field. Making the playing field suitable for children and the adults who work with them is equally important, if not more urgent.

The issues that are being raised have profound implications. First, will government now fund programs at the real cost of service delivery? Second, will government eliminate or modify some standards that could lessen program quality? Those are big questions, but the White House office must tackle them.

Implications for faith-based organizations. The foregoing information describes a fairly complex, if not complicated, situation for faith-based organizations. For example, many of the country's leaders now are presenting faith-based organizations' involvement in social service delivery as if it were a new phenomenon. It is not. Second, for faith-based organizations to do their work well and truly meet the needs of children and youth, they need to be fully funded. Third, full funding requires faith-based organizations to be able to manage both the increase in funding and expanded service provision. Failure to focus on enhancing their capacity guarantees the failure of effective program delivery. Finally, faith-based organizations must be partners with government, not a substitute for government, in meeting the needs of children and youth.

CONCLUSION

The short- and long-term implications of involving faith-based organizations in child-care and after-school programs are multiple, complex, and often contradictory. For example, running cost-effective child-care programs often means not paying caregivers a living wage. The cynical side of human nature says that the establishment of the White House office and the attendant rhetoric constitute the ultimate political spin and that many good and sincere faith-based organizations are being set up to fail. The more optimistic side wants the new emphasis on the spirit of community to make a measurable difference. Did not President Bush himself have a positive transformation through a faith-based connection?

Imagine that in the year 2003 President Bush were to visit a "Reverend Michaels," who ministers to a small congregation in north Philadelphia, to find out what impact receiving government money has had on the reverend's programs. Reverend Michaels received two grants—one to reduce juvenile delinquency, the other to run an after-school program. The reverend operated both initiatives with great success. Juvenile crime was reduced in her catchment area, and in the first year of her after-school program, thirty children were doing better in school.

By year two, the reverend's catchment area no longer qualifies for funding for the delinquency prevention program and the youth in the after-school program hit a learning plateau. The reverend visits their schools and discovers wretched physical conditions, few books, and teachers who are not certified to teach in their subject areas. In addition, the youth that were in the juvenile delinquency prevention program no longer have their outreach worker, and two young people in the group cannot live at home. Moreover, the city cannot restore the local park, open the library on weekends, or maintain a Saturday bus route. Armed with this information, Reverend Michaels prepares to give a sermon in a suburban church in Chestnut Hill, a wealthy neighboring suburb.

The Chestnut Hill congregation is horrified by what they hear, and they are moved to action. One Chestnut Hill congregation member does a sophisticated fiscal analysis comparing his and the reverend's resources. Youth in Chestnut Hill receive about twice as many government resources (for example, funds for education, parks, street maintenance) as the reverend's youth. Chestnut Hill engages in a successful statewide campaign to increase resources to Reverend Michaels's community so her youth have economic equality with Chestnut Hill . . . and everyone grows and prospers developmentally and spiritually ever after.

That scenario may be apocryphal, but it does dramatize some of the realities the nation needs to address if we want better outcomes for all of our youth. But better outcomes will elude us until we figure out how much money we need to develop each child in the United States and ensure that that amount is made available. A small church with or without limited government resources cannot make up for years of neglect of education and community infrastructure. It is dangerous to imply that poor communities can turn around their youth and families if government provides a limited amount of money directly to faith-based organizations. We have been trying to do this for years, and we have some wonderful anecdotes and some true success stories. What we have not done is the math to determine what it would take to support the models that we have seen work in a ten-block radius and then expand that scale to include all children and youth in a community. The challenge for President Bush and like-minded leaders is this: Are you willing to do the math?

NOTES

1. Catholic Charities USA, "Our Story in Stats" (http://www.catholiccharitiesusa.org/who/stats.html [February 2001]).

2. David Ackerman, "Charitable Choice: Background and Selected Legal Issues." CRS Report for Congress (Congressional Research Service, Library of Congress, September 2000).

3. The C-SPAN congressional glossary explains the term *bully pulpit* as follows: "This term stems from President Theodore Roosevelt's reference to the White House as a 'bully pulpit,' meaning a terrific platform from which to persuasively advocate an agenda."

4. National Child Care Information Center, "Child Care for Young Children: Demographics," *Child Care Bulletin*, no. 17 (September/October 1997).

5. U.S. Bureau of the Census, March 1998 Current Population Survey, P20-514, table 6, 1998 (http://www.census.gov/population/www/socdemo/ms-la.html).

6. Jared Bernstein, Edie Rasell, John Schmitt, and Robert E. Scott, "Tax Cuts No Cure for Middle Class Economic Woes" (Washington: Economic Policy Institute, 1999).

7. Jeffrey Capizzano, Kathryn Tout, and Gina Adams, "Child Care Patterns of School-Age Children with Employed Mothers," Occasional Paper 41 (Washington: The Urban Institute, September 2000).

8. See for example Sandra Hofferth, "Family Reading to Young Children: Social Desirability and Cultural Biases in Reporting," paper presented at Workshop on Measurement of and Research on Time Use, Committee on National Statistics (Washington: National Research Council, May 1999).

9. Sandra Hofferth, Zita Jankuniene, and Peter Brandon, "Self-Care among School-Age Children," paper presented at the biennial meeting of the Society for Research on Adolescence, Minneapolis, 2000.

10. Sanford Newman, James Alan Fox, Edward A. Flynn, and William Christeson, *America's After-School Choice: The Prime Time for Juvenile Crime, or Youth Enrichment and Achievement* (Washington: Fight Crime: Invest in Kids, 2000).

11. Gregory S. Pettit and others, "Patterns of After-School Care in Middle Childhood: Risk Factors and Developmental Outcomes," *Merrill-Palmer Quarterly*, vol. 43 (1997), 515–38.

12. Karen Schulman, *The High Cost of Child Care Puts Quality Care out of Reach for Many Families* (Washington: Children's Defense Fund, 2000).

13. Robert Halpern, "After-School Programs for Low-Income Children: Promises and Challenges," *Future of Children*, vol. 9, no. 2 (Los Altos, Calif.: David and Lucile Packard Foundation, 1999).

14. Mark Dynarski, principal investigator of the National Longitudinal Study of the 21st Century Community Learning Centers Program, Mathematica Policy Research, personal communication, June 2000.

15. *Future of Children*, vol. 9, no. 2.

16. Marcy Whitebook, Laura Sakai, and Carollee Howes, "NAEYC Accreditation as a Strategy for Improving Child Care Quality: An Assessment," Final Report (Washington: National Center for the Early Childhood Work Force, 1997).

17. Deborah Lowe Vandell and Barbara Wolfe, *Child Care Quality: Does It Matter and Does It Need to Be Improved?* (Office of the Assistant Secretary for Planning and Evaluation, U.S. Department of Health and Human Services, May 2000).

18. Joyce Shortt, *Spotlight on MOST: Building a Stable High-Quality After-School Work Force* (Wellesley, Mass.: National Institute on Out-of-School Time, 2001).

19. The Afterschool Alliance, *Afterschool Alert Poll Report No. 3* (Washington: June 2000).

20. "More Than Two-Thirds of Public Say Boosting Investments in Kids Is Higher Priority Than Tax Cut" (http://www.fightcrime.org/pressdocs/taxcutrelease.html [February, 2001]).

21. Steve Farkas and others, *For Goodness' Sake: Why So Many Want Religion to Play a Greater Role in American Life* (New York: Public Agenda, 2001).

22. Susan K. E. Saxon-Harrold and others, *America's Religious Congregations: Measuring Their Contribution to Society* (Washington: Independent Sector, November 2000).

23. Halpern, "After-School Programs for Low-Income Children."

24. Catholic Charities USA, "Our Story in Stats."

25. Saxon-Harrold and others, "America's Religious Congregations."

26. Ram Cnaan, "Our Hidden Safety Net: Social and Community Work by Urban American Religious Congregations," *Brookings Review* (Spring 1999), pp. 50–53.

27. Karen J. Pittman, Ray O'Brien, and Mary Kimball, *Youth Development and Resiliency Research: Making Connections to Substance Abuse Prevention* (Washington: Center for Youth Development and Policy Research/Academy for Educational Development, 1993), p. 8.

28. Ibid., p. 9.

29. Ibid.

30. Robert W. Blum and Peggy Mann Rinehart, *Reducing the Risk: Connections That Make a Difference in the Lives of Youth* (University of Minnesota, Division of General Pediatrics and Adolescent Health, 1997); Bonnie Benard, *Fostering Resiliency in Kids: Protective Factors in the Family, School, and Community* (San Francisco: Far West Laboratory for Educational Research and Development and the Western Regional Center for Drug-Free Schools and Communities, 1991).

31. Emmy Werner and Ruth S. Smith, *Vulnerable but Invincible: A Study of Resilient Children* (New York: McGraw-Hill, 1982).

32. Harold Dean Trulear, *Faith-Based Institutions and High-Risk Youth* (Philadelphia: Public/Private Ventures, Spring 2000); Demetra Smith Nightingale and Nancy Pindus, *Privatization of Public Social Services: A Background Paper* (Washington: Urban Institute, October 1997).

33. Trulear, *Faith-Based Institutions and High-Risk Youth;* Saxon-Harrold and others, *America's Religious Congregations.*

34. Nightingale and Pindus, *Privatization of Public Social Services.*

35. The Afterschool Alliance, *Afterschool Alert Poll Report No. 3.*

36. Trulear, *Faith-Based Institutions and High-Risk Youth.*

37. Mark Chaves, "Congregations' Social Service Activities," *Charting Civil Society,* no. 6 (Washington: Center on Nonprofits and Philanthropy, Urban Institute, December 1999).

38. Ibid.

39. "Bush Establishes White House Office of Faith-Based and Community Initiatives," *White House Bulletin,* January 29, 2001.

40. George W. Bush, "No Child Left Behind," The White House, January 22, 2001, p. 21.

41. John J. DiIulio Jr., "Compassion 'In Truth and Action': How Sacred and Secular Places Serve Civic Purposes, and What Washington Should—and Should Not—Do to Help," speech delivered before the National Association of Evangelicals, Dallas, Texas, March 7, 2001, p. 26.

42. Chaves, "Congregations' Social Service Activities."

43. Saxon-Harrold and others, *America's Religious Congregations: Measuring Their Contribution to Society.*

44. Joseph P. Tierney, Jean Baldwin Grossman, and Nancy L. Resch, *Making a Difference: An Impact Study of Big Brothers/Big Sisters* (Philadelphia: Public/Private Ventures, 1995).

45. Richard Snyder, *The Protestant Ethic and the Spirit of Punishment* (Grand Rapids, Mich.: Eerdmans Publishing Company, 2001), p. 12.

46. Erik H. Erikson, *Identity: Youth and Crisis* (New York: Norton, 1968).

47. Henry Ward Beecher, *Proverbs from Plymouth Pulpit: Selected from the Writings and Sayings of Henry Ward Beecher, by William Drysdale. Revised in Part by Mr. Beecher, and Under Revision by Him at the Time of His Death* (New York: D. Appleton and Company, 1887).

48. Frank S. Mead, *Handbook of Denominations in the United States,* 10th ed., revised by Samuel S. Hill (Nashville: Abingdon Press, 1995), p. 194.

49. M. Jack Suggs, Katharine Doob Sakenfeld, and James R. Mueller, *The Oxford Study Bible: Revised English Bible with the Apocrypha* (Oxford University Press, 1992), Amos 5:24.

50. Ibid., Micah 6:8.

51. Ibid., Isaiah 1:17, 23; Jeremiah 7:6, 22:3.

52. Johannes Lindblom, *Prophecy in Ancient Israel* (Philadelphia: Fortress Press, 1962), p. 215.

53. Mark Chaves, "Religious Congregations and Welfare Reform: Who Will Take Advantage of 'Charitable Choice'?" Working Papers Series, Nonprofit Sector Research Fund (Washington: Aspen Institute, 1998).

54. Chaves, "Congregations' Social Service Activities."

CHAPTER FIFTEEN

Sacred Places? Not Quite.
Civic Purposes? Almost.

EILEEN W. LINDNER

Some of you may remember *The Children's Cause*, by Gilbert Steiner, published by the Brookings Institution at a time when some other similar institutions failed to consider children's issues a serious matter. It records, among other things, the development, advocacy, passage, and ultimate veto of the 1971 omnibus child-care bill. You may remember that President Nixon vetoed it, saying that it was "the broadest plan yet advanced for the Sovietization of American children." I say that not to ridicule or belittle, but to note how far we have come in our understanding of the role of child care in rearing children in this society. Thirty years ago the debate, heated and ideological, still raged. Today, while there is still some debate, the vast majority of parents see child care as a tool to use in their own good parenting.

I am a pastor who happened to take up the issue of child care, not a child advocate who happened to take up the ministry. I want to be straightforward about that because I think that it conditions how I see things. It was as a pastor that I undertook the study of church-housed child care twenty years ago. The results were reported in *When Churches Mind the Children*,[1] and are, of course, central to Mary Bogle's findings.

Twenty years ago we had a hunch that the church was playing a role in child care; we came to find out that we were the McDonald's of the industry. Our share of the market for child care and McDonald's share of the market for hamburgers were roughly analogous. In 1980, for every child in our sample attending church school on Sunday, there were nine children at the church on Monday morning. That is especially important when we recall that the sample consisted of 120,000 congregations, making ours the largest study of child care in the

United States. We hope to undertake a twentieth-anniversary study to see what has changed in the intervening years.

Mary Bogle's chapter does a fine job of summarizing the findings of our study of church-housed child care. In addition to discovering the primacy of church as a provider, we learned that several broadly held assumptions about church-housed care were not borne out by empirical evidence. Very few congregations limit child-care provision to their own members and virtually none fail to make some form of financial contribution to the child-care centers they house. Often that is done by the contribution of in-kind services or through a reduction in costs of utilities, custodial services, and the like. Generally speaking, child care does not serve as a membership outreach or evangelical program. In the aggregate, churches provide a staggering array of child-care services within church-owned properties.

In a final introductory comment I want to say that I have adapted the book's title, *Sacred Places, Civic Purposes,* to explore the hypothesis "Sacred Places? Not Quite. Civic Purposes? Almost."

First, the issue of sanctity. The churches and congregations that provide space for child care generally do not use their most sacred space for that activity. It does not take place in the nave or the sanctuary—that is, in the worship space. There would be many more issues to consider if that were the space that was used. Such space often is laden with religious artifacts and symbols and reverentially maintained, and by custom it is a place of specialized behaviors. Child care is more commonly offered in educational rooms and all-purpose facilities. So it is important to understand that the space is not quite "sacred." It is, for example, the educational wing that was built and mortgaged along with the sacred space, often space in the basement underneath the sanctuary. The congregants do not feel about that space quite the way they feel about what is truly a sacred worship space. That may seem like hair splitting, but I don't think it is. Few congregations that have only worship space offer child-care services. It is important to note here that I am not making a legal distinction. The whole of the church property is exempt from taxation. Sacred activities, such as prayer, counseling, hymn singing, and so forth do take place in such spaces. Yet I believe that in the present discussion of faith-based initiatives subtle differences will be very important. The precise location—classroom or altar—makes a difference to the provider of the service and perhaps to the recipient.

Now, as for the civic nature of the purposes. I think that we have almost phrased this correctly, but many congregants might disagree, because the question of motivation is important. In the Christian tradition we would say, with regard to child care, for example, that we allow our buildings to be used in that capacity so that children might live the lives for which they were created. Now, I'm not sure that that would meet the test of a civic purpose. It really is a theologically informed call to a mission and ministry of faithfulness. What is true of child care may prove to be true of many social services offered by religious organizations. Pastors and congregations perceive and talk about the services they offer as "ministries and missions." They are more apt to ask "Is it faithful for us to provide this service?" than to ask "Should we provide this social service to the community?" Both religious and secular parties need to take special care in describing and discussing these issues, making allowances for different perspectives and vocabulary. When we look at these things from inside the religious community they do not quite square with how we look at them from a secular perspective.

It therefore matters what questions we ask and how we ask them. If we ask, "Can churches provide child care?" the answer is yes. In fact, they will continue to provide more child care than any single institution in this land. "Should they, and under what terms?" Those are different questions, and they are the questions that are really before us.

What have we learned about child care that may be instructive as we look at the broader range of faith-based initiatives? Church-housed child care grew up in direct response to local needs all across the United States. Not one single denomination suggested to its congregations that they provide child care. Not one single national parent church organization suggested it, nor did any ecumenical agency. Perhaps more significant is that no financial incentives or technical assistance was offered to local churches. The fact that child care is so prevalent in churches is evidence that congregations are highly responsive to local needs.

In contrast, we have worked hard to get churches to respond to Habitat for Humanity and other initiatives, such as Crop Walks, in which participants walk on behalf of the hungry. No one asked for local congregations to start child-care programs. As it says in the Book of Judges, "There was no king in the land, and everyone did what was right in their own eyes." In the eyes of many, many congregations during the 1960s and 1970s, it was right to provide some weekday child program. Following World War II, as you may know, the church either suffered or profited from what has been called "the edifice complex." It was a time of the highest religious affiliation rate in American history; as a result, church infrastructure was significantly developed at mid-century.

In order to enhance the quality of life in new communities, builders during that time left the corner lots open so that churches and banks could use the space to build. Initially most child-care programs were "mother's morning out" programs that offered women a place to leave their children for a few hours. The fittings and furnishings of the buildings were just right, and the space was available during the week. Over time the programs evolved into three-day nursery schools, often run on a co-op basis. It was a very common pattern throughout the 1950s and into the 1960s. The baby boomers, the largest age cohort ever to reach parenthood, were enrolled there in nursery school. The initiative was authentically local, and its evolution was by and large responsive to community need and interest.

The degree to which pastors were unaware of these services is startling. Most of the programs evolved under the leadership of laywomen and did not involve the pastors, in contrast to today's faith-based efforts. We wrote to all those pastors to ask whether they had child care or daycare, writing almost half a page to describe what it might look like. We asked them to specify whether they had infant care, toddler care, or preschool care. As returns began to come in, it began to look as if we had more infant care available than there were infants in America. To sort out our findings we made some follow-up calls. A typical exchange follows:

"Good morning, Reverend. I'm from the National Council of Churches. You responded that you have a child-care program."

"Yes, we do. It's Noah's Ark Preschool. We're very, very proud of it."

"Fine, Reverend. Just a few simple questions. How old are the children in your program? Is it an infant program, or a toddler program, or a preschool program?"

"They're little."

"Yes, Reverend. How little are they?" [Pause] "Do they talk?"

"Kind of."

And so it went. We would talk some more. Sometimes the pastor would say things like, "Well, I'd go down and ask them how old they are, but they're on a field trip to a zoo today." Well, we know that infants don't take field trips to the zoo!

I am not saying this to poke fun at male pastors, but to say that the church in its ecclesiastical and theological manifestation had almost nothing to do with the rise of child care in its midst. That ought to be the first lesson here—not only for child care but for drug counseling or any other services that we might consider. If there is not an authentic need in the community the program will not succeed. If there is an authentic need, the program in some rudimentary form already exists.

We learned that the quality of child-care programs varies not only by socioeconomic class but also by the sponsoring denomination. Churches that run their own child-care programs rather than allow their space to be used by other providers are a distinct subset, and they tend to be more conservative, both theologically and socially. Other churches are more apt to use a Maria Montessori or Head Start–based curriculum than a church-based curriculum. In the case of child care, churches tend to offer programs that are consistent with the social class of their members and with community standards rather than with their denominational identity. For example, in terms of curriculum, class size, and program characteristics, a child-care program in a Methodist or Episcopal church in a conservative upper-middle-class community is more apt to resemble other child-care programs in the community than it is to resemble Methodist or Episcopal child-care centers nationwide.

When it comes to issues of quality and standards there often has been great confusion about church-housed programs. While some church programs are of poorer quality than secular programs, generalizations have to be avoided. Most mainline Protestant churches have a national policy requiring church-housed programs in their congregations to comply voluntarily with state regulations even in states that exempt church-based programs from compliance. Other denominations and independent churches often actively advocate exemption from licensing standards for church-housed programs.

The licensing issue illustrates the complex interaction of theology, ideology, and practical considerations in church-based social service provision. Some well-meaning attempts to improve church-housed child care by insisting that churches meet licensing standards were misdirected at the very churches that complied voluntarily while ignoring those that used the religious exemption to avoid costly features such as appropriate group size. We do not want churches to slip away from adhering to quality standards because they are exempt from licensing standards. It is a very difficult problem.

That brings me to another point that I think is terribly significant. It is very important to underscore that the faith community brings three things to any social undertaking; in ascending order, they are as follows: First, they bring their material resources, that is, the physical plan. Religious organizations have parking spaces and cribs, small tables, and other furnishings and fittings needed, for example, for a child-care program. Sometimes they are not so nice, but quality has to be measured not by some absolute, unrealistic standard, but in relation to what is available in the community.

Second, religious organizations bring human resources, sometimes in the person of volunteers. The third thing that they bring is moral authority. That moral authority is a terribly underestimated but highly significant characteristic of religiously sponsored programs. Sometimes moral authority is consciously and intentionally exercised by the sponsoring organization; other times it is simply bestowed by the fact of religious sponsorship and its impact on the outcome of programs is little recognized or studied.

We conducted research so that we would have a basis for saying to churches that it is unethical—nay, immoral—to use their church status to exempt themselves from health and safety regulations that were established to safeguard all children, including those in their care. Churches that seek exemption to offer substandard care generally are outside the universe that we sampled here. That, in turn, tells us whom we ought to be talking to in the religious world. We do not have to say the same things to all the different churches and religious organizations. That suggests that those who wish to see churches provide more publicly funded social services will need a sophisticated understanding of religious communities and how they differ from one another.

Now, on the matter of church-state relations. Child care has a lot to offer all of us by way of instruction in the nature of church-state relations. For example, the organizational life of the church is altered by the provision of services to those outside the congregation. Why have there not been more lawsuits? There are two realities that we need to recognize. When Aunt Hester walks out of the church on Sunday morning, slips on ice, breaks her hip, and ruins her new dress, she praises the Lord because she lived through it. She does not sue the church.

People who bring their children to the child-care center may not have such devotion. And one of the realities that churches are going to have to grapple with is the issue of ascending liability. Nobody has ever successfully sued a local child-care center. They could succeed, of course, but the net worth of a child-care center would be too low for any financial incentive to exist. Let's talk instead about liability ascending to the Episcopal Church in America. Now, there are some pretty deep pockets! So one of the questions is whether in the era before us child-care centers will be welcome in church facilities. Will they be too expensive? Will they raise new questions about the need for churches to indemnify themselves?

Just as a cautionary note, in recent discussions we have been speaking as though a separate 501(c)(3) organization is a magic tonic. It isn't. It is a good first step. When the pastor's, priest's, or rabbi's study becomes a social services administration office, it may not matter. Faith groups need to know that they will have to alter more than their legal status to comply with the law. That is just one example of how providing a service can ultimately change the character of a religious organization.

In light of these issues, what is the future of church-housed child care itself? Church-housed child care does not exist in a vacuum. Indeed, it exists as a feature in the highly dynamic, ever-changing religious landscape of the American people. You all have heard the statistic that there are more Muslims than Episcopalians in America.[2] That is an indication of what I mean by change.

In March 2001, a Hartford Seminary study found that just over half of all congregations in the United States now have fewer than 100 adults participating in their worship services. Those small congregations still have the educational wing that was there when they had 800 people at worship on Sunday. They still have the space, but they lack other characteristics that they need to offer and manage social programs. In many congregations there also are notable differences that we have not begun to explore, such as socioeconomic status, racial factors, and geographical location. Again, just about half of all churches today are in towns or in suburbs, not in inner-city communities.

I am not qualified to speak for the Jewish community or the Muslim community, but I think that I can speak for child care. Church-based child care is a local response to need at the door. There is a danger in allowing each congregation to respond in any way it wishes to that need. I think there is a distinct possibility that two hermetically sealed strains of church-housed child care may emerge in the United States: one that incorporates child care as a part of its witness and ministry, in faith formation and faith development; and one that offers it as part of its mission identity, unrelated to faith training. The struggle for those of us who care about the whole field of child care will be to understand how the issues of quality, availability, and affordability can be addressed within that two-part picture.

It also is likely that before- and after-school programs will continue to burgeon, as they have since the time of this study. All over the country, congregations, sometimes at the behest of their local school boards and sometimes at the behest of parents, have initiated various after-school programs.

Historic black churches recently developed an extraordinary number of after-school programs in tutoring that are well worth our attention. For so many in the black community, the public school has been a place and an instrument of failure. The church has been a very different place. In the black churches and in nearly every quarter, after-school programs are more numerous.

Another factor in the provision of faith-based services is that available property is often in inverse proportion to need. To use the New York area as an example, a church in affluent Larchmont in Westchester County is likely to have a lot of parking spaces and excellent furnishings, finishings, and so forth. However, there probably are few people looking for entry-level keyboarding skills there. And those who need drug rehabilitation check into some place like a spa in Hilton Head.

Now, the Temple of El Redentor on 167th Street in Manhattan is a storefront church. Its members and friends have need of such programs, but they have very little space. So before we get too excited about the threat of faith-based initiatives breaking down the wall of separation between church and state that we have so long cherished, we ought to remember the inverse proportion of facilities to population in need and scale back our estimate of what is possible.

Continuing with church-state relations, I remember the days in early childhood education when we used to make sure that the churches removed the pictures of Jesus to preserve the secular nature of the services they offered. Every Monday morning those pictures would be put away in a drawer, and every Friday afternoon they would be hung up again so that they were there for Sunday school. We never seemed to bother with the $3.2 million dollar steeple with the crucifix on top that stayed in place all week long. Children are short, and they are young, but they are not stupid! They probably cannot tell you the difference between blood theories and substitutional theories of atonement, but when they see a steeple, they know they are in a church. Hiding the 69-cent picture of Jesus is not what ensures children's religious freedom. It is what is expected, even demanded, of them by adults that determines whether or not their right to religious freedom is honored. And we cannot regulate that with a few ill-conceived rules.

I want to say one final word. Church-housed child care has been a wonderful laboratory for research into and development of child care in America. When we did the National Council of Churches study, we were hampered in some ways that we would not be now, given the advances in computer science. At the time of the study, we sorted the responses into infant care, child care, preschool, and the like. Then we had a box that was labeled "other." In that leftover box, we found magnificent programs. One was in a church in Cherry Valley, Colorado. When we asked them what kind of child care they offered, they said that they had everything, from birth to age 16. When we asked them about their hours of operation, they said that they were open from 5:00 a.m. to 7:00 p.m.—and then they noted, "for four months a year." It turned out that for those four months, women of the church arise at 4:00 a.m. and go out to the fields to pick up the children of the migrant workers who are in town because the crop is ready to be picked. They take the children to the church, where they provide child care, some tutoring, a family meal in the evening, and the like. That is completely off our radar, but it is a great program. Of course, it is operated with private, not public, funds.

There was another place in Florida, across the street from a children's hospital, where a group of senior citizens provide respite care for children with terminal illnesses. They wrote on their form, "We, like the children, are near life's end. Their predicament is not nearly as frightening to us as it is to their parents." They provide child care on a drop-in basis from 10:00 a.m. to 3:00 p.m., three days a week. Parents do not have to say why they need the time off: it may be to fill out insurance forms, to go home to cry, to deal with their other children, to go get their hair done, or to pretend that the whole horrible dream is not happening. We don't know. But because the church is the church, it wants to respond. If those children also are poor, we want them to be fed. And if the church is too poor to feed them, we want a program like Women, Infants, and Children to be available. Those are not programs with religious content, unless kindness and courtesy are considered religious content. So, you can see that sacred places and civic purposes are not as easily distinguished as some have suggested. The venerable example of church-housed child care can offer us much wise counsel as we seek to find our way.

NOTES

1. All data from the National Council of Churches study are reported in Eileen W. Lindner and others, *When Churches Mind the Children: A Study of Day Care in Local Parishes* (National Council of Churches of Christ in the U.S.A., 1983).

2. All church membership data are drawn from the annual *Yearbook of American and Canadian Churches* (Nashville, Tenn.: Abingdon Press, 2001).

Ensuring Quality and Accountability in Faith–Based Child Care

FLOYD FLAKE

After twenty-five years of experience in religion, politics, and a variety of social services, I have reached the conclusion it is possible for faith-based institutions to deliver almost any community or social service. Certainly that is true for daycare. The issue becomes one of delivering daycare without requiring parents to make a faith statement or any statement whatever about their religious beliefs. Religious content of the program should be kept to a minimum, but it should not be a disqualifier.

I have discovered that parents are not looking for religious- or non–religious-based daycare, but quality daycare. If it happens to be religious based and they do not subscribe to that particular religion, it is irrelevant, as long as the child receives a quality daycare education.

Allen Christian School opened on March 1, 2001, offering two kinds of daycare: a private, church-sponsored program with a tuition of $3,800 and a government-funded Head Start program. The programs are operated under separate corporations, and a clear distinction is maintained between the church program and the Head Start program in terms of financial accountability.

If a child cannot be accommodated in the limited spaces in our funded program or any of the other funded programs in the community, parents find the means to pay for our private daycare center. Our church-sponsored daycare center's phenomenal growth is evidence of that: on opening day, people were lined around the corner and we had a waiting list of more than 150 people after filling our spots. The religious devotional programming clearly was not of primary concern to those parents.

What was essential was that the school has a good reputation and that once a child is enrolled, he or she has nearly automatic acceptance into our first-through eighth-grade program. We rarely reject a child who has been inculcated in the system—not the religion, but the system. Parents realize that their child is better able to survive by enrolling in our daycare center because the foundation of the multilayered educational pyramid is sound daycare.

Although I am a supporter of faith-based initiatives and of charitable choice, I have some concerns. I remember the precariousness of the Model Cities era, and I do not want to see a replay of the mistakes that led to the destruction of that program. The process was much too open. People came into the business to provide funding, but once the funds were lost, people who were benefiting from services suddenly were left without them. We do not want to get children, especially, involved in programs that will not survive.

There are three important principles for setting up faith-based daycare. First, there must be some way to analyze capacity. Not every group that wants to deliver daycare services has the pedagogical, academic, or material wherewithal to do so. Not being able to do a qualitative analysis to determine whether providers actually have the capability and capacity to properly run a daycare center ultimately results in failure. There still must be a request for proposals (RFP) process to ensure that capacity can be determined ahead of time.

Second, it is imperative to have a firewall in place once the program is established. Generally, a firewall is maintained by having a congregation's service arm incorporate separately as a 501(c)(3) corporation that speaks specifically to its needs. I have eleven corporations, in part because I run a $29 million operation and I am trying to protect the interests of all components. My child-care component is a totally separate corporation. If the daycare center is involved in a lawsuit because a child got hurt, I do not want the lawsuit to affect the church. So, my liability constraints required that I set up the 501(c)(3). I would argue that, if we are serious about making these programs work, partnerships, which would allow us to serve more children, make sense. However, firewalls must be in place.

Third, I know of too many churches that do not have adequate accounting or bookkeeping procedures. If you commingle federal, state, and city dollars with church dollars, you are headed for disaster. The number of churches that are in operation but remain unincorporated amazes me. I am afraid that those unincorporated entities will see charitable choice as an opportunity to expand, by way of daycare or another program, without recognizing the importance of getting their books straight. If they do not understand accounting principles and refuse to hire professional help, they can open themselves up to some very serious problems.

I would summarize my position this way: I strongly support faith-based child-care initiatives and I strongly support charitable choice, but with a cautionary note: *we have to do this in a way that ensures accountability and quality programs.* We must set standards that do not reflect negatively on the overall principle of involving faith-based institutions in daycare and guarantee that whatever has been promised in response to an RFP is in fact delivered to our children.

Harnessing the Potential of Partnerships without Violating Cherished Values

LISBETH B. SCHORR

Two urgent social problems are central to the discussion of child care in this volume: many more families need good, affordable, out-of-home child care than are now able to obtain it, and many disadvantaged children are arriving at school with the odds already stacked against them because their early needs were neglected. The research and experience of the last few decades can illuminate strategies that could involve faith-based organizations in addressing these problems without violating constitutional or other cherished values.

The data make clear that the nation could not do without church-based child care, in large part because churches offer conveniently located, usually safe, and often inexpensive physical space. The country's dependence on faith-based child care also is related to the many motivations that faith-based organizations have for engaging in child care in the first place. They range from the Jewish mandate to contribute to "repairing the world" to the evangelical view of child care as a way to recruit new members to a particular faith. They also include service to members of the congregation or the neighborhood; the desire to instill the traits, norms, values, and beliefs of a particular culture or faith; the determination to promote pride and hope among marginalized ethnic and racial groups; and the pursuit of social justice by serving low-income or immigrant families and special-needs children.

While some of those motivations make liberals nervous, it is important to note that they are more than incidental to achieving valued social purposes. Motivations to serve, to instill values, and to promote social justice all are potentially powerful promoters of quality services. Many efforts to intervene systematically to improve child and family outcomes are more effective when those making the effort *believe* in what they are doing and when they are *driven by a mission* that transcends the self—characteristics that are sharply at odds with an impersonal, bureaucratic model of service delivery. That means that we have to find ways of promoting urgently needed quality standards in the child-care field without imposing regulations that make it harder to do the job right.

Dorothy Stoneman, founder of YouthBuild, a marvelous youth development and training program, says that YouthBuild encourages staff to bond with trainees by responding to their needs in a way that goes well beyond their job descriptions. Staff give trainees their home telephone numbers and are on call twenty-four hours a day. If youngsters have a personal emergency, such as a death or illness in the family, staff accompany them to funerals and hospitals. Stoneman says, "When staff simply do what they are paid to do, trainees remain agnostic or negative concerning whether the staff really care . . . and can be trusted not to betray or to abandon them." Almost every successful human service program I have studied points in some way to the importance of going above and beyond the call of duty if staff are to help participants learn to trust. An obvious show of caring is an important signal to parents and youth that this experience will be different.

Professionals, managers, and agencies seeking to redefine professionalism to ensure quality standards while supporting more personal interaction do not simply go with whatever feels right. Rather, they function within the boundaries of well-developed standards and theories of effective practice while pushing the constraints imposed by job descriptions and bureaucracies.

That is why I believe that we have to contend not only with the church-state problem, but also with the tension between bureaucracy and effectiveness. When churches or other organizations that pride themselves on their flexibility and responsiveness worry that their effectiveness will be undermined once they become subject to government rules and regulations, theirs is a realistic fear. The landscape is littered with social programs that were highly successful as pilots but that were demolished, or at the very least diluted into ineffectiveness, as soon as they scaled up. The need for child care is so urgent and so widespread that we have to make sure, on one hand, that every source of care that meets quality standards and protects constitutional, individual, and civil rights is enlisted. On the other, we have to make sure that mainstream funding does not bring with it inappropriate, self-defeating regulations that undermine the very attributes that made a pilot program effective.

The Bush administration is shining a spotlight on the government rules, regulations, funding patterns, and accountability requirements that can interfere with the effective operation of promising faith-based initiatives. I join E. J. Dionne Jr. in his hope that "these faith-based efforts might become a small oasis of nonpartisan possibility." But I would like to see that oasis enlarged. I am hopeful that the new interest in flexible programming also will encourage the search for ways to make government more supportive of all community-based initiatives—faith-based and others—that produce results because they are mission driven, relationship oriented, and responsive to local needs . . . and because their staffs believe in what they are doing.

My plea, then, is that we pay attention not just to the church-state problem, but also to the bureaucracy-effectiveness issue. We must figure out how to harness those aspects of bureaucracy that are essential to promoting both quality and accountability (as the military has done so successfully in the child-care field) while shedding those aspects that undermine our best efforts.

If we want to see models that have worked in a ten-block radius enlarged in scale to serve all the community's children, we have to face up to the funding implications. We have to stop thinking that we can get the same results when the inputs are diminished because we are determined to do it on the cheap. We also must face up to the equally formidable barriers raised by the rules that govern how money is spent, who is eligible, what the service mix is, who determines compliance, and how results are measured.

Let us commit new energy and resources to figuring out how programs operating with public funds can promote the values of love, respect, and service (which, as many authors in this book point out, can transcend dogma and doctrine) while protecting participants from being coerced into conversion.

Let us commit new energy and resources to figuring out how to ensure that program providers can hire people who share the program's convictions about the possibilities of human redemption and how to prevent them from hiring people on the basis of sectarian convictions or affiliation.

Let us commit new energy and resources to figuring out how to monitor and evaluate programs that are truly community based, that change every day in response to changing circumstances, and that operate with a significant number of what social scientists call "unobservables."

In my work in a variety of successful social programs, I repeatedly have seen evidence that being part of a movement that transcends the individual's material needs contributes to success—whether the movement springs from religious, political, ethnic, or ideological roots. Paul Light, director of governmental studies at the Brookings Institution, has written that one cannot underestimate the importance of faith as a core value that makes it possible to persevere in the face of stress, uncertainty, and disappointment. That faith, he found in his study of effective organizations, may be "rooted in formal religion, culture, one's vision of a just society, or simply confidence in human capacity." I would like to think that together we can find ways to permit all organizations operating on principles that rise above the forces of the marketplace to become a solid and significant part of the effort to alleviate our most urgent social problems.

>━━●━━<

Church–Based Child Care in Rural Areas

DIANA JONES WILSON

Although the need for child care is great in rural areas, the supply is scarce. Child care is less available in rural than in urban areas, and even when it does exist, rural parents are less able to afford it. Public dollars are failing to reach many poor rural families that are eligible for child-care subsidies, yet working mothers make significant contributions to their families' income and to the rural economy.

The North Carolina Rural Economic Development Center established the Church Child Care Initiative in 1993. Its goal was to increase the number of church-based child-care programs available to rural children, with special emphasis on helping children from poor families that were eligible for but not currently receiving help from Head Start and other public programs.

The Rural Economic Development Center looked to the one entity that existed in most communities—the church. Through a policy forum and a series of meetings and workshops, we began to understand the issues and myths that prevented the church from engaging in subsidized child care. During the early 1990s in North Carolina, where eighty-five of the state's 100 counties are considered rural, counties were returning subsidies because they had no child-care centers in which to use them. A significant number of families, however, needed child care. The establishment of the Child Care Loan Guarantee Fund by the state legislature as a pilot program for distressed counties addressed some of the capital requirements for rural child-care programs, including faith-based programs. We initiated efforts to equip churches to offer licensed programs capable of addressing the issues of child-care quality and affordability.

Discussions regarding quality care often reference the *Cost, Quality, and Child Outcomes in Child Care Centers* study released in 1995. A secondary analysis indicates there are two categories of churches involved in child care: those that operate child-care programs as a mission and those that operate them as a source of income. Richard Clifford, a researcher at the University of North Carolina–Chapel Hill and coauthor of the study, recently stated, "It looks like there are some churches that operate child care as a mission, and they tend to be pretty high quality. Other churches operate child care as a business to increase church revenue; they do not seem as concerned about quality."[1]

The Church Child Care Initiative joins organizations such as the Ecumenical Child Care Network at the national level to encourage faith-based child-care programs to operate as separate 501(c)(3) nonprofit corporations. The nonprofit designation gives rural faith-based programs the option of tapping the community for expertise that might not otherwise be available to a small rural congregation, increasing the likelihood of quality programs, sound program management, and fiscal accountability.

Policymakers and funders should not make the mistake of pitting child-care programs in rural areas against those in the inner cities when they decide how to allocate funds. The need for child care exists in both places. However, rural children and providers may have "extra-special" needs because of the limited resources available for and within rural communities. And when engaging the faith community in child care, you cannot craft one set of policies for one denomination and another set for another denomination—or exclude any groups, whether formal denominations or faith-based groups that are not affiliated with a formal denomination. The needs of children transcend that kind of categorizing of care as rural or urban, denominational or nondenominational.

How do you get denominations and independent churches to understand that they have a calling to deal with the needs of "the least of these"? You demystify child care. You help churches understand quality; you introduce them to child-care licensing experts as "partners," as a resource to help them provide quality programs. You take a program that might be extremely complex and technical and break it down as we have in the guidebook *A Child at the Door*. This guidebook helps churches understand how to embrace child care—how to prepare a sound needs assessment and business plan and how to deal with licensing, sanitation, and health issues in the planning process. Introducing regulatory issues and personnel at the beginning establishes a resource base and builds partnerships, thereby enabling churches to avoid costly mistakes.

The Church Child Care Initiative also provides consultants to facilitate planning sessions. How do you equip churches so that planning takes place, so that the congregation has a sense of ownership in the program, so that there is a partnership? The resources of the church must be recognized so that the advantages of providing faith-based child care are recognized and facilities that can offer services to children are no longer empty.

The initiative has worked to provide those services. We have built partnerships along the way. When we talk to members of the state general assembly about resources, we do not say that we want to take child-care funds from the fifteen urban counties to give them to our eighty-five rural counties. We ask how we can come together to deal with the needs of all the children. We say let us find more dollars for the urban areas if there is a greater need; however, let us also provide adequate resources to meet the rural child-care crisis. We believe that a thoughtful discussion of the church's ministry to children among policymakers and leaders of the faith community can prove to be a turning point—one that will open eyes, challenge complacency, and stimulate personal as well as collective action.

NOTE

1. Personal telephone conversation, spring 2001.

The Child-Care Trilemma
and Faith-Based Care

JUDITH C. APPELBAUM

The "trilemma" of child care summarized in Mary Bogle's chapter—the challenge of addressing availability, affordability, and quality without sacrificing any of those goals in the service of the others—is well known. In an era when more than 70 percent of American women with children are in the paid labor force, the demand for child care is at an all-time high. But for many, high-quality care is too expensive or just not available.

There is no mystery about how to tackle these problems effectively. Several European countries have done it. Closer to home, the U.S. military's transformation of the military child-care system into a model for the nation demonstrates that a comprehensive system of affordable, high-quality child care is attainable if the necessary steps are taken—such as improving caregiver training and compensation to increase professionalism and reduce turnover, implementing and enforcing comprehensive standards, and subsidizing the cost so that all families have access to good care.[1]

In the civilian realm, the Child Care and Development Block Grant (CCDBG), enacted in 1990, addresses at least part of the child-care trilemma by providing funds to the states for child-care subsidies for low- and moderate-income families. A critically needed program, the CCDBG remains severely underfunded; the U.S. Department of Health and Human Services estimates that currently CCDBG subsidies reach only 12 percent of eligible families.

There is little doubt that faith-based organizations make an important contribution to meeting the need for child care. Sectarian child care expands the array of options for parents, although to the extent that it entails the inculcation of religious teachings, it cannot be a serious option for families that do not share those beliefs. And sectarian care may offer affordable care for some families, especially to the extent that faith-based providers take advantage of public subsidies, as the CCDBG allows them to do when the funds flow through certificates (vouchers) to the parents, rather than through direct state grants to or contracts with providers.

Some quality concerns do arise, however. Bogle indicates that the quality of child care in at least some faith-based settings tends to be lower than in other settings. That is undoubtedly related to the fact that in many states, religious child care is exempt from the licensing requirements and regulations that apply generally to child care—notwithstanding strong evidence that vigorous enforcement of strong standards, as in the military system, is essential to ensuring high-quality care.

Another problem is that quality cannot be addressed effectively through a voucher-based system, which is the only way that public funds are permitted to flow to sectarian care under the CCDBG. Quality improvements are possible only through investments in the system's infrastructure, for example, by allocating funds to help states with licensing and enforcement or to help individual programs meet higher standards. Vouchers that enable individual families to defray the cost of care will never lead to systemic reforms.

Moreover, when public dollars flow to sectarian institutions, the church-state issues do not evaporate just because support is provided through vouchers. When the CCDBG was passed, some supporters were uncomfortable with the voucher approach for that reason and some legal scholars expressed doubts about its constitutionality. Others cited precedents suggesting that the Constitution permits public support for sectarian institutions when the individual recipient of assistance makes an independent choice about where to spend the money, as is the case with vouchers. The constitutionality of vouchers for religious child care under the CCDBG has not been tested in the courts.

Legal issues aside, those with misgivings about the appropriateness of spending public funds directly on sectarian activities could raise the same concerns about support provided through vouchers. Whether spent directly or provided through vouchers, public funds can end up paying for materials or services with religious content, such as an overtly religious curriculum. The chapter by Fred Davie and his colleagues suggests one of the benefits of faith-based child care is that within most faith traditions there are universal values (like respect for oneself and one's neighbors) that transcend dogma and doctrine. But there is no guarantee that those values, or only those values, are transmitted by every sectarian program—as opposed to, for example, promoting the subordination of women or antipathy to other religions or to racial minorities. Indeed, the fact that a child-care program is sectarian is neither necessary nor sufficient to ensure that the positive values identified by Davie and others will be inculcated in the children.

Finally, concerns about employment discrimination also arise when public funds are used to support sectarian programs that hire and fire employees on the basis of religion or religious tenets (which CCDBG allows when the funds flow through vouchers) or programs that in effect discriminate on the basis of sex by, for example, refusing to employ unmarried mothers—but not unmarried fathers—because of a religious objection to the women's conduct.

The CCDBG has become a cornerstone of federal child-care policy and indeed should be significantly expanded. However, the balancing act that it embodies, which aims to maximize parental choice while avoiding direct public funding of sectarian activities, is not perfect. More extensive analysis should be done before a similar approach is considered for areas beyond the complicated and unique world of child care.

NOTE

1. See National Women's Law Center, *Be All That We Can Be: Lessons from the Military for Improving Our Nation's Child Care System* (Washington: 2000), available at www.nwlc.org.

PART SIX

Should Government Help
Faith-Based Charity?

CHAPTER SIXTEEN

Compassion in Truth and Action: What Washington Can Not Do to Help

JOHN J. DiIULIO JR.

In "Rallying the Armies of Compassion," the blueprint for the White House Office on Faith-Based and Community Initiatives, President George W. Bush states:

> Government cannot be replaced by charities, but it can and should welcome them as partners. We must heed the growing consensus across America that successful government social programs work in fruitful partnership with community-serving and faith-based organizations—whether run by Methodists, Muslims, Mormons, or good people of no faith at all.[1]

The consensus cited by the president runs wide and deep. Americans of every socioeconomic status and demographic description have faith in faith-based and community approaches to solving social problems.

Solid survey data compiled over several decades by George Gallup Jr. and associates indicate that most citizens—including 86 percent of blacks and 60 percent of whites in 1995—believe that religion can help "answer all or most of today's problems." The same week that the president signed my office into being, the Pew Charitable Trusts released a national poll showing that most Americans believe that "local churches, synagogues, or mosques," together with "organizations such as the Salvation Army, Goodwill Industries, and Habitat for Humanity," are top problem-solving organizations in their communities. Americans appreciate our community helpers and healers, and so should our government.

This chapter was adapted from a speech delivered before the National Association of Evangelicals, Dallas, Texas, March 7, 2001.

Metaphorically speaking, community-serving faith-based organizations are the army ants of civil society, daily leveraging ten times their human and financial weight in social good. Or, as I have elsewhere described them, they are the paramedics of urban civil society, saving lives and restoring health, answering emergencies with miracles.

But, make no mistake: while faith-based organizations can supplement and strengthen public social service programs, they can by no means substitute for government support. To dramatize the point, just consider that even if all 353,000 religious congregations in America doubled their annual budgets and devoted them entirely to the cause and even if the cost of government social welfare programs was magically cut by one-fifth, the congregations would barely cover a year's worth of Washington's spending on those programs and never even come close to covering total program costs.

Compassionate Conservatism for Church-State Separation

President Bush has been steadfast in articulating a caring, common-sense vision of compassionate conservatism, one that enlists government effort but resists government growth. His vision comprehends both the strengths and limits of faith-based and community initiatives. It calls on the rest of us to help those who help the "least of these" by giving them more of our own time and more of our own money.

Compassionate conservatism warmly welcomes people of faith back into the public square while respecting and upholding, without fail, our constitutional traditions governing church, state, and civic pluralism. It fosters model public-private partnerships so that community-based organizations, religious and non-religious, can work together and across racial, denominational, urban-suburban, and other divides to achieve civic results.

And it challenges Washington to work overtime and in a bipartisan fashion to ensure that tax-supported social programs and the nonprofit organizations that help to administer those programs are performance managed, performance measured, and open to competition from qualified community-serving organizations, large or small, new or old, sacred or secular.

Why an Office of Faith-Based and Community Initiatives?

The White House Office of Faith-Based and Community Initiatives aims to do several interrelated things.

First, we aim to boost charitable giving, of both human and financial resources. The first financial boosts are in the president's budget plan, which

among other things would permit the 80 million taxpayers who do not itemize deductions—70 percent of all taxpayers—to deduct charitable contributions. The human boosts are embodied in the president's use of the bully pulpit
to affirm the value of volunteers and in the hopes of Stephen Goldsmith, former mayor of Indianapolis, for retooling AmeriCorps in ways that put col-
lege-educated, public-spirited young adults at the disposal of the small
faith-based and community organizations that need them. (AmeriCorps already has people in urban community-serving ministries and such, but we aim
to refine and enlarge their participation on behalf of needy children, youth,
and families.)

Second, we are authorized to form centers and conduct program audits in
five Cabinet agencies—Justice, Labor, Education, Health and Human Services,
and Housing and Urban Development. That is easily the most crucial but least
well understood part of our mission. It is about paving the path to civic results
through greater government solicitude for faith-based and community organizations—the real civic rationale for charitable choice.

In sum, since the end of World War II, virtually every domestic program that
Washington has funded in whole or in part has been administered not by federal civil servants alone (there are about 2 million of those today, roughly the
same number as in 1960), but by federal workers in conjunction with state and
local government employees, for-profit firms, and nonprofit organizations.

Certain nonprofit organizations, both religious and secular, have long been
funded in whole or in part through this federal "government-by-proxy" system.
Some, no doubt, deserve their privileged positions in that system because they
have produced measurable civic results. Others, however, are in simply because
they are in. Despite a far-reaching 1993 federal law requiring federal agencies
to do performance-managed, performance-measured grant making, you still can
count on your fingers and toes the number of government-by-proxy programs
that have really put nonprofit providers to the test.

If many nonprofits in the government-by-proxy network have never had any
meaningful performance evaluation; if their claims of greater capacity are based
mainly on their bigger staffs; and if their public pose as providers of "up close
and personal" services to the citizens whom they serve are belied by the fact
that they have more personnel in the suites than on the streets, then—purely
in the interest of helping those in need while generating a better return on the
public's investment in social programs—why should the leaders of qualified
community and faith-based organizations, local groups that really do serve the
poor and have been doing so for years, not be able, if they so choose, to seek
partial government funding on the same basis as any other nongovernment
provider of social services?

WHAT IS CHARITABLE CHOICE FOR?

Community and faith-based groups *should* be able to seek government funding, and that is why President Bush has directed my office to help level the federal funding playing field to "encourage and support the work of charities and faith-based and community groups," including small ones "that offer help and love one person at a time."

> These groups are working in every neighborhood in America, to fight homelessness and addiction and domestic violence, to provide a hot meal or a mentor or a safe haven for our children. Government should welcome these groups to apply for funds, not discriminate against them.[2]

That is also precisely what charitable choice is about. What, exactly, is charitable choice, how does it "welcome" faith-based organizations to the federal government-by-proxy fold, and what, if any, real church-state or other problems does it pose? Let me highlight some of the main points.

In brief, President Clinton signed charitable choice into law on August 22, 1996; thus it has been on the books for five years now. It was a largely bipartisan and by-consensus provision in the otherwise uproarious debate over the 1996 federal welfare law (the Personal Responsibility and Work Opportunity Reconciliation Act of 1996). Essentially, it covered temporary assistance to needy families and welfare-to-work funding. Another charitable choice provision passed in 1998 (part of the Community Services Block Grant), and yet another, reaching some faith-based drug treatment programs, passed in two separate bills last year. Five years ago, charitable choice was a little-noticed landmark. Today, it is a much-noticed, mainstream, landmark.

Under charitable choice legislation, both religious and secular community-serving organizations can seek federal support on the same basis as any other nongovernment for-profit or not-for-profit provider of services. Sacred places that serve civic purposes can seek federal (or federal-state) funding without having to divest themselves of their religious iconography.

As Stephen Monsma has documented, for decades the sacred and secular have mixed in the administration of hundreds of taxpayer-supported programs. By some estimates, for example, one-third or more of all daycare programs in low-income urban neighborhoods with high concentrations of welfare-to-work recipients are provided by faith-based organizations.[3]

However, as Monsma shows, all too many other laws and regulations do not clearly authorize such involvement. Charitable choice gives community-serving religious nonprofits and government officials specific guidelines that legitimate and guide the participation of faith-based organizations in federally funded programs.

To wit, faith-based providers that receive any public money cannot discriminate against beneficiaries on the basis of race, color, gender, age, national origin, disability, or religion. Regarding religion, charitable choice reinforces federal antidiscrimination laws by explicitly prohibiting participating faith-based organizations from denying service to anyone "on the basis of religion, a religious belief, or refusal to actively participate in a religious practice."

Moreover, government must provide beneficiaries with religious objections to receiving services from a faith-based organization with an equivalent secular alternative, without placing an undue burden on the beneficiary (no ridiculously long drives and such). And, according to the statutes, if government fails to provide ample and equivalent secular alternatives, if its actions have the effect of "diminishing the religious freedom of beneficiaries of assistance," then beneficiaries may enforce their rights against the government in a private cause of action for injunctive relief.

In addition, federal law has long required an independent audit by a certified public accountant of any group, religious or secular, that receives more than $300,000 a year in government funds. Charitable choice flatly prohibits federal funds from being used "for sectarian worship, instruction, or proselytization." In the case of faith-based groups, charitable choice favors segregated accounts—so do I—and only the walled-off government accounts used for public purposes may be audited.

Despite these hefty and wholesome protections, critics variously charge charitable choice with seven supposedly deadly sins. To alliterate, let's call them "huge leaks, horrible louts, hiring loopholes, and hijacked faith," plus "bogus alternatives, bloated agencies, and beltway business-as-usual."

Huge leaks? Some critics of charitable choice assert that, even when religious organizations form 501(c)(3) entities, there is no effective way to segregate fiscal accounts. Money, they remind us, is fungible, and tax dollars will leak between Bible studies and soup kitchens.

Well, money is fungible in the entire government-by-proxy network. Anyone who has ever worked in or studied secular nonprofits that get government grants knows that funds sometimes leak between projects. But government has adequate ways to detect and minimize that leakage, and there is nothing about religious or secular community-based organizations that places them beyond the reach of personnel, procurement, and other relevant protocols.

Horrible louts? Others wrongly suppose that disagreeable, even hate-mongering, individuals and organizations that call themselves religious somehow will suddenly become eligible for federal funding under charitable choice. For starters, what the Constitution requires of government is equal treatment, neither favoring nor disfavoring groups because they are religious. The federal government will not distribute funds on a religious basis. Funds must go to nongovernment providers, religious or secular, that meet all relevant anti-discrimination laws, procurement procedures, and performance protocols.

Second, before charitable choice, any organization that could fill out a grant application and afford the postage to send it in could apply for federal support. Some religious or quasi-religious groups that many citizens find offensive did so, and some got contracts for particular services. With and since charitable choice, the law still applies. But by making it easier for all qualified community-based organizations to become part of Washington's government-by-proxy network, charitable choice will, if anything, increase competition, raise performance standards, and thereby make it less likely than before that groups more interested in advocacy than in service will obtain grants.

Third, currently there are many federally funded secular nonprofits that represent ideological (as opposed to theological) worldviews that are offensive to many Americans (for example, the American Civil Liberties Union and Planned Parenthood). In some cases, their approach to service delivery is rather plainly anchored more in their ideology than in any empirical evidence about what works or in any independent confirmation of the efficacy of their program.

Still, the Constitution gives taxpayers no right to insist that government decisions, including procurement decisions, not offend their sense of morality. Evenhanded performance standards, not illegal, a priori blacklists, have been and continue to be the best constitutional method for keeping horrible louts, religious or secular, out of the game.

Hiring loopholes? Under section 702, Title VII, of the Civil Rights Act of 1964, religious organizations are permitted to discriminate in employment decisions on the basis of religion. Charitable choice preserves that thirty-seven-year-old right. Should receiving public money require religious organizations to hire people who are not co-religionists and who may be actively opposed to their beliefs, benevolent traditions, and service goals? As Jeffrey Rosen pointed out in an essay in the *New Republic*:

> Without the ability to discriminate on the basis of religion in hiring and firing staff, religious organizations lose the right to define their organizational mission enjoyed by secular organizations that receive public funds. . . . Planned Parenthood may refuse to hire those who don't share its views about abortion; equal treatment requires that churches, mosques, and synagogues have the same right to discriminate. The Supreme Court accepted this reasoning in 1988, when it upheld religious nonprofits' exemption from the federal law prohibiting religious discrimination. And by extending this exemption to religious groups that receive government funds, the charitable-choice law is careful to insist that these groups can discriminate in the hiring of staff but not in the treatment of beneficiaries.[4]

Critics who contend that Title VII furnishes religious organizations with a special hiring loophole are simply wrong, unless by "hiring loophole" they mean "equal treatment." To accept ideological reasons for employment discrimination as legitimate while rejecting theological ones out of hand is to arbitrarily, unfairly, and—or so I believe the courts will find—unconstitutionally relegate the civil rights of religious individuals in the public square to a limbo of lesser moral, intellectual, and civic significance. Besides, all government-funded nonprofit organizations ought to be judged by whether they follow all relevant laws and achieve measurable, positive civic results.

Furthermore, the Title VII controversy is so heated because critics assume that the extent to which community-serving ministries engage in religion-based employment discrimination is so vast. Especially in urban America, that is not a safe assumption. For starters, remember that we are talking mainly about volunteer organizations. "Employment," save for the minister and an assistant pastor or two, often is a moot issue, and any organization with fifteen or fewer paid employees can take religion into account in hiring without having to invoke the exemption. The vast majority of urban community-serving ministries and faith-based organizations have far fewer than fifteen paid employees; most have only one or two.

Next, while no reliable data are yet available, my last six years studying the ways and means of urban community-serving ministries all across the country tell me that typically theirs is an all-hands-on-deck world in which people of all faiths—and of no faith—are "employed," as volunteers or paid staff, as long as they will enter the prisons, change the bedpans, counsel the probated juvenile, tutor the inner-city child, and so on.

Finally, among other "areas of agreement concerning government funding of religious organizations to provide social services," the American Jewish Committee's *In Good Faith* document, which also appears in this volume, correctly advises:

> The Supreme Court has not addressed whether a religious organization retains the liberty to make employment decisions on the basis of religion in the case of employees who work in programs or activities funded (in whole or in part) by, or paid with, government money. [W]e agree that religious organizations retain their ability to use religious criteria in employment for those positions in nongovernmental programs that are wholly privately funded, regardless of whether other programs or activities of the organization receive government funds.[5]

That is right, and it is important. We will defend the right of religious organizations to take religion into account in making employment decisions. When and if the Court rules, we naturally will follow its decision and reasoning both in letter and in spirit. Even if the Court ruled that a church-based program that receives public funds thereby loses its Title VII exemption, it would not follow that in all "non-governmental programs that are wholly privately funded" the parent church itself would, too. And neither, of course, would the long-standing tax-exempt status of religious organizations be affected.

Hijacked faith? Some religious leaders, especially of conservative evangelical Christian communities of faith, have worried out loud that religious bodies that receive government support will, over time, become dependent on Caesar's coin. In turn, they fear, partnerships of government and faith-based organizations will enervate the spiritual nature of the participating churches and stifle their prophetic voices. Even if public support is strictly applied to specific social service programs, they fear, the resulting secularizing influence will put churches on the super-slippery slope to losing the "faith" in "faith-based." And, despite the fact that charitable choice protects participating religious organizations from having to divest themselves of their religious symbols and such, it does, as they correctly note, require them to meet all relevant federal antidiscrimination and other laws, to ensure that program funds are not spent for religious worship, and so on.

Such concerns are entirely understandable, and for many faith communities they should be the deciding factor. Charitable choice ought to be open to all qualified community-serving groups, but not all groups ought to participate. Faith leaders, organizations, and communities that perceive the slope as slippery and secularizing simply ought to opt out.

But, in all fairness, let's remember that the types of public-private partnerships that America's faith communities form are as diverse as their theological understandings. In particular, compared with predominantly ex-urban white evangelical churches, urban African American and Latino communities of faith have traditions and histories that make them generally more dedicated to the mission of serving the community and generally more confident about engaging public and secular partners in achieving that mission without compromising their spiritual or religious identity. To be sure, there also are many urban clergy who want nothing whatsoever to do with government. But the "hijacked faith" fears expressed by some are less pointed and less prevalent in metropolitan America. Finally, the concern that nonprofit organizations can grow overly dependent on government funds must be taken seriously, but no more seriously for religious than for secular ones. While there are no well-researched rules for avoiding that fate, it seems clear that once any organization, religious or secular, receives more than one-quarter to one-half of its funding from any single source, it risks its independence and ability to remain faithful to its core values and original missions. Among other reasons, that is why, as I will explain, performance-based contracting should be short term and why, with respect to the so-called Compassion Capital Fund proposed by President Bush, the federal contribution would constitute no more than one-quarter of the total funds of any model public-private community-serving program, religious or secular.

Bogus alternatives? As discussed, charitable choice requires government to provide beneficiaries of services with an equivalent secular alternative to faith-based programs. Still, some worry that even with the best intentions and most stringent administration, the government will not be able to honor that guarantee.

Providing an alternative in rural areas might be quite a challenge. So far, though, as a Center for Public Justice study last year by Amy Sherman shows, officials are doing just fine.[6] In the nine states she investigated, there were only two instances in which a person needing help requested a secular alternative to the faith-based provider, and officials immediately provided that alternative. Since in the past officials typically contracted with secular programs, charitable choice most likely will increase the options available in rural and urban areas rather than diminish them. In any case, charitable choice requires government officials to find a way to provide that secular alternative. We will hold to that requirement.

Bloated agencies? I have heard reports and read magazine articles asserting that my office would have more than 100 employees, mostly new hires, and require an explosion in state and local government employment to monitor and manage the billions of dollars that will come coursing through the Department of Education alone. Not so.

The office opened on February 20, 2001. The core office staff, me included, is composed of nine people, including support staff. The five Cabinet centers, when fully operational, will have a total of fewer than forty workers (they now have only five), many of them assigned career public servants, not new hires. The five audits will recommend changes in regulations that discriminate against qualified community-based providers, religious and secular. Those recommendations could be accepted or rejected. If accepted, they could in due course result in changes that affect the granting of billions of dollars. The White House office does not disburse grants itself, but rather works to help ensure that federal programs are as accessible, open, and hospitable to faith-based groups as they are to others.

Beltway business-as-usual? Some have asserted or insinuated that, because charitable choice provisions have passed four times and despite the problems that we ourselves have identified with its implementation to date, our "real endgame" is simply to ram another set of charitable choice laws through Congress, claim political credit, pacify interested constituencies, and, win or lose, be able to say that we made good on President Bush's campaign promises.

Anyone who believes that does not understand how close to the president's heart faith-based and community initiatives are. That is why we are taking a deliberative approach, first conducting our audits, studying competing ideas, and assessing other perspectives and looking forward to forging model public-private partnerships later. That is why we are following our principles, correcting misconceptions, and reaching out widely.

COMPASSION CAPITAL: SEEDING PUBLIC-PRIVATE PROGRAMS

In addition to increasing charitable giving, leveling the federal funding playing field, and improving government-by-proxy programs through performance-based grant making and charitable choice, our fourth goal is to seed or expand selected model public-private programs that involve community-based organizations in meeting civic needs.

Washington must look for such models beyond the beltway. It must look to mayors and local leaders like Philadelphia's Mayor John F. Street, who beat the president to the punch by establishing his own Office of Faith-Based and Voluntary Action in city hall last year. On New Year's Day of 2001, Mayor Street, joined by four-score of local clergy, visited inmates in the city's prisons.

The Compassion Capital Fund proposed by the president would provide federal matching funds to model public-private initiatives that harness the strengths of community-based organizations, religious and secular, and hold promise of being able to address unmet civic needs on a citywide or national scale. While we are still discussing the framework of the fund (there are several federal precedents worth examining), my hope and expectation is that it will be structured and administered so as to implement the president's idea of devolution: "Resources are to be devolved, not just to the States, but to the neighborhood healers who need them most."[7]

Ideally, beyond any seeding phase, fund support would never constitute more than twenty-five cents of any fully operational, at-scale program dollar, with the rest coming from local government, private, corporate, or philanthropic support. Where possible and appropriate, secular nonprofits could serve as lead agencies.

POSTSCRIPT: *ENLIGHTENED STATESMEN* V. *FACTIONS*

The foregoing essay was adapted from the much longer text of a speech that I gave in March 2001. In the half-year between then and September 2001:

—The U.S House of Representatives passed the Community Solutions Act, which is broadly consistent with the principles and goals of President Bush's plan to encourage faith-based and community initiatives.

—The five Cabinet centers completed their first annual departmentwide performance audits, documenting various barriers to the full and fair participation of qualified grassroots groups in federal social service delivery programs. The White House Office of Faith-Based and Community Initiatives summarized the main findings of the audits in an aptly entitled report, *Unlevel Playing Field,* which was released at a Brookings Institution public forum.

—Former mayor of Indianapolis Stephen Goldsmith, board chairman of the Corporation for National Service (CNS), worked with me in identifying ways to increase technical assistance for community-serving, volunteer-based organizations, both sacred and secular. CNS and the White House Office planned a joint task force.

—Hundreds of independent sector leaders, religious and secular, representing virtually every race, ethnic group, religion, and region, endorsed the president's call for more public-private partnerships to benefit the needy and neglected, as did organizations such as the U.S. Conference of Mayors.

—The faith initiatives debate raged among the policy elite, in the press, and in Washington, D.C., but awareness of and support for providing more public help to sacred places serving civic purposes exploded in communities from coast to coast. One indicator: Our early town meetings on the issue in cities across the country drew crowds of a few hundred, but by July, during my last town meeting at a church in Brooklyn, New York, nearly 3,000 folks came—early on a Saturday morning.

—Sticking with the 180-day plan that brought me to the White House in January—and with the legislative, administrative, and outreach missions that President Bush had asked me to initiate all duly launched or accomplished—I announced in August that I would be returning home to Philadelphia once a new director was in place.

A week after the House bill passed in July, I joined the president and my good friends U.S. Senator Joseph Lieberman, Democrat of Connecticut, and U.S. Senator Rick Santorum, Republican of Pennsylvania, in the Oval Office to discuss the next steps. Shortly thereafter, Senator Santorum announced that, as far as he was concerned, the charitable choice (or, as he prefers, "beneficiary choice") provisions of any Senate bill should neither add to nor subtract from the existing body of civil rights and, to the extent possible, ought to mirror kindred provisions enacted previously, with bipartisan majorities, under President Clinton. Likewise, earlier in July, Senator Lieberman, speaking at a Democratic Leadership Council meeting, exhorted his fellow Democrats to express whatever differences they may have with specific provisions of the House bill—or with the president's broader vision—but to do so in a manner that caused no one to suppose that Democrats are somehow uniformly and reflexively hostile to fellow citizens who (as the Senator has so eloquently phrased it) "serve God with gladness" by serving their own communities' disadvantaged children, youth, and families.

Numerous Democratic leaders, including former United Nations Ambassador and mayor of Atlanta Andrew Young and Philadelphia Mayor John Street, have strongly echoed Senator Lieberman's intraparty counsel. As the senator told *USA Today* in early September, "It won't be easy, but I do think that we can come together and find common ground."

In President Bush and Senator Lieberman, we are blessed to have genuinely public-spirited leaders who truly care about increasing support—public and private, human and financial—for community-serving organizations, both religious and secular, that truly do the Lord's work among the least, the last, and the lost of our society. The president has consistently stressed that while "government cannot be replaced by charities, it must welcome them as partners, not resent them as rivals." The senator has consistently argued that government at all levels should become more open to addressing social problems by partnering with faith-based and community organizations.

Thus, much common ground already exists; but, as Founding Father and chief author of the Constitution James Madison himself might advise, in this case whether it can be built on must depend largely on the extent to which our most "enlightened statesmen" can overcome the "factions" that beset their respective parties.

In Federalist Paper Number Ten, Madison defines a "faction" as any group of citizens, whether it encompasses a vast majority or a tiny minority, that attempts to advance its ideas or interests at the expense of other citizens' rights and well-being and that does so in ways that conflict with "the permanent and aggregate interests of the community," or the greater "public good." The "causes of faction" are "sown" into human nature, and the most fertile soil for factions include "a zeal for different opinions concerning religion." Wise and public-spirited leaders, Madison says, must "adjust these clashing interests and render them all subservient to the public good."

The issue of the role of sacred places in serving public purposes presently is beset by at least two species of minority factions that, for lack of better appellations, may be termed *orthodox secularists* and *orthodox sectarians*.

Many individuals and organizations have legitimate concerns about the implications of both existing and proposed charitable choice laws for Americans' constitutional rights, civil rights, and civil liberties. They are to be distinguished from orthodox secularists, mostly on the political left, who—while often paying lip service to the good works done by faith-based organizations and the right of religious people to enter the public square, *as religious people,* and participate fully in civic life—insist that government foster or fund religious activities and programs only if they are nominally religious or thoroughly secularized.

Likewise, many individuals and organizations have legitimate concerns about keeping the "faith" in "faith-based," including many Christian conservatives who have venerable theological reasons for avoiding any other than incidental contact with government. They are to be distinguished from orthodox sectarians who, far from insisting on strict church-state separation, insist that public social welfare service delivery funds be used for expressly religious purposes, including worship services and proselytization, who further insist that the programs they favor are far more efficacious than less pervasively sectarian and strictly secular alternatives, and who dismiss any constitutional, empirical, or other arguments to the contrary as antireligious.

The minority factions are magnets for other factious individuals and groups that threaten to turn the healthy debate over how best to support sacred places in advancing civic purposes into a bloody battleground over other issues—supporting or opposing homosexual rights and state and local laws governing the same; supporting or opposing delivery of social welfare programs funded in whole or in part by the federal government, the vast majority of which now are statutorily administered through direct grants and indirect disbursement arrangements including vouchers; and so on.

Each minority faction, it seems, issues weekly or monthly political ultimatums. The best way for our enlightened statesmen—and the rest of us—to respond is with corresponding invitations to search for common ground in accordance with what President Bush himself has repeatedly referred to as his own guiding principles on the issue: evenhandedness, neutrality, nondiscrimination, a desire for better civic results, and a respect for pluralism.

Take, for example, Title VII and the question of faith-based organizations' right to take religion into account in hiring. In principle, President Bush, Senator Lieberman, most other leaders, and most Americans agree that that right ought to be upheld, but they may differ on how to balance it against competing rights and liberties when public funds are involved. Those differences, however, except at the factious extremes, do not appear to be so broad as to prevent bipartisan cooperation in the public interest. *In Good Faith*, a document developed by the American Jewish Committee and included in this volume, as well as statements prepared by the constitutional and legal beagles in the White House Office of Faith-Based and Community Initiatives and available upon request are roadmaps for resolving reasonable Title VII differences. I think the actual differences can be measured in inches, not miles, and accommodated along the lines advocated by Senator Santorum.

Or, take the issue of how literally thousands of government social welfare programs are presently administered. In principle, President Bush, Senator Lieberman, most other leaders, and most Americans want them to be administered through whatever legally appropriate fiscal or other arrangements result in the most cost-effective results. Most of those programs now work through direct grants, some work through both direct grants and vouchers, and a small fraction work through vouchers only. Overall, nobody seems truly satisfied with the results, but policy decisions about whether to change a given program's disbursement procedures or other administrative features ought not to be the basis of all-purpose ideological or nebulous sentiments for or against "big government." Fortunately, except at the factious extremes, everyone seems inclined to make administrative reform decisions consistent with reasonable case-by-case, program-by-program assessment of how such changes might result in better performance. I have no doubt that, if such reforms are pursued, relatively more programs, but by no means most or all programs, would feature indirect disbursement procedures, or vouchers.

As I said in the conclusion to my March speech, to me, the essential Christian social teaching is that there are no "strangers," only brothers and sisters whom we have yet to meet, greet, get to know, and come to love. As the Bible says in I John 18, "Little children, let us love, not in word or speech, but in truth and action."[8] If our enlightened statesmen focus on poor children and others in need, then the mischief wrought by factions will cease to bedevil the bipartisan push to enlist our national government more squarely in the support of America's diverse community helpers and healers.

NOTES

1. George W. Bush, "Rallying the Armies of Compassion," January 29, 2001.

2. Quotation from George W. Bush's speech to Congress, February 28, 2001.

3. Stephen Monsma, *When Sacred and Secular Mix* (Lanham, Md.: Rowman and Littlefield, 1996).

4. Jeffrey Rosen, "Religious Rights: Why the Catholic Church Shouldn't Have to Hire Gays," *New Republic*, February 26, 2001.

5. "In Good Faith: A Dialogue on Government Funding of Faith-Based Social Services," a statement arising from discussions convened by the American Jewish Committee and the Feinstein Center for American Jewish History at Temple University (2001).

6. Amy Sherman, *The Growing Impact of Charitable Choice* (Annapolis, Md.: Center for Public Justice).

7. Bush, "Rallying the Armies of Compassion."

8. John 3:18, New Revised Standard Version.

CHAPTER SEVENTEEN

Testing the Assumptions: Who Provides Social Services?

MARK CHAVES

The establishment of the White House Office of Faith-Based and Community Initiatives by the Bush administration is part of a larger initiative to expand the role of religious organizations in the U.S. social welfare system. Beyond enacting and enforcing charitable choice legislation of the sort that began with section 104 of the Personal Responsibility and Work Opportunity Reconciliation Act of 1996, that initiative seeks to fight poverty by encouraging religious organizations—including those that have never engaged in social services in a serious way—to start, expand, and seek public support for social service activities.

This chapter assesses the soundness of several assumptions behind the initiative by discussing empirical evidence about the provision of social services by congregations. Religious congregations—members of churches, synagogues, mosques, temples, and so forth—constitute only a subset of the faith-based organizations involved in social services, and in most respects they are far less important actors than are faith-based social service agencies like the Salvation Army and Catholic Charities. Still, congregations are the core religious groups in American society, and advocates of faith-based social services often point to congregation-based programs as models. Furthermore, congregations are the prototypical "pervasively sectarian" organization; their inclusion in large numbers in our publicly supported social welfare system would constitute a qualitative change in church-state relations regarding social services. It is therefore appropriate to examine the provision of social services by congregations in the context of charitable choice initiatives.

This chapter addresses several specific questions: What social services do congregations typically offer? Do congregations provide social services in distinctive ways? Which types of congregations provide more social services? To what extent are congregations inclined to take advantage of funding available under charitable choice? With whom do congregations collaborate? Does collaboration affect their activities? The answers to those questions are sometimes surprising. They dispel certain assumptions about congregations and their provision of social services and provide a more realistic view of congregations' current and potential role in our social welfare system.[1]

WHAT SOCIAL SERVICES DO CONGREGATIONS PROVIDE?

Charitable choice advocates sometimes argue that congregations already are an important component of the U.S. social welfare system, giving the impression that the vast majority actively and intensively engage in social service delivery. The truth is somewhat different. Although virtually all congregations engage in what might be considered social service activities and although a majority—57 percent—support provision of some type of more or less formal social service, community development, or neighborhood organizing projects, the intensity of congregational involvement varies widely. For example, congregations may donate money to a community food bank, supply volunteers for Meals on Wheels, organize a food drive every Thanksgiving, or operate an independent food pantry or soup kitchen. They may supply volunteers to do occasional home repairs for the needy, assist first-time homebuyers with congregational funds, participate in neighborhood redevelopment efforts, or build affordable housing for senior citizens. They may donate money to a neighborhood shelter, provide volunteers to prepare dinner at a shelter on a rotating basis with other congregations, or actually provide shelter for homeless women and children in the congregation's facilities.

One measure of the depth of congregational involvement in those activities is the percentage having a staff person who devotes at least 25 percent of his or her time to social service projects. *Only 6 percent of all congregations and only 12 percent of those reporting some degree of social service involvement have such a staff person.* Other measures also are informative. The median dollar amount spent by congregations in direct support of social service programs is approximately $1,200, or 3 percent of the median congregation's total budget. In the median congregation with some sort of involvement in social service activities, only ten individuals are involved in those activities as volunteers. The basic picture is clear: although most congregations participate in some sort of social service activity, only a small minority actively and intensively engage in such activity.

Congregations also favor certain types of projects. Housing, clothing, and, especially, food projects are more common than programs dealing with health, education, domestic violence, tutoring/mentoring, substance abuse, or job training. Fewer than 10 percent of congregations have programs in any of the latter areas. By comparison, 11 percent have clothing projects, 18 percent have housing/shelter projects, and 33 percent have food projects. Eight percent of congregations report providing services to homeless people.

In other words, *congregations are much more likely to engage in activities that address the immediate needs of individuals for food, clothing, and shelter than to engage in projects or programs that require sustained involvement to meet longer-term goals.* Programs that appear to involve only short-term or fleeting contact with clients are far more common (36 percent of congregations) than programs that involve more intensive, long-term, or sustained face-to-face interaction (10 percent of congregations).

Those results contradict the widely held assumption that religious organizations provide social services in a distinctively holistic or personal way. There is indeed substantial congregational involvement in social services, but not of the sort usually envisioned. Congregational social service provision is much more commonly characterized by attention to short-term emergency needs, especially for food, clothing, and shelter, than by more personal and intensive interaction or by holistic attention to cross-cutting problems. That pattern is found in *every* extant survey of congregations that provide social services.[2]

How Do Congregations Provide Social Services?

Beyond the tendency to focus on short-term, emergency needs, congregations tend to structure their social service involvement in a distinctive way. When they do more than donate money, canned goods, or old clothes, they are most apt to organize small groups of volunteers to perform relatively well-defined tasks on a periodic basis: fifteen people spending several weekends renovating a house; five people cooking dinner at a homeless shelter one night a week; ten young people spending two weeks in the summer painting a school in a poor community; and so on. When congregations do provide social services, virtually all— 90 percent—do so with volunteers from the congregation. At the same time, the total number of volunteers provided by the typical congregation is rather small. As mentioned above, in the median congregation that engaged in some level of social service activity, only ten congregants volunteered to participate in those activities. In 80 percent of the congregations, fewer than thirty volunteers participated. In light of that, it probably is no accident that congregational involvement in social services is highest in areas in which organizations such as

homeless shelters or Habitat for Humanity have emerged to exploit congregations' capacity to mobilize relatively small numbers of volunteers to carry out
well-defined and delimited tasks.

Research thus points to a more modest—and realistic—vision for congregational involvement in social services than is sometimes trumpeted. That more
realistic vision does not deny that some congregations engage in important antipoverty projects and programs—those are the congregations that have received
the most media attention in recent years—nor does it trivialize the contribution
that they make to the U.S. social welfare system. If only 1 percent of congregations deliver social services in an intensive way, that still represents about 3,000
congregations across the nation. Nevertheless, it is important to recognize that
they are the exception rather than the rule. Understanding that congregations
that are deeply engaged in providing social services are very uncommon—and
likely to remain so—does not minimize their contributions, but it should cau-
tion all parties against making sweeping claims about the capacities of idealized
congregations. A more realistic assessment would recognize that, on one hand,
only a very small percentage of congregations is likely to play an active role under a new welfare regime and, on the other, that most congregations' social service activity is now and will continue to be limited to organizing small groups
of people to perform specific tasks on a periodic basis.

WHICH CONGREGATIONS PROVIDE MORE SOCIAL SERVICES?

Although the percentage of congregations that are deeply engaged in social service activity is rather low, some congregations participate intensively. Which
congregations are most active? Four patterns emerge. The first is unsurprising
but important: larger congregations do more than smaller congregations. Although only about 1 percent of congregations have more than 900 regularly participating adults, the largest 1 percent account for about one-quarter of all the
money spent directly by congregations on social service activities. Only about
10 percent of congregations have 250 or more regular participants, but that 10
percent accounts for more than half of all the money that congregations spend
on social service activities. *Clearly, the minority of large congregations provide the
bulk of social services carried out by congregations.*

The second pattern is less obvious. On one hand, congregations located in
poor neighborhoods tend to engage in more social service activity than those located in nonpoor neighborhoods. On the other hand, congregations with more
middle-class members engage in more social service activity than those with
more poor members, *and that is true even of congregations in poor neighborhoods.*
Taken together, those two findings imply that congregations located in poor

neighborhoods but composed of less poor or more middle-class people engage in the most social service and community activity. That pattern suggests that a congregation's own resources are crucially important in generating social service activity. Congregations located in poor neighborhoods, but without the internal resources that come with middle-class constituents, do not engage in as much social service activity as congregations with more of those resources.

The third pattern suggests that religious tradition matters. Congregations associated with mainline Protestant denominations provide more social services than conservative Protestant congregations, and Catholic congregations are neither more nor less active than conservative Protestant congregations. Beyond denomination, self-described theologically liberal congregations provide more social services than self-described conservative congregations. That pattern is consistent with previous research that shows that theologically more liberal individuals and congregations are, in a variety of ways, more connected to their surrounding communities than are more evangelical or conservative individuals and congregations.[3]

The fourth pattern indicates that race also matters. Although African American congregations do not, in general, provide more social services than white congregations, African American congregations are more likely to be engaged in certain key types of social services, such as education, mentoring, substance abuse, and job training or employment assistance programs.

Beyond the intrinsic importance of identifying the most active congregations, these findings take on special significance when combined with data on which congregations are inclined to take advantage of new opportunities for public funding and government collaboration that might emerge from current initiatives.

WHO WILL TAKE ADVANTAGE OF CHARITABLE CHOICE?

The current involvement of congregations in social service delivery is only part of the story. We also might ask about congregations' interest in expanding their participation by taking advantage of funding opportunities presented by charitable choice legislation. Whatever social services they currently provide and whatever their current level of collaboration with secular and government agencies, are religious congregations inclined to take advantage of new funding opportunities?

The National Congregations Study collected data from congregations through sixty-minute interviews with a key informant (a minister, priest, rabbi, or other leader) from each congregation. Informants were asked whether they thought that their congregation would apply for government money to support its human services programs. Fifteen percent of congregations had a congregational policy against taking government money; 36 percent, however, indicated interest in applying for government support.

That should not be taken to mean that more than one-third of U.S. congregations are likely to apply for government grants and contracts in the coming years. That a member of the clergy expressed interest in moving in that direction is not at all the same thing as willingness among members of the congregation. Other research shows that clergy tend to be more supportive of such a move than parishioners. That number probably should be interpreted as a maximum—an estimate of the percentage of U.S. congregations that *might* apply for government funds if given the opportunity. Since only about 3 percent of congregations currently receive government money for social service projects, even a small increase—say, 5 percentage points—in the proportion of congregations receiving public funds could represent a major increase in the participation of religious congregations in the U.S. social welfare system and a major change in church-state relations. The overall level of expressed willingness to seek government support indicates that potential exists for increasing the numbers of government-congregation partnerships in social service delivery. There is a market for charitable choice.

Whatever the absolute level of interest among congregations, which subsets of congregations are likely to take advantage of the opportunities presented by charitable choice? The basic patterns are similar to those described above regarding which congregations provide more social services; once again, size, religious tradition, and race are the key factors. Again, it is not surprising that large congregations are considerably more likely to express interest in seeking government funds. The most interesting findings, however, demonstrate the enduring power of both race and ideology in determining the engagement of U.S. congregations in state and society.

A congregation's ethnic composition is by far the most powerful predictor of willingness to apply for government funds. Informants from 64 percent of predominantly African American congregations expressed a willingness to apply for government funds compared with only 28 percent from predominantly white congregations. Controlling other congregational features, predominantly black congregations are *five times* more likely than other congregations to seek public support.

The importance of this finding is enhanced when it is viewed in the context of two other facts about African American congregations. First, there already is a lower wall—both culturally and institutionally—between church and state in African American than in other religious communities in the United States. Second, clergy in predominantly black churches enjoy greater power than their counterparts in predominantly white churches to initiate and implement congregational programs of their own choosing. Both of those features increase the likelihood that clergy-reported interest in seeking government funding will translate into concrete action. In light of that, if charitable choice initiatives successfully redirect public monies to religious congregations, African African congregations are likely to be substantially overrepresented among those who take advantage of those initiatives.

Catholic and liberal/moderate Protestant congregations are significantly more likely to apply for government funds to support social service activities than are conservative/evangelical congregations. Forty-one percent of congregations in liberal/moderate Protestant denominations said that they would be willing to apply for government funds compared with 40 percent of Catholic congregations and only 28 percent of congregations in conservative/evangelical denominations. Furthermore, when informants were asked to classify their congregations as liberal leaning, conservative leaning, or middle-of-the-road, congregations identified as theologically and politically conservative were significantly less likely to express willingness to apply for government funds, and that was true even after controlling for denominational affiliation and other characteristics. Although denominational affiliation remained salient, liberal/conservative ideology crosscut denominational lines in important ways, and that divide mattered when it came to expressed willingness to pursue charitable choice opportunities.

Combining the results reported in this section with those in the previous section yields an important conclusion: the assumption that charitable choice initiatives are likely to involve *new* sorts of religious congregations in providing publicly funded social services—those that have not been involved before—is questionable. Larger congregations, African American congregations, and Catholic and liberal/moderate Protestant congregations are more likely to apply for funds, and those are exactly the congregations that already are most likely to be more deeply involved in social services.

WITH WHOM DO CONGREGATIONS COLLABORATE AND WHAT ARE THE CONSEQUENCES?

Congregations provide social services primarily in collaboration with other organizations. Eighty-four percent of congregations that provide social services have at least one collaborator on at least one program. Seventy-two percent of all programs are operated in collaboration with others. Although other congregations are the single most common type of collaborator, congregations are as likely to collaborate with some sort of secular organization (59 percent of congregations) as with some sort of religious organization (58 percent of congregations).

Although only 3 percent of congregations currently receive government financial support for their social service activity, about one-fifth of those with programs collaborate in some fashion with a government agency. Clearly, when congregations offer social services it is mainly in collaboration with others, including secular and government agencies in nontrivial numbers.

Congregations are not equally likely to collaborate. Large, mainline Protestant, theologically liberal congregations with more college graduates are significantly more likely than others to collaborate on social services. Interestingly, although there is no race difference in the likelihood of collaborating in general, predominantly African American congregations are significantly more likely than white congregations to collaborate with *secular* organizations.

When congregations collaborate with secular, especially government agencies, are they less likely to engage in the longer-term, more holistic or transformational kinds of social services some claim to be their special purview? The answer is no. Looking first at individual programs, congregational social service programs involving secular collaborators of any sort are slightly *more* likely (10 percent versus 7 percent) than programs involving nonsecular collaborators to be personal and long-term, and they are significantly *less* likely (25 percent versus 35 percent) to be fleeting and superficial. Programs involving government collaborators are significantly *less* likely to be fleeting and superficial (21 percent versus 32 percent). The pattern is similar for congregations as a whole: with many other variables controlled, congregations with secular collaborators are significantly *more* likely to be engaged in longer-term, personal, face-to-face kinds of social service activities than are congregations without such collaborators. Congregations with government collaborators are no less likely than congregations without government collaborators to participate in or support such programs. None of the differences is large, and these results alone do not indicate that secular collaborations actually encourage more holistic kinds of social services. Still, they clearly do not support the notion that such collaborations are likely to discourage holistic social services.

Thus, research on provision of social services by congregations contradicts yet another common assumption about charitable choice initiatives: that a distinctively holistic or personal approach to social services is potentially threatened by collaboration with secular, and especially government, agencies. That assumption is sometimes used to justify calls for allowing religious organizations, when collaborating with government, to operate under looser accountability and monitoring standards than those imposed on secular social service organizations. But there is no evidence that collaborating with government agencies makes congregations less likely to engage in the more personal and longer-term social service activities that some think are more likely to occur within a religious organization that guards its autonomy. If the call for loosening the regulatory environment in which religious organizations deliver social services is based on the assumption that a stricter environment threatens their holistic approach to social services, that call is on shaky empirical ground. In the main, congregations do not employ a holistic approach to social services, and the minority that do are not discouraged from doing so by government collaborations, including financial collaborations.

CONCLUSION

We are in a moment of enthusiasm about the role that religious organizations may be able to play in our social welfare system, a moment also of considerable interest in expanding that role and creating new kinds of partnerships between government and religious organizations. This chapter has tried to present a realistic, pragmatic, and clear-headed assessment of the possibilities—and limits—of religious congregations' current and likely future role. Research indicates that congregations do indeed engage in a wide range of social services and that many congregations already collaborate with secular and government-funded groups in providing those services. But only a tiny minority of congregations engage in social services in more than a superficial way, and the congregations that are most likely to take advantage of charitable choice initiatives and the activities of the White House Office of Faith-Based and Community Initiatives are those that already are most actively involved in social services: large, African American, Catholic, and liberal/moderate Protestant congregations in poor neighborhoods. From that perspective, it is difficult to see how charitable choice initiatives might succeed in involving new sorts of congregations in social services, publicly funded or not.

Perhaps most important, some of the results described in this chapter speak to one of the fundamental ambiguities within the charitable choice movement: is the goal of this initiative, including the White House Office of Faith-Based and Community Initiatives, to remove discrimination against religious organizations in public funding or is it to actively prefer religious organizations? The activities sponsored and encouraged by charitable choice initiatives sometimes go well beyond rooting out discrimination, as when state or federal agencies favor religious organizations in competition for funding—perhaps even setting aside public funds for which only religious organizations are eligible to apply—or when religious organizations are allowed to operate in a looser regulatory environment than secular organizations while delivering the same services. Even if that sort of preference for faith-based over secular social service agencies were to pass constitutional muster, it can be justified on pragmatic grounds only by assuming that the social services provided by religious organizations are distinctive and ultimately more effective than those provided by secular organizations. But there is little reason to think that congregations—or, for that matter, other types of religious organizations—deliver social services that are distinctively holistic, more focused on individuals' long-term needs, or generally more effective than those provided by secular organizations. Even if the charitable choice movement succeeds in institutionalizing a preference for religious organizations in awarding public funds—either by favoring religious organizations in funding competitions or by allowing them to operate under laxer standards and regulations—there is little reason to believe that doing so will advance the battle against poverty in our society.

NOTES

1. This chapter uses data from the National Congregations Study (NCS), a 1998 survey of a nationally representative sample of 1,236 religious congregations. For more information about the National Congregations Study methodology, see Mark Chaves and others, "The National Congregations Study: Background, Methods, and Selected Results," *Journal for the Scientific Study of Religion*, vol. 38 (1999), pp. 458–76. This chapter is a condensed version of two articles: Mark Chaves, "Religious Congregations and Welfare Reform: Who Will Take Advantage of Charitable Choice?" *American Sociological Review*, vol. 64 (1999), pp. 836–46, and Mark Chaves and William Tsitsos, "Congregations and Social Services: What They Do, How They Do It, and with Whom," *Nonprofit and Voluntary Sector Quarterly*, vol. 30 (2001, forthcoming). Readers interested in more detail should consult those articles.

2. See, for example, Ram A. Cnaan, *Social and Community Involvement of Religious Congregations Housed in Historic Religious Properties: Findings from a Six-City Study* (Philadelphia: University of Pennsylvania School of Social Work, 1997), and *Keeping Faith in the City: How 401 Urban Religious Congregations Serve Their Neediest Neighbors* (Philadelphia: Center for Research on Religion and Urban Civil Society, 2000); Tobi J. Printz, *Faith-Based Service Providers in the Nation's Capital: Can They Do More?* Charting Civil Society, no. 2 (Washington, D.C.: The Urban Institute, 1998); Nancy T. Ammerman, *Doing Good in American Communities— Congregations and Service Organizations Working Together: A Research Report from the Organizing Religious Work Project* (Hartford, Conn.: Hartford Seminary, 2001a); Lester M. Salamon and Fred Teitelbaum, "Religious Congregations as Social Service Agencies: How Extensive Are They?" *Foundation News* (September/October 1984); Carol Silverman, "Faith-Based Communities and Welfare Reform," in *Can We Make Welfare Reform Work? California Religious Community Capacity Study* (Sacramento: California Council of Churches, 2000), pp. 66–84; Melissa Stone, "Scope and Scale: An Assessment of Human Service Delivery by Congregations in Minnesota," paper presented at the annual meeting of the Association for Research on Nonprofit Organizations and Voluntary Action, New Orleans, 2000; Robert J. Wineburg, "Local Human Services Provision by Religious Congregations: A Community Analysis," *Nonprofit and Voluntary Sector Quarterly*, vol. 21 (1992), pp. 107–17.

3. Concerning individuals, see Robert Wuthnow, "Mobilizing Civic Engagement," in Theda Skocpol and Morris Fiorina, eds., *Civic Engagment in American Democracy* (Brookings, 1999), pp. 331–63. Concerning congregations, see Chaves and others, "Religious Variations in Public Presence: Evidence from the National Congregations Study," forthcoming in Robert Wuthnow and John H. Evans, eds., *Quietly Influential: The Public Role of Mainline Protestantism* (University of California Press, 2001), and Nancy Ammerman, "Connecting Mainline Protestant Churches with Public Life, " also forthcoming in Wuthnow and Evans, eds., *Quietly Influential*.

CHAPTER EIGHTEEN

Appropriate and Inappropriate Use of Religion

DAVID SAPERSTEIN

Religious individuals and organizations have the constitutional right to practice their religion however they please. If a religious organization wants to create a religious political party, there is no constitutional bar to doing so, although it would likely lose its tax exemption. If a presidential candidate wants to do nothing but proselytize, she or he may do so, although much of the electorate will be alienated. The 2000 presidential campaign dramatized the need to draw a line between "appropriate" and "inappropriate" religious rhetoric and activity in U.S. political life. The terms "appropriate" and "inappropriate" are used intentionally rather than "legal" or "not legal." In the United States, we have a right to do a lot of things—including things that may be, in the views of others, wrong or inappropriate. And religious and political groups and leaders (including candidates for office) may well do things that are within their rights—and even within the short-term interests of a political campaign—but that are bad for religion, bad for America, or bad for democracy. So what, then, are appropriate uses of religion in political life? Let me suggest three.

First, discussion of religion can help explain who candidates and political leaders are and what they are about. Profiles of George W. Bush, Al Gore, or Joseph Lieberman (we learned less about Dick Cheney's religious beliefs in the 2000 campaign) would be neither accurate nor complete if they did not describe the candidate's religious beliefs and the role that religion plays in his life. And since Americans knew comparatively little about Orthodox Jews and Orthodox Judaism before Senator Lieberman's selection as Vice President Gore's running mate, it was legitimate to seek more explanations than usual.

Second, candidates for election not only can but should express their views on policy issues concerning religion. Such views need to be part of the public debate. The American people have a right to know where candidates stand on crucial proposals that arise at the intersection of religion and public policy. Present proposals include religious freedom legislation; constitutional amendments to weaken the establishment clause of the First Amendment; and legislation on school prayer, scientific creationism, the posting of the Ten Commandments, protection of the religious rights of American workers on their jobs, and charitable choice.

Third, the American people have a right to know how candidates' religious beliefs and values will inform their views on a whole range of issues beyond what are broadly seen as "religious issues," such as school prayer and charitable choice. In that respect, while the Anti-Defamation League's (ADL's) public letter to Senator Lieberman complaining of his frequent use of religious rhetoric on the campaign trail raised vital concerns and sensitized the public and the candidates to the dangers of misusing religious rhetoric, the ADL was woefully off base in its subsequent assertion that it is inappropriate for candidates to suggest that their religious beliefs shape or inform their public policy perspectives and that religion "belongs in the church, in the synagogue, in the home and in the heart; it doesn't belong on a political campaign, and certainly not in politics or government."

Almost every member of Congress and public figure with whom I have worked in my twenty-seven years in Washington has been influenced by his or her religious beliefs. Religion has a long tradition of inspiring American political values, and much of Senator Lieberman's language resonated with the rhetoric of the Declaration of Independence, Abraham Lincoln, and Martin Luther King Jr. While using religion to establish the moral context for their views, those leaders went on to explain their policies in terms that were open political debate and that included all Americans, regardless of faith. Thus, the Declaration of Independence roots our rights in our Creator, but the Constitution, in formally setting forth our rights, does not mention God. King presented his views in nonsectarian, inclusive religious language to prick the conscience of the nation and to establish a moral context for the powerful public policy arguments he would then make—arguments made in secular language that all people could relate to.

Politicians and candidates have asserted in recent years that God's "pervasive preference for the poor" should animate our welfare policy; that respect for God's creation should deepen our concern for endangered species; and that religious "just war theory" can provide moral insight into U.S. policies in the Gulf War or Kosovo conflict. To suggest that such assertions are by virtue of their religious nature inappropriate is to foist on political discourse an artificial straightjacket that has no place in American history or law. It morally weakens much of the vital debate our nation needs. Lieberman was well within the bounds of propriety in stating that the Fifth Commandment to "Honor your father and your mother" strengthened his resolve to ensure prescription drug benefits for the elderly. Not only do our candidates and leaders have a *right* to talk about their faith, they have a *responsibility* to explain how their religious views shape their political agenda. Such use of religious language in the public forum can serve to goad the conscience of the nation.

What uses of religious rhetoric are not appropriate? Let me again suggest three guidelines. First, it is inappropriate to suggest that one should support or oppose a policy on the basis of religious belief exclusively. Policies justified by belief alone cannot be tested in the free marketplace of ideas, and they must be tested if democracy is to work and if meaningful public policy debate is to flourish. Had Lieberman dropped his strong policy justification for prescription drug benefits to argue that we should adopt such a policy only because the Ten Commandments enjoins us to, he would have stepped over the line and greatly weakened the case for a policy he supports.

Second, it is never appropriate for candidates, explicitly or implicitly, to suggest that there is a religious test for holding office. While Article VI of the Constitution expressly prohibits only the government from creating such tests, the spirit of that prohibition should extend to political statements and policies. Article VI, together with the First Amendment's religion clauses, led to one of America's greatest contributions to political thought: that one's status as a citizen does not depend on one's religious beliefs or practices. That concept has provided more rights, freedoms, and opportunities to religious minorities in the United States than are available in any other nation. That concept made it possible for Joseph Lieberman to be nominated for vice president.

The religious test also arises when candidates suggest that their religious beliefs or practices qualify them for office or that others' beliefs or practices disqualify them. That occurs not only when someone like Pat Robertson asserts it directly, as he did when he said, "The Constitution of the United States is a marvelous document for self-government by Christian people. But the minute you turn the document into the hands of non-Christian people and atheist people, they can use it to destroy the very foundation of our society"[1]—and as he did when he said, ten years later, "When I said during my presidential bid that I would only bring Christians and Jews into the government . . . the media challenged me . . . 'How dare you maintain that those who believe the Judeo-Christian values are better qualified to govern America than Hindus and Muslims?' [they asked]. My simple answer is, 'Yes, they are.'"[2] It also happens when candidates put forward their religious beliefs so persistently that those beliefs become a political tool that implies that such beliefs are an inherent qualification for office. For example, if a candidate asserts that he or she is a born-again

Christian in an interview, it helps the electorate to understand the candidate; making that assertion at a prayer breakfast is likewise appropriate. In contrast, repeatedly inserting that identifier in every political speech or debate suggests that the candidate is saying to the public, "Vote for me because my belief in Jesus as savior makes me better qualified for office than someone who believes otherwise." In the 2000 presidential election, many candidates who ran in the primary and general elections either crossed or came perilously close to crossing that line.

Finally, candidates should minimize their use of divisive and exclusive language. While some religious language is far less sectarian and divisive than other language, all religious speech excludes some people. As a general principle, Americans should not be made to feel like outsiders because of their political leaders' rhetoric. (That is the key idea behind Supreme Court Justice Sandra Day O'Connor's "endorsement test," now widely used to determine whether the government has acted in a manner that violates the establishment clause.)

Is there a double standard in tolerating Senator Lieberman's religious rhetoric while condemning the use of religious rhetoric by some conservative Christians during the campaign? No, there is a consistent standard, and it applies to remarks rather than to individuals. Inclusive, aspirational, historically resonant comments like Bush's "our nation is chosen by God and commissioned by history to be a model to the world of justice" or Lieberman's "our equality . . . was an endowment of our creator" contrast starkly with the sectarian and divisive tone of Bush's suggestion that he could not explain how Jesus had affected his political views if listeners had not themselves been changed by Jesus and Bush's declaration of "Jesus Day" in the state of Texas. Exclusivity also was the major problem with Franklin Graham's Christological invocation and benediction at President Bush's inauguration. He absolutely had the "right" to give that invocation, and the president had a right to ask him to give it. But it made many Americans feel like outsiders.

On a political level, the president needs to confront the problem of exclusivity, because the concern about rhetoric is not just about the language used. It is, at its core, about the policies the language represents and justifies. Depending on how a candidate's political agenda is perceived, the same religious rhetoric may sound different. From the mouth of a candidate who is identified with religious tolerance, explicitly religious language is less likely to be seen as code for religious intolerance. From a candidate who is perceived as being religiously exclusive or intolerant, the same language might well be fairly seen as offensive. Not just the words themselves, but what the words are seen to represent, define public reaction.

Thus those who contend that separation of church and state is essential to ensuring freedom of religion did not hear in Lieberman's rhetoric an abandonment of that principle or a justification for changing or violating the Constitution. But in the rhetoric of the religious right, separationists hear an agenda that would change the Constitution, impose organized school prayer on children, and mandate teaching biblical creationism. Likewise, when Lieberman borrowed one of the religious right's favorite phrases—"the Constitution guarantees freedom for religion, not freedom from religion"—not only was he factually wrong, his words legitimized the religious right's legislative agenda, which smacks of exclusivity.

As long as religious rhetoric is aimed at inspiring the conscience of the nation, is inclusive, is not transformed into a political tool, and is not aimed at justifying an agenda that would alter the constitutional protections that make the United States the most religiously free and vibrant democratic country in the world, we should celebrate and not fear its presence in our political process.

THE DEBATE OVER CHARITABLE CHOICE

How does the foregoing discussion apply to charitable choice? First, opposing voices in the debate are equally committed to a robust role for religion in American public life and in providing social services. They differ profoundly on how to achieve that goal and on what is best for religion.

Currently, two types of social service programs are offered by the religious community. The first type is operated by religiously affiliated entities created by religious communities to act on their theological obligation to help the poor and needy, often more professionally and effectively than any individual church could do. Such programs do not proselytize, engage in worship, or promote religious education, nor do they discriminate in whom they serve or hire. These programs represent a constitutional way for government and faith-based organizations to work together, and they receive enormous amounts of government assistance. The second type is offered by churches, synagogues, and mosques—that is, "pervasively sectarian" institutions—and they engage in religious worship, proselytization, and education. They can discriminate in whom they hire and serve as long as they are not funded with government money.

Members of the Bush administration deserve credit for offering some revolutionary and visionary new ways for government and faith-based organizations, even pervasively sectarian institutions, to strengthen their partnership. The major issue is whether the government should directly fund pervasively sectarian entities to provide social service programs of the second type.

Is direct funding bad for religion? First, direct funding can exert a secular influence on religious organizations because government money comes tied to government rules, regulations, restrictions, audits, monitoring, and interference. The specter of government intrusion in the bookkeeping and daily operation of religious institutions frightens some people who care about religion. But equally alarming is the reverse: having the federal government fund religious organizations with tax dollars and not monitor those organizations. We know that the inherent religious mission and culture of many pervasively sectarian institutions will exert significant pressure on those churches that receive government funding to discriminate, to proselytize, and to fulfill their complete religious mandate. There is documented evidence of that pattern in churches that received funding under earlier charitable choice provisions. The only way to counterbalance that pressure and ensure that government regulations are met is through extensive government monitoring, which threatens religious autonomy.

Second, dependence on government money weakens religious organizations in several ways. An obvious consequence is that reliance on government funding obviates the need for individuals to support their own churches, synagogues, and mosques. But it also results in the weakening of distinctive legal protections that religious organizations enjoy. Take the debate over whether programs taking government money should be allowed to discriminate in hiring. There is a constitutional right and policy need for religious groups to select people to run their programs who share their religious identity and beliefs. But there are serious concerns over whether government-funded programs should be allowed to discriminate. One way to avoid the problem is to deny government funding to those programs. Another way is to deny a program a religious exemption if it receives significant amounts of government money. That, however, would force religious institutions to sacrifice their unique constitutional and legal status for the privilege of lining up at the public trough to fight with one another over scarce federal dollars. As tempting as having government funding to assist in meeting the church budget may be, it is an enormous price to pay for very little in return. Further, when churches voluntarily give up such exemptions and protections in one set of circumstances, it gives political weight to the arguments of those who seek to strip them of such exemptions in all circumstances.

Third, charitable choice will do little to help and will undoubtedly harm the recipients of social services. Not only will charitable choice divert money from successful programs to pervasively sectarian programs (some of which may be great successes but many of which may, at least at first, struggle to meet their goals), the religious rights of recipients will be compromised as they are forced to turn to programs with religious content to receive government-supported services. Those pitfalls are magnified by the government's refusal to increase existing funds. The money will necessarily be taken out of strong, successful faith-based entities such as Catholic Charities, Lutheran Social Services, and Jewish Federations and distributed among the approximately 350,000 churches, synagogues, and mosques in the United States that may decide to seek government funding. If one-tenth of those eligible apply, there will be 35,000 pervasively sectarian institutions competing with each other for limited government grants. That kind of competition will undermine the fabric of religious tolerance that has served our nation so well and dilute, if not altogether eradicate, funding for long-standing, effective, religiously affiliated social service programs.

Finally, the fungibility argument has been central to the Supreme Court's refusal to uphold direct government funding of pervasively sectarian institutions. Charitable choice proponents insist that as long as funding flows only to the secular components of programs run by pervasively sectarian institutions, no harm will be done. But they have to be honest about that. Even in a pervasively sectarian institution where government funds support only secular social services, every dollar in the church budget freed up by government funding is going to be used for religious activities. That is problematic. If a church literacy program receives government money to run the program and to help rehabilitate the classroom and that classroom is used on Sunday for religious instruction, the government has helped to fund the underlying religious nature of the institution. Thomas Jefferson said it well when addressing a taxing scheme over 200 years ago: "[T]o compel a man to furnish contributions of money for the propagation of opinions which he disbelieves is sinful and tyrannical."[3]

President Bush must recognize in the charitable choice debate a far-reaching test of his intention to unify and heal the nation. He faces a choice. If he rallies the nation around the substantial parts of his faith-based initiative on which almost everyone agrees he can forge a new, constitutionally permissible partnership between the faith community and government. If he insists on including a major funding program aimed at supporting houses of worship in their social service efforts, he will draw the nation into a painful, divisive, sectarian dispute that will mar his legacy. Reverend Jerry Falwell's attack on Islam and the attack by Reverend Eugene Rivers, who runs wonderful inner-city programs, on conservative evangelicals as racist is just a foretaste of what might be before us. Thousands of local churches, synagogues, and mosques competing for limited government funds in coming years will only exacerbate such rancor.

There are many simple, constitutional ways to achieve our common goals: using the tax system to encourage more charitable giving; providing technical assistance and staff training for all programs; sharing best practices; researching possible program improvements; diminishing or eliminating fees for all small organizations, including religious organizations, to establish separate 501(c)(3) corporations. With mutual respect and some hard work, we can ensure religious liberty, protect our Constitution and our religious institutions, maintain religion's vital role in the public square, and promote the excellent work that our religious institutions do in carrying out their prophetic mission to help those in need.

NOTES

1. Pat Robertson, *Washington Post*, March 23, 1981.
2. Pat Robertson, *The New World Order* (Dallas, Tex.: Word Publishing, 1991).
3. Excerpts from Jefferson's *Virginia Statute for Religious Freedom*, 1786.

CHAPTER NINETEEN

In Good Faith:
Government Funding
of Faith-Based Social Services

A Statement Arising from Discussions Convened by the
American Jewish Committee and the Feinstein Center
for American Jewish History at Temple University

The project that became In Good Faith *began in what may be seen as the dawn of
the national discussion on government funding of faith-based social service programs.
The project took shape in the wake of the enactment of the first charitable choice provision, which was part of the 1996 welfare reform legislation.*

*While the group drafted the document, charitable choice provisions were added to
several more federal laws and both presidential candidates called for extending them
to cover new streams of federal social service funding. Since the release of the document,
President Bush has unveiled a spate of new policy proposals through his Office of Faith-
Based and Community Initiatives, and his agenda has come under close scrutiny and
triggered heated debate. A bill has been introduced in the House of Representatives to
cover a number of new sources of federal social service funds under charitable choice
legislation while a bill introduced in the Senate would create new tax incentives for
charitable giving without extending charitable choice provisions. Many more voices
have joined the dialogue, and the political winds have shifted in sometimes surprising directions.*

*None of us could have predicted the ways in which the dialogue on this subject has
evolved. Nonetheless,* In Good Faith *continues to set forth the relevant issues and helps
to clarify the contours of an often-confusing debate on the principle of separation of
church and state. Those of us who were involved in the project continue to work on*

these issues in various ways. In Good Faith *surely does not represent the end of the dialogue, but it may fairly represent the beginning.*

Melissa Rogers

The debate over the 1996 welfare reform legislation turned national attention to a question of critical and enduring importance—what is the best way for our nation to assist those in need? This question has triggered many wide-ranging discussions about the role of the federal and state governments in social services, the most effective way to move people from welfare to work, and how better to coordinate government services with the business sector, nonprofit organizations, and community groups. Another issue about which welfare reform has generated debate is financial collaboration between government and faith communities to serve the needy. This issue has sparked great interest and also strong concern. It is this question that is the focus here.

The conversation regarding cooperative efforts between government and religious organizations occurs at a time when there is great enthusiasm for the contribution of faith communities to social well-being, and a sense that some on the Supreme Court of the United States are moving toward a narrower interpretation of the Establishment Clause of the First Amendment. This conversation also occurs, however, in the context of concern that some forms of collaboration between religious organizations and the government could seriously undermine the religious freedom of social service beneficiaries, religious providers, and taxpayers generally.

This document originated in two discussions: a project to seek common ground concerning government funding of faith-based groups to provide social services, organized by The American Jewish Committee and the Feinstein Center for American Jewish History at Temple University and underwritten by The Pew Charitable Trusts;[1] and monthly meetings of persons who in 1998 were participants at a conference on welfare reform and faith-based organizations organized by the J. M. Dawson Institute of Church-State Studies at Baylor University. The two groups merged in the fall of 1999 to work on this document in a process that has included a series of consultations with experts and practitioners with a range of views.

The group formed in an effort to provide guidance to those involved in the policy process. We hope also to provide illumination to others interested in government's relations with religious organizations and the shifting structure of the social safety net. While each participating organization has formulated its own policy statement, we recognized the unique value of forming a representative panel of the various points of view on these issues. By engaging in sustained conversation we worked to identify areas both of agreement and disagreement regarding collaboration between the government and religious organizations. This document is the fruit of that labor.

INTRODUCTION

The shape and scope of government collaboration with faith-based organizations[2] has been undergoing a historic transformation. The legislative focal point for this attention has been "charitable choice." "Charitable choice" is a term of art that refers to a specific legislative proposal first enacted by Congress in the 1996 federal welfare reform law. Although the concept is often used loosely to refer to government funding of faith-based social service programs in general, in fact it refers more particularly to the new statutory conditions under which states may enter into funding relationships with religious organizations that provide social services[3] using federal or state funds that originated with enactment of the TANF[4] Program in 1996. Other legislative initiatives also popularly referred to as "charitable choice" have since been introduced in Congress and the states, and some have been enacted.[5] These apply variations of the TANF language to other program areas, such as drug rehabilitation or housing.

The new idea represented by "charitable choice" is not the involvement of faith communities in the social service arena, as many religious organizations have a history of involvement in such services. Nor is government funding of religious social service providers in itself an innovation, as many organizations with a religious affiliation have long received government funds[6] to carry out their work. Before "charitable choice," governments at all levels awarded grants and contracts to religiously affiliated organizations. There are no uniform statutory provisions regarding the participation of religious providers, and there was and remains controversy over whether an organization could be a pervasively religious entity[7] (such as a house of worship) and receive government money to provide social services.

"Charitable choice" alters previous practice through new federal statutory language that specifically addresses the participation of religious providers. "Charitable choice" permits all faith-based organizations to compete for government social service funding, regardless of their religious nature. Thus "charitable choice" significantly broadens the scope and extent of government financial collaboration with faith-based organizations. This change is welcome to some but highly problematic to others. The legal, philosophical, and ethical dimensions of the change have generated substantial controversy.

People who care deeply both about religious liberty and about the provision of effective social services disagree about the constitutionality and advisability of "charitable choice." Some believe that "charitable choice" is a long overdue correction to the discriminatory exclusion of some religious providers on the basis of an unconstitutional judgment about their religious character, and that the changes benefit society by expanding the capacity of faith communities to address social problems. Others believe that by allowing government funds to flow to pervasively religious entities like houses of worship, or to religiously affiliated programs without appropriate safeguards, "charitable choice" unconstitutionally and unwisely opens the door to government advancement of religion, excessive government entanglement with religion, government support of religious discrimination, and a general weakening of religious autonomy.

Our dialogue has been undergirded by the following common core values:

—Concern for human needs, particularly those of the economically and socially disadvantaged, and for the social health of the nation.

—Affirmation that promoting the well-being of the nation is a responsibility jointly of the private sector, faith communities, nonprofit organizations, and government, and that religious organizations cannot replace government's role in upholding the social safety net.

—Preservation of religious liberty under the Constitution of the United States.

—Identification of common ground while bringing clarity and civil discourse to bear on areas of significant disagreement.

—Recognition that the support by businesses, philanthropies, and other nongovernmental organizations of the good work done in society by religious organizations is valuable, and, of course, constitutional.

Within this broad framework, this document discusses specific areas of agreement regarding government collaboration with faith-based social service programs. The discussion bears on relationships structured by "charitable choice," but it is not limited to this concept and it is not an attempt to interpret any statute. The document also outlines areas of substantive disagreement on matters of constitutional interpretation and policy implementation related to collaboration.

We hope that this document will produce several benefits for policymaking and policy implementation. First, we hope that those who design and implement policies will be guided by the significant points of agreement we have forged as a way to promote healthy cooperation between government and religious organizations in the social service realm. Second, we hope that the document will provide a clear statement about where the agreements and disagreements lie in a complex area of the law as an aid for readers to develop their own informed conclusions. Third, we hope that the document will obviate the need for decision makers to collect from different sources the various positions on this matter. While we continue to differ about what is constitutional and advisable on some points, all of us believe that religious organizations and the government can work together in productive ways to bring about the greater good of society.

This topic will continue to be at the forefront of policy debates. Those engaged in the debate should acknowledge that no one side is the sole protector of the poor or of religious liberty. The most fruitful public debate will result when all acknowledge our shared stake in both the general welfare of our nation and the flourishing of religious freedom.[8]

AGREEMENT CONCERNING GOVERNMENT NONFINANCIAL COOPERATION WITH RELIGIOUS ORGANIZATIONS

Regardless of one's position on the constitutionality and advisability of "charitable choice," certainly government may, in many ways, include religious organizations among the community organizations with which it cooperates. Legitimate nonfinancial support includes:

—Providing information to the public and to persons in need about the availability of programs offered by religious and other community organizations.

—Providing access to education and training opportunities for program staff and volunteers of religious and other community organizations.

—Inviting faith community representatives to join community wide program task forces.

—Calling attention to the successful work of religious as well as secular providers.

—Providing letters of recommendation for faith-based and other community organizations that can help them raise funds from other sources.

—Advising social service beneficiaries of mentoring, support, and advocacy resources available from community organizations, including religious nonprofit agencies or houses of worship.

—Listing houses of worship and religious nonprofit agencies among the organizations that may provide community service placements to welfare recipients.

—Making information about the community, such as census tract data, directories of service providers, or needs assessments, available to help community service providers, including religious organizations, do planning, networking, and grassroots organizing.

—Encouraging charitable contributions through appropriate tax relief.

In addition, last year's enactment of the Religious Land Use and Institutionalized Persons Act (Public Law No. 106-274 [2000]) prevents zoning and other land use authorities from discriminating against or unnecessarily burdening the religious practices of houses of worship and other religious institutions, including their ability to provide social ministries.

AREAS OF AGREEMENT CONCERNING GOVERNMENT FUNDING OF RELIGIOUS ORGANIZATIONS TO PROVIDE SOCIAL SERVICES

Our shared values lead us to agree on the following important considerations, even as there remain strong differences among us as to the constitutionality and advisability of "charitable choice" (see Section IV):

1. *Government funding for social services provided by religiously affiliated entities.* Organizations that are affiliated with a house of worship or other religious body but are separate institutions performing secular functions should continue to be permitted to receive government money to fund their secular work.

2. *Availability of a secular alternative.* Beneficiaries have a right to a secular alternative if they do not wish to receive services from a religious organization. When government contracts with or awards grants to religious organizations for services, it must have a mechanism in place to provide a readily accessible secular service of equal value should any beneficiary require it. When the service is provided via a voucher mechanism, government should seek to include at least one secular alternative. If that is not possible, then government must have a mechanism in place to supply a readily accessible, equal value secular service in some other way.

3. *Notice to prospective and current beneficiaries.* Government must inform prospective and current beneficiaries about the religious nature of any participating programs and providers and of their right to receive equivalent services from a secular provider if they want.

4. *Nondiscrimination in the provision of government-funded social services.* Religious providers of government-funded social services should not discriminate against beneficiaries on the basis of religion or religious belief, either in admitting them into a program or in providing the government-funded services.

5. *Ability of beneficiaries to opt out of religious activities.* Whenever social service programs are funded by government, or participation in such programs is mandated by government, beneficiaries have the right not to participate in religious activities. Beneficiaries should be able to exercise this right within a program that has a religious component or dimension by declining active and passive participation in religious activities.

We disagree about the threshold question of whether government should fund programs where religious exercise is an integral element of the program. Notwithstanding the underlying objection of some of us to any government funding of these programs at all, if such programs do receive government funds, beneficiaries should be given notice of the religious and integral nature of the program, their right to choose between such a program and programs which do not require religious participation (including secular programs), and their option to leave the integral program at any time. If government does fund an integral program, then a beneficiary's religious liberty should be protected by ensuring choice between readily accessible programs of equal value, rather than through the right to opt out of the religious activities in a particular program.

6. *Prohibition on use of government grant or contract funds for religious activities.* The Supreme Court has held that organizations may not constitutionally use government grant or contract funds for religious activities. In federal statutes, this proscription is commonly expressed as a requirement not to use government funds for worship, religious instruction, or proselytizing. It is difficult, if not impossible, to define these concepts. In most situations, determining whether particular activities fall into these categories will depend on the facts and circumstances of each case. Some situations will present difficult questions.

Teaching values or beliefs as religious tenets constitutes religious instruction or proselytizing. An example would be urging a beneficiary to accept Jesus Christ or some other religious faith as the only way to move from welfare into employment. Discussing with a beneficiary commonly held values such as abiding by the law and being honest does not automatically represent religious instruction or proselytizing, although most, if not all, religions also teach these values. Worship includes such acts as offering prayers and reading scripture, but observing a neutral moment of silence does not constitute worship.

7. *Privately funded religious activities.* A provider that receives government contract or grant money may offer religious activities as well as the government-funded services as long as the religious activities are privately funded, purely voluntary, and clearly separate from the activities funded by government. For example, a religious provider that offers government-funded welfare-to-work counseling may post notices about support groups that engage in prayer and Bible study as long as the support groups are privately funded, participation in them is voluntary, and it is clear that the groups are separate from the welfare-to-work counseling. A provider that offers government-funded services may leave religious literature on tables in waiting rooms if the religious literature is paid for with private funds and it is clear that acceptance of the materials is voluntary and not a part of the government-funded program.

8. *Employment decisions on the basis of religion.* Federal law does not prohibit religious organizations from taking religious beliefs and practices into account in making decisions about hiring, promotion, termination, and other conditions of employment. The Supreme Court has not addressed whether a religious organization retains the liberty to make employment decisions on the basis of religion in the case of employees who work in programs or activities funded (in

whole or in part) by, or paid with, government money. Although the law is not settled in this area of government-funded positions, we agree that religious organizations retain their ability to use religious criteria in employment for those positions in nongovernmental programs that are wholly privately funded, regardless of whether other programs or activities of the organization receive government funds.

9. Display of religious art and use of a religious name. A religious provider receiving government funds is permitted to display religious art, icons, symbols, and scripture under certain conditions. Religious providers should not be required to eliminate religious references from their names (e.g., government should not require a St. Vincent de Paul Center to be renamed the Mr. Vincent de Paul Center). In constitutional rulings, the presence of religious art, icons, symbols, and scripture within a private organization offering social services has not, by itself, disqualified an entity from receiving government funds. However, the presence of such art, icons, and symbols has been considered by the Supreme Court in the overall determination of whether an entity is constitutionally permitted to accept government funding.[9]

10. Fiscal accountability. The federal government has the right to audit the funds it disburses. If a religious organization does not segregate the government contract and grant funds it receives, all of its accounts could be subject to an audit. Segregating the government money will decrease a religious organization's risk that all of its funds will be examined in a government audit.

11. Creation of a separately incorporated organization. Government is not precluded from requiring a pervasively religious organization to create a separate organization to provide government-funded services.[10] Even if government does not require such a separate organization, houses of worship and other pervasively religious organizations may wish to (and, some of us believe, should) create one. A separate organization facilitates keeping separate accounts to limit audits and helps to shield them from certain federal requirements that otherwise are triggered by the receipt of federal funds (see paragraph 12 below). Separate incorporation can also afford protection for the religious organization against liabilities incurred by the separate corporation.

12. Civil rights regulation of social service providers receiving government funds. Receipt of federal funds triggers the application of a number of federal civil rights statutes. These laws prohibit discrimination on the basis of race, color, national origin, sex, age, disability, and visual impairment.[11] Religious organizations that receive federal funds are subject to these laws. Religious organizations should consult legal counsel regarding the requirements of these laws and other regulations that may apply, including other federal, state, and local laws and ordinances.

CONFLICTING PERSPECTIVES ON GOVERNMENT FUNDING OF RELIGIOUS ORGANIZATIONS TO PROVIDE SOCIAL SERVICES

Notwithstanding the broad areas of agreement noted above concerning government funding of religious social-service organizations, the groups involved in this discussion remain deeply divided about "charitable choice." Some are strong supporters of "charitable choice"; others are equally strong opponents of this change in law and policy. The disagreements involve political philosophy, interpretation of current law, beliefs about the best way to protect and support the work of religious institutions, and pragmatic concerns. The contrasting positions are briefly sketched below both to illuminate the importance of the concerns raised on the two sides and to highlight the importance of the agreements we have reached after extensive discussion.

In Favor of "Charitable Choice"

"Charitable choice" is an innovative and carefully crafted means to expand government financial collaboration with religious organizations to meet critical social needs, while protecting beneficiaries, providers, the public trust, and constitutional values.

The past approach was, roughly, for government to permit funds only to religiously affiliated organizations providing secular services in a secular setting. "Pervasively religious" organizations, which displayed an integral religious character, were excluded. "Charitable choice" instead permits religious and secular organizations alike to participate as government-funded social service providers. "Charitable choice" enables government to fulfill its constitutional obligation not to establish religion and its constitutional duty to protect the religious liberty of beneficiaries without imposing illegitimate secularizing requirements on religious social service providers.

"Charitable choice" is constitutional. The U. S. Supreme Court, which has never wholly excluded "pervasively religious" organizations from government funding, has turned away from the strict separationist concept that undergirds opposition to "charitable choice." Recently, the Court did not use the "pervasively religious" criterion as the determining factor in deciding whether a religious organization may receive government funded services.[12] Even before this decision the Court had upheld direct governmental cash reimbursements for secular services performed by institutions that had been considered pervasively religious.[13]

"Charitable choice" ends government discrimination in the treatment of religious providers. The new standard is government neutrality. Government may now select from among all providers, based only on their ability to supply the needed

social services. "Charitable choice" does not guarantee funds to religious organizations; it creates a level playing field, removing the past bias against religious providers whose faith visibly shapes the organization's staff, character, and service delivery. This is not government endorsement of religion, but rather the end of the presumption that government should endorse only secular prescriptions for poverty and need.

"Charitable choice" protects the religious character of faith-based providers without establishing religion. It safeguards their autonomy by protecting their religious character if they accept government funds. They may maintain a religious environment and continue to select staff of like beliefs as long as they provide the assistance that government seeks and do not spend direct government funds on inherently religious activities. They may accept vouchers to aid beneficiaries who seek faith-based help. Providers are accountable for how they spend government funds, but without excessive government entanglement. They may limit government audits by establishing a separate account for government funds; government may require them to establish a separate organization for the government-funded services. When government buys services, it is not aiding the religious organization, but rather obtaining needed social services.

"Charitable choice" protects the religious liberty of beneficiaries. Beneficiaries may not be denied help on account of their religion nor be forced to participate in inherently religious activities to obtain help. Government must ensure that a secular alternative is available. These are specific requirements of "charitable choice" as enacted in the 1996 federal welfare law and they are crucial to guard against religious coercion. Early experience shows that beneficiaries have not had to bend to someone else's faith in order to receive help, but rather have enjoyed an expanded range of services and providers.[14]

"Charitable choice," prudently implemented, enhances social provision. Religious organizations are not required to contract with government nor to stop seeking donations and voluntary support. They should evaluate carefully the new funding opportunities, being mindful of the risk of dependency on government funds, the paperwork and regulatory burden, and the temptation to mute criticism of government or to adapt their mission to whatever government will fund. They should reject government money if accepting it will compromise their convictions or undermine their effectiveness. Government officials, for their part, should welcome the opportunity to select whichever provider offers the most effective help and the chance to offer a greater diversity of services. They must ensure that their rules effectively protect both the religious character of providers and the religious liberty of beneficiaries.

"Charitable choice" serves the needy. Government's desire for effective social services often coincides with faith-based organizations' ability to serve the poor

with excellence and respect. There is no need to choose between the First Amendment and the expanded involvement of faith-based providers. "Charitable choice" is a constructive alternative to an inequitable strategy which sought to protect beneficiaries and prevent religious establishment but at the price of excluding many religious providers. It is constitutionally sound, socially valuable, and pragmatically wise that such organizations are now permitted to use government funds, as other providers do, to provide the services government desires and that hurting families, individuals, and communities need.

Opposed to "Charitable Choice"

"Charitable choice" undermines governmental neutrality toward religion and promotes government funded discrimination. It also jeopardizes beneficiaries' rights to religious liberty, and threatens the autonomy and vitality of religion and religious liberty.

"Charitable choice" undermines governmental neutrality toward religion. "Charitable choice" is designed to allow houses of worship and other organizations that integrate religion into their social services to receive funds generated through taxation. When the government funds these institutions, it inevitably results in governmental funding and advancing religion itself, which is unconstitutional. Every member of the current Supreme Court has expressed concern about government funds flowing directly to pervasively religious organizations.[15]

Governmental advancement of religion is not just some abstract legal problem. It creates resentment when taxpayers are forced to support religions they reject. Legal and ethical claims are triggered when taxpayers are denied tax-funded employee positions because they aren't the "right" religion or don't hold the "right" religious beliefs. Furthermore, by requiring elected leaders to pick and choose among competing religions to award a limited number of social service grants and contracts, "charitable choice" creates an opportunity for using religion as a political tool and heightens religious divisions.

"Charitable choice" promotes government-funded discrimination. "Charitable choice" expressly allows religious organizations that receive government funds for their services to discriminate on the basis of religion in their employment practices. We believe that this results in government-funded discrimination and violates the Establishment Clause by using taxpayer money to advance a particular religious viewpoint. While churches and religious agencies retain the ability to make employment decisions on the basis of religion for privately funded positions, that right should not extend to those who provide the services that are funded by the government.

"Charitable choice" jeopardizes beneficiaries' rights to religious liberty. By making it possible to integrate tax-funded secular services with religious ones, "charitable

choice" practically invites the use of social service beneficiaries as a captive audience for proselytizing and other religious activities. Although "charitable choice" ostensibly requires access to alternative providers and a limited right to opt-out from religious activities, it will be very difficult for some beneficiaries to exercise these rights. Our concern is not with religious activities themselves, of course, but with governmental coercion in religious matters.

"Charitable choice" threatens the autonomy and vitality of religion and religious liberty. It is the government's obligation to demand accountability for its funds. When government funds flow to houses of worship and other pervasively religious groups, this obligation will invite excessive and unconstitutional entanglement between the institutions of church and state. If a house of worship accepts government money, for example, the regulation that attaches to the government money could bind the entire church, the church's books could be audited, and "charitable choice" lawsuits could jeopardize the church's assets.

Furthermore, we are concerned about religion's dependency on government funds and the effect that this will have on religion's willingness to serve as a prophetic critic of government. We also fear that, as many policymakers come to view religion as simply a cog in the vast engine of social reform, religion will be distorted, distracted, and demeaned. Religion in America is vibrant because it is fully owned and operated by believers, rather than by any governmental bureaucracy.

"Charitable choice" is part of several laws; therefore, we offer the following general recommendations to religious organizations:

—Houses of worship and other pervasively religious organizations (those that cannot or do not wish to clearly separate any privately funded religious activities from secular activities and refrain from discrimination on the basis of religion in hiring with government funds) should refrain from seeking government funds. Houses of worship and other pervasively religious institutions should remain self-supporting to protect taxpayers' consciences, governmental neutrality, and religious vitality. These organizations may cooperate with the government in nonfinancial ways (see areas of agreement) and seek funding from various private sources, including charitable foundations and corporate sponsorships.

—If houses of worship or other pervasively religious organizations would like to create separate organizations to receive tax funds, they must ensure that the secular services that are offered are clearly distinct from any privately funded religious activities, that tax money is not used for religious activities, including discrimination on the basis of religion in hiring, and that any participation in religious activities by beneficiaries is purely voluntary. These organizations must be prepared to be subject to the same general regulations that apply to any other recipient of government funds. Many organizations already operate in this fashion and we strongly recommend that other religious organizations create such religious affiliates.

Because government officials are charged not only with implementing "charitable choice," but also with upholding the Constitution, we urge them to seek guidance from an attorney because "charitable choice" conflicts in many respects with the Constitution.

APPENDIX: NON-GOVERNMENT COMMUNITY SUPPORT FOR FAITH-BASED ORGANIZATIONS

Regardless of one's position on the constitutionality and advisability of "charitable choice," partnerships and sources of funding in the private sector are available to religious organizations that desire to serve members and neighbors in need.

Funding possibilities include special appeals within houses of worship or denominations, grants from charitable foundations, and corporate giving alliances. Partnerships with various other sectors in the community could include

—Partnerships with banks to create non-profit housing programs.

—Partnerships with businesses in job training and placement programs.

—Partnerships with private hospitals in staffing and supplying congregation-based health clinics.

—Partnerships with community organizations in adult education, literacy, ESL, childcare and youth violence intervention programs.

—Partnerships with national social service coordinating organizations (such as Catholic Charities or United Jewish Communities) that facilitate local community work.

Signatories

The undersigned are a diverse group of religious, charitable, civil rights, and educational organizations. Each recognizes and respects the historical and contemporaneous importance of the role that religious freedom, as embodied in the Free Exercise and Establishment Clauses of the First Amendment, has played and will continue to play in the life of this country. Each also recognizes that government and the private sector, including religious organizations, have legitimate, distinct, and important responsibilities in addressing societal needs. Organizations that share these core assumptions may nevertheless have differing interpretations of the United States Constitution, particularly as applied to the question of government funding for the social work of religious organizations. The legislative provisions known as "charitable choice," which represent a particular approach to the participation of religious organizations in the delivery of government-funded social services, have focused attention on this controversial area. Some of the organizations listed below supported the "charitable choice" provision; some opposed it and some took no position. While not every organization listed below agrees with every statement in this document, it is their hope that the document will provide useful insights for government officials, social service providers, and beneficiaries in this complex and sensitive area.

Signatories

American Baptist Churches USA; American Jewish Committee; Baptist Joint Committee; The Becket Fund; Call to Renewal; Catholic Charities USA; The Center for Public Justice; Columbus School of Law, Catholic University of America; Evangelicals for Social Action; Feinstein Center for American Jewish History, Temple University; First Amendment Center, The Freedom Forum World Center; Friends Committee on National Legislation (Quaker); General Board of Church and Society, The United Methodist Church; Islamic Supreme Council of America; National Association of Evangelicals; National Council of Churches of Christ in the USA; The Salvation Army; Sikh Mediawatch and Resource Task Force (SMART); Soka Gakkai International–USA Buddhist Association; United States Catholic Conference

Draftees

Professor Marshall Breger, *Columbus School of Law, Catholic University of America;* Stanley Carlson-Thies, *Director of Social Policy Studies, The Center for Public Justice;* Professor Robert A. Destro, *Acting Dean, Columbus School of Law, Catholic University of America;* Richard T. Foltin, *Legislative Director and Counsel, American Jewish Committee;* Dr. Murray Friedman, *Director of the Philadelphia Chapter of the American Jewish Committee and Director of the Feinstein Center for American Jewish History, Temple University;* Nancy Isserman, *Associate Director, Feinstein Center for American Jewish History, Temple University;* John A. Liekweg, *Associate General Counsel, United States Catholic Conference;* Forest D. Montgomery, *Counsel, NAE Office for Governmental Affairs, National Association of Evangelicals;* Melissa Rogers, *former General Counsel, Baptist Joint Committee;* Duane Shank, *Issue and Policy Advisor, Call to Renewal;* Julie Segal, *former Legislative Counsel, Americans United for Separation of Church and State;* Jeffrey Sinensky, *Director of Domestic Policy and General Counsel, American Jewish Committee;* Dr. Stephen Steinlight, *Senior Fellow and Director of Publications, American Jewish Committee;* Heidi Unruh, *Policy Analyst, Evangelicals for Social Action.*

NOTES

1. The opinions expressed herein do not necessarily reflect the views of The Pew Charitable Trusts.

2. The terms "faith-based organization" or "religious organization" are used here as umbrella terms encompassing any organization that is motivated by faith, affiliated with a faith tradition, or that incorporates religion in its activities in any way. The term applies, therefore, to a range of organizational forms including houses of worship as well as separately incorporated nonprofits.

3. For the purposes of this document, the phrase "social services" includes services such as job training, counseling, child care, and job search assistance, but does not include elementary and secondary education.

4. TANF is Temporary Assistance for Needy Families, the program that in 1996 replaced the long-standing Aid to Families with Dependent Children (AFDC) welfare program.

5. The "charitable choice" provision applies to the following government funds (as of December 31, 2000): the Temporary Assistance to Needy Families (TANF) funds provided in the Personal Responsibility and Work Opportunity Reconciliation Act (Public Law 104-193 [1996]); the Community Services Block Grant funds provided in the Community Opportunities, Accountability, and Training and Educational Services Act (Community Services Block Grant Act, Public Law 105-285 [1998]); the Children's Health Act of 2000 (Public Law 106-310 [2000]); and the New Markets Venture Capital Program Act (Public Law 106-554 [2000]).

6. Government funds means any funds received by government by taxation or any other means.

7. The phrase "pervasively sectarian" has been used by the Supreme Court in some of its decisions. Some have criticized the term "sectarian" as being pejorative and reflecting bias. See the plurality opinion in *Mitchell* v. *Helms,* 530 U.S. 793 (2000). Because the term "sectarian" is controversial, this document will use the phrase "pervasively religious" in place of "pervasively sectarian." The concept of religious pervasiveness is discussed in the "Conflicting Perspectives" section, below.

8. This document does not constitute legal advice, nor does it create any attorney-client professional relationship. A knowledgeable attorney should be consulted for specific advice about religious organizations and government funding.

9. The Supreme Court has in some cases used the presence of religious symbols as one of the indicators of whether an organization is, in the Court's words, "pervasively sectarian." This concept of "pervasively sectarian" and its validity are discussed in the "Conflicting Perspectives" section below.

10. In cases where separate organizations are created, we disagree about whether they have to be secular. Some of us believe the Constitution requires that a separate organization cannot be pervasively religious if it is to receive government funds. Others of us believe that the Constitution does not permit government to require such a separate organization to have a particular religious or secular character.

11. 20 U.S.C. Section 1681 et seq. (1990), 29 U.S.C. Section 794 (1985), 42 U.S.C. Section 2000d et seq. (1994), 42 U.S.C. Section 6101 et seq. (1995).

12. *Mitchell* v. *Helms,* 530 U.S. 793 (2000).

13. *Committee for Public Ed. And Religious Liberty* v. *Regan,* 444 U.S. 646 (1980).

14. A. Sherman, "The Growing Impact of Charitable Choice," Center for Public Justice, (March 2000).

15. In *Mitchell* v. *Helms*, 530 U.S. 793 (2000) (upholding a program of government-funded loans of computers to religious schools), a four-justice plurality of the Court observed: "Of course, we have seen 'special Establishment Clause dangers' [cite omitted], when money is given to religious schools or entities directly rather than . . . indirectly [cites omitted]. But direct payments of money are not at issue in this case. . . ." 530 U.S. at ___ (Thomas, J., for the Court). The views expressed by the five concurring and dissenting justices were even firmer on the Establishment Clause concerns that are presented when taxpayers' funds flow to religious institutions. As Justice O'Connor has noted, "our concern with direct monetary aid is based on more than just [concern about] diversion [of tax-funded aid to religious use]. In fact, the most important reason for according special treatment to direct money grants is that this form of aid falls precariously close to the original object of the Establishment Clause's prohibition." 530 U.S. at ___ (O'Connor, J.) (concurring).

CHAPTER TWENTY

The Breaking Points:
When Consensus Becomes Conflict

MELISSA ROGERS

Americans are engaged in a vigorous and multifaceted debate on government funding of the provision of social services by religious groups. There is significant agreement and also strong disagreement in this area, and some of the differences represent multiple and competing visions of religious freedom.

Even people with vastly different perspectives on the appropriate relationship between church and state can agree on certain methods of cooperation between the government and religious social service providers. They can agree, for example, that the government may create certain tax incentives, such as the one that would allow taxpayers who do not itemize to take a deduction for charitable giving. Similarly, there is strong agreement that the government may call upon corporations and foundations to give more to those in need. President Bush has noted, "[c]urrently, six of the ten largest corporate givers in America explicitly rule out or restrict donations to faith-based groups." Even those who vehemently disagree about some church-state issues agree that those restrictions are unnecessary and in many cases unwise. Virtually everyone agrees that the institutions of religion and government may share information, serve on task forces together, and work in nonfinancial cooperation.

Increasing government-supported technical assistance to nongovernmental organizations, including religious ones, is another important yet largely unheralded point of agreement. The government may offer workshops to help nongovernment social service providers learn how to apply for grants and contracts and educate them about the substantive opportunities and obligations created by various laws and regulations.

Government funds may be used and the government itself may train volunteers gathered by and from houses of worship and other community groups for service in tax-funded social service programs. The government also may assist in the formation of new nonprofit organizations. Although some providers may choose not to take advantage of those opportunities, there does not appear to be opposition to offering that kind of assistance.

There is even some agreement relating to the most difficult and important questions in the debate. How religious may a group or program be and remain eligible to receive government funding to provide social services? There is widespread agreement that religious providers may retain their religious name and receive tax funds to provide secular services that stem from religious motivation. Despite President Bush's complaint that "[s]ome critics [of charitable choice] object to the idea of government funding going to any group motivated by faith," the right of groups to provide services because they feel a religious motivation to do so is not a matter of serious debate. Many also agree that a religious provider should not be required to clear its buildings of all religious symbols in order to be eligible to receive tax money.

Nonetheless, there is serious debate on how the religious activities and character of a social service provider coexist with the tax-funded aid or program. The debate is squarely raised by the charitable choice provision that President Bush wishes to expand. As *In Good Faith* notes, charitable choice "is a term of art that refers to a specific legislative proposal first enacted by Congress in the 1996 federal welfare reform law." It refers specifically "to the new statutory conditions under which states may enter into funding relationships with religious organizations that provide social services" and "permits all faith-based organizations to compete for government social service funding, regardless of their religious nature." One of the premises of charitable choice, therefore, is the notion that it is unfair and discriminatory to label certain religious organizations "too religious" to compete for tax funds. The Bush administration is pursuing an expansion of the charitable choice concept through legislation as well as through revision of existing regulations regarding certain social service providers.

The charitable choice provision of the 1996 welfare reform law states that a religious organization may receive government money for its provision of social services while retaining "control over the definition, development, practice, and expression of its religious beliefs." It also states that no grant or contract money may be spent on "sectarian worship, instruction, or proselytization" and that no beneficiary may be discriminated against on the basis of religion.

Although many agree that the charitable choice safeguards against government establishment of religion are necessary, they disagree over whether they are sufficient. Some believe that ensuring that tax money is not used to buy Bibles or force conversion is important but that it leaves significant issues open regarding the coexistence of tax aid and privately funded religious activity.

More specifically, those critics worry that tax money will flow to churches and other institutions that weave religious activities and emphases into tax-funded ones, creating captive audiences for religious outreach and indoctrination and resulting in government establishment of and excessive entanglement with religion.

The Bush administration has proposed further safeguards to address some of those dangers. With respect to government grants and contracts, the administration has suggested that any privately funded "sectarian worship, instruction, or proselytization" activities should be separate from government-funded activities and voluntarily attended by beneficiaries. Critics are skeptical that such safeguards could or would be adequately implemented and are resolute in their belief that other constitutional dangers remain.

Meanwhile, the last thing some conservatives want is more regulation of religious providers who participate in the faith-based initiative. Indeed, a vocal band of conservatives believe that its safeguards regarding religious activities are unnecessary and unacceptable. The problem with charitable choice, according to those critics, is that it does not go far enough toward allowing any religious group to receive government money free of rules and restrictions.

Michael Horowitz and Marvin Olasky have jointly called for certain modifications of charitable choice. They argue that "[g]overnment officials with the power to award or withhold discretionary grants should be unconditionally barred from directly or indirectly influencing or dictating the form or frequency of prayers offered by or required of participants in faith-based grant programs, and they should never be permitted to exercise any authority over the religious content of such programs."

Indeed, such concerns have led some conservatives to urge that any government faith-based initiative be conducted entirely through tax incentives or individual social service vouchers; their belief is that doing so greatly diminishes the risk of government regulation. As mentioned earlier, most parties can find some common ground on certain tax incentives, like the deduction for nonitemizers. Vouchers, however, are controversial for a number of reasons, some of which are related to church-state concerns.

Charitable choice vouchers are not subject to any restrictions on expenditures for "sectarian worship, instruction and proselytization." Further, some proposals would not provide a beneficiary with the right to opt out of religious activities if the beneficiary uses a voucher. For those reasons, vouchers provide multiple points for debate. On one side are those who believe that vouchers are on firm constitutional ground, pointing to the Supreme Court's recognition that individual choice may function as a sort of "circuit breaker" in the link between government and religion in particular cases. On the other side are those who question whether truly voluntary choices can be made in certain situations and who emphasize other Supreme Court cases in which the Court seems to have laid the groundwork to reject vouchers. It is important to note that the Supreme Court has recently agreed to decide whether it is constitutional to include religious schools in a tax-supported voucher program. The decision in the case will be closely scrutinized for its impact on the debate over religious organizations and tax-funded social services.

Another crucial question in the debate concerns the regulation of religious providers that receive tax funds. The Bush administration has released an "audit" of five federal agencies for "barriers" to the participation of faith-based and community organizations. Some limited agreement may emerge on the topic of regulatory reform. All can agree, for example, that because constitutional principles do not vary from program to program or agency to agency, regulations—to the extent that they express constitutional principles—should not either. All will also agree that there should be no religious set-asides—in other words, no money should be reserved for use only by religious social service providers. And, if the church-state debate is put to the side, there may be more significant agreement about regulatory reform efforts aimed broadly at nongovernment social service providers.

But some of the items that the administration identifies as unnecessary "barriers" to the participation of religious social service providers are what others consider crucial constitutional protections or necessary requirements of public policy. The administration, for example, counts as a barrier regulatory prohibitions on hiring on the basis of religion with regard to tax-funded employee positions within religious groups. There is strong agreement that religious groups have the right to hire on the basis of religion for positions that are wholly privately funded, but fierce debate about whether that right does or should exist in hiring for tax-funded positions.

Those who count that type of regulation as a barrier believe that robust religious autonomy need not and should not be diminished when a religious organization receives tax funds. Successful results are an important form of accountability to the taxpayer, they say, and such results can best be produced when the organization's members are united by shared religious belief. Furthermore, they point to a Supreme Court decision that upholds the statutory right of religious organizations to hire on the basis of religion.

Critics of the idea acknowledge that the Supreme Court has upheld that right as a general matter in a case that did not involve tax funds, but they stress that the Court has not addressed the issue of whether a religious organization may hire on a religious basis for tax-funded positions. They argue that an organization offends basic notions of taxpayer accountability when it makes religious distinctions in employee positions supported by tax funds. These critics believe that when such conflicts arise between the right to religious autonomy and the obligation of accountability for tax funds, the organization should either refuse to accept the funds or give way to the government.

A host of related regulatory issues may come into sharper focus as new religious providers, including houses of worship, enter the tax-funded social service delivery system. While charitable choice promises religious providers that they can maintain their independence from government, including "control over the definition, development, practice, and expression of [their] religious beliefs," the receipt of tax funds will create new accountability obligations for first-time participants in the "government-by-proxy" system. Novel issues will arise regarding the strength of the right to religious autonomy when tax funds are involved.

The government's obligation to protect beneficiaries' rights to religious liberty when tax money flows to religious social service providers is another key area of discussion. There is widespread agreement that an alternative should be available for anyone who wants one and that beneficiaries should not be turned away from tax-funded programs because they are not of the "right" religion. Many on different sides of the debate also agree that some work must be done to ensure that theoretical rights in that area translate into practical ones.

But differences emerge here as well. There is disagreement over whether the alternative must be a clearly secular one or one that is "unobjectionable to the individual on religious grounds." And, while all oppose barring beneficiaries from tax-funded programs on the basis of their religious beliefs, some argue that funding certain religious programs without adequate safeguards will effectively result in discriminating against some beneficiaries in that way.

One of the most fundamental disagreements is over the issue of whether a beneficiary should have a choice only *among* providers or whether that choice should be married with a choice *within* particular tax-funded, faith-based programs about whether to participate in religious activities. Some believe that there is no need to provide a right to opt out of religious activities in a faith-based program if there is an adequate alternative program. Others insist that opt-outs are critical in all cases, in part because there will be many times, they argue, when the beneficiary will not know about or have easy access to a secular alternative that is of equal value. Still others find opt-outs necessary when the tax-supported program is conducted through grants and contracts, but not when participants pay with vouchers.

Philosophical divisions on these issues also are reflected on the Supreme Court. The Court is deeply divided, for example, over the meaning of government neutrality toward religion on funding questions. A plurality of the justices define this neutrality as requiring that the government aid itself must be secular and offered in an evenhanded way to religious and nonreligious bodies alike. The plurality argues that the government is decidedly not neutral toward religion when it gives any consideration to whether the potential recipient institution is pervasively religious in nature. On the other side of the debate are three justices who argue that, while evenhandedness in the distribution of aid has been an important factor in particular cases, neutrality also describes the obligation of the government to occupy the middle ground between governmental encouragement and discouragement of religion. These justices claim that this middle ground is lost if there can be no consideration of the pervasively religious character of the recipient institution or if the government cannot apply the safeguards necessary to ensure that the aid will not be used to advance religion. The justices between these two camps find the plurality's neutrality factors to be significant and agree that there should be no presumption that aid to certain religious institutions will inevitably result in governmental aid for religion. But these justices argue that the plurality's factors cannot be assigned singular importance because they ignore such issues as whether aid was direct or indirect and whether it has been diverted to advance a religious mission.

There are many ways in which the government and religious social service providers may cooperate that do not implicate these fundamental divisions. When proposals touch on these fundamental issues, however, we will continue to witness the clash of multiple visions of religious freedom.

CHAPTER TWENTY-ONE

Holy Waters: Plunging into the Sea of Faith-Based Initiatives

PETER STEINFELS

Is there anyone who has not, as child or adult, stood fascinated on a beach, trying to predict which of the ceaseless, crisscrossing ranks of foam-specked waves would prove the largest? Which swells, converging or coming quickly on one another, would break modestly and quietly flow back? Which would rear up and, with a huge splash, dash farthest up the sand?

Why are we so easily transfixed by that seaside drama? Surely one reason is the tension it creates between fear and delight. We never entirely shed that instinctive wariness, the tremor that braces us, on all but the calmest days, to dodge back from the oncoming surf. We never lose the small, secret dread that this breaker will be the monster that sucks everything out to sea. But then there is a counterimpulse, the sheer exuberance in being part of the pounding, rhythmic wash, the anticipation of new patterns drawn in the sand, new bits of sparkling shells and well-worn shining pebbles left behind.

It now is evident that the current debate over government support for faith-based initiatives is just such a big breaker, one that could be seen building, wave by wave, from a long way off—and one that for me, but obviously not for everyone, has produced far more delight than anxiety.

Everyone recognizes that one swelling force contributing to the current debate was the political resurgence in the late 1970s of conservative Christianity—the "religious right," to use the useful shorthand for the most outspoken and militant sector of a larger, more diffuse movement. Reactions to that resurgence, pro and con, fed a national discussion about the role of religion in public life, a discussion already stimulated by periodic civil libertarian challenges to government-sponsored displays of Christmas trees and other religious symbols, by conservative attempts to restore or defend religious activities in public school settings, and most seriously by the question of whether opposition to the 1973 legalization of abortion by the Supreme Court in *Roe* v. *Wade* constituted an illegitimate intrusion of religious belief in political life. That discussion added new phrases to our political vocabulary: "naked public square" and "culture of disbelief" joined older imagery like "wall of separation."

Meanwhile, another movement had been growing since the 1960s, one of dissatisfaction with large-scale government agencies and programs of all kinds, from highway building to urban renewal, from public housing and welfare to big-city school systems, from institutions for the mentally disabled to the Army Corps of Engineers. Initially, many of the critiques came from the "new left" of civil rights and antipoverty activists. Then, as affirmative action programs and environmental controls complicated business operations, traditional antigovernment and pro-market advocates began to inspire a new array of policy proposals. The left talked grass roots and community control; the right talked entrepreneurship and privatization. Both revived Toquevillian notions of intermediate associations.

Two other currents reinforced the wave. American conservatives have always emphasized moral discipline as essential to social cohesion—even while they promoted a market economy that, as Daniel Bell noted in *The Cultural Contradictions of Capitalism*, has had few equals in undermining established patterns of living. By contrast, many liberals viewed that moral emphasis, often associated with traditional religion, as one of the tools by which the powerful maintained an unjust status quo: pie in the sky when you die, but caffeine, clean living, and hard work to keep you productive in the meantime. The suggestion that social policy should address matters of personal character or living habits among those in need was quickly labeled "blaming the victim." By the late 1970s, however, political backlash from the countercultural outbreaks of the preceding decade had forced liberals, if only for self-protective reasons, to acknowledge that social policy could not ignore issues of character, conduct, and moral norms. By the 1990s, a good number were maintaining without embarrassment that liberalism's emphasis on economic improvement had to operate in tandem with attention to personal responsibility and personal transformation.

Not unrelated to that shift in liberalism were developments among the African American leadership. Once at the center of national soul-searching and consequent political upheaval, black leaders increasingly appeared to be running in place. Their by-now familiar concerns were accepted as predictable components of interest-group politics; their consistent demands for expanded federal programs were registered or ignored as confidence in those programs rose or fell. Black politics often seemed distant, except rhetorically, from the most obvious needs of the black community and the persistent disparities between black and white. The compelling identification of the civil rights movement with ordinary people struggling mightily to retain or regain their dignity in oppressive circumstances seemed attenuated. The story is a complicated one of generational transition, of economic change, and, to borrow from Max Weber, of inevitably routinized charisma, and the end is by no means clear. In the meantime, however, new energy has flowed from what was always the wellspring of African American leadership, the church. If momentum was stalled at the national level, it would pick up again in the neighborhood and on the street corner. If faith-based initiatives have resonated far beyond the church basements, it is because of their link with the most morally significant movement in American politics of the last century.

Each one of these forces—the reentry of conservative Christians into active citizenship, the intense discussion of religion's legitimate place in political discourse and civic life, the criticism of entrenched bureaucracies by advocates of entrepreneurship and of community, the "re-moralization" of social policy, the religious reincarnation of the black drive for dignity and equality—strikes me as essentially healthy. Not that I do not find problematic aspects—of the religious right's emergence, for example, and the free marketeers' enthusiasm for privatization. Others may have different worries. Nonetheless, much of what is freshest and best in American politics has converged in the debate about faith-based initiatives, and almost no matter how the debate turns out, I rather expect to be happy that it has taken place.

If nothing else, the debate has allowed religion to "get some respect." It may sound strange to suggest, in one of the world's most publicly religious nations, where no presidential speech ends without mention of God, that religion is in any way wanting for respect. Yet for all the public professions of faith and overt or covert appeals to religious voters, when it comes to designing social policy, religion and religious institutions ordinarily have been bracketed. The reason is not antireligious sentiment (I will get to that in a moment), but the deeply bred conviction that faith is essentially personal and private, no more to be hauled into conscious policymaking than to be recorded in the census. At one level, most people have probably assumed that religious beliefs and affiliation might have a great deal to do with work habits and family stability, without knowing precisely what. At another level, that very big hunch was not considered pertinent to policymaking or to policy-oriented research, any more than, one suspects, the current administration considered religion and faith-based initiatives something to be factored into its energy policy.

So while many religious leaders may be feeling satisfied at the very public acknowledgment of faith's social role inherent in charitable choice proposals, their satisfaction reveals a measure of religion's new weakness as well as its continuing strength. After all, there was a time when no one required statistical proof of faith's efficacy in shaping lives. That was taken for granted, so much so as normally to escape notice. Fish aren't aware of water until it begins to drain away. Nonetheless, even a somewhat diminished and contested religious presence in American life remains enormously powerful, and recognizing that fact simply enlarges our political elite's grasp of reality.

But the debate about government and faith-based initiatives also has given us a new, and I think helpful, way of approaching a long-standing American quandary recently rendered ever more complicated. How does a society so dramatically diverse—and so committed to the rights of the venturesome, free-wheeling individual—maintain the minimal degree of moral consensus any society needs to survive? Two centuries ago, the United States effectively invented religious pluralism in spite of the general belief that such an arrangement could end only in religious, moral, and social chaos. That didn't happen. Instead, religion flourished as in few comparable societies; morality and social norms, rooted in religion, held firm. The truth, however, is that for much of that time, religious diversity in the United States was only a fraction of what it has become today. Throughout the nineteenth century, a broad evangelical Christianity was established culturally if not politically, and despite some surface squabbling and at least one major conflict—Prohibition—it managed to graft Roman Catholics and Jews into what became, up through the middle of the twentieth century, a successor "Judeo-Christian" establishment, quite similar in its moral and cultural function. Only recently have we had to imagine getting along without any such establishment. Only recently have we had to contemplate the meaning not only of true religious pluralism but also of moral pluralism. Does our generally positive experience with the government's religious neutrality now extend logically to a kind of moral neutrality on the part of official institutions that increasingly touch all aspects of our lives, from genetic experimentation to child care and education, from economic security to health care and treatment for terminal illnesses? Would such a position really be neutral or constitute itself a morality of a particular sort, although probably packaged in the superficially amoral quantitative language of polls, markets, cost-benefit analysis, or utilitarianism? And if we back away from such a questionable neutrality, do we inevitably stumble back into the tangle of religious traditions from which the vast majority of citizens draw their moral sense?

All this may seem quite distant from the concrete, very human concerns about teenage pregnancy, child care, public schooling, addiction, crime control, housing, and employment addressed by contributors to this volume. "Oh no," I can hear them saying. "We never wanted to get into questions so grand and theoretical as those." But it is precisely because they have not begun with grand, theoretical questions but with very concrete, human realities, on the street and in the neighborhood, that the proposals about faith-based initiatives have injected a new creativity into the thinking on larger problem of juggling government, religion, religion-linked morality, diversity, and pluralism. Maybe small experiments will be the stepping-stones to a new social wisdom.

Here, however, I must add my disappointments with the current debate to my enthusiasm for it. It has been disappointing to hear the debate often cast in alarmist terms that detect First Amendment conflicts even before the varying specifics of different faith-based initiatives can be set out. There is no denying potential First Amendment problems. But the speed and emotion with which they have sometimes been evoked suggests to me a desire to cut off discussion at the earliest stage possible. I admit that my attitude is shaped by the conviction that the vast majority of Americans, including those who support faith-based initiatives, are deeply committed to separation of church and state; in my view, we run no great risk if the public is allowed time and tranquillity to assess the legitimately contending ways that this fundamental Constitutional principle can be applied to ambiguous cases.

It also has been disappointing to encounter the occasional antireligious response that is truly visceral, fortified with a store of stereotypes, historical images, and worst-case scenarios defying rational explanation. Similarly disappointing is the way in which "horrible possibilities" have been paraded in this debate—will tax money go into the coffers of the Nation of Islam, Scientologists, witches' covens, goddess worshipers? The prospect of money going to, say, a Wiccan group, since it cannot absolutely be ruled out, is supposed to shock us into opposition to the proposal. There is nothing wrong, indeed there is everything right, with following out the logical implications, however unlikely, of a policy proposal. But such appeals to our supposedly common sense of the "unthinkable" are just too reminiscent of past evocations of other once-marginal groups like Catholics, Jews, Mormons, Jehovah's Witnesses, and Pentecostals. And, when all is said and done, the possibilities being paraded today might be no more horrible than those paraded in the past. In that respect, my final disappointment has been the sudden loss of interest by Pat Robertson and some other conservative Christian leaders in government assistance to faith-based programs when they realized that faiths that they did not approve of would be treated as equals of their own. There is a first lesson here about religious pluralism that apparently they have not learned.

There is one other aspect of the debate that I might find disappointing, were my disappointment not drowned by my sheer puzzlement: the weight given to the two most recurrent objections to government support for faith-based initiatives.

The first common objection is to the possibility that such support would fund religious proselytizing. The second common objection is to the possibility that such support would (indeed, as presently conceived, quite likely would) permit discriminatory hiring by faith-based organizations that require employees to affirm certain beliefs or adhere to certain moral codes. What puzzles me is that the second of these two issues has been given a weight in recent debates at least equal to, if not greater than, that of the first. After all, the first objection—proselytizing people with government funds—touches on the very heart of the First Amendment prohibition of any official establishment of religion. The second objection—religious discrimination in staffing—is a much more recent concern and much less thoroughly founded.

Let me explain. From early in our constitutional history, the power to tax has been recognized as the power to destroy, and the recognition of that power underlies one of the arguments for exempting religious bodies from taxation. The power to determine whom an association or organization employs can also be the power to destroy. That is why, while we have laws barring employment discrimination of various kinds, those barriers against discrimination have to stop short of insisting that enterprises employ people who are unable or unwilling to carry on the enterprise's core activity. Restaurants do not have to hire as chefs people who cannot cook or as waiters people who cannot serve. Hospitals do not have to hire unqualified physicians or nurses who are not devoted to health care.

How should competing protections for hiring organizations and potential hires apply to religious groups? Religious organizations should not be required to hire people, at least in key positions or in significant numbers, if hiring them risks altering the nature of the organization as reflected in its beliefs and practices. Southern Baptist congregations can "discriminate" by ordaining only Southern Baptists. Catholic schools can "discriminate," if they wish, by hiring only Catholics as principals. That principle is reflected in the many exceptions for religious organization found in antidiscrimination statutes, although there remain complicated and unresolved cases in this area. (If the director of an Orthodox Jewish school converts to Pentecostalism, no one doubts the school's right to dismiss him—but what about the school janitor or an athletic coach?) Without such exemptions, prohibitions against religious discrimination could very well work to undermine the capacity of religious organizations to maintain their core identity. The courts have recognized that the power to determine employment would be the power to destroy.

But what happens when a religious body offers services eligible for government funding, such as many of the secular social services mentioned in this volume? One workable model for minimizing the problem of religious discrimination in those cases has been to offer the services through nonprofit organizations that are affiliated with the religious body or its tradition but also organizationally distinct from the worshipping (and possibly proselytizing) community. Leading organizations of that sort that receive government funds include many religiously affiliated hospitals, universities, relief organizations, and social service agencies such as Catholic Charities and Lutheran World Service. They can, and do, hire staff on strictly professional grounds without regard to religious requirements—at least to an extent that has diminished, without entirely eliminating, questions of discrimination.

Critics of expanded government involvement with faith-based organizations have pointed to decades of cooperation with such "secular" affiliates and asked, "If it ain't broke, why fix it?" Certainly, no one would claim that those impressive organizations are "broke." Yet questions have been justly raised about their capacity to make full use of the resources of their own religious traditions in delivering social services and ultimately about their long-term viability. Have they really resolved the dilemma inherent in reducing or removing religious staffing requirements while maintaining a strong religious identity and a strong link to their religious communities? More than one observer, including some within those organizations themselves, have worried that they have been steadily moving away from their religious roots toward becoming generic and thoroughly professionalized human services agencies. Is that bad? At the very least, it means a reduced ability to draw on the energy and resources of religious volunteers. At the most, it threatens the organizations' very raison d'être.

Why should we pretend that we have worked out a good model for cooperation between government and faith-based groups ("It ain't broke") if working with government funds means that Catholics operating Catholic Charities must accept a high risk that the "Catholic" in the title will become meaningless and that, over time, the organization will mirror the Red Cross, the public housing authority, or the state welfare bureau? Why should the Catholic Church run, support, or maybe merely lend its name to an essentially secular or pseudo-state agency? The relationship between a religious group's convictions and its social service agencies and their activities must at some point be maintained by personnel who share those convictions.

Who or what, on the other hand, would be threatened if faith-based organizations that are receiving government funds employed religious criteria in hiring more directly than generally occurs with such nonprofit affiliates? Some professional social workers, perhaps. Gays and lesbians who are struggling to bring themselves under the umbrella of anti-discrimination sentiment and who are aware of religious strictures on homosexuality, perhaps. Maybe anyone who feels that any justification whatsoever for discrimination in hiring, *even* religious discrimination for religious organizations, undermines the general principle of nondiscrimination and eventually harms racial minorities, women, the elderly, the handicapped, and so on. I do not find it puzzling that concern over discrimination against those groups might obscure what to me are weighty considerations in the other direction (that is, concern for protecting the fundamental character or mission of the religious organizations that are making the hires). I do find it puzzling, frankly, that so much of the public goes along with it and apparently shares little of my sense that, when it comes to hiring by religious groups, the objection to discrimination on religious grounds is not only less founded in our Constitutional tradition than the objection to proselytizing but actually runs athwart the First Amendment rights of religious bodies.

The sentiment that no one should be barred from employment without good cause is a sound one, but when it comes to defining "good cause," it almost seems that religion is especially suspect. I do not think that the general public considers hiring on the grounds of a potential employee's "fit" with the hiring organization to be objectionable per se. Other forms of values-related discrimination in hiring appear to be accepted. Suppose that a Planned Parenthood clinic receiving public funds chose not to hire an antiabortion accountant, or a community housing program for low-income elderly people rejected an applicant who opposes government subsidies in general (or doesn't like seniors), or a subsidized arts group refused to consider someone who thinks the arts are a waste of time and money. Whatever the legal status of such decisions, the public would find such "discrimination" understandable, even if the person's performance of the particular job in question was not affected by his or her views. Religious groups, however, appear to be held to a different standard: just as long as a job candidate can do the daily tasks of the position competently, a Southern Baptist group, for example, has no business refusing to hire someone who thinks that the Southern Baptist Convention's approach to the Bible is preposterous and a Catholic group has no business refusing to hire someone who considers the papacy a nefarious institution.

According to a poll taken in March 2001 by the Pew Forum on Religion and Public Life along with the Pew Research Center for the People & the Press, more Americans (78 percent) are troubled by allowing government-funded faith-based groups "to only hire people who share their religious beliefs" than are concerned about proselytizing (60 percent). The question was tweaked for an independent sample that was asked simply whether such groups "should be allowed to hire people on the basis of their religious beliefs." Although the word "only" was dropped in this version and the vaguer "on the basis of their religious beliefs" substituted for "share," 69 percent still said no. That sample also answered yet a third variation, asking whether "religious organizations using government funds to provide social services" should be allowed to hire only people "who share their moral values." Although "moral values" is a broader notion than "religious beliefs," again the respondents overwhelmingly (62 percent) said no.

On this point, then, people of my outlook have a lot of persuading to do. The entire discussion of faith-based initiatives makes little sense, except as a short-run policy fix, if the faith communities mounting such initiatives cannot maintain strong, vibrant identities. There is good evidence that religious groups without distinctive beliefs and practices, preaching nothing but a generic Golden Rule religiosity, cannot mobilize the energies and resources needed even to pass on their faith, let alone address the kind of human problems described in this volume or create and reinforce the civic bonds that any society requires. Most religious charities were founded and are still run on the basis of very distinctive beliefs and practices, very strong group loyalties, and the convictions inculcated by each group's history rather than on the basis of abstract, universal principles or general good will. There is also good evidence, although it is by no means conclusive, that many religious groups are using up that stock of "religious capital"—analogous to the "social capital" that Robert Putnam argues is being depleted[1]—and that it is not being renewed.

The challenge of maintaining religious communities with distinctive and compelling identities will not be met by any program to bolster faith-based initiatives with government aid. The challenge goes well beyond anything that government can or should do. Yet the awareness stirred by the contemporary debate, however it turns out, may help. Already it has turned bright lights on programs and congregations that are brashly uninterested in disguising their religious commitment with a veneer of professional neutrality. And if the debate ends by affirming sharp limits on government involvement with faith-based organizations, it may encourage involvement of private foundations, corporate donors, and individual philanthropists.

The breaker rising up before us may be an imposing one, but not, I am convinced, a destructive one. To those who feel panic, who view the current debate only as menace, who may even be tempted to call the lifeguard to clear the beach, my response is twofold. Relax. Plunge in.

NOTE

1. Robert Putnam, *Bowling Alone* (Simon & Schuster, 2000).

Contributors

ABDULWAHAB ALKEBSI is the executive director of the Islamic Institute. Previously he served as deputy director of the American Muslim Council, executive director of the American Muslim Association for Democracy, and director of international affairs at the Islamic Institute.

JUDITH C. APPELBAUM is vice president and director of employment opportunities at the National Women's Law Center, a nonprofit organization in Washington, D.C. She is an attorney specializing in employment-related issues such as sex discrimination in the workplace and child-care policy.

MARY M. BOGLE serves as a private consultant on early childhood development, youth development, and nonprofit management. Before that she was executive director of Grantmakers for Children, Youth & Families; program specialist for the Head Start Bureau; and a member of the Early Head Start design team. She is co-author of *The Statement of the Advisory Committee on Services for Families with Infants and Toddlers*.

THE REVEREND DR. JOHN BUEHRENS served as president of the Unitarian Universalist Association of Congregations from 1993 to 2001. He is a leader in interfaith cooperation and theological education who helped draft the "Religious Declaration on Sexual Morality, Justice, and Healing."

MARK CHAVES is an associate professor in the Sociology Department of the University of Arizona and principal investigator of the National Congregations Study. His research focuses on the interaction between religion and formal organizations.

MING HSU CHEN, a Paul and Daisy Soros Fellow at New York University Law School, served as a research assistant at the Brookings Institution and as a

337

research fellow at the Pew Forum on Religion and Public Life, where she focused on American politics, civil society, and faith and public life.

ERNESTO CORTES JR. is the executive director of the Southwest Region of the Industrial Areas Foundation (IAF). He founded a network of twelve IAF organizations in Texas and additional IAF projects in Arizona, New Mexico, Louisiana, Nebraska, and the United Kingdom.

FRED DAVIE is vice president for faith-based programs at Public/Private Ventures and an ordained minister in the Presbyterian Church. Previously, he served with the New York City Mission Society, the Brooklyn Ecumenical Cooperatives, and the Presbytery. He also was a program officer in the Community and Resource Development program at the Ford Foundation; Charles H. Revson Fellow at Columbia University; chief of staff to the deputy mayor for community and public affairs in New York City; and deputy borough president of Manhattan.

WILLIAM T. DICKENS is a senior fellow at the Brookings Institution specializing in economics, poverty, trade, income support, labor markets, unemployment, and monetary policy.

JOHN J. DIIULIO JR. is a professor of politics, religion, and civil society and professor of political science at the University of Pennsylvania and nonresident senior fellow at the Brookings Insitution. During his leave from Penn in academic year 2000-2001, he served as assistant to the president of the United States and as the first director of the White House Office of Faith-Based and Community Initiatives. He also serves as senior fellow at the Manhattan Insitute, where he founded the Jeremiah Project, and as board member and senior counsel at Public/Private Ventures.

E. J. DIONNE JR. is a senior fellow at the Brookings Institution, where he focuses on American politics, civil society, and faith and public life. He is a columnist with the *Washington Post* and co-chair, with Jean Bethke Elshtain, of the Pew Forum on Religion and Public Life. He is the author of *Why Americans Hate Politics* and *They Only Look Dead*. He is editor or co-editor of several Brookings volumes: *Community Works*; *What's God Got to Do with the American Experiment?* with John DiIulio; and *Bush v. Gore*, with William Kristol.

CUSHING DOLBEARE is the founder and chair emeritus of the National Low Income Housing Corporation. She currently is a freelance housing policy consultant and a member of the Millennial Housing Commission.

PATRICK F. FAGAN is the William H.G. FitzGerald Fellow in family and culture issues at the Heritage Foundation. His work documents the relationship between marriage and family and national trends, such as teen pregnancy.

THE REVEREND FLOYD FLAKE is a senior fellow at the Manhattan Institute; senior pastor of the Allen African Methodist Episcopal Church; and the president of Edison Charter Schools. From 1986-1997, Reverend Flake served as a representative in the U.S. Congress.

WILLIAM A. GALSTON is a professor at the Maryland School of Public Affairs and director of the Institute for Philosophy and Public Policy. He is a member of the board of the National Campaign to Prevent Teen Pregnancy and serves as chair of the campaign's task force on religion and public values.

JOSEPH R. HACALA is rector of the Jesuit Community and special assistant to the president at Wheeling Jesuit University. From 1997-2001 he served as special assistant to Secretary Andrew Cuomo and director of the Center for Community and Interfaith Partnerships at the U.S. Department of Housing and Urban Development (HUD). Formerly he was the executive director of the Catholic Campaign for Human Development at the United States Catholic Conference.

DEBRA W. HAFFNER is the codirector of the Religious Institute for Sexual Morality, Justice, and Healing and the former president and CEO of the Sexuality Information and Education Council of the United States. She is the author of four books, including the award-winning *From Diapers to Dating: A Parent's Guide to Raising Sexually Healthy Children.*

CHARLES C. HAYNES is senior scholar at the Freedom Forum First Amendment Center in Arlington, Virginia. He is best known for helping schools and communities throughout the United State find common ground on First Amendment issues.

DAVID HORNBECK serves as chairman of the board of directors for both the Children's Defense Fund and the Public Education Network, and he was Philadelphia's superintendent of schools from 1994 through August 2000. He has served as state superintendent of schools in Maryland, executive deputy secretary of education and deputy counsel to the governor in Pennsylvania, and executive director of the Philadelphia Tutorial Project.

GEORGE L. KELLING is a professor at the School of Criminal Justice, Rutgers University; a research fellow at the Kennedy School of Government, Harvard University; and a senior fellow at the Manhattan Institute.

JOYCE A. LADNER is a senior fellow at the Brookings Institution. She specializes in disadvantaged women and children, governance of urban public institutions, race/ethnic relations, and social welfare policy. She is the author most recently of *The New Urban Leaders.*

SUZANNE LE MENESTREL, a developmental psychologist, is a senior program officer in the Center for Youth Development and Policy Research at the Academy for Educational Development, where she directs a project that identifies and disseminates information on promising after-school program practices.

MONSIGNOR WILLIAM J. LINDER developed New Community Corporation (NCC) after the civil disturbances in Newark, New Jersey, in 1967. NCC became the largest community development organization in the United States.

THE REVEREND DR. EILEEN W. LINDNER is the deputy general secretary for research and planning in the Office of the General Secretary of the National Council of Churches of Christ in the USA and editor of the *Yearbook of American and Canadian Churches*. Before that she served as director of the Child Advocacy Office and director of the Child and Family Justice Project; she also was an adviser to the Children's Defense Fund and a member of the board of directors of Stand for Children.

JOAN LOMBARDI is the director of the Children's Project. She served as the deputy assistant secretary for children and families in the U.S. Department of Health and Human Services and as the first associate commissioner of the Child Care Bureau. She is co-author of *Right from the Start* and *Caring Communities*.

SISTER MARY ROSE MCGEADY is a clinical psychologist and president of Covenant House, which maintains international shelters and rehabilitation centers for teenage runaways and homeless children. She is a board member of the National Campaign to Prevent Teen Pregnancy.

ROBERT MUCCIGROSSO has served as the principal of two Catholic high schools and as the associate superintendent for schools in his native Diocese of Brooklyn. Most recently, he served as principal of Nazareth Regional High School in New York..

RICHARD MURPHY is a vice president at the Academy for Educational Development (AED) and the director of the Center for Youth Development and Policy Research. Before joining AED, Murphy served as commissioner of New York City's Department of Youth Services and was the founder and director of the Rheedlen Centers for Children and Families.

PIETRO NIVOLA is a senior fellow at the Brookings Institution. His research focuses on energy policy, federalism, regulatory politics, trade policy, and urban policy.

JEREMY NOWAK is the president of the Reinvestment Fund, a development finance institution that specializes in inner-city real estate and business lending.

KEITH PAVLISCHEK is a fellow at the Center for Public Justice and director of the *Civitas* Program in Faith and Public Affairs.

EUGENE F. RIVERS III is pastor of the Azusa Christian Community, a Pentecostal church affiliated with the Church of God in Christ. He is founder of the National Ten Point Leadership Foundation, president of the Ella J. Baker House, and general secretary of the Pan African Charismatic Evangelical Congress.

MELISSA ROGERS is executive director of the Pew Forum on Religion and Public Life, a project supported by the Pew Charitable Trusts that serves as a clearinghouse for information on issues relating to religion and public affairs. Rogers is a lawyer who has been active in the discussion of government funding and religious social service providers since 1996.

MAVIS G. SANDERS holds a joint appointment as research scientist at the Center for Research on the Education of Students Placed at Risk (CRESPAR) and assistant professor in the graduate division of education at Johns Hopkins University. Her research and teaching interests include school reform, parent and community involvement in education, and African American student achievement.

RABBI DAVID SAPERSTEIN is director of the Religious Action Center of Reform Judaism. A First Amendment lawyer, he teaches church-state law at Georgetown University Law Center.

ISABEL SAWHILL is a senior fellow at Brookings and the codirector of the Welfare Reform and Beyond Initiative. She also is the president of the National Campaign to Prevent Teen Pregnancy.

LISBETH B. SCHORR is director of the Project on Effective Interventions at Harvard University and co-chair of the Aspen Institute's Roundtable on Comprehensive Community Initiatives. Her work focuses on identifying policies and practices that improve outcomes for disadvantaged children, families, and neighborhoods.

JULIE A. SEGAL is an adjunct professor of government at the American University. As the former legislative counsel of Americans United for Separation of Church and State, she led the national coalition against charitable choice legislation.

DENNIS SHIRLEY is associate dean in the Lynch School of Education at Boston College. He has written several books on the role of faith-based groups in improving public schools, including *Community Organizing for Urban School Reform* and *Valley Interfaith and School Reform: Organizing for Power in South Texas*.

He is the director of the Massachusetts Coalition for Teacher Quality and Student Achievement.

PETER STEINFELS was the senior religion correspondent at the *New York Times* from 1988 to 1998 and continues to write a biweekly column for the paper on religion and ethics. He is a codirector of American Catholics in the Public Square, a project funded by the Pew Charitable Trusts.

THE REVEREND CARLTON W. VEAZEY, president of the Religious Coalition for Reproductive Choice since 1997, is founder of the coalition's Black Church Initiative and a national leader on progressive religious issues. Reverend Veazey is pastor of Fellowship Baptist Church in Washington, D.C., and a former chair of the Theological Commission of the National Baptist Convention. He also was a member of the Washington, D.C., City Council from 1970-73.

AVIS C. VIDAL is principal research associate in the Metropolitan Housing and Communities policy center at the Urban Institute. Her research focuses on community development and building community capacity.

DARREN WALKER is chief operating officer of the Abyssinian Development Corporation, a faith-based community development corporation in Harlem. He is a member of the boards of the National Low-Income Housing Coalition, National Housing Institute, and Association for Neighborhood Housing and Development, Inc.

JIM WALLIS is editor of *Sojourners*, convener of Call to Renewal, and author of *Faith Works: Lessons from the Life of an Activist Preacher* and *The Soul of Politics: Beyond 'Religious Right' and Secular Left.*

DIANA JONES WILSON is senior director for work force development for the North Carolina Rural Economic Development Center. She directs the Communities of Faith Initiative and the Church Child Care Initiative. She has served as a member of the N.C. Child Care Commission for the last seven years.

CHRISTOPHER WINSHIP is a professor of sociology at Harvard University. For the past seven years he has been working with and studying the Ten Point Coalition.

Index